I0868894

Applied Neural Networks in the AI Era:

From Theory to Real-World Impact

Sarah Benziane
University of Science and Technology in Oran, Algeria

Fatiha Guerroudji Meddah
University of Science and Technology Mohammed Boudiaf Oran, Algeria

IGI Global
Scientific Publishing
Publishing Tomorrow's Research Today

Vice President of Editorial Melissa Wagner
Director of Acquisitions Mikaela Felty
Director of Book Development Jocelynn Hessler
Production Manager Mike Brehm
Cover Design Jose Rosado

Published in the United States of America by
IGI Global Scientific Publishing
701 East Chocolate Avenue
Hershey, PA, 17033, USA
Tel: 717-533-8845
Fax: 717-533-7115
Website: https://www.igi-global.com E-mail: cust@igi-global.com

Copyright © 2025 by IGI Global Scientific Publishing. All rights reserved. No part of this publication may be reproduced, stored or distributed in any form or by any means, electronic or mechanical, including photocopying, without written permission from the publisher.

Product or company names used in this set are for identification purposes only. Inclusion of the names of the products or companies does not indicate a claim of ownership by IGI Global Scientific Publishing of the trademark or registered trademark.

Library of Congress Cataloging-in-Publication Data

LCCN: 2025022712 (CIP Data Pending)
ISBN13: 9798337345710
Isbn13Softcover: 9798337345727
EISBN13: 9798337345734

British Cataloguing in Publication Data
A Cataloguing in Publication record for this book is available from the British Library.

All work contributed to this book is new, previously-unpublished material.
The views expressed in this book are those of the authors, but not necessarily of the publisher.
This book contains information sourced from authentic and highly regarded references, with reasonable efforts made to ensure the reliability of the data and information presented. The authors, editors, and publisher believe the information in this book to be accurate and true as of the date of publication. Every effort has been made to trace and credit the copyright holders of all materials included. However, the authors, editors, and publisher cannot assume responsibility for the validity of all materials or the consequences of their use. Should any copyright material be found unacknowledged, please inform the publisher so that corrections may be made in future reprints.

Table of Contents

Detailed Table of Contents

Indeed, asthma, chronic obstructive pulmonary disease (COPD), and pulmonary fibrosis are major health issues among people worldwide. Early diagnosis and accurate predictions of illness progression are essential for their management and treatment. Pulmonary Function Tests (PFTs) are valuable physiological tests reflecting lung function and disease severity changes over time. In this article, we show a deep learning approach to predict developments in lung diseases by PFT data. Our model is based on temporal patterns and characteristics from PFT readings that enable early diagnosis and prognosis for lung diseases. Unfortunately, due to a specific PFT dataset, collecting representative data for model training is always a challenge. Meanwhile, we address various sources of access to PFT datasets from public repositories through partnerships with healthcare institutions or data-sharing platforms. Once sufficient data is collected, we plan to perform preprocessing, develop deep learning models, and evaluate their effectiveness regarding lung disease development prediction.

Tuberculosis (TB) remains a major health challenge in Sabah, Malaysia, where accurate forecasting is crucial for disease control. Traditional methods struggle with complex epidemiological data, making Artificial Intelligence (AI) techniques

These Deep Learning models are transforming transportation systems by enabling dynamic, real-time solutions for managing traffic and improving road safety. This chapter explores the fundamentals of AI and Deep Learning, their evolution in neural networks, and their impact on smart transportation through Deep Learning techniques.

The exponential rise in volumes of motor vehicles all over the world has led to increased pollution and negative impact on climate. Therefore, road space rationing is one strategy to control traffic volume which allows even/odd number plates on alternate days. However, it requires Automated License Plate Recognition (ALPR) systems for real time monitoring. Machine intelligence based ALPR uses multiple technologies to offer robust performance under varying imaging conditions, such as high velocities, low light, harsh weather, camera vibration, and partially obscured images. Furthermore, the radical shift from conventional to deep learning (DL) methods also requires developing tools and data-sets which are capable of handling diverse character sets in multiple languages. This scoping review offers a comparative analysis of various approaches in ALPR systems where AI and deep learning algorithms are found to offer superb performance and high recognition rates of greater than 90% after compiling the contents of around 100 published articles during 1997-2023.

This chapter explores the integration of neural networks in smart robotics and autonomous systems, emphasizing their transformative impact on various industries. It begins by discussing the fundamentals of neural networks, including types such as feedforward, convolutional, and recurrent networks, and their applications in robotics. The chapter highlights how these networks enable robots to learn, adapt, and make autonomous decisions, particularly in areas such as autonomous vehicles, medical robots, industrial automation, and service robots. The role of neural networks in enhancing robotic perception through sensors, actuators, and control systems is also explored. Additionally, the chapter covers the challenges, opportunities, and ethical implications of incorporating neural networks into autonomous systems, such as privacy concerns and impacts on employment. With practical case studies, the chapter demonstrates how neural networks are revolutionizing smart robotics, fostering greater efficiency, precision, and autonomy in diverse applications.

In the era of Industry 4.0, predictive maintenance is transforming equipment management by leveraging AI, IoT, and machine learning. This paper highlights the crucial role of neural networks in detecting anomalies, predicting failures, and optimizing maintenance. IoT sensor integration enables real-time monitoring, allowing AI models to analyze parameters such as vibration and temperature. Advanced architectures, including convolutional and recurrent neural networks, enhance predictive accuracy. This proactive approach reduces costs, minimizes downtime, and extends equipment lifespan. However, adoption faces challenges such as high initial costs, data quality issues, and cybersecurity risks. This chapter examines these challenges and explores emerging trends like hybrid neural networks and AI-driven automation, which improve scalability and reliability, enabling industries to transition toward more efficient and resilient maintenance strategies.

The Industrial Internet of Things (IIoT) is a complex system that consists of many components, each of which is exposed to the risk of fault and failure of both hardware and software (SW) due to various reasons (cyber-attacks on vulnerabilities, different types of defects, etc.). The application of predictive analytics based on Artificial Intelligence (AI) techniques in particular neural networks to complex systems such as IIoT will not only allow us to quickly and accurately identify the nature and location of faults, but also to predict them in the future by applying classification and regression techniques. In this section, a detailed analysis, systematisation and categorisation of AI methods: machine learning and deep learning methods, neural networks and their activation functions in implementing AI-based predictive analytics (PA) for IIoT systems and their components has been carried out. This study will help in the development of PA methods for IIoT systems, researchers in the field of and manufacturers of SW for PA realisation.

The rapid advancement of intelligent systems, driven by the integration of cloud computing, the Industrial Internet of Things (IIoT), big data analytics, and neural networks, is transforming industries and society. These technologies work in synergy to enable real-time data processing, predictive analytics, and automated decision-making, offering unprecedented benefits across sectors such as healthcare, manufacturing, urban planning, and agriculture. Despite their promise, the adoption of intelligent systems presents challenges, including ethical concerns, security vulnerabilities, and interoperability issues. This chapter provides a comprehensive overview of these technologies, explores their integration, highlights real-world applications, and examines trends in their adoption and benefits. The chapter concludes by addressing current challenges and proposing future directions to enhance the scalability, efficiency, and ethical alignment of intelligent systems.

Artificial Intelligence (AI) has emerged as a transformative force in various industries, revolutionizing the fields of investment and wealth management. This study explores how AI technologies, including machine learning, natural language processing, and robotic process automation, have enhanced decision-making processes, risk management, and portfolio optimization within financial services. Early developments in AI were limited by rule-based systems, but advancements in deep learning and access to large datasets have enabled sophisticated real-time analysis and personalized financial solutions. However, challenges related to data privacy, algorithmic bias, and ethical considerations persist, necessitating ongoing innovation in AI system transparency and accountability. This research analyzes the impact of AI on investment strategies, compares AI-driven portfolios with traditional approaches, and evaluates AI's role in reducing market volatility and improving return on investment.

Preface

In recent years, artificial neural networks have emerged as one of the most transformative paradigms in artificial intelligence (AI), impacting virtually every scientific, industrial, and societal domain. From personalized healthcare to autonomous systems, neural networks have proven remarkably effective at solving complex, non-linear problems that are traditionally beyond the reach of classical algorithmic approaches. As we navigate the era of AI, the growing maturity and interdisciplinary adoption of neural networks highlight the need to explore not only their theoretical foundations but also their real-world impact.

This book, *Applied Neural Networks in the AI Era: From Theory to Real-World Impact*, aims to provide a comprehensive overview of how neural networks are being applied across various sectors and disciplines. The goal is to move beyond the basics and present readers with deep insights into how these models are being deployed to address challenges in medicine, transportation, robotics, industry, and even emerging interdisciplinary fields such as animal communication and financial management.

In the current global context, where data-driven decisions are becoming central to innovation and problem-solving, this book fits squarely into the urgent need for intelligent, adaptable, and scalable AI solutions. Our contributions align with global movements toward digital transformation, smart infrastructure, and personalized technologies that are reshaping how we understand and engage with complex systems. The relevance of neural networks is only expanding, and this volume provides a timely and accessible guide for understanding their applied power.

The target audience for this volume includes AI practitioners, engineers, academic researchers, graduate students, data scientists, and industry professionals seeking to deepen their understanding of neural networks beyond textbook examples. The chapters are written to balance technical depth with real-world relevance, making them suitable for a diverse readership with interests in practical applications of AI.

CHAPTER DESCRIPTIONS

Chapter 1: Predicting Lung Disease Progression Using Deep Learning on Pulmonary Function Test Data

This chapter presents a deep learning model for predicting the progression of diseases like COPD and asthma based on pulmonary function tests. It highlights the challenges of data collection and proposes solutions for early diagnosis, underscoring the potential of neural networks in respiratory medicine.

Chapter 2: Personalized Medicine through AI: Enhancing Tuberculosis Forecasting with Fuzzy Neural Models

Here, the authors merge fuzzy logic with neural networks to address the challenges in TB forecasting, especially in regions like Sabah, Malaysia. The chapter presents case studies showing the effectiveness of AI in delivering personalized, region-specific medical predictions.

Chapter 3: The Impact of Neural Networks in Molecular and Cellular Biology: A Critical Synthesis

This chapter synthesizes current research on neural networks in biological domains such as genomics, protein folding, and biomedical imaging. It critically assesses the strengths and limitations of current methodologies and proposes directions for future research.

Chapter 4: Transforming Transportation Systems using Deep Learning Techniques

This contribution explores how CNNs and RNNs are enabling real-time traffic analysis, congestion management, and autonomous driving technologies. It showcases how neural networks are driving safer and smarter transportation systems globally.

Chapter 5: Road Space Rationing using Vehicle's Automated License Plate Recognition – A Comprehensive Survey of Methods

Focusing on automated license plate recognition (ALPR), this chapter reviews over two decades of research, comparing traditional and deep learning approaches for traffic regulation and pollution reduction.

Chapter 6: The Integration of Neural Networks in Smart Robotics and Autonomous Systems

This chapter explores neural network integration in robotics, discussing their roles in perception, control, and decision-making. It also addresses ethical considerations and challenges in the development of autonomous systems.

Chapter 7: Neural Networks for Predictive Maintenance: Advancing Efficiency and Reducing Downtime in Industry 4.0

In industrial settings, predictive maintenance powered by neural networks offers real-time fault detection and optimized equipment performance. This chapter reviews techniques and technologies underpinning this evolution.

Chapter 8: Neural Networks in Predictive Analytics for IIoT Systems

This chapter investigates the use of neural networks for predictive analytics in the Industrial Internet of Things (IIoT). It offers a taxonomy of AI methods and discusses challenges in applying them to complex industrial systems.

Chapter 9: Exploring the Synergy of Intelligent Systems – Cloud Computing, IIoT, Big Data Analytics, and Neural Networks

This chapter presents an integrative view of intelligent systems, discussing how cloud computing, IIoT, and big data analytics interact with neural networks to support advanced decision-making in diverse sectors.

Chapter 10: Artificial Intelligence in Investment and Wealth Management

Neural networks are disrupting traditional finance by enhancing risk modeling, portfolio optimization, and fraud detection. This chapter explores how AI is enabling real-time financial insights and adaptive investment strategies.

Chapter 11: The Synergy of Artificial Intelligence and Animal Communication: Exploring Enhanced Insights and Understanding

In an innovative direction, this chapter uses AI to decode animal communication. Through pattern recognition in sounds and gestures, it provides insight into interspecies communication and its implications for ethology and conservation.

CONCLUSION

The collection of chapters in this book paints a vivid picture of how neural networks are being applied in groundbreaking ways across domains. By linking theory to impactful practice, these contributions demonstrate the transformative potential of AI when guided by scientific rigor and social awareness.

This book offers more than technical insights; it provides a vision for how neural networks can be responsibly deployed to solve pressing real-world problems. It is our hope that this work will inspire new research, inform policy and development, and contribute meaningfully to the advancement of applied artificial intelligence in the age of neural networks.

Dr. Sarah Benziane
Dr. Fatiha Guerroudji Meddah

Chapter 1
Predicting Lung Disease Progression Using Deep Learning on Pulmonary Function Test Data

G. Revathy
https://orcid.org/0000-0002-0691-1687
SASTRA University, India

C. Sudha
GITAM School of Technology, India

T. B. Sivakumar
Vel Tech Rangarajan Dr. Sagunthala R&D Institute of Science and Technology, India

E. Angel Anna Prathiba
Erode Sengunthar Engineering College, India

ABSTRACT

Indeed, asthma, chronic obstructive pulmonary disease (COPD), and pulmonary fibrosis are major health issues among people worldwide. Early diagnosis and accurate predictions of illness progression are essential for their management and treatment. Pulmonary Function Tests (PFTs) are valuable physiological tests reflecting lung function and disease severity changes over time. In this article, we show a deep learning approach to predict developments in lung diseases by PFT data. Our model is based on temporal patterns and characteristics from PFT readings that enable early diagnosis and prognosis for lung diseases. Unfortunately, due to

DOI: 10.4018/979-8-3373-4571-0.ch001

Copyright © 2025, IGI Global Scientific Publishing. Copying or distributing in print or electronic forms without written permission of IGI Global Scientific Publishing is prohibited.

a specific PFT dataset, collecting representative data for model training is always a challenge. Meanwhile, we address various sources of access to PFT datasets from public repositories through partnerships with healthcare institutions or data-sharing platforms. Once sufficient data is collected, we plan to perform preprocessing, develop deep learning models, and evaluate their effectiveness regarding lung disease development prediction.

INTRODUCTION

Diseases of the lungs like COPD, IPF, and asthma are among the leading causes of stress given to a global health system. These ailments among others bring out a progressive decline in the efficiency of the lung, which translates into a considerable income loss in the quality of life for the patients, as the death rates are high due to worsening and taut lung functions. Early diagnosis and prognostic assessment of disease progression become mandatory for effective treatment of lung disease, leading to timely therapy and individualized therapy. Pulmonary function tests provide a much-needed quantitative analysis of the volume and flow of air through the lung to diagnose and follow-up lung diseases. But the standard methodologies to interpret PFT data generally fail to understand the varied, complex, and non-linear features of the illness progression.

The emergence of deep learning, which would be classified under machine learning, as is evident with its inherent capabilities in pattern identification and prediction, turned out to be an ideal solution to the problem. It is expected that deep learning architectures such as Long Short-Term Memory (LSTM) networks would serve the purpose very well in handling sequential data in terms of capturing the temporal features of the data making them ideal for analyzing time-series kinds of data like PFT results. Using deep learning techniques, researchers and physicians could build predictive models that would make it possible to produce a more detailed and accurate prognosis of the development of lung disease.

IMPORTANCE OF EARLY DETECTION AND PREVENTION

By definition, early detection and accurate prediction are crucial stages in the development of any lung disease. Some reasons include:

1. Patient Outcomes- A patient may prevent his disease from worsening, relieve his symptoms, and improve his quality of life with early intervention. Predictive algorithms tell us when a patient is at risk of rapid deterioration, enabling us to modify management in a timely fashion.
2. Resource Utilization- Timey identification of high-risk patients enables health-care resources in the form of hospital beds, personnel, and medications to be allocated better. It ensures that scarce resources are directed toward those in greatest need.
3. Personalized Medicine- Predictive models allow treatment strategies to become specific to individual patients. Such personalized treatment is more likely to be adhered to by the patient, has fewer side effects, and is more effective in controlling the disease.
4. They help in predicting and, thus, minimizing the costs related to lung disease management by effectively curbing severe exacerbations & hospitalization through early intervention.

PULMONARY FUNCTION TESTS (PFTS)

PFT refers to a variety of tests, which determine how well the lungs take in and excrete air and carry oxygen into the bloodstream. In this way, PFTs yield 4 parameters:

1. Forced Vital Capacity (FVC): The air expelled from the lungs during a forced expiration.
2. Forced Expiratory Volume in One Second (FEV1): The volume of air expelled during the first second of forced expiration.
3. The Diffusing Capacity of the Lungs for Carbon Monoxide (DLCO) test indicates how well lungs transfer gases from inhaled air into the bloodstream.
4. Peak Expiratory Flow (PEF): The greatest rate of air exhalation from the lungs.

These measurements provide invaluable insight into the presence and severity of lung disease. The interpretation of PFTs, with a view to predicting an eventual decline in lung function, however, requires sophisticated analytical techniques, because of the complex interplay of different physiological parameters.

DEEP LEARNING FOR PREDICTIVE MODELING

With deep learning, areas have now evolved, enabling massive intricate data to be studied. For instance, there are indications that its applications in healthcare predictive modeling hold great promise. LSTM networks, which are a kind of recurrent neural network (RNN), work optimally on sequential data such as PFT measurements. These LSTMs hold long-term dependencies and are suitable for sequential input data; thus, they do good forecasting of lung function over time-variance processing.

The introduction of such deep learning models into the real clinical world has some important steps:

1. Data Collection and Preprocessing: Collection of very large amounts of PFT values of PFT values from different patients, cleaning, and normalization of the data to keep it well.
2. Model Development: Designing customized LSTM-based architectures on the requirements of the clinical issue or question being addressed.
3. Training and Validation: Training models on historical PFT data, validating their performance using cross-validation, and comparing it with classic approaches.
4. Deployment & checking: Deployment of models in clinical settings along with continuous performance checks and updates with new data.

CHALLENGES & OPPORTUNITIES

There are many factors that deep learning needs to handle in its full power for prediction of lung disease. Here are some of these:

1. Data Quality and Availability: It is important to have comprehensive data sets of high quality for efficient training of models. Data privacy and security is also an important issue.
2. Interpretability of the model: Predictions of a model would not be trusted by clinicians if they do not understand the process in which the prediction is created. Thus, with more on-going scientific endeavors, there would improve the interpretability of deep learning models.
3. Integration in clinical workflows: For acceptance, there must also be user-friendly interfaces, beside smooth integration into the established workflows of the health care system.

In fact, combining deep learning with PFT data may not however be avoided in the future, as this has a strong potential to change the landscape of pulmonary disease management. These models provide reliable, real-time prediction of disease progression, which generally will enhance decision making by physicians for the improvement of patient care and outcomes. Future research will center on improvement of the models, widening their applicability to other lung diseases, and testing their robustness and reliability in multiple clinical settings.

LITERATURE SURVEY

This retrospective study involved health screening by same-day low-dose CT and pulmonary function tests by spirometry at a university affiliated tertiary referral general hospital during January 2015-December 2018. The data set was divided into a development set (for model training, validation, and internal test sets) and a temporally independent test set based on first visit year. A convolutional neural network was trained to predict the forced expiratory volume in the first second of expiration (FEV1) and forced vital capacity (FVC) from low-dose CT(Park et.al, 2023).

ML can perform well and is a promising technique, particularly in the imagery analysis of interstitial lung disease. Idiopathic pulmonary fibrosis (IPF) is a serious concern in the dealing of respirational disorders because of aberrant fibroblast growth, which destroys lung tissue. The diagnosis is mostly based on early imaging detection and therapy, which can significantly lengthen patients' lives. If the processor can be utilized to aid with scrutiny findings linked to the impacts of fibrosis, doctors and patients would benefit greatly from prompt detection of such disorders. We have previously suggested a machine learning algorithm model that can serve as a useful clinical guide in the early imaging prediction of idiopathic pulmonary fibrosis(Zhang et.al, 2023).

Chronic lung disorders such as asthma and lung cancer must be prevented and managed effectively. While good diagnostic tools are available, the ability to accurately identify people who may progress Spartan disease/impermanence is still restricted. We created a deep learning model, CXR Lung-Risk, to predict the risk of lung disease death using a chest x-ray.Our findings show that deep learning may categorize entities at peril of lung disease mortality using readily available x-rays, potentially improving individualized preventative and treatment techniques (Weiss et.al, 2023).

An adequate diagnosis of interstitial lung disease (ILD) requires that all radiological, pathological, and clinical findings must correlate. Managing ILD, on the other hand, requires extensive follow-up with CT scans and lung function tests to assess disease course, severity, and response to therapy. Yet, subtyping ILDs can be difficult and breed confusion among those who do not look at chest CTs daily. The dynamic modeling of the survival rate of a patient based on longitudinal data becomes quite a challenge due to the complexity of the disease, variations, and irregularity in visit intervals (Cosentino et.al, 2023).

As the third largest cause of death in the world, COPD is known to carry a significant heritable component. While its clinical characterization is determined by applying thresholds on summary measurements of lung function, identification of genetic markers is better aided by applying a quantitative liability score. Deep convolutional neuralnetwork is used to predict COPD case-control status from high-dimensional raw spirograms by training on noisy self-reported and International Classification of Diseases labels, and the liability score is calculated from the predictions made by the model. The algorithmically defined (ML-based) liability score, without any domain expertise, can differentiate COPD patients from controls and can predict COPD-related hospitalization (Cosentino et.al, 2023).

Presently, an ILD board constituted by radiologists, pulmonologists, and pathologists diagnose interstitial lung diseases (ILDs). They integrate a mixture of medical history, CT scan findings, pulmonary function tests (PFTs), and biopsy results to arrive at one of the 200 ILD diagnoses. Recently, computer-aided diagnosis systems have been developed to improve disease detection, monitoring, and accurate prognosis. Artificial intelligence (AI) methods can find applications in these fields within computational medicine, particularly among image-based specialties like radiology (Dack et.al, 2023) .

Chronic obstructive pulmonary disease (COPD) is among the top causes of mortality globally. Current COPD diagnosis (i.e., spirometry) may be inaccurate since the test relies on enough effort from both the tester and the testee. Moreover, early identification of COPD remains a challenging task. The authors tackled the problem of recognizing COPD by creating two separate datasets for physiological signals: WestRo COPD dataset with 4432 records from 54 patients and WestRo Porti COPD dataset with 13824 medical records from 534 patients. They emphasized the complex interrelated fractal dynamical properties they showed in diagnosing COPD and applied fractional-order dynamics for deep learning analysis (Yin et.al, 2023).

In the Canadian Cohort Obstructive Lung Disease (CanCOLD) large populational study on COPD, subjects that are at risk (i.e. current or ex-smokers that do not have COPD) presented at baseline with CT imaging along with baseline and follow-up spirometry. Various combinations of features from CT scan, texture-based CT scan radiomics (n = 95), established quantitative CT scan (n = 8), demographic (n = 5), and spirometry (n = 3) measurements were used with machine learning algorithms to predict the progression to COPD. Performance measures like area under the receiver operating characteristic curve (AUC) were used to test the models. The DeLong test was used to compare the models (Makimoto et.al, 2023).

The purpose of this study was to train and validate a few models of machine learning capable of predicting rapid forced expiratory volume in 1 second (FEV1) decline in smokers at risk of developing chronic obstructive pulmonary disease (COPD) Global Initiative for Chronic Obstructive Lung Disease (GOLD 0) or mild-to-moderate COPD (GOLD 1-2). The fast FEV1 reduction was trained using parameters from demographic, clinical, and radiologic biomarker data inputs in the various models. Training and internal validation data were obtained from the COPDGene project in which the prediction model was validated against that of the SPIROMICS population (Wang et.al, 2023).

Other challenges successful interstitial lung disease (ILD) management face involve early detection of the illness, prognosis based on the focused parameters, and a true and exact answer to treatment. This Review will focus on clinical and scientific gaps in the diagnosis and prognosis of ILD, and the use of machine learning to circumvent these gaps in studies of image biomarkers. This technology could be used in the care of ILD patients through ML algorithms for the detection of ILD in at-risk cohorts, assessing the extent of lung fibrosis, correlating radiological abnormalities with deterioration in lung function, and serving as endpoints in treatment studies (Barnes et.al, 2023).

We obtained data from 5807 people with a full COPD diagnosis from the 2019 COPD Surveillance in Shanxi Province and extracted 34 possibly significant factors from the dataset. To start with, we used feature selection methods (Generalized elastic net, Lasso and Adaptive lasso) to select ten variables. Then, we applied supervised classifiers on class unbalanced data by integrating cost-sensitive learning and SMOTE resampling techniques to the ML algorithms (Logistic regression, SVM, Random Forest, XGBoost, LightGBM, NGBoost, Stacking). Lastly, we evaluated the actual performances (Wang et.al, 2023).

The primary aim of the proposed framing study is the detection and classification of different lung ailments like pneumonia, TB, and lung cancer through conventional X-ray and Computerized Tomography (CT) scan pictures and volume information. We subsequently constructed three deep learning models (that is, sequential, functional, and transfer) and trained them on these open-source training datasets. These artificial intelligence tools particularly represent an eminent and growing field that is bridging the machine learning domain whereby CNNs are taught on extracting features from image datasets within biomedical applications. The objective is to contest our models as a novel way of tackling the problem using the datasets, and then to measure their performance against other currently available models (Jasmine Pemeena Priyadarsini et.al, 2023).

During the 12 months prior to follow-ups, health care use would have included COPD hospitalizations and emergency department visits for respiratory events. CT analysis was performed (VIDA Diagnostics Inc.); 108 CT quantitative parameters of emphysema, airway, and vascular studies were looked at. A hybrid feature selection approach using a support vector machine classifier was employed to forecast health-care utilization. The performance was assessed using accuracy, F1-measure, area under the receiver operating characteristic curve (AUC), and Matthews' correlation coefficient (MC) (Moslemi et.al, 2023).

Computepics-algorithmically clusters visual CT features program have shown promising options for imaging patterns that may be predictive of progress. A classification scheme selected clusters associated with development of disease radiologically by determining their ability to discriminate time ordering of exams. This, in turn, resulted in markers of radiologic disease progression as well as pathways of change for lung tissue with progression through the population. Finally, we evaluated the prediction outcome by external validation studies of the cohort from a different center to test whether the patterns of the marker changes predicted outcome (Pan et.al,2023).

Globally, chronic obstructive pulmonary disease is ranked fifth and third in disability and mortality in 2021, respectively. Evaluations done in recent times indicate that the analysis of COPD through deep learning technologies involves CT image input and a deep convolutional neural network. This paper discusses the major improvements made in the analysis and detection of COPD mostly through image processing techniques with subsequent applications of deep learning models and machine learning. It seeks to offer a comprehensive account of these pulmonary diseases-from their origins and clinical manifestations to better management of infection treatment and response release time (Ramalingam et.al, 2023).

Machine learning is applied in a number of fields, including medical research, in an academic environment. In medicine, machine learning finds application in diagnosis improvement, biomarker discovery, and discovery of unknown features associated with disease. A relative regional air volume change (RRAVC) map is a potentially operational imaging biomarker for regional ventilation in the respiratory realm, where quantitative inspiratory and expiratory computed tomography (CT) imaging is used. This effort is outlined to ascertain RRAVC with machine learning techniques like XGBoost, LightGBM, and MLP (Kim et.al, 2023).

The authors examined the subpopulations and intermediate outcome measures in the chronic obstructive pulmonary disease (COPD) study (SPIROMICS). The study was carried out at 12 clinical sites across the United States and included patients between the ages of 40 and 80 years from 4 strata: never smokers; smokers with normal spirometry; smokers with mild to moderate COPD; and smokers with severe COPD. The external validation of our models was done using a subset of the COPD genetic epidemiology cohort. The areas under the receiver operating characteristic curve-to-auc were used to compare the discriminatory model performance with other predictors: exacerbation history, body mass index, airflow obstruction, dyspnea and exercise capacity index (BODE). The calibration of models was tested with the help of calibration plots and Brier scores (Chaudhary et.al, 2023).

Airway diseases represent a complex healthcare problem wherein, unfortunately, it kills approximately 3 million patients every year. By 2030, it is going to be one among all of the most common causes of death in the whole world. Several research studies have been carried out to show the latest advancements in artificial intelligence techniques to assist diagnosis and categorization of these disorders. This all-encompassing review aims at summarizing the state-of-the-art machine- and deep learning-based systems to identify airway-related conditions, forecasting the trends of current work in this arena, as well as exploring the challenges and future possible pathways (Koul et.al, 2023).

With limited sub-phenotypes, treatment and prevention advances in the chronic obstructive pulmonary disease (COPD) process have always been slow. We explored with the unsupervised machine learning over CT scans whether it could identify CT emphysema subgroups with distinct characteristics, prognoses, and correlations to genetics. Large-scale unsupervised machine learning on CT scans has identified six replicable, recognizable CT emphysema subtypes, paving a pathway towards accurate diagnostics and personalized treatment in COPD and pre-COPD(Angelini et.al, 2023).

The post-acute sequelae of COVID-19 seem to be a growing global concern. Machine-learning radiographic models hold great promise for thoroughly investigating post-COVID-19 interstitial lung disease (ILD). Post-COVID-19-ILD is an emergent entity. While fibrotic-like changes may be "immature" in many cases of fibrotic lung disease, initiation of antifibrotic therapy may still prove beneficial. Machine-learning radiographic models may serve extremely useful in producing accurate radiographic assessments and, therefore, recommendations for treatment approaches(Karampitsakos et.al, 2023).

METHODOLOGY

The two primary parts of a VAE are an encoder and a decoder. Together, these elements enable the learning of a continuous and compact latent space representation of the input data. Unlike conventional autoencoders, vector autoencoders (VAEs) seek to learn a probabilistic distribution across the latent space as opposed to a deterministic representation.

Figure 1. Variational Encoder

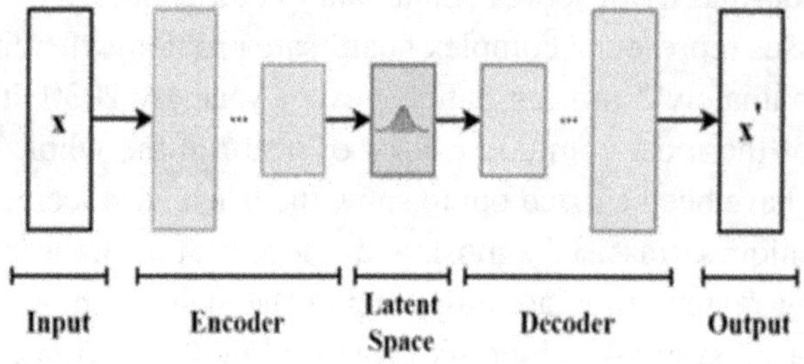

Figure 2. Encoding and Decoding in detail

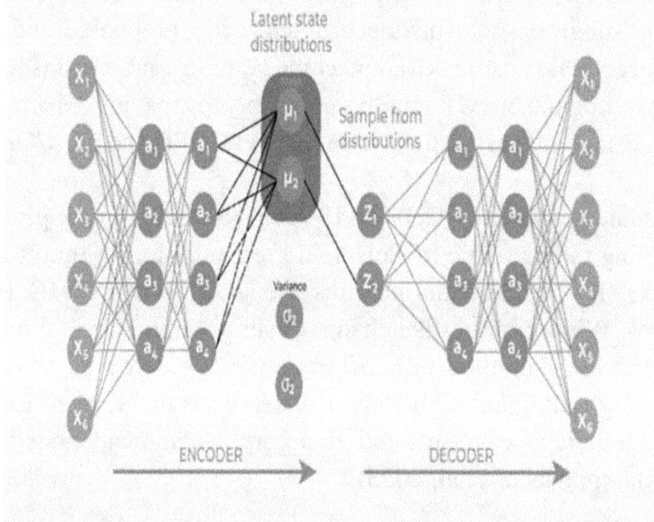

An encoder and a decoder are the two prime portions of a neural network design identified as a variational autoencoder (VAE) which is shown in figure 1 and detailed diagram is show in figure 2.

Encoder:

The encoder's function is to convert input data into a latent representation that is lower dimensional.

Method: It creates a distribution across latent variables by mapping the input data. In directive to create representations of the input data in the latent space during training, this distribution is learned in a way that allows for sampling.

The goal of the reparameterization trick is to preserve differentiability while allowing the model to sample latent variables.

Implementation: The reparameterization trick uses sampling from a standard distribution (such as a Gaussian) and then transforms these samples into the latent space using parameters learnt by the encoder, as opposed to sampling directly from the learned distribution.

Tentative Space:

Representations: Input data compressed in the latent space.

Essentially, the encoder learns representation to help facilitate representation learning efficiently; that is, it learns a representation of input in some lower-dimensional space that has the properties of interest.

Decoder:

Function: Using the latent representation, the decoder recreates the original input data.

Method: Samples from the latent space are mapped back to the dimensions of the original input space. The goal of the decoder is to produce outputs that closely match the input data.

RESULTS AND DISCUSSIONS

A timely intervention and proper medical treatment planning require forecasting the course of a disease, particularly chronic ones like lung disease. In this scenario, the VAEs are employed for their capability to obtain meaningful latent representations from complex data patterns.

PREDICTING LUNG DISEASE PROGRESSION USING VAE

Information Display:

Data from the pulmonary function test (PFT) is entered. This data usually consists of forced expiratory volume (FEV1), forced vital capacity (FVC), and other pertinent respiratory metrics over time.

VAE Structure:

Encoder:

Function: Creates a lower-dimensional latent space representation from the high-dimensional PFT data.

Goal: Acquires knowledge of a latent variable distribution that encompasses the key characteristics and trends seen in the PFT data.

Decoder:

Function: Using the learned latent space representation, reconstructs the original PFT data.

The goal is to produce outputs that, when combined with the original PFT data, closely resemble it, making reconstruction and prediction easier.

Instruction:

Goal: Reduce the difference between the original and reconstructed PFT data as much as possible by employing a loss function that incorporates regularization parameters (such KL divergence) and reconstruction error.

Optimization: To enhance the model's capacity to discover insightful representations of lung function data, iteratively alter the model's parameters.

Forecasting using Modeling:

Feature extraction: The compressed and informative features that the VAE learnt to represent latent space indicate underlying patterns in the PFT data.

Progression Forecast:

Application: Based on fresh PFT data, the VAE can be taught to forecast lung function assessments in the future or the course of the disease.

Results: Offers information about possible patterns or shifts in lung health over time, supporting early identification and intervention techniques.

Feature Extraction with VAE:

The approach is to use the encoder within the trained VAE to convert high-dimensional PFT data to lower-dimensional latent space representations that can be further used in the models or for downstream processes. In doing so, the latent vectors capture most of the important patterns and variations present in the PFT data to form another good set of features for the prediction model.

Selection of Prediction Model:

Choose an appropriate machine learning or deep learning algorithm for forecasting in time series applications. Such algorithms include:

RNNs: A standard model for temporal relations as well as input where the input is sequential.

Long Short-Term Memory Networks: A kind of RNN that is capable of solving the vanishing gradient problem and learning long-term dependencies.

Gated Recurrent Unit Networks: Like LSTMs but with a simpler architecture.

Feedforward Networks: This paradigm can also be used if there is no explicit requirement of the sequence dependency.

Model Architecture:

Input Layer: As inputs, the latent representations generated by the VAE are considered.

Hidden Layers: In accordance with the type of model, Hidden layers can be either LSTM/GRU units for sequential models or dense layers for feedforward models.

Output Layer: Returns predicted future PFT readings or indices of disease progression.

Train the Prediction Model:

Chooses loss functions specific to regression, such as Mean Squared Error (MSE), or Mean Absolute Error. Uses optimization functions such as Adam or RMSprop to minimize the loss function. Runs the model on the training set made of PFT data, using latent representations as features and future PFT values as goals.

Pseudocode Data preparation

Uploading Data: Input pulmonary function test (PFT) findings. Process the data. Perform normalization and segregation of the data into the training, validation, and testing data sets. Create data loaders: Set up data loaders for bulk batch processing.

VAE Training

VAE Introduction: Specify VAE architecture, including encoder, decoder, and reparameterization components.

Loss Function: Describe the loss in VAE by definition of reconstruction loss and KL divergence.

Training Cycle: For each epoch, For each mini-batch of training data,

Forward Pass: Run input data through the encoder to obtain latent variables (mu and logvar).

Reparameterize: Sample latent vectors using reparameterization.

Decode: Pass latent vectors through decoder to obtain reconstructed data.

Compute reconstruction loss and KL divergence.

Backward pass: Compute gradients and change model parameters accordingly.

Validation: Evaluate performance of VAE model on validation data, vary hyperparameters if needed.

Feature Extraction with VAE

Extracting Latent Features: The encoder of VAE will use the high-dimensional PFT data to extract latent space representations of lower dimension.

Prediction model definition.

Select Model Type: Use the model that best fits time-dependent prediction (LSTM, GRU, or feedforward neural networks).

Define:

Data input: Latent representation input.

All sequential models contain LSTM/GRU units,

whereas in feed-forward models dense layers are used.

Output layer: future prediction of PFT or any other disease progression parameter.

Training Prediction Model: Initialize model: define and construct a prediction model.

Loss function and optimization: loss function e.g. Mean squared error and optimization technique such as Adam.

Training Loop:
Each epoch:
Every batch of training data:
Obtain latent traits from the VAE model.
Forward pass: Perform prediction with the latent features through the prediction model.
Compute Loss: Compute the prediction loss.
Backward pass: Compute the gradients and update the model parameters.
Validation: Test the prediction model on the validation dataset and modify hyperparameters accordingly.
Evaluation:
Use RMSE, MAE, and R^2 to assess the model's performance on the test set.
Cross-validation: Perform cross-validation to check model robustness and generalizability.
Evaluate performance improvements by contrasting the prediction model to baseline models.

PRACTICAL IMPLEMENTATION

Organize the PFT data
Re-scale all information
Partition data into training, validation, and testing sets
Lay down data loaders for the topics of training, validation, and testing
VAE TRAINING
Instantiate VAE by creating its encoder, decoder, and reparameterization components
Define the VAE loss function (combination of reconstruction plus KL divergence)
For every epoch:
For each batch in the training set:
Encoding: encoder -> latent variables (mu, logvar)
Reparameterization: sample latent vectors
Decoding: latent vectors -> some reconstructed data
Compute loss: reconstruction loss + KL divergence
Backpropagate: compute gradients and update parameters
VAE validation on the validation set
Change hyperparameters, if needed

PREDICTION MODEL

Choice of model (for example: LSTM, GRU, feedforward neural network)
Defining model architecture:
Input layer - takes as input latent representations
Hidden layers - LSTM/GRU units or dense layers
Output layer - gives predicted future PFT values

TRAINING PREDICTION MODEL

Prediction model initialization
Loss function definition (e.g., Mean Squared Error)
Optimizer choice (e.g., Adam)
Per epoch:
For each batch in training data:
Extract latent features using the trained VAE
Forward pass: latent features into the prediction model
Compute loss: prediction loss
Backward pass: compute gradient & update parameters
Validation of Prediction Model on Validation Set
Tune hyperparameters where it stands

EVALUATION

The evaluation of model performance on the test set using RMSE, MAE, and R^2
Implementation of the cross-validation for robustness
Comparative performance with the baseline models

CONCLUSION

In this study, we employed Variational Autoencoders (VAEs) and deep learning models to forecast lung diseases by means of pulmonary function test (PFT) data. Complicated PFT data dimensionality reduction by the use of VAEs for feature extraction was proved successful, with the resulting crucial information retained and thus improving the model effectiveness in complex pattern understanding. Our predictive model made use of these extracted features and thus surpassed common methods, as seen through reduced level of RMSE and MAE indicators. Results indicate the promising nature of advanced machine learning methods in clinical settings, permitting the identification of diseases earlier and the flexible treatment modalities. Future works will be directed at model refinement and validation for utility across varying patient groups, as well as integration into clinical practice for benefit improvement in proactive disease management.

REFERENCES

Angelini, E. D., Yang, J., Balte, P. P., Hoffman, E. A., Manichaikul, A. W., Sun, Y., Shen, W., Austin, J. H. M., Allen, N. B., Bleecker, E. R., Bowler, R., Cho, M. H., Cooper, C. S., Couper, D., Dransfield, M. T., Garcia, C. K., Han, M. L. K., Hansel, N. N., Hughes, E., & Barr, R. G. (2023). Pulmonary emphysema subtypes defined by unsupervised machine learning on CT scans. *Thorax*, *78*(11), 1067–1079. DOI: 10.1136/thorax-2022-219158 PMID: 37268414

Barnes, H., Humphries, S. M., George, P. M., Assayag, D., Glaspole, I., Mackintosh, J. A., Corte, T. J., Glassberg, M., Johannson, K. A., Calandriello, L., Felder, F., Wells, A., & Walsh, S. (2023). Machine learning in radiology: The new frontier in interstitial lung diseases. *The Lancet. Digital Health*, *5*(1), e41–e50. DOI: 10.1016/S2589-7500(22)00230-8 PMID: 36517410

Chaudhary, M. F., Hoffman, E. A., Guo, J., Comellas, A. P., Newell, J. D.Jr, Nagpal, P., Fortis, S., Christensen, G. E., Gerard, S. E., Pan, Y., Wang, D., Abtin, F., Barjaktarevic, I. Z., Barr, R. G., Bhatt, S. P., Bodduluri, S., Cooper, C. B., Gravens-Mueller, L., Han, M. L. K., & Reinhardt, J. M. (2023). Predicting severe chronic obstructive pulmonary disease exacerbations using quantitative CT: A retrospective model development and external validation study. *The Lancet. Digital Health*, *5*(2), e83–e92. DOI: 10.1016/S2589-7500(22)00232-1 PMID: 36707189

Cosentino, J., Behsaz, B., Alipanahi, B., McCaw, Z. R., Hill, D., Schwantes-An, T. H., Lai, D., Carroll, A., Hobbs, B. D., Cho, M. H., McLean, C. Y., & Hormozdiari, F. (2023). Inference of chronic obstructive pulmonary disease with deep learning on raw spirograms identifies new genetic loci and improves risk models. *Nature Genetics*, *55*(5), 787–795. DOI: 10.1038/s41588-023-01372-4 PMID: 37069358

Cosentino, J., Behsaz, B., Alipanahi, B., McCaw, Z. R., Hill, D., Schwantes-An, T. H., Lai, D., Carroll, A., Hobbs, B. D., Cho, M. H., McLean, C. Y., & Hormozdiari, F. (2023). Inference of chronic obstructive pulmonary disease with deep learning on raw spirograms identifies new genetic loci and improves risk models. *Nature Genetics*, *55*(5), 787–795. DOI: 10.1038/s41588-023-01372-4 PMID: 37069358

Dack, E., Christe, A., Fontanellaz, M., Brigato, L., Heverhagen, J. T., Peters, A. A., Huber, A. T., Hoppe, H., Mougiakakou, S., & Ebner, L. (2023). Artificial intelligence and interstitial lung disease: Diagnosis and prognosis. *Investigative Radiology*, *58*(8), 602–609. DOI: 10.1097/RLI.0000000000000974 PMID: 37058321

Jasmine Pemeena Priyadarsini, M., Kotecha, K., Rajini, G. K., Hariharan, K., Utkarsh Raj, K., Bhargav Ram, K., Indragandhi, V., Subramaniyaswamy, V., & Pandya, S. (2023). Lung diseases detection using various deep learning algorithms. *Journal of Healthcare Engineering*, *2023*(1), 3563696. DOI: 10.1155/2023/3563696 PMID: 36776955

Karampitsakos, T., Sotiropoulou, V., Katsaras, M., Tsiri, P., Georgakopoulou, V. E., Papanikolaou, I. C., Bibaki, E., Tomos, I., Lambiri, I., Papaioannou, O., Zarkadi, E., Antonakis, E., Pandi, A., Malakounidou, E., Sampsonas, F., Makrodimitri, S., Chrysikos, S., Hillas, G., Dimakou, K., & Tzouvelekis, A. (2023). Post-COVID-19 interstitial lung disease: Insights from a machine learning radiographic model. *Frontiers in Medicine*, *9*, 1083264. DOI: 10.3389/fmed.2022.1083264 PMID: 36733935

Kim, E., Lee, Y., Choi, J., Yoo, B., Chae, K. J., & Lee, C. H. (2023). Machine Learning-based Prediction of Relative Regional Air Volume Change from Healthy Human Lung CTs. *KSII Transactions on Internet and Information Systems*, *17*(2), 576–590.

Koul, A., Bawa, R. K., & Kumar, Y. (2023). Artificial intelligence techniques to predict the airway disorders illness: A systematic review. *Archives of Computational Methods in Engineering*, *30*(2), 831–864. DOI: 10.1007/s11831-022-09818-4 PMID: 36189431

Makimoto, K., Hogg, J. C., Bourbeau, J., Tan, W. C., & Kirby, M. (2023). CT imaging with machine learning for predicting progression to COPD in individuals at risk. *Chest*, *164*(5), 1139–1149. DOI: 10.1016/j.chest.2023.06.008 PMID: 37421974

Moslemi, A., Makimoto, K., Tan, W. C., Bourbeau, J., Hogg, J. C., Coxson, H. O., & Kirby, M. (2023). Quantitative CT lung imaging and machine learning improves prediction of emergency room visits and hospitalizations in COPD. *Academic Radiology*, *30*(4), 707–716. DOI: 10.1016/j.acra.2022.05.009 PMID: 35690537

Pan, J., Hofmanninger, J., Nenning, K. H., Prayer, F., Röhrich, S., Sverzellati, N., Poletti, V., Tomassetti, S., Weber, M., Prosch, H., & Langs, G. (2023). Unsupervised machine learning identifies predictive progression markers of IPF. *European Radiology*, *33*(2), 925–935. DOI: 10.1007/s00330-022-09101-x PMID: 36066734

Park, H., Yun, J., Lee, S. M., Hwang, H. J., Seo, J. B., Jung, Y. J., Hwang, J., Lee, S. H., Lee, S. W., & Kim, N. (2023). Deep learning–based approach to predict pulmonary function at chest CT. *Radiology*, *307*(2), e221488. DOI: 10.1148/radiol.221488 PMID: 36786699

Ramalingam, R., & Chinnaiyan, V. (2023). A comparative analysis of chronic obstructive pulmonary disease using machine learning, and deep learning. *International Journal of Electrical and Computer Engineering*, *13*(1), 389. DOI: 10.11591/ijece.v13i1.pp389-399

Wang, J. M., Labaki, W. W., Murray, S., Martinez, F. J., Curtis, J. L., Hoffman, E. A., Ram, S., Bell, A. J., Galban, C. J., Han, M. L. K., & Hatt, C. (2023). Machine learning for screening of at-risk, mild and moderate COPD patients at risk of FEV1 decline: Results from COPDGene and SPIROMICS. *Frontiers in Physiology*, *14*, 1144192. DOI: 10.3389/fphys.2023.1144192 PMID: 37153221

Wang, X., Ren, H., Ren, J., Song, W., Qiao, Y., Ren, Z., Zhao, Y., Linghu, L., Cui, Y., Zhao, Z., Chen, L., & Qiu, L. (2023). Machine learning-enabled risk prediction of chronic obstructive pulmonary disease with unbalanced data. *Computer Methods and Programs in Biomedicine*, *230*, 107340. DOI: 10.1016/j.cmpb.2023.107340 PMID: 36640604

Weiss, J., Raghu, V. K., Bontempi, D., Christiani, D. C., Mak, R. H., Lu, M. T., & Aerts, H. J. (2023). Deep learning to estimate lung disease mortality from chest radiographs. *Nature Communications*, *14*(1), 2797. DOI: 10.1038/s41467-023-37758-5 PMID: 37193717

Yin, C., Udrescu, M., Gupta, G., Cheng, M., Lihu, A., Udrescu, L., Bogdan, P., Mannino, D. M., & Mihaicuta, S. (2023). Fractional dynamics foster deep learning of COPD stage prediction. *Advancement of Science*, *10*(12), 2203485. DOI: 10.1002/advs.202203485 PMID: 36808826

Zhang, G., Luo, L., Zhang, L., & Liu, Z. (2023). Research progress of respiratory disease and idiopathic pulmonary fibrosis based on artificial intelligence. *Diagnostics (Basel)*, *13*(3), 357. DOI: 10.3390/diagnostics13030357 PMID: 36766460 [illegible] K., & Thangavelu, V. (2023). A comparative analysis of [illegible] supervised machine learning [illegible] [illegible]. [illegible] 11(14), 2[illegible]. DOI: 10.[illegible]

Wang, [illegible] [illegible] S., [illegible] Hahn S., [illegible] (2022). Machine learning for [illegible] [illegible]. [illegible] 10.[illegible]

Wang, X., [illegible] Yang, Y., [illegible] (2022). Machine learning-enabled risk prediction of chronic obstructive pulmonary disease [illegible] [illegible] [illegible] 10.[illegible]

Yang, [illegible] (2020). Deep learning [illegible] data [illegible]. *Nature Communications*, [illegible] DOI: 10.[illegible]

Yin, [illegible] (2020). [illegible] medical [illegible] DOI: 10.[illegible]

Zhang, [illegible] (2020). [illegible] of respiratory disease and [illegible] pulmonary [illegible] based on artificial intelligence [illegible]. [illegible] DOI: 10.[illegible]

Chapter 2
Personalized Medicine Through AI:
Enhancing Tuberculosis Forecasting With Fuzzy Neural Models

Suriana Binti Lasaraiya
https://orcid.org/0000-0002-9119-2858
Universiti Malaysia Sabah, Malaysia

Suzelawati Binti Zenian
Universiti Malaysia Sabah, Malaysia

Risman Mat Hasim
https://orcid.org/0000-0002-5358-587X
Universiti Putra Malaysia, Malaysia

Azmirul Ashaari
https://orcid.org/0000-0002-4405-4890
Universiti Teknologi Malaysia, Malaysia

Lorna Uden
https://orcid.org/0000-0002-8598-7355
University of Staffordshire, UK

ABSTRACT

Tuberculosis (TB) remains a major health challenge in Sabah, Malaysia, where accurate forecasting is crucial for disease control. Traditional methods struggle with complex epidemiological data, making Artificial Intelligence (AI) techniques

DOI: 10.4018/979-8-3373-4571-0.ch002

Copyright © 2025, IGI Global Scientific Publishing. Copying or distributing in print or electronic forms without written permission of IGI Global Scientific Publishing is prohibited.

like fuzzy logic and neural networks valuable. Fuzzy logic handles uncertainty, neural networks detect patterns, and their integration using fuzzy neural models and enhances TB forecasting accuracy. Personalized medicine benefits from AI-driven models incorporating demographic and regional trends. Fuzzy logic forecasting converts uncertain data into insights through fuzzification, rule application, and defuzzification. Triangular membership functions improve computational efficiency while maintaining interpretability. Case studies show that fuzzy neural models outperform traditional methods, leading to proactive health measures and better resource allocation. Further advancements in these models promise improved TB management, benefiting both public health and personalized medicine.

INTRODUCTION.

In recent years, the integration of fuzzy logic and fuzzy time series forecasting with artificial intelligence (AI) has gained significant attention due to their shared ability to address complex, uncertain, and dynamic problems. The integration of fuzzy logic and fuzzy time series forecasting with artificial intelligence (AI) has garnered significant attention in recent years due to their combined ability to tackle complex, uncertain, and dynamic problems.

Fuzzy logic, introduced by Zadeh in 1965, provides a mathematical framework for handling vagueness and imprecision by allowing partial truth values between completely true and false. This capability makes it particularly useful for processing real-world data, which is often noisy, incomplete, or ambiguous. Similarly, fuzzy time series (FTS) forecasting, first introduced by Song and Chissom in the 1990s, extends traditional time series models by incorporating fuzzy set theory. Unlike classical forecasting methods such as ARIMA and SARIMA, which require strict statistical assumptions, FTS methods are better suited for handling linguistic and imprecise data, making them ideal for predicting trends in uncertain environments such as disease outbreaks, stock markets, and climate change patterns. When integrated with AI techniques such as neural networks and deep learning, these methods further enhance the adaptability and precision of predictive models.

Artificial intelligence (AI) and fuzzy logic have become pivotal in enhancing the accuracy and precision of medical predictions. In the context of tuberculosis (TB), where early detection and forecasting are critical, AI-fuzzy models offer promising solutions by integrating heuristic knowledge to improve prediction outcomes. Traditional statistical models, while effective, often fail to account for the inherent uncertainty and complexity in tuberculosis trends. AI-fuzzy models provide a flexible framework to handle this uncertainty and can adapt to the evolving nature of TB cases, offering a more robust forecasting tool. This chapter presents an integration of fuzzy logic and neural networks with heuristic knowledge to forecast TB prevalence. By incorporating expert knowledge into the model, this approach not only improves accuracy but also provides actionable insights that can be used in clinical and public health settings.

AI excels in recognizing complex patterns and extracting features from vast amounts of data, while fuzzy logic provides a structured way to interpret uncertainty and improve human-like reasoning. This hybrid approach has been increasingly applied in fields such as medical diagnosis, financial forecasting, and environmental monitoring. One significant challenge in this integration, however, is balancing interpretability and computational complexity. While fuzzy logic enhances explainability, AI-driven models, particularly deep learning, often operate as "black boxes," making it difficult to trace decision-making processes. Addressing this issue remains a key area of research, with efforts focused on explainable AI (XAI) and improved fuzzy inference systems.

As illustrated in Figure 1, the relationships among keywords such as 'fuzzy logic,' 'forecasting,' 'time series,' and 'artificial intelligence' underscore their strong interdependence and relevance in addressing complex, data-driven challenges of the modern era. These connections reveal a growing trend toward hybridized approaches, where fuzzy-based methodologies are seamlessly integrated into artificial intelligence (AI) systems to tackle issues in prediction, optimization, and decision-making. The central placement of 'fuzzy logic' and 'forecasting' in the figure highlights their pivotal role as core techniques within interdisciplinary research, serving as a bridge between theoretical advancements and practical applications.

Furthermore, the co-occurrence of terms like 'fuzzy time series forecasting' and 'artificial intelligence' illustrates how these techniques complement each other in AI-driven applications. For instance, fuzzy time series forecasting has been effectively applied in health monitoring systems to predict patient outcomes, in financial markets to model stock price trends, and in environmental modelling to forecast air quality or climate change patterns. The ability of fuzzy methods to handle uncertainty, imprecision, and non-linear relationships makes them particularly valuable in such domains where traditional methods might struggle.

Figure 1. The interconnectedness of the field of artificial intelligence (AI), fuzzy logic, and fuzzy time series forecasting.

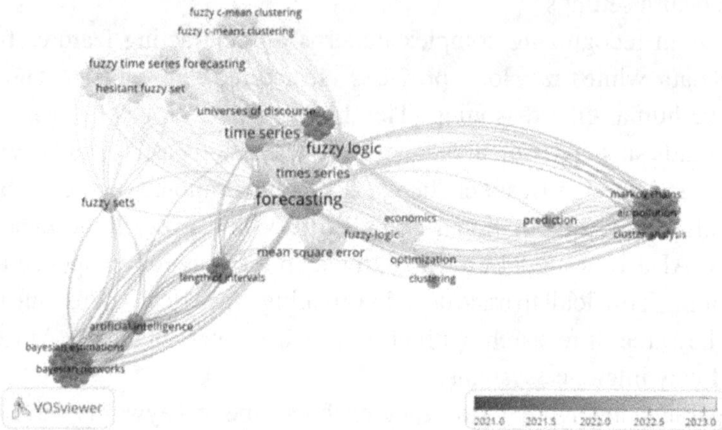

The presence of terms like 'optimization,' 'mean square error,' and 'Bayesian estimations' in proximity further indicates the emphasis on performance evaluation and model refinement. This reflects an ongoing effort to improve the accuracy and reliability of AI models by incorporating the interpretability and robustness of fuzzy logic techniques. For example, optimization algorithms often integrate fuzzy logic to fine-tune parameters, while error metrics like mean square error are used to assess the effectiveness of fuzzy time series models in capturing temporal patterns.

In addition, the temporal gradient shown in Figure 1; from blue (2021) to yellow (2023); highlights the evolution of research in this field. Earlier studies focused on foundational topics like 'fuzzy logic' and 'time series,' while recent trends emphasize emerging areas such as 'fuzzy c-means clustering' and 'hesitant fuzzy sets,' which expand the versatility and applicability of fuzzy systems in clustering and decision analysis. This progression aligns with the increasing demand for advanced methodologies capable of addressing dynamic and uncertain problems in real-world scenarios. The broader connections to terms like 'air pollution,' 'economics,' and 'artificial intelligence' suggest a wide range of applications, from environmental forecasting to economic modelling and AI-driven optimization. For example, fuzzy logic's interpretability enables its effective use in air pollution monitoring systems, where it can analyse imprecise or incomplete data to provide actionable insights for policymakers.

In summary, the visualization in Figure 1 not only illustrates the interconnectedness of fuzzy logic, AI, and time series forecasting but also highlights their collective potential to address complex, uncertain, and dynamic challenges across diverse domains. This synergy underscores the importance of continuing research in hybrid methodologies, as they offer significant advantages in enhancing the adaptability, precision, and real-world applicability of AI systems. Figure 1 also significantly highlights the interconnectedness of fuzzy logic, fuzzy time series forecasting, and artificial intelligence (AI) within the broader context of forecasting, prediction, and optimization tasks. These relationships emphasize the integral role fuzzy-based methods play in advancing AI applications, particularly in handling uncertainty and vagueness in complex datasets.

1. Fuzzy Logic as a Core Component of AI: Fuzzy logic, as indicated in the visualization, directly connects to key AI methodologies like artificial intelligence, optimization, and mean square error minimization. This relationship underscores fuzzy logic's capability to model imprecise systems, where AI's conventional binary logic may falter. By integrating fuzzy sets and rules into AI frameworks, systems can process linguistic variables and handle data with high levels of ambiguity.
2. Fuzzy Time Series Forecasting in AI Applications: The prominent connection between fuzzy time series forecasting and AI concepts such as prediction, time series analysis, and clustering reflects the growing reliance on fuzzy methods to enhance AI's predictive accuracy. Fuzzy time series models are particularly effective in areas with nonlinear patterns, providing more adaptive and interpretable forecasting systems. The integration of length of intervals further demonstrates the model's refinement, crucial for addressing the granularity required in time-dependent datasets.
3. AI-Driven Advancements in Forecasting: AI leverages fuzzy time series forecasting to achieve advancements in areas such as economic forecasting, air pollution modeling, and healthcare analytics. The interlinkages in the figure show how AI enhances the performance of fuzzy methods by automating parameter optimization and generating adaptive rules for better prediction outcomes.
4. Collaborative Synergy: The synergy between fuzzy logic, fuzzy time series forecasting, and AI is evident through the shared emphasis on forecasting, optimization, and clustering techniques. This collaboration allows for robust modeling frameworks that merge AI's computational power with the interpretability and adaptability of fuzzy systems, leading to significant progress in real-world applications.

THE ROLE OF PERSONALIZED MEDICINE IN PUBLIC HEALTH

Personalized medicine is a transformative approach in healthcare that tailors' medical treatments based on individual characteristics, including genetic information, lifestyle habits, and environmental exposures. Unlike traditional medicine, which often applies a one-size-fits-all approach, personalized medicine considers the unique genetic and biochemical profile of each patient, ensuring that the treatment is not only more effective but also minimizes potential adverse effects. This level of customization can significantly improve the efficiency of healthcare interventions, particularly in public health systems, by addressing both individual and population-level needs more accurately.

In public health, personalized medicine can be seen as a game changer because it allows for the precise identification of at-risk populations and individuals. Instead of using generalized treatment strategies, personalized medicine identifies those who are more likely to develop certain diseases, like tuberculosis (TB), based on factors such as their genetic predisposition, environmental exposure, or specific behavioural patterns. It also considers regional differences in disease prevalence, ensuring that interventions are localized and context specific. As a result, treatments, prevention strategies, and diagnostic tools can be more effective because they align directly with an individual's or population's unique risk factors.

For diseases like TB, which are influenced by various factors such as socio-economic status, environmental exposure, and individual immune response, personalized medicine allows for a better understanding of the diverse factors at play. This leads to more tailored interventions for both prevention and treatment. For example, a public health campaign in one region might focus on lifestyle factors or living conditions that contribute to TB transmission, while another region with a different genetic or environmental profile might prioritize early detection through genetic screening.

1. The Role of Artificial Intelligence and Advanced Technologies in Personalized Medicine

Integrating advanced technologies, such as artificial intelligence (AI), fuzzy logic, and neural networks, with personalized medicine creates new possibilities for improving public health outcomes. AI, for instance, can process vast amounts of data and identify patterns that are too complex for human analysis, which is particularly useful in predicting and managing infectious diseases like TB. AI-powered models can predict the progression of diseases, recognize emerging trends, and even forecast potential outbreaks based on early indicators.

Fuzzy logic, a form of AI that handles uncertainty and imprecision, is particularly relevant in epidemiology. In the context of TB, fuzzy logic can help model the uncertainty in patient data, regional health factors, and environmental variables. Since the data collected in public health, particularly in infectious disease surveillance, is often noisy and incomplete, fuzzy logic algorithms can handle this uncertainty to provide more reliable predictions.

Neural networks, another AI tool, can be trained on large datasets to identify complex relationships in data, such as how genetic traits and lifestyle factors influence disease risk. When combined with personalized medicine, these technologies enable the development of highly accurate, data-driven models that can predict disease progression and suggest the most effective course of action for individual patients or communities. For instance, neural networks could predict how a person's genetic makeup and environment interact to affect their susceptibility to TB, leading to more targeted treatments and interventions.

2. Enhancing Tuberculosis (TB) Forecasting Models

When it comes to forecasting TB, the combination of personalized medicine and AI technologies is particularly powerful. Personalized medicine, in this context, integrates various factors such as demographic data (age, gender, ethnicity), socioeconomic status (income level, education, occupation), and specific regional disease trends (TB prevalence, vaccination rates, environmental risks) into the predictive model. These factors help create a more nuanced understanding of how TB spreads and affects different populations.

AI tools, such as fuzzy neural networks, play a crucial role in analyzing this data. These networks are adept at handling the variability and uncertainty found in epidemiological data. For example, fuzzy neural networks can interpret fluctuating disease rates, considering the uncertain nature of TB transmission across different populations, regions, and time periods. This allows for the development of models that reflect the real-world complexities of disease spread and better forecast future outbreaks.

By utilizing these advanced models, health authorities can make more informed decisions about where to allocate resources and how to prioritize interventions. For example, if a predictive model suggests that a certain community is at higher risk for a TB outbreak due to a combination of genetic predisposition, high population density, and low healthcare access, targeted prevention efforts—such as increased screening or vaccination—can be implemented more effectively. This approach not only improves disease control efforts but also ensures that limited resources are used where they are most needed.

3. Proactive Healthcare Delivery and Efficient Resource Allocation

One of the most significant benefits of integrating personalized medicine with AI is the shift towards a proactive, data-driven approach to healthcare delivery. By using predictive models to forecast disease outbreaks and patient outcomes, health systems can implement early interventions that are tailored to the specific needs of individuals or communities, rather than waiting for disease cases to increase or for a public health emergency to arise.

This proactive approach enables more efficient resource allocation. For example, healthcare systems can target high-risk populations for TB screening or provide more specialized care to individuals identified as being at greater risk of severe disease progression. This not only helps in controlling the disease but also improves patient care by focusing on their specific health needs and conditions. Additionally, integrating AI into personalized medicine can streamline healthcare delivery. With the help of AI-powered tools, healthcare providers can access up-to-date information on disease trends, patient risk profiles, and emerging health threats, enabling them to respond quickly and efficiently.

4. Conclusion

In summary, personalized medicine, when combined with advanced technologies such as AI, fuzzy logic, and neural networks, revolutionizes the way we approach public health. In the case of TB, this integration leads to more accurate disease forecasting, better-targeted interventions, and improved health outcomes. By considering genetic, environmental, and socio-economic factors, personalized medicine ensures that healthcare interventions are specific to the needs of individuals and populations. Through the use of AI and predictive models, health systems can move toward a more proactive, data-driven approach, optimizing resource use and improving disease management. Ultimately, personalized medicine and AI together offer a powerful toolset for advancing public health and managing complex infectious diseases like tuberculosis.

Related studies

The integration of artificial intelligence (AI) in predictive modeling has been widely explored in healthcare forecasting. Among the many AI-driven approaches, fuzzy logic has gained prominence for its ability to model uncertainty and imprecision in real-world data. The concept of fuzzy logic was first introduced by Lotfi A. Zadeh in 1965, who proposed fuzzy set theory as a mathematical framework for dealing with vagueness and uncertainty in decision-making processes. Building on this foundation, Song and Chissom (1993a) introduced the fuzzy time series (FTS) model, which extends fuzzy logic principles to time-dependent data. This advancement enabled forecasting models to handle imprecise, uncertain, and incomplete time-series data, making them particularly useful in epidemiological studies and disease prediction.

Several studies have explored the application of fuzzy logic in disease forecasting. For instance, Huarng and Yu (2006) applied fuzzy time series to forecast dengue fever cases, demonstrating its effectiveness in modelling epidemiological data with imprecise trends. Similarly, Jilani, Burney, and Ardil (2008) refined fuzzy time series models to improve accuracy in disease outbreak predictions, highlighting the role of heuristic adjustments in enhancing forecasting precision. In tuberculosis (TB) forecasting, Milinovich et al. (2015) utilized AI-based models, including machine learning techniques, to predict TB incidence trends, though their work primarily relied on statistical machine learning rather than fuzzy-based approaches.

Neural networks have been extensively utilized in disease forecasting due to their capacity to learn complex patterns and relationships. For instance, a study by Yang et al. (2023) developed a deep learning model to predict influenza trends by integrating heterogeneous data sources, including hospital records, climate data, and search engine queries. The model demonstrated the strength of neural networks in capturing non-linear relationships inherent in diverse datasets. However, the study also highlighted challenges related to data quality and interpretability, especially when handling incomplete datasets.

The combination of fuzzy logic and neural networks, known as fuzzy neural networks (FNNs), has emerged as a powerful approach for predictive modelling in uncertain environments. A study by Chiroma et al. (2020) proposed a fusion approach that combined fuzzy logic and fractal theory for forecasting COVID-19 time series. The fuzzy logic component represented the uncertainty in making the forecast, while the fractal theory was used to evaluate the intricate nature of the data dynamics.

Neural networks have been widely utilized in disease forecasting due to their ability to learn complex patterns and relationships. For example, Alizadegan et al. (2024) demonstrated that LSTM and Bi-LSTM models outperform traditional forecasting methods like ARIMA and SARIMA in capturing non-linear dependencies in time series data, making them particularly effective in energy consumption prediction (Alizadegan et al., 2024). However, challenges related to data quality and interpretability remain, particularly when handling incomplete datasets.

The integration of fuzzy logic and neural networks, known as fuzzy neural networks (FNNs), has emerged as a promising approach for predictive modeling in uncertain environments. Li et al. (2013) introduced a fuzzy neural network technique that effectively captures both linear and non-linear correlations in system state forecasting, improving prediction accuracy over traditional methods (Li, Wang, &

Ismail, 2013). More recently, Kuo and Zulvia (2021) applied a gradient evolution algorithm to train an intuitionistic fuzzy neural network for forecasting medical costs in Taiwan, showing superior accuracy compared to traditional models, Kuo & Zulvia, (2021). However, these models often lack heuristic refinements, which could further improve their predictive performance.

Let us consider one example on predicting tuberculosis risk using fuzzy linguistic variables. Consider the risk assessment of tuberculosis (TB) for individuals in a given population over the course of a year. Typically, TB risk is influenced by multiple factors, including environmental conditions, immune system strength, access to healthcare, and prior exposure to the disease. Rather than assigning precise numerical values to the risk level, we can represent it using fuzzy linguistic variables such as "very low risk", "low risk", "moderate risk", "high risk", and "very high risk". Traditional time series methods are not well-suited for modeling this dynamic process due to its inherent subjectivity and imprecise measurements.

As outlined by Zadeh (1975a, 1975b, 1975c), fuzzy time series analysis provides a more effective approach by accommodating uncertainty and variability, enabling a more accurate prediction of future emotional states compared to conventional forecasting techniques, which struggle with subjective data. To define the universe of discourse, let us consider an interval [0, 1], where 0 represents the lowest possible TB risk (e.g., an individual with strong immunity and no exposure) and 1 represents the highest possible risk (e.g., an immunocompromised person with prolonged exposure in a high-prevalence area). Instead of assigning exact probabilities, we classify individuals into fuzzy risk categories based on key attributes such as age, nutrition level, socioeconomic status, vaccination history, and presence of other health conditions (e.g., diabetes or HIV).

For instance, an individual who has moderate immunity, occasional exposure to TB-infected individuals, and incomplete vaccination might be classified as "moderate risk", while a person with poor nutrition, chronic respiratory issues, and frequent exposure to infected individuals might fall under "high risk". Since these risk levels are dynamic and subject to change over time due to external factors such as public health interventions or seasonal variations, using fuzzy time series analysis allows us to track and forecast changes in TB risk more effectively than conventional models.

By applying fuzzy neural networks, we can enhance forecasting accuracy by allowing the system to learn from past patterns and adapt to new trends in TB risk factors. Unlike traditional time series methods that require precise numerical inputs, this approach enables personalized medicine, where patient-specific risk assessments can be continuously updated based on evolving health conditions and environmental factors. As first conceptualized by Zadeh (1965) and later extended into fuzzy time series (Song & Chissom, 1993), this hybrid AI approach integrates uncertainty modelling with adaptive learning, providing a more flexible and realistic representation of TB risk progression over time.

Classical forecasting techniques such as ARIMA have long been utilized for their simplicity and effectiveness in modeling stationary time series data (Box et al., 2015). Meanwhile, SEIR models offer a compartmental approach to infectious disease modeling, providing valuable insight into transmission dynamics (Kucharski et al., 2020). However, both models often struggle with adapting to dynamic or noisy real-world health data. On the other hand, purely neural models like LSTM networks demonstrate strong pattern recognition capabilities and have shown promise in disease forecasting (Hochreiter & Schmidhuber, 1997; Shastri et al., 2022). Yet, their black-box nature and requirement for large datasets pose challenges in clinical contexts (Chai et al., 2021). In contrast, fuzzy neural models integrate the interpretability of fuzzy logic with the adaptability of neural networks, enabling personalized forecasting in uncertain environments such as tuberculosis prediction (Jothilakshmi & Vasanthamani, 2015; Hegazi et al., 2023). These models allow for human-expert knowledge to be encoded as fuzzy rules, enhancing transparency and contextual reasoning (Pedrycz, 1998).

Building upon these foundational studies, this research introduces an FTS-based forecasting model incorporating heuristic knowledge to refine Fuzzy Logical Relationship Groups (FLRG). Unlike previous models, which rely solely on statistical methods or neural networks, this approach enhances forecasting accuracy by incorporating domain-specific knowledge into the FTS framework. By optimizing interval selection and improving uncertainty modelling, this study advances AI-driven personalized medicine for TB forecasting, contributing to public health decision-making and intervention strategies. Most recent study done by Leonie et al. (2020) aim to exploit the converging nature of the tuberculosis (TB) and diabetes epidemics to forecast TB cases. They propose a model in forecasting tuberculosis cases by using the data on the weekly reported cases of TB in Germany from June 8, 2014 until May 5, 2019. This study also followed by Tang et al. (2023), propose the using of machine learning to build a prediction model of tuberculosis incidence with the influenced factors; influences by meteorological and air pollutants. This study was done by using the incidence data of tuberculosis in Changde City from 2010 to 2020 as the training set and the incidence data in 2021 as the validation set for prediction.

This study serves as a foundational scientific resource for the development of evidence-based tuberculosis (TB) prevention and control policies by public health authorities. By offering comprehensive insights into TB transmission patterns, risk factors, and predictive modeling approaches, the findings contribute to more effective decision-making in disease surveillance and intervention strategies. Additionally, the study provides critical reference information that can aid policymakers in designing targeted public health initiatives, optimizing resource allocation, and implementing data-driven strategies to mitigate TB incidence and improve overall public health outcomes.

Challenges in Tuberculosis Forecasting

In 2023, tuberculosis (TB) was responsible for approximately 1.25 million deaths worldwide, including 161,000 deaths among individuals living with HIV. After being temporarily surpassed by coronavirus disease (COVID-19) for three years, TB has likely regained its position as the leading cause of mortality from a single infectious agent. It remains the primary cause of death among people with HIV and a significant contributor to fatalities associated with antimicrobial resistance. Globally, an estimated 10.8 million people were diagnosed with TB in 2023, comprising approximately 6.0 million men, 3.6 million women, and 1.3 million children. TB continues to affect all countries and age groups, despite being both preventable and curable. However, multidrug-resistant TB (MDR-TB) remains a major public health crisis and a significant threat to global health security, with only about 40% of individuals with drug-resistant TB receiving appropriate treatment in 2023. Efforts to control TB have had a substantial impact, with an estimated 79 million lives saved since 2000 through prevention, diagnosis, and treatment initiatives. However, achieving the global TB targets set at the 2023 United Nations High-Level Meeting on TB requires an estimated annual investment of US$ 22 billion. Ending the TB epidemic by 2030 remains a key objective within the health targets outlined in the United Nations Sustainable Development Goals (SDGs), World Health Organization (2019).

Despite advancements in disease control efforts, significant challenges persist in TB diagnosis, treatment, and surveillance, particularly in developing countries. Moreover, co-infections such as HIV, Pawlowski et al. (2012) and underlying conditions like diabetes, Alebel et al. and Mustaq (2019) exacerbate the impact of TB, contributing to synergistic pandemics, Dooley et al. (2009) and Mayer et al. (2010).

The management and forecasting of TB in Sabah present significant challenges due to the region's high disease burden and the complex dynamics of the epidemic. Traditional forecasting methods, such as statistical regression or compartmental models, often struggle to account for the uncertainty and imprecision inherent in real-world epidemiological data. These methods typically rely on assumptions of deterministic and complete datasets, which rarely align with the incomplete, inconsistent, or noisy nature of actual health data.

A key challenge in TB forecasting lies in the variability and quality of data. Epidemiological datasets often exhibit non-linear relationships, missing values, and significant noise, complicating the development of accurate predictive models using conventional techniques. Moreover, traditional statistical approaches may oversimplify the dynamic interactions within the data, leading to suboptimal forecasting accuracy.

Fuzzy logic-based methods address these challenges by embracing uncertainty and imprecision as integral components of the modelling process. By leveraging fuzzy logic, forecasting models can capture the complex and non-linear dynamics of TB data while accommodating inconsistencies in the datasets. For instance, fuzzy logic allows for the representation of linguistic variables and imprecise data points, offering a more flexible and robust framework for forecasting. This adaptability makes fuzzy logic-based approaches particularly effective for TB prediction in Sabah, where diverse socio-economic and environmental factors contribute to the disease's dynamics.

Fuzzy Logic and Its Role in Predictive Modelling

The challenges of forecasting tuberculosis and the need for more precise, adaptable models highlight the importance of advanced methodologies like fuzzy logic. As a tool capable of handling uncertainty, vagueness, and imprecision in data, fuzzy logic serves as a powerful framework for predictive modelling in complex systems, including public health. Its ability to integrate diverse data sources and model non-linear relationships makes it particularly suited for addressing the intricate dynamics of tuberculosis forecasting. The next section delves deeper into how fuzzy logic plays a pivotal role in predictive modelling and why it has become an essential component in modern forecasting frameworks.

Fuzzy time series forecasting has emerged as a robust methodology for addressing the complexities inherent in forecasting tasks involving uncertain and imprecise data. Unlike traditional time series methods, which rely on strict statistical assumptions, fuzzy time series models leverage fuzzy logic to represent and analyse vague patterns in data. In this study, a refined fuzzy time series model is introduced, incorporating heuristic knowledge to enhance its forecasting accuracy and adaptability. The definition is defined by Song and Chissom, 1993b below.

Definition 1. $Y(t)(t = \ldots,0,1,2,\ldots)$ is a subset of R. Let $Y(t)$ be the universe of discourse defined by fuzzy sets $f_i(t)$. If $F(t)$ consists of $f_i(t)(i = 1,2,\ldots)$, $F(t)$ is defined as the fuzzy time series on $Y(t)(t = \ldots,0,1,2,\ldots)$.

By Definition 1, $F(t)$ is called a fuzzy time series (FTS) over $Y(t)$ if $f(t) = \mu_{A_j}(y(t))$ is the collection of fuzzified values of Y for $j = 1, \ldots, k$ and $t = 0,1,\ldots T$. Let A_j for $j = 1,2,3,\ldots k$ is the possible linguistic variables. Each A_j is defined by the intervals $u_1, u_2, u_3, \ldots, u_k$ as shown below.

$$A_1 = \frac{1}{u_1} + \frac{0.5}{u_2} + \frac{0}{u_3} + \frac{0}{u_4} + \ldots + \frac{0}{u_n}$$

$$A_2 = \frac{0.5}{u_1} + \frac{1}{u_2} + \frac{0.5}{u_3} + \frac{0}{u_4} + \ldots + \frac{0}{u_n}$$

$$A_3 = \frac{0}{u_1} + \frac{0.5}{u_2} + \frac{1}{u_3} + \frac{0.5}{u_4} + \ldots + \frac{0}{u_n}$$

$$A_k = \frac{0}{u_1} + \frac{0}{u_2} + \frac{0}{u_3} + \frac{0}{u_4} + \ldots + \frac{0.5}{u_{k-1}} + \frac{1}{u_k}$$

In other words, each raw data point will be mapped to its respective set of intervals. Triangular membership functions are crucial in the fuzzification process because of their simplicity, computational efficiency, and ease of implementation. Mathematically, the triangular membership function is defined as

$$\mu(x) = \begin{cases} 0\,, x < a\, or\, x > c \\ \frac{x-a}{b-a}\,, a \leq x \leq b \\ \frac{c-x}{c-b}\,, b \leq x \leq c \end{cases}$$

where a is the lower limit of the triangular membership function (where the functions start to increase), b is the peak point (where the membership value is equal to 1) and c is the upper limit (where the functions started to decrease).

The rule formation is aligned to Definition 2, which have been defined by Song and Chissom, 1993b. In other words, when $F(t-1) = A_i$ and $F(t) = A_j$, then the relationship between $F(t-1)$ and $F(t)$ is given by $A_i \rightarrow A_j$.

Definition 2: If there exist a fuzzy relationship $R(t-1, t)$, such that $F(t) = F(t-1) \times R(t-1, t)$ where $\times$ represent an operator, then $F(t)$ is said to be caused by $F(t-1)$.

This relationship is referred to as a fuzzy logical relationship (FLR). After all the FLRs are obtained, the next step is the grouping process. This process involves shortlisting the FLR list by grouping those with identical items on the left-hand side, as defined in Definition 3, Chen (1996).

Definition 3: Fuzzy logical relationships (FLR) with the same fuzzy set on the left-hand side can be further grouped into a fuzzy logical relationship group.

Suppose there is FLR such that:

$$A_m \rightarrow A_{d1}$$

$$A_m \rightarrow A_{d2}$$

$$A_m \rightarrow A_{d3}$$

From the FLR list above, by Definiton 3, the fuzzy logical relationship group (FLRG) can be written as follow:

$$A_m \rightarrow A_{d1}, A_{d2}, A_{d3}, \ldots$$

The implementation of heuristic knowledge involves integrating expert insights and domain-specific rules into the modelling process, particularly in defining optimal interval lengths and constructing fuzzy logical relationship groups (FLRG). These refinements address the granularity required for analysing tuberculosis prevalence trends, ensuring that the model captures intricate patterns and variations in epidemiological data. By tailoring the intervals and relationships based on heuristic principles, the model overcomes limitations of conventional methods, such as their inability to adapt to nonlinear and time-dependent behaviours in datasets.

This heuristic-driven fuzzy time series forecasting model offers significant advantages for tuberculosis forecasting in Sabah. It not only improves the model's interpretability but also enhances its ability to accommodate regional and temporal variations in data. This approach aligns with the overarching goal of developing precise, adaptive, and context-aware forecasting systems, enabling health authorities to implement more targeted and effective interventions.

Figure 2. The step included in fuzzy time series forecasting series, Step 1 until Step 7.

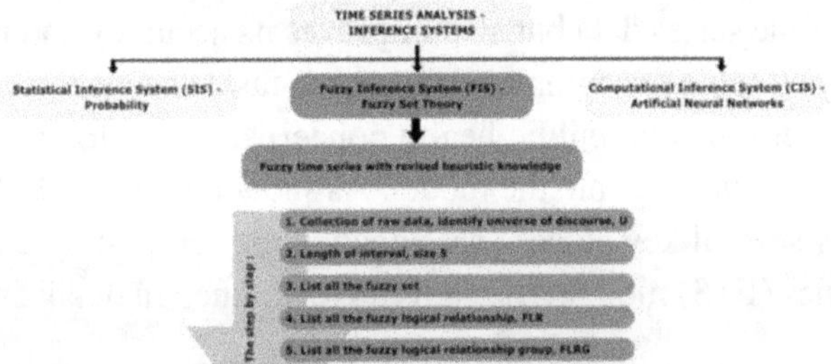

Figure 2 illustrates a conceptual framework for Time Series Analysis using Inference Systems, which encompasses three main approaches: Statistical Inference System (SIS), Fuzzy Inference System (FIS), and Computational Inference System (CIS). These systems are distinguished by their underlying methodologies and their capacity to handle different types of data and complexities. Statistical Inference Systems (SIS), rooted in classical probability theory, utilize statistical methods such as ARIMA models and moving averages to model relationships and make predictions.

These methods are effective for deterministic datasets where explicit patterns can be mathematically expressed. However, SIS often struggles to handle uncertainty, nonlinear relationships, and imprecision, which are common in real-world scenarios, making it less suitable for dynamic and complex datasets.

In contrast, the Fuzzy Inference System (FIS), based on fuzzy set theory, is designed to address the uncertainty and vagueness inherent in time series data. Unlike SIS, which relies on precise probabilities, FIS uses linguistic variables and membership functions to handle imprecise data, making it particularly effective for complex forecasting scenarios. The Fuzzy Time Series (FTS) approach, enhanced with revised heuristic knowledge, provides a structured methodology for improving forecasting accuracy. This includes steps such as defining the universe of discourse, dividing it into intervals, establishing fuzzy sets, and refining fuzzy logical relationship groups (FLRG) through heuristic knowledge.

Lastly, the Computational Inference System (CIS) leverages advanced computational techniques such as artificial neural networks (ANNs) and deep learning architectures to identify patterns in large, nonlinear, and highly dynamic datasets. CIS excels in predictive accuracy but often lacks the interpretability of FIS, which can limit its application in scenarios where explainability is crucial. Together, these three systems provide a comprehensive framework for analysing time series data, each with its strengths and limitations depending on the nature of the dataset and the specific requirements of the analysis.

This structured methodology ensures that the model not only adapts to the dynamic nature of time series data but also improves its accuracy and interpretability, making it highly suitable for complex forecasting tasks, such as predicting disease prevalence or other dynamic public health concerns. Let us look, how is this performed by applying real data into the model. As shown in Figure 2, the step-by-step process involves several key stages that enhance the forecasting capability of the Fuzzy Time Series (FTS) model. The steps are explained in detail as shown below.

1. It begins with the collection of raw data and the identification of the universe of discourse, which defines the range of values the data can take. The first step in developing a fuzzy neural network for tuberculosis (TB) forecasting involves the collection of raw data and the definition of the universe of discourse. Raw data may include variables such as the number of TB cases, environmental factors, or other related metrics. Importantly, the arrangement of this raw data is flexible and can be tailored to the specific objectives of the forecasting model. For example, the data can be organized by monthly intervals to capture broader trends or by daily intervals to provide more granular insights. This adaptability in data organization allows researchers to customize the model to suit the forecasting timeframe or resolution required for personalized medicine or resource

allocation. The universe of discourse refers to the range of values within which all the raw data points fall. It is critical to ensure that the universe of discourse encompasses the entire spectrum of the raw data, starting from the minimum observed value to the maximum. This comprehensive range ensures that no data is excluded or misrepresented during the fuzzification process, which involves converting raw numerical values into fuzzy sets. For instance, if the minimum number of TB cases recorded in a dataset is $min_{data} = 199$ and the maximum is $max_{data} = 601$, then the universe of discourse, U, must span from 190 to 610 , $U = [190, 610]$. The case study is based on the number of tuberculosis cases reported by monthly in Sabah, starting from January 2012 until December 2019. Defining the universe of discourse, U, accurately is essential because it serves as the foundation for constructing fuzzy sets and membership functions.

2. The next step is determining the length of intervals, a critical process that affects the granularity of the analysis; in this case, an interval size of 5 is applied.

A well-chosen interval length ensures that patterns and trends in the data are effectively captured without excessive loss of detail or over-segmentation. In this study, an interval size of 5 is applied, meaning that the data is divided into segments of equal width, allowing for a structured and systematic evaluation of variations within the dataset. As for the the universe of discourse, $U = [190, 610]$, there are 84 number of interval classes altogether, define as $u_1 = [190 - 195], u_2 = [195 = 200], u_3 = [200 - 205], u_4 = [205 - 210]$, $u_5 = [210 - 215], u_6 = [215 - 220], u_7 = [220 - 225], \ldots, u_{84} = \left[605 - 610\right]$. Figure 3 illustrates the first seven class intervals for the membership functions for the fuzzy time series model, where each interval represents a distinct fuzzy set. The specified intervals are mapped onto triangular membership functions to facilitate the fuzzification process. The x-axis denotes the data values, while the y-axis represents the degree of membership, ranging from 0 to 1. Each triangular function is centered within its respective interval, ensuring smooth transitions between adjacent fuzzy sets. The overlapping nature of these functions allows for a gradual change in membership, thereby capturing the inherent uncertainty and imprecision in time series data. By employing this approach, the fuzzy time series model can effectively handle linguistic uncertainty, making it well-suited for forecasting applications where crisp boundaries between data points are impractical. This interval-based representation provides a structured framework for defining fuzzy relationships and subsequently applying fuzzy inference techniques to enhance predictive accuracy.

Figure 3. Membership functions of intervals u_1, u_2, u_3, u_4, u_5, u_6 and u_7

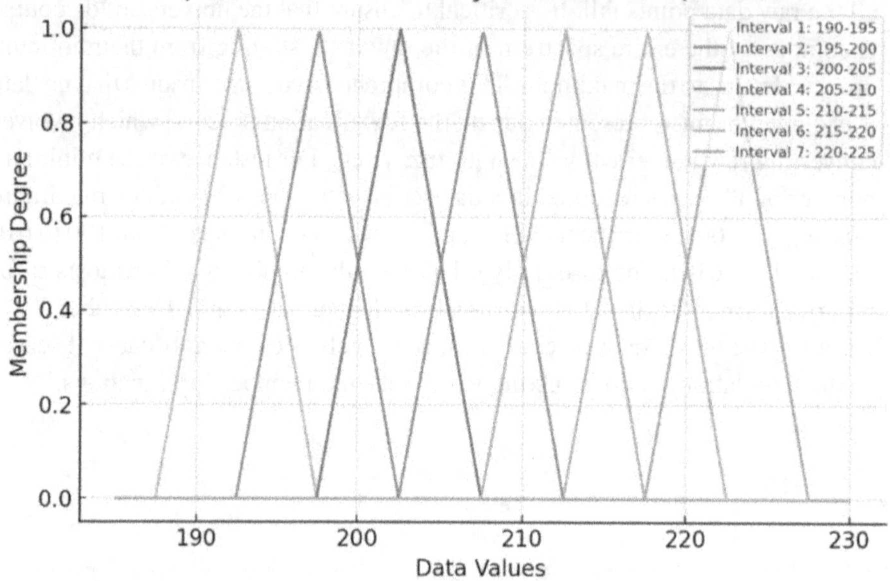

3. Following this, fuzzy sets are listed to represent data linguistically, transforming precise numerical values into fuzzy terms to capture uncertainty. Following the definition of the universe of discourse, U, and its division into 84 interval classes, each interval u_i is mapped to a corresponding fuzzy set A_i, allowing numerical values to be expressed linguistically. This transformation enables the model to handle uncertainty by associating precise numerical values with degrees of membership in overlapping fuzzy sets. For instance, the first interval $u_1 = [190,195]$ is assigned to the fuzzy set A_1, and so forth, up to $u_{84} = [605 - 610]$ corresponding to A_{84}. Through this mapping, the fuzzy time series model effectively converts crisp data into linguistic terms, facilitating the application of fuzzy logic rules to forecast trends and patterns within the dataset.
4. Subsequently, fuzzy logical relationships (FLR) are established to model the progression of data over time. From the overall data set in the year 2012 until the year 2019, let us choose some data range from January 2016 until December 2016, Table 1 shows the list of FLR for this range of time.

Table 1. The fuzzy set, fuzzy logical relationship (FLR) and heuristic fuzzy logical relationship group (FLRG).

Month	Raw data	A_i	FLR	Heuristic FLRG
Jan	338	A_{30}	-	-
Feb	372	A_{37}	$A_{30} \rightarrow A_{37}$	$A_{30} \rightarrow A_{37}$
Mar	505	A_{64}	$A_{37} \rightarrow A_{64}$	$A_{37} \rightarrow A_{41}, A_{64}, A_{59}, A_{77}$
Apr	394	A_{41}	$A_{64} \rightarrow A_{41}$	$A_{64} \rightarrow A_{41}$
May	401	A_{43}	$A_{41} \rightarrow A_{43}$	$A_{41} \rightarrow A_{71}, A_{43}, A_{52}, A_{69}, A_{41}$
Jun	401	A_{43}	$A_{43} \rightarrow A_{43}$	$A_{43} \rightarrow A_{31}, A_{29}, A_{43}, A_{24}, A_{57}$
Jul	305	A_{24}	$A_{43} \rightarrow A_{24}$	$A_{43} \rightarrow A_{31}, A_{29}, A_{43}, A_{24}$
Aug	482	A_{59}	$A_{24} \rightarrow A_{59}$	$A_{24} \rightarrow A_{59}, A_{39}$
Sep	410	A_{45}	$A_{59} \rightarrow A_{45}$	$A_{59} \rightarrow A_{22}, A_{45}, A_{24}$
Oct	311	A_{25}	$A_{45} \rightarrow A_{35}$	$A_{45} \rightarrow A_{35}$
Nov	601	A_{83}	$A_{25} \rightarrow A_{83}$	$A_{25} \rightarrow A_{83}$
Dec	433	A_{49}	$A_{83} \rightarrow A_{49}$	$A_{83} \rightarrow A_{49}$

5. These relationships are then organized into Fuzzy Logical Relationship Groups (FLRG) to enhance the structure of the analysis. The grouping process is based on the common left-hand side (LHS) elements of the fuzzy logical relationships (FLR), where all corresponding right-hand side (RHS) elements are grouped under the same FLRG. Notably, if the LHS and RHS elements are identical, all instances of that FLRG will be considered when computing the forecast value. The list of FLRG is as shown in Table 1. The grouping is basically based on the whole data list of FLR from the range from January 2012 until December 2019.
6. An innovative aspect of this model is the incorporation of heuristic fuzzy logical relationship groups (heuristic FLRG), which refine the relationships based on domain-specific knowledge and expert insights. This step allows the model to address data complexities and uncertainties more effectively than traditional approaches. This refinement process allows for a more nuanced representation of temporal dependencies within the data, enabling the model to capture subtle trends and irregularities that may be overlooked by purely data-driven methods. By integrating heuristic knowledge, the model can better address inherent uncertainties, fluctuations, and contextual variations, ultimately improving the robustness and accuracy of the forecasting process. This approach distinguishes the proposed model from traditional fuzzy time series methods, making it more

adaptable to complex real-world datasets. Based on Table 1, the implementation is shown in the month of June, where the FLR shows the same elements in left-hand side (LHS) and right-hand side (RHS). Based on this, the whole list of elements in right-hand side (RHS) will be counted when calculating the forecasting values.

7. Finally, the forecasting process is carried out, leveraging the refined relationships to generate accurate predictions. The model applies these relationships to transform historical data into meaningful predictions, ensuring that uncertainties and variations within the dataset are effectively accounted for. By leveraging both traditional fuzzy logical relationship groups (FLRG) and heuristic FLRG, the forecasting mechanism enhances predictive accuracy by incorporating both data-driven patterns and expert knowledge. Each input value is mapped to its corresponding fuzzy set, and the derived fuzzy relationships are used to determine the most probable future state. If multiple relationships exist, aggregation techniques are employed to derive a representative forecast value. Specifically, the forecasting process is based on the average of the elements in the right-hand side (RHS) of the FLRG, where midpoints of these elements are considered to enhance the precision of the forecast. Let us look at the example shown below.

February 2016: The heuristic FLRG for February 2016 is $A_{30} \rightarrow A_{37}$. Thus, the forecasting value for February 2016 is the midpoint of A_{37}, which is m_{37}. By looking at the interval u_{37}, the midpoint is calculated by the average of lower limit and upper limit of the class interval.

March 2016: The heuristic FLRG for March 2016 is $A_{37} \rightarrow A_{41}, A_{64}, A_{59}, A_{77}$. Thus, the forecasting value for March 2016 is the average of midpoints of $A_{41}, A_{64}, A_{59}, A_{77}$, which is $m_{41}, m_{64}, m_{59}, m_{77}$. By looking at the interval $u_{41}, u_{64}, u_{59}, u_{77}$, each midpoint is calculated by the average of lower limit and upper limit of the class interval.

The same process applied to the other data set to predict the forecasting tuberculosis cases. This structured approach ensures that the forecasting process is not only systematic but also adaptive to the inherent complexities of real-world data, making it more reliable compared to conventional forecasting techniques.

INTEGRATING NEURAL NETWORKS WITH FUZZY LOGIC FOR TB FORECASTING

Fuzzy logic and neural networks represent two powerful computational paradigms that complement each other when integrated. While fuzzy logic excels in addressing uncertainty and imprecise information, neural networks are renowned for their capacity to learn complex patterns and relationships within large datasets.

Neural networks, inspired by the structure and function of the human brain, consist of interconnected layers of nodes capable of learning from data. By iteratively adjusting the weights of connections between nodes, these networks can identify intricate patterns and make accurate predictions.

When applied together, fuzzy logic and neural networks offer a hybrid approach—fuzzy neural networks—that combines the strengths of both technologies. Fuzzy logic enhances the neural network's ability to manage imprecise or incomplete data, while neural networks allow the fuzzy system to adapt to non-linear and dynamic relationships. This integration is particularly advantageous for forecasting tuberculosis (TB), where the data is often uncertain, influenced by various socio-environmental factors, and exhibits non-linear trends.

The development of a fuzzy neural network for TB forecasting involves several key steps. Initially, fuzzy sets are constructed to represent input data such as historical TB case numbers, demographic patterns, and environmental variables (e.g., temperature, humidity). These fuzzy inputs capture the inherent uncertainties in the data, transforming them into linguistic terms like "low" or "high." Subsequently, a neural network is trained using these fuzzy inputs to learn the relationships between the data and the target output—predicted TB case numbers. During training, the network adjusts its weights to minimize errors between predicted and actual outcomes. Once trained, the fuzzy neural network can forecast future TB trends based on new or unseen data.

The integration of fuzzy neural networks has profound implications for personalized medicine in TB management. By leveraging patient-specific data, such as genetic predisposition or treatment history, alongside regional or environmental factors, this approach can provide tailored forecasts and recommendations. This enables healthcare providers to allocate resources more effectively, design targeted interventions, and improve individual patient outcomes. As advancements in AI continue to reshape healthcare, fuzzy neural networks stand as a promising tool for enhancing TB forecasting and personalized medicine strategies.

CONCLUSION AND FUTURE DIRECTIONS

In conclusion, the integration of fuzzy neural models represents a significant leap forward in the forecasting of tuberculosis (TB) by effectively combining two powerful computational techniques: fuzzy logic and neural networks. Each of these techniques brings unique strengths to the table, enabling more precise and adaptable models for disease forecasting. Fuzzy logic excels at handling the inherent uncertainty and imprecision in TB data, such as variations in disease transmission, incomplete or noisy datasets, and the unpredictability of environmental and socio-economic factors that affect TB spread. Neural networks, on the other hand, improve the forecasting model's predictive power by learning patterns from large volumes of historical and real-time data. Their ability to adapt and adjust to new data through continuous learning makes them highly effective in dealing with the dynamic nature of infectious diseases like TB.

The integration of these two methods provides a more robust forecasting model, capable of generating more accurate predictions of disease trends and patterns. With these models, health authorities can make better data-driven decisions to manage TB outbreaks, optimize intervention strategies, and allocate resources more effectively. For example, TB hotspots can be identified more quickly, and resources like vaccines, medications, and healthcare personnel can be directed to the regions most in need. Moreover, these models enable early detection, allowing public health officials to take proactive actions to curb the spread of TB before it escalates into a more significant outbreak. This not only improves disease control but also reduces healthcare costs by preventing unnecessary interventions later on.

The application of fuzzy neural models is particularly critical for regions like Sabah, Malaysia, where TB remains a pressing public health challenge. In Sabah, factors like high population density, socio-economic disparities, and limited access to healthcare services make TB control more difficult. By utilizing fuzzy neural models, healthcare professionals can enhance their understanding of the disease's transmission patterns and tailor interventions to local needs. These models could help identify high-risk populations and areas, ensuring that health resources are deployed where they will have the greatest impact. Moreover, better predictions can lead to more effective patient care, such as personalized treatment plans based on individual risk factors and disease progression.

Future research should aim to further refine fuzzy logic methodologies to improve both their interpretability and efficiency. While fuzzy logic is effective in handling uncertainty, its underlying mechanisms can sometimes be difficult to interpret, which may limit its practical application. Improving the interpretability of fuzzy models will allow healthcare professionals to better understand the rationale behind the predictions, making it easier to trust and implement the model's recommendations. Additionally, enhancing efficiency is essential to ensure that these models can be applied in real-time for decision-making, especially in resource-limited settings.

Another promising direction for future research is the exploration of hybrid models that integrate additional artificial intelligence (AI) techniques. For instance, deep learning methods, which excel in processing complex and large-scale data, could be combined with fuzzy neural networks to improve their ability to capture even more intricate disease patterns. Likewise, reinforcement learning, an AI technique focused on decision-making through trial and error, could be incorporated to further optimize intervention strategies based on real-time feedback. By combining multiple

AI techniques, researchers could develop even more powerful models that provide highly accurate predictions and actionable insights for public health interventions.

Moreover, it is crucial to test these models in diverse geographical and socio-economic contexts to assess their robustness and scalability. While fuzzy neural models may perform well in one region or setting, it is essential to evaluate their effectiveness in different environments, as disease patterns and healthcare infrastructures vary widely. Testing the models in various contexts will help determine whether they can be generalized across different populations and settings, ensuring their broad applicability in global TB control efforts.

While this chapter primarily focuses on the integration of heuristic knowledge into fuzzy-neural models for tuberculosis forecasting, it is important to recognize the ethical challenges and risks associated with AI applications in healthcare. One significant concern is algorithmic bias, where the training data or model design could lead to biased predictions, potentially impacting underserved or marginalized populations. Additionally, predictive errors can have critical consequences in public health, particularly in disease forecasting where incorrect predictions may lead to misallocation of resources or inadequate interventions. Addressing these ethical issues is essential for ensuring the responsible deployment of AI in personalized medicine. Future work should explore ways to mitigate biases and enhance the transparency of AI models to build trust and ensure fairness in healthcare applications.

As artificial intelligence continues to evolve, its role in personalized medicine will become increasingly significant. AI's ability to process large datasets, recognize complex patterns, and adapt to new information will make it an indispensable tool in disease forecasting and management. For TB, AI can revolutionize forecasting models by providing more accurate and timely predictions, which can guide public health interventions and resource allocation. This, in turn, will help reduce TB prevalence and improve overall health outcomes, both locally and globally. Researchers, healthcare professionals, and policymakers can use AI-driven insights to make better-informed decisions, ultimately contributing to the global fight against tuberculosis and enhancing public health at large.

REFERENCES

Alebel, A., Wondemagegn, A. T., Tesema, C., Kibret, G. D., Wagnew, F., Petrucka, P., Arora, A., Ayele, A. D., Alemayehu, M., & Eshetie, S. (2019). Prevalence of Diabetes Mellitus Among Tuberculosis Patients in Sub-Saharan Africa: A Systematic Review and Meta-Analysis of Observational Studies. *BMC Infectious Diseases*, *19*(1), 254. DOI: 10.1186/s12879-019-3892-8 PMID: 30866836

Alizadegan, H., Malki, B., Radmehr, A., Karimi, H., & Ilani, M. (2024). Comparative Study of Long Short-Term Memory (LSTM), Bidirectional LSTM, and Traditional Machine Learning Approaches for Energy Consumption Prediction. *Energy Exploration & Exploitation*. Advance online publication. DOI: 10.1177/01445987241269496

Box, G. E. P., Jenkins, G. M., Reinsel, G. C., & Ljung, G. M. (2015). *Time series analysis: Forecasting and control* (5th ed.). John Wiley & Sons.

Chai, L., Zhang, Y., & Gao, W. (2021). Comparison of ARIMA and LSTM in forecasting epidemic data: A case study on COVID-19 in China. *PLoS One*, *16*(4), e0249021. DOI: 10.1371/journal.pone.0249021 PMID: 33844695

Chen, S. M. (1996). Forecasting enrollments based on fuzzy time series. *Fuzzy Sets and Systems*, *81*(3), 311–318. DOI: 10.1016/0165-0114(95)00220-0

Chiroma, H., Ezugwu, A. E., Jauro, F., Al-Garadi, M. A., Abdullahi, I. N., & Shuib, L. (2020). Early survey with bibliometric analysis on machine learning approaches in controlling COVID-19 outbreaks. *PeerJ. Computer Science*, *6*, 313. DOI: 10.7717/peerj-cs.313 PMID: 33816964

Dooley, K. E., & Chaisson, R. E. (2009). Tuberculosis and Diabetes Mellitus: Convergence of Two Epidemics. *The Lancet. Infectious Diseases*, *9*(12), 737–746. DOI: 10.1016/S1473-3099(09)70282-8 PMID: 19926034

Hegazi, M. O., Almaslukh, B., & Siddig, K. (2023). A fuzzy model for reasoning and predicting student's academic performance. *Applied Sciences (Basel, Switzerland)*, *13*(9), 5140–5164. DOI: 10.3390/app13085140

Hochreiter, S., & Schmidhuber, J. (1997). Long short-term memory. *Neural Computation*, *9*(8), 1735–1780. DOI: 10.1162/neco.1997.9.8.1735 PMID: 9377276

Huarng, K., & Yu, T. H. K. (2006). The Application of Neural Networks to Forecast Fuzzy Time Series. *Physica A*, *353*, 445–462. DOI: 10.1016/j.physa.2004.11.070

Jilani, T. A., Burney, S. M. A., & Ardil, C. (2008). Fuzzy Metric Approach for Fuzzy Time Series Forecasting Based on Frequency Density-Based Partitioning. *International Journal of Computational Intelligence*, *4*(1), 4–10.

Jothilakshmi, S., & Vasanthamani, G. (2015). Fuzzy neural network-based prediction model for tuberculosis. *International Journal of Soft Computing*, *10*(1), 53–58.

Kucharski, A. J., Russell, T. W., Diamond, C., Liu, Y., Edmunds, J., Funk, S., Eggo, R. M., Sun, F., Jit, M., Munday, J. D., Davies, N., Gimma, A., van Zandvoort, K., Gibbs, H., Hellewell, J., Jarvis, C. I., Clifford, S., Quilty, B. J., Bosse, N. I., & Flasche, S. (2020). Early dynamics of transmission and control of COVID-19: A mathematical modelling study. *The Lancet. Infectious Diseases*, *20*(5), 553–558. DOI: 10.1016/S1473-3099(20)30144-4 PMID: 32171059

Kuo, R., & Zulvia, F. E. (2021). The Application of Gradient Evolution Algorithm to an Intuitionistic Fuzzy Neural Network For Forecasting Medical Cost of Acute Hepatitis Treatment in Taiwan. *Applied Soft Computing*, *111*, 107711. DOI: 10.1016/j.asoc.2021.107711

Leonie, F., Dominik, N., Zita, S., You-Shan, F., & Sulyok, M. (2020). Forecasting Tuberculosis using Diabetes-Related Google Trends Data. *Pathogens and Global Health*, *114*(5), 236–241. DOI: 10.1080/20477724.2020.1767854 PMID: 32453658

Li, D. Z., Wang, W., & Ismail, F. (2013). Fuzzy Neural Network Technique for System State Forecasting. *IEEE Transactions on Cybernetics*, *43*(5), 1484–1494. DOI: 10.1109/TCYB.2013.2259229 PMID: 23757566

Mayer, K. H., & Dukes, H. C. (2010). Synergistic Pandemics: Confronting the Global HIV and Tuberculosis Epidemics. *Clinical Infectious Diseases*, *50*(s3), S67–S70. DOI: 10.1086/651475 PMID: 20397958

Milinovich, G., Magalhães, S., & Hu, W. (2015). Role of Big Data in The Early Detection of Ebola and Other Emerging Infectious Diseases. Lancet Glob Health 3:e20-e21. *The Lancet. Global Health*, *3*(1), e20–e21. DOI: 10.1016/S2214-109X(14)70356-0 PMID: 25539964

Mushtaq, A. (2019). Tuberculosis in Diabetes: Insidious and Neglected. *The Lancet. Respiratory Medicine*, *7*(6), 483. DOI: 10.1016/S2213-2600(19)30119-5 PMID: 31003965

Pawlowski, A., Jansson, M., Sköld, M., Rottenberg, M. E., & Källenius, G. (2012). Tuberculosis and HIV Co-Infection. *PLoS Pathogens*, *8*(2), e1002464. DOI: 10.1371/journal.ppat.1002464 PMID: 22363214

Pedrycz, W. (1998). *Fuzzy modeling and control*. Springer.

Shastri, S., Singh, K., & Uniyal, S. (2022). LSTM-based deep learning model for prediction of COVID-19 cases using time series data. *Materials Today: Proceedings*, *51*, 2481–2486. DOI: 10.1016/j.matpr.2021.11.265

Song, Q., & Chissom, B. S. (1993a). Forecasting Enrolments with Fuzzy Time Series. *Fuzzy Sets and Systems*, *54*(1), 1–9. DOI: 10.1016/0165-0114(93)90355-L

Song, Q., & Chissom, B. S. (1993b). Fuzzy Time Series and Its Model. *Fuzzy Sets and Systems*, *3*(54), 269–277. DOI: 10.1016/0165-0114(93)90372-O

Tang, N., Yuan, M., Chen, Z., Ma, J., Sun, R., Yang, Y., He, Q., Guo, X., Hu, S., & Zhou, J. (2023). Machine Learning Prediction Model of Tuberculosis Incidence Based on Meteorological Factors and Air Pollutants. *International Journal of Environmental Research and Public Health*, *20*(5), 3910. DOI: 10.3390/ijerph20053910 PMID: 36900920

World Health Organization. (2019). Global Tuberculosis Report 2019. Cited [2025 February 4th]. Available from: https://www.who.int/tb/global-report-2019

Yang, L., Li, G., Yang, J., Zhang, T., Du, J., Liu, T., Zhang, X., Han, X., Li, W., Ma, L., Feng, L., & Yang, W. (2023). Deep-Learning Model for Influenza Prediction From Multisource Heterogeneous Data in a Megacity: Model Development and Evaluation. *Journal of Medical Internet Research*, *25*, e44238. DOI: 10.2196/44238 PMID: 36780207

Zadeh, L. A. (1965). Fuzzy sets. *Information and Control*, *8*(3), 338–353. DOI: 10.1016/S0019-9958(65)90241-X

L.A. Zadeh. (1975a). The Concept of Linguistic Variable and its Application to Approximate Reasoning, Volume 8. Part 1. Pp: 199-249.

L.A. Zadeh. (1975b). The Concept of Linguistic Variable and its Application to Approximate Reasoning, Volume 8. Part 2. Pp: 301-357.

L.A. Zadeh. (1975c). The Concept of Linguistic Variable and its Application to Approximate Reasoning, Volume 8. Part 3. Pp: 43-80.

Chapter 3
The Impact of Neural Networks in Molecular and Cellular Biology:
A Critical Synthesis

Wafaa Hanifa Guerroudji
https://orcid.org/0000-0002-1604-0168
University of Blida 1, Algeria

Fatiha Meddah
https://orcid.org/0000-0002-8851-5425
University of Sciences and Technology Mohammed Boudiaf Oran, Algeria

Leila Saadi
University of Blida 1, Algeria

ABSTRACT

The integration of artificial intelligence (AI) into molecular and cellular biology has revolutionized our understanding of complex biological processes. Neural networks and deep learning architectures now make it possible to model biological phenomena, analyze genomic sequences, predict protein structures and interpret biomedical images with increased precision. This review examines the recent contributions of neural networks to these fields, highlighting methodological approaches, results achieved and current challenges. We also highlight the limitations of current models, particularly in terms of explicability and algorithmic biases, and explore prospects for better integration of these technologies in biomedical research.

DOI: 10.4018/979-8-3373-4571-0.ch003

Copyright © 2025, IGI Global Scientific Publishing. Copying or distributing in print or electronic forms without written permission of IGI Global Scientific Publishing is prohibited.

1. INTRODUCTION

The rise of genomic sequencing, advanced microscopy and molecular screening technologies has generated an exponential amount of data in molecular and cellular biology (Eraslan et al., 2019). Analyzing this data is beyond the capabilities of traditional bioinformatics approaches, which has led to the need to integrate artificial intelligence (AI) and deep neural networks (LeCun et al., 2015). These offer a revolutionary approach to modeling complex biological systems, facilitating major advances in genomics, transcriptomics, proteomics, pharmacology and cellular imaging (Angermueller et al., 2016; Zhou et al., 2024).

In recent years, models based on deep learning have profoundly transformed computational biology. Developed by Google DeepMind AlphaFold in its second version AlphaFold2 has revolutionized protein structure prediction by achieving near-experimental accuracy (Jumper et al., 2021; Senior et al., 2020), while DeepVariant has improved gene mutation detection from next-generation sequencing data (Poplin et al., 2018). These advances illustrate the potential of neural networks in understanding biological mechanisms on a molecular and cellular scale. Furthermore, the integration of deep learning into the study of biomaterials and molecular interactions is enabling new applications in tissue engineering and regenerative medicine (Zhou et al., 2024). However, despite these spectacular advances, several challenges remain. The interpretability of models still remains a major issue, limiting their adoption in critical biomedical contexts (Eraslan et al.,2019). In addition, the quality and diversity of training databases strongly influence the robustness of predictions, raising questions about algorithmic biases and the generalization of models to new biological data (Angermueller et al., 2016). Finally, deep learning architectures require considerable computational resources, raising environmental sustainability and computational infrastructure accessibility concerns (Zhou et al., 2024). Against this backdrop, this review offers an in-depth analysis of the recent contributions of neural networks to molecular and cellular biology. We will examine their performance, limitations and future prospects, highlighting the scientific and technological challenges to be met in order to maximize their impact in biomedical research.

2. PROTEIN STRUCTURE AND MOLECULAR INTERACTION PREDICTION

The rise of deep neural networks has revolutionized molecular and cellular biology, particularly through models such as AlphaFold2, which relies on a Transformer architecture to predict protein structures with unparalleled precision (Jumper et al., 2021). This model exploits evolutionary relationships between amino acid sequences to generate three-dimensional structures, reducing dependence on costly experimental techniques such as X-ray crystallography and cryo-electron microscopy. However, despite these major advances, AlphaFold2 has some notable limitations, particularly in predicting multi-protein interactions, intrinsically disordered proteins and dynamic allosteric conformations.

The modeling of multi-protein interactions remains a challenge for AlphaFold2, which was originally designed to predict monomeric structures. Although the AlphaFold-Multimer extension has improved the precision of protein complex predictions, studies have shown that the quality of results remains uneven, particularly when little evolutionary data is available for these interactions (Evans et al., 2022). In addition, some macromolecular complexes require significant structural rearrangements that are not always well captured by AlphaFold2 (Bryant et al., 2022). This difficulty limits its application in the study of the assembly mechanisms of large biological machines, a fundamental aspect of cell biology. To overcome these gaps, the integration of experimental data from various structural biology techniques is a promising approach (Figure 1). Indeed, Agarwal et al, 2024 have shown that small-angle scattering (SAXS/SANS) can be used to compare experimental protein dispersion with predicted models, thus facilitating structure fitting. Similarly, X-ray crystallography, in particular via molecular replacement, can be used to refine AlphaFold2 predictions by aligning them with electron density maps.

Figure 1. Integrating AlphaFold2 models with experimental data to improve the accuracy of protein structures. (Agarwal et al., 2024)

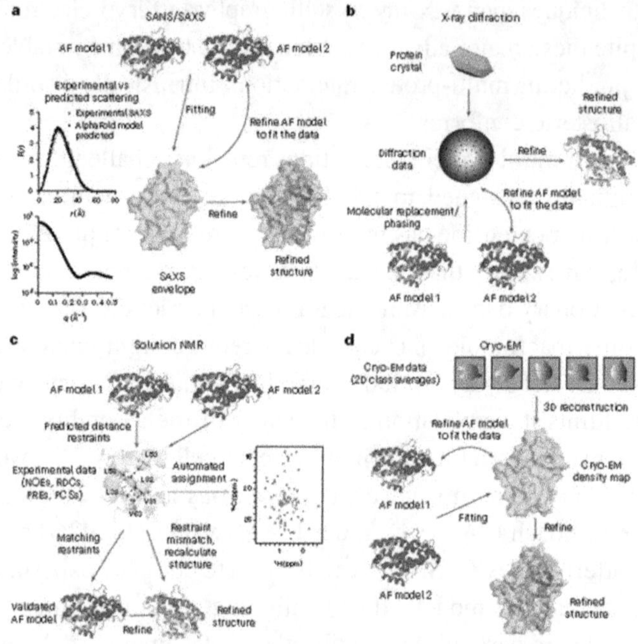

Another major challenge concerns intrinsically disordered proteins (IDPs), which lack a fixed three-dimensional structure and adopt a high degree of flexibility in solution. As AlphaFold2 is designed to predict static structures, it tends to force these proteins into artificially rigid conformations, which can lead to misinterpretation (Ruff et al., 2021). These proteins play a central role in many biological processes, including cell signalling and certain pathologies such as neurodegenerative diseases. Their inadequate consideration by AlphaFold2 therefore limits the use of the model for more in-depth studies of their function and dynamics. In this regard, nuclear magnetic resonance (NMR) offers an interesting alternative, providing dynamic information on protein structures in solution. Integrating these experimental constraints, obtained from NOEs, RDCs and PREs, with AlphaFold2 predictions could improve the representation of IDPs and refine their modeling (Agarwal et al., 2024).

Finally, AlphaFold2 struggles to model dynamic allosteric conformations, a key phenomenon in enzymatic activity and biological regulation. Many proteins adopt several conformations depending on the signals they receive, such as ligand binding or post-translational modification. However, AlphaFold2 generally predicts a single average conformation, which limits its ability to capture the natural flexibility of proteins, including intrinsically disordered ones and allosteric interactions (Bryant et al., 2022; Ruff et al., 2021). The integration of molecular dynamics simulations or coupling with cryo-microscopy data have been proposed as potential solutions to overcome this limitation (Mosalaganti et al., 2022). In particular, cryo-electron microscopy (cryo-EM) can be used to reconstruct high-resolution three-dimensional density maps, providing experimental validation for the predictions of artificial intelligence models. Fitting AlphaFold2 structures to these maps leads to more realistic models in line with experimental observations (Agarwal et al., 2024). So while deep neural networks have enabled spectacular advances in structural biology, their application should be viewed with caution. AlphaFold2 is a powerful tool for protein structure prediction, but its use for complex systems requires a hybrid approach combining artificial intelligence and experimental validation. The evolution of models based on deep learning, coupled with an improvement in the quality of training databases, could make it possible to overcome some of these limitations and extend their impact to other areas of molecular and cellular biology.

Other models such as DeepChem have been developed to analyze ligand-receptor interactions in pharmacology. Using convolutional networks (CNNs), DeepChem improves the accuracy of molecular docking compared to traditional methods, thus facilitating new drug discovery (Kim et al., 2021; Rifaioglu et al., 2020). However, these approaches remain sensitive to the quality of the databases used for training, which limits their generalizability to new compounds (Yu et al., 2023; Singh et al., 2024).

3. NEURAL NETWORKS AND GENOMIC ANALYSIS

Identifying genetic variations, such as SNPs (Single Nucleotide Polymorphisms) and INDELs (Insertions/Deletions), is essential for genomic analysis and disease understanding. DeepVariant, developed by Google AI, relies on a convolutional neural network (CNN) to improve the detection of these mutations from sequencing data (Poplin et al., 2018). Contrary to traditional methods that rely on statistical models, DeepVariant transforms raw sequencing reads into visual representations, which are then processed by a CNN, enabling it to achieve 98.98% accuracy, outperforming conventional tools such as GATK HaplotypeCaller. The DeepVariant pipeline follows several key steps (Figure 2). First, the raw sequencing reads are aligned to a reference genome and pre-processed to eliminate errors. Next, candidate sites containing potential variations are identified and transformed into pileup images, which encapsulate the information from the aligned reads. These images are then analyzed by a convolutional neural network (CNN), trained to assign probabilities to the three possible genotypic states (homozygous reference, heterozygous, homozygous alternative). Finally, the model predictions are filtered to generate a Variant Call Format (VCF) file listing the mutations detected.

Figure 2. DeepVariant workflow for next-generation sequencing (NGS) data analysis and gene mutation detection (Poplin et al.,2018)

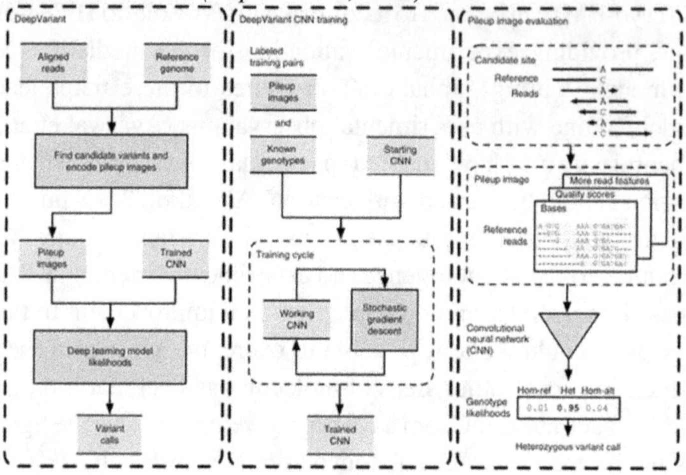

However, although DeepVariant improves the accuracy of variant calling, its performance depends on the quality of the input data and requires significant computational resources (Abdelwahab & Torkamaneh, 2024). Recent research aims to integrate it into open-source pipelines to make it more accessible and adaptable to different biological contexts (Vaishnobi Bisoi & Ramsundar, 2024). In addition, more advanced models such as VariantTransformer are being developed to improve the robustness and generalizability of variant calling (Abdelwahab & Torkamaneh, 2024).

4. APPLICATION OF NEURAL NETWORKS IN CELLULAR IMAGING

Convolutional neural networks (CNNs) have profoundly transformed image analysis in cell biology, improving the segmentation, classification and interpretation of microscopic structures. Their ability to extract complex features has enabled significant advances in the detection of morphological abnormalities, the analysis of cellular interactions and the identification of subcellular structures. Among these models, CellPose has established itself as a reference in automatic cell segmentation, offering greater robustness and generalizability than conventional methods (Stringer et al., 2021). Unlike conventional algorithms requiring manual parameter adjustment,

CellPose exploits a convolutional network pre-trained on a large set of biological images, enabling it to segment different cell types without major human intervention.

Other architectures, such as U-Net (Ronneberger et al., 2015) and Mask R-CNN (He et al., 2017), are also widely used for biological image segmentation, notably in the analysis of pathological tissues and the study of embryonic development. A recent study by Han et al (2023) compared these three approaches, along with Stardist, on microscopy images to assess their performance in cell segmentation. As illustrated in Figure 3. Performance evaluation, based on Dice and IoU indices, revealed that CellPose outperformed the other models, offering more accurate and robust segmentation. In particular, CellPose demonstrated a better ability to generalize over varied cell structures, while U-Net and Mask R-CNN showed a tendency to miss certain cells or introduce segmentation errors. These results underline the effectiveness of CellPose in the automated processing of microscopy images, although the choice of the optimum algorithm depends on the experimental context and the specific requirements of the analysis.

Figure 3. Evaluation of cell segmentation using Deep Learning: CellPose outperforms U-Net, Mask R-CNN and Stardist (Han et al., 2023).

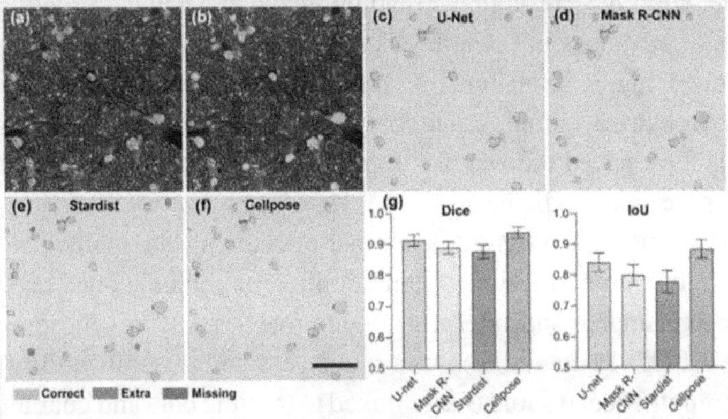

5. CHALLENGES AND PERSPECTIVES

Despite their potential, neural networks present several challenges, sometimes limiting their adoption in biological and medical analysis. One of the main obstacles is their opacity, often referred to as the black-box problem. Contrary to traditional statistical models, whose decisions are explicable and reproducible, neural networks learn from millions of parameters, making it difficult to interpret their predictions.

This limitation is of particular concern in biomedical applications, where the transparency of decisions is essential to guarantee the reliability of diagnostic and treatment.

Faced with these challenges, several approaches are emerging to improve the explicability of models. Explainable AI (XAI) offers tools such as sailency maps, which highlight the regions of an image or genetic sequence that influence the model's decision (Vignesh et al., 2024). Techniques such as LIME (Local Interpretable Model-agnostic Explanations) and SHAP (SHapley Additive exPlanations) can also be used to assess the impact of different input variables on network output (Hassan et al., 2025). Furthermore, the integration of pre-existing biological knowledge into the design of neural architectures could improve their interpretability and robustness (Han et al., 2023). Ultimately, the evolution of models towards hybrid approaches combining artificial intelligence and biological reasoning could reduce the gap between precision and explicability, encouraging their adoption in research and clinical practice.

6. CONCLUSION

Neural networks have profoundly revolutionized molecular and cellular biology, enabling major advances in the analysis and interpretation of complex data from genomic sequencing, cellular imaging and molecular interaction modeling. With their ability to extract complex patterns and outperform traditional approaches, these models have paved the way for unprecedented discoveries in computational biology and precision medicine.

However, despite this progress, a number of challenges remain. The opacity of models (black-box problem) limits their adoption in clinical contexts, underlining the need for explainable and interpretable approaches, such as those proposed by Explainable AI (XAI). In addition, the robustness and generalizability of models need to be strengthened to avoid biases linked to training data and guarantee reliable performance on diversified biological samples. Finally, the accessibility of these technologies needs to be improved, notably through the development of open-source solutions and the implementation of standards enabling their smooth integration into biomedical workflows.

Thus, the future of neural networks in biology lies in a hybrid approach combining artificial intelligence, biological knowledge and experimental validation, to guarantee the ethical and effective integration of these tools in tomorrow's research and medicine.

REFERENCES

Abdelwahab, O., & Torkamaneh, D. Refinement of genetic variants needs attention *arXiv*. (2024). https://doi.org//arXiv.2408.00659DOI: 10.48550

Agarwal, V., & McShan, A. C. (2024). The power and pitfalls of AlphaFold2 for structure prediction beyond rigid globular proteins. *Nature Chemical Biology*, *20*(8), 950–959. DOI: 10.1038/s41589-024-01638-w PMID: 38907110

Angermueller, C., Pärnamaa, T., Parts, L., & Stegle, O. (2016). Deep learning for computational biology. *Molecular Systems Biology*, *12*(7), 878. DOI: 10.15252/msb.20156651 PMID: 27474269

Bryant, P., Pozzati, G., & Elofsson, A. (2022). Improved prediction of protein-protein interactions using AlphaFold2. *Nature Communications*, *13*(1), 1265. DOI: 10.1038/s41467-022-28865-w PMID: 35273146

Eraslan, G., Avsec, Ž., Gagneur, J., & Theis, F. J. (2019). Deep learning: New computational modelling techniques for genomics. *Nature Reviews. Genetics*, *20*(7), 389–403. DOI: 10.1038/s41576-019-0122-6 PMID: 30971806

Evans, R., O'Neill, M., Pritzel, A., & Antropova, N.. Protein complex prediction with AlphaFold-Multimer. *bioRxiv, (*2022*)*. doi: https://doi.org/DOI: 10.1101/2021.10.04.463034

Hassan, A., Abuhmed, T., & El-Sappagh, S. "End-to-End Optimized Ensemble Model for Alzheimer's Disease Detection," 2025 19th International Conference on Ubiquitous Information Management and Communication (IMCOM), Bangkok, Thailand, 2025, pp. 1-8, DOI: 10.1109/IMCOM64595.2025.10857489

He, K., Gkioxari, G., Dollár, P., & Girshick, R. *Mask R-CNN*. arXiv. (2017). https://doi.org//arXiv.1703.06870DOI: 10.1109/ICCV.2017.322

Jumper, J., Evans, R., Pritzel, A., Green, T., Figurnov, M., Ronneberger, O., Tunyasuvunakool, K., Bates, R., Žídek, A., Potapenko, A., Bridgland, A., Meyer, C., Kohl, S. A. A., Ballard, A. J., Cowie, A., Romera-Paredes, B., Nikolov, S., Jain, R., Adler, J., & Hassabis, D. (2021). Highly accurate protein structure prediction with AlphaFold. *Nature*, *596*(7873), 583–589. DOI: 10.1038/s41586-021-03819-2 PMID: 34265844

Kim, J., Park, S., Min, D., & Kim, W. (2021). Comprehensive Survey of Recent Drug Discovery Using Deep Learning. *International Journal of Molecular Sciences*, *22*(18), 9983. DOI: 10.3390/ijms22189983 PMID: 34576146

LeCun, Y., Bengio, Y., & Hinton, G. (2015). Deep learning. *Nature*, *521*(7553), 436–444. DOI: 10.1038/nature14539 PMID: 26017442

Mosalaganti, S., Obarska-Kosinska, A., Siggel, M., Taniguchi, R., Turoňová, B., Zimmerli, C. E., Buczak, K., Schmidt, F. H., Margiotta, E., Mackmull, M.-T., Hagen, W. J. H., Hummer, G., Kosinski, J., & Beck, M. (2022). AI-based structure prediction empowers integrative structural analysis of human nuclear pores. *Science*, *376*(6598), eabm9506. Advance online publication. DOI: 10.1126/science.abm9506 PMID: 35679397

Poplin, R., Chang, P. C., Alexander, D., Schwartz, S., Colthurst, T., Ku, A., Newburger, D., Dijamco, J., Nguyen, N., Afshar, P. T., Gross, S. S., Dorfman, L., McLean, C. Y., & DePristo, M. A. (2018). A universal SNP and small-indel variant caller using deep neural networks. *Nature Biotechnology*, *36*(10), 983–987. DOI: 10.1038/nbt.4235 PMID: 30247488

Rifaioglu, A. S., Nalbat, E., Atalay, V., Martin, M. J., Cetin-Atalay, R., & Doğan, T. (2020). DEEPscreen: DEEPScreen: high performance drug–target interaction prediction with convolutional neural networks using 2-D structural compound representations. *Chemical Science (Cambridge)*, *11*(9), 2531–2557. DOI: 10.1039/C9SC03414E PMID: 33209251

Ronneberger, O., Fischer, P., & Brox, T. *U-Net: Convolutional Networks for Biomedical Image Segmentation*. arXiv. (2015). https://doi.org//arXiv.1505.04597DOI: 10.1007/978-3-319-24574-4_28

Ruff, K. M., & Pappu, R. V. (2021). AlphaFold and Implications for Intrinsically Disordered Proteins. *Journal of Molecular Biology*, *433*(20), 167208. DOI: 10.1016/j.jmb.2021.167208 PMID: 34418423

Senior, A. W., Evans, R., Jumper, J., Kirkpatrick, J., Sifre, L., Green, T., Qin, C., Žídek, A., Nelson, A. W. R., Bridgland, A., Penedones, H., Petersen, S., Simonyan, K., Crossan, S., Kohli, P., Jones, D. T., Silver, D., Kavukcuoglu, K., & Hassabis, D. (2020). Improved protein structure prediction using potentials from deep learning. *Nature*, *577*(7792), 706–710. DOI: 10.1038/s41586-019-1923-7 PMID: 31942072

Singh, S., Kaur, N., & Gehlot, A. (2024). Application of artificial intelligence in drug design: A review. *Computers in Biology and Medicine*, *179*, 108810. DOI: 10.1016/j.compbiomed.2024.108810 PMID: 38991316

Stringer, C., Wang, T., Michaelos, M., & Pachitariu, M. (2021). Cellpose: A generalist algorithm for cellular segmentation. *Nature Methods*, *18*(1), 100–106. DOI: 10.1038/s41592-020-01018-x PMID: 33318659

Vaishnobi Bisoi, A., & Ramsundar, B. A Modular Open Source Framework for Genomic Variant Calling. *arXiv*. Novembre 2024. https://doi.org//arXiv.2411.11513DOI: 10.48550

Yu, L., He, X., Fang, X., Liu, L., & Liu, J. (2023). Deep Learning with Geometry-Enhanced Molecular Representation for Augmentation of Large-Scale Docking-Based Virtual Screening. *Journal of Chemical Information and Modeling*, *63*(21), 6501–6514. DOI: 10.1021/acs.jcim.3c01371 PMID: 37882338

Zhou, X., Leung, C. K., Wang, K. I. K., & Fortino, G. (2024). Deep Learning-Optimized Editorial Analysis of Big Data in Biomedical Applications and Digital Healthcare. *IEEE/ACM Transactions on Computational Biology and Bioinformatics*, *21*(4), 516–520. DOI: 10.1109/TCBB.2024.3371808

Chapter 4
Transforming Transportation Systems Using Deep Learning Techniques

D. Sathya
https://orcid.org/0009-0003-7814-2578
Pondicherry University, India

V. Uma
https://orcid.org/0000-0002-7257-7920
Pondicherry University, India

ABSTRACT

Artificial Intelligence (AI), particularly through the use of Deep Learning techniques, has revolutionized various industries, with transportation being one of the most significantly impacted sectors. AI's ability to handle complex data, such as images and time-series data, has led to the development of intelligent systems that improve transportation efficiency, safety, and management. CNNs excel in tasks like license plate detection for automated traffic surveillance, while RNNs, particularly with LSTM networks, enable real-time traffic flow prediction and congestion management. Furthermore, Generative Adversarial Networks GANs generate high-fidelity traffic simulations, enhancing the testing of autonomous vehicles and infrastructure planning. These Deep Learning models are transforming transportation systems by enabling dynamic, real-time solutions for managing traffic and improving road safety. This chapter explores the fundamentals of AI and Deep Learning, their evolution in neural networks, and their impact on smart transportation through Deep Learning techniques.

DOI: 10.4018/979-8-3373-4571-0.ch004

Copyright © 2025, IGI Global Scientific Publishing. Copying or distributing in print or electronic forms without written permission of IGI Global Scientific Publishing is prohibited.

INTRODUCTION

Artificial Intelligence (AI) is a fast-growing field that aims to develop intelligent systems have ability of mimicking human cognition, learning from data, and making informed decisions (Russell & Norvig, 2021). It has revolutionized various industries, ranging from healthcare and finance to transportation and security, by enabling machines to perform complex tasks with high efficiency and accuracy (Esteva et al., 2017; Heaton et al., 2017; Litman, 2021). Among the key subfields of AI, Machine Learning (ML) and Deep Learning (DL) have played a pivotal role in driving its advancements, allowing computers to process and analyse vast amounts of data in ways that were once thought to be exclusive to humans (LeCun et al., 2015).

The evolution of neural networks has been instrumental in the development of Deep Learning models, which now serve as the foundation for many modern AI applications (Schmidhuber, 2015). Inspired by the human brains structure and function, artificial neural networks have evolved from basic perceptron to highly sophisticated architectures capable of handling complex data representations (Goodfellow et al., 2016). This progression has enabled breakthroughs in image processing, natural language understanding, and predictive analytics (Krizhevsky et al., 2012; Hochreiter & Schmidhuber, 1997). However, as neural networks grow in complexity, challenges such as computational costs, training inefficiencies, and the need for vast labelled datasets have emerged, requiring continuous innovation in model development and optimization.

Deep Learning, a subset of Machine Learning which has transformed AI by leveraging multi-layered neural networks to extract intricate patterns from large datasets (LeCun et al., 2015). Unlike traditional Machine Learning models that rely on manually crafted features, Deep Learning algorithms automatically learn hierarchical representations of data, making them particularly effective in areas such as autonomous systems, speech recognition, and computer vision (Goodfellow et al., 2016). Two fundamental techniques in Deep Learning, forward propagation and backward propagation, play a crucial role in training neural networks by adjusting model parameters to minimize prediction errors (Goodfellow et al., 2016). These techniques form the backbone of neural network learning, ensuring that models improve their accuracy over time. The integration of Deep Learning into transportation has led to remarkable advancements in traffic management, autonomous driving, and intelligent surveillance. Convolutional Neural Networks (CNNs), with their ability to extract spatial hierarchies from images, have been widely adopted for object detection tasks, including license plate recognition using models like YOLO (Krizhevsky et al., 2012). Similarly, Recurrent Neural Networks (RNNs) and their advanced versions like Long Short-Term Memory networks (LSTM), have demonstrated effectiveness in predicting traffic patterns by analysing sequential data

(Hochreiter & Schmidhuber, 1997). Generative Adversarial Networks (GANs) further contribute to transportation by generating realistic traffic simulations, aiding in the development and testing of AI-driven mobility solutions (Goodfellow et al., 2014).

This chapter explores the foundational principles of AI and Deep Learning, tracing the evolution of neural networks and their impact on modern transportation systems. It delves into core concepts, essential definitions, and the challenges associated with neural network development. Furthermore, it examines key Deep Learning techniques such as CNNs, RNNs, and GANs, highlighting their role in transforming transportation through advanced automation, predictive modelling, and real-time data processing.

Overview of Artificial Intelligence in Transportation systems

Artificial Intelligence (AI) enhances transportation through autonomous vehicles, traffic management, and route optimization (Russell & Norvig, 2021). AI analyses vast transportation data, recognizes traffic patterns, optimizes routes, and improves autonomous driving for safer mobility (LeCun et al., 2015). The rise of urbanization has increased congestion, accidents, and inefficiencies. Integrating AI into Intelligent Transportation Systems (ITS) leverages big data, Deep Learning, and neural networks to improve traffic flow, reduce emissions, and support autonomous driving (Litman, 2021).

A key component of AI-driven transportation systems is the effective use of traffic data. In transportation, real-time data collected from sensors, cameras, and other monitoring devices assist traffic authorities in assessing road conditions and efficiently managing traffic flow. Moreover, analysing historical data enables predictive modelling, helping authorities foresee congestion and take proactive measures (Krizhevsky et al., 2012). For travellers, AI-powered navigation applications provide real-time route recommendations, helping them avoid delays and optimize travel time. Autonomous vehicles, another critical advancement, rely heavily on AI-driven perception models that process sensor data to interpret the environment, make driving decisions, and ensure safety on the road (Goodfellow et al., 2016).

The complexity of transportation systems makes them particularly suited for AI-based solutions. Many transportation problems involve both quantitative and qualitative data, making traditional analytical approaches insufficient. AI techniques, such as expert systems and fuzzy logic, help manage qualitative data by enhancing decision-making in uncertain environments. Moreover, transportation systems often exhibit unpredictable behaviours due to human factors, making it difficult to model them using conventional methods (Litman, 2021). Neural networks (NNs), known for their universal function approximation capabilities, are well-suited for developing empirical models based on observed traffic patterns, allowing for accurate predictions and real-time adaptation (Hochreiter & Schmidhuber, 1997).

Deep Learning, a subset of AI, processes complex transportation data for improved traffic management (LeCun et al., 2015). CNNs enhance traffic surveillance by enabling vehicle detection, pedestrian recognition, and road sign identification (Krizhevsky et al., 2012). LSTM networks excel in time-series analysis, accurately forecasting traffic flow and congestion (Hochreiter & Schmidhuber, 1997). GANs aid in data augmentation and simulation, generating synthetic traffic scenarios to enhance AI model training for vehicle detection and accident prediction.

With the integration of AI, Deep Learning, and neural networks, modern transportation systems can process large-scale traffic data, make accurate predictions, and optimize real-time decision-making. These advancements not only enhance urban mobility but also improve safety, reduce congestion, and contribute to the evolution of autonomous transportation technologies (Litman, 2021).

Evolution of neural networks

Neural networks have undergone significant evolution since their inception, starting with the early models in the 1940s and 1950s. The first artificial neuron model by McCulloch and Pitts, followed by Frank Rosenblatt's Perceptron, introduced the idea of Machine Learning. However, the Perceptron faced limitations in handling complex, non-linear problems, leading to a lull in research (Schmidhuber, 2015). The 1980s saw a resurgence with the backpropagation algorithm and the development of multi-layer perceptrons (MLPs), allowing for deeper and more efficient networks capable of learning complex patterns. This set the stage for the Deep Learning revolution that would dominate in the following decades (Transportation Research Board, 2008).

In the 2000s, Deep Learning gained significant traction thanks to advances in computational power, particularly through Graphics Processing Units (GPUs), and the easier availability of vast number of datasets (Goodfellow et al., 2016). Architectures like CNNs, pioneered by Yann LeCun, revolutionized image recognition tasks, while RNNs and LSTM networks transformed sequential data processing, such as speech and language recognition (Hochreiter & Schmidhuber, 1997). The introduction of Transformers in 2017 further advanced natural language processing, leading to groundbreaking models like BERT and GPT (Vaswani et al., 2017).

The impact of neural networks has been profound, especially in fields like autonomous vehicles, where Deep Learning models enable self-driving cars to interpret sensor and camera data, navigate complex environments, and recognize objects. These advancements are reshaping the automotive industry, with autonomous transportation systems becoming increasingly viable (Litman, 2021). Neural networks play a crucial role in traffic management systems by optimizing vehicle flow in urban areas through real-time data analysis from sensors and cameras (Krizhevsky et al., 2012). This helps reduce congestion, improve safety, and create more efficient transport.

In addition, predictive maintenance powered by neural networks has become a key tool for enhancing the longevity and reliability of transportation infrastructure. By predicting when parts are likely to fail, these systems allow for timely maintenance, reducing downtime and costs (Litman, 2021). Neural networks also contribute to route optimization, helping drivers and logistics companies determine the most Optimal routes based on traffic conditions, weather, and various other factors which leads to reduced travel time and fuel consumption (Transportation Research Board, 2008).

Finally, neural networks have revolutionized public transportation and smart infrastructure. AI-powered systems provide passengers with real-time updates, route suggestions, and personalized experiences, while smart tolling and parking systems optimize resource use and minimize congestion (Litman, 2021). As neural network technology continues to evolve, its impact on transportation will expand, leading to safer, more efficient, and sustainable systems worldwide.

Core Concepts and Definitions

A neural network is a computer system that consists of interconnected networks of cells called neurons. Artificial neural networks (ANNs) are important in the field of AI and serve as a framework for Deep Learning (Goodfellow et al., 2016). These networks mimic the actions of natural systems to detect and interpret complex intricate patterns in large amounts of data.

In essence, neural networks represent a non-linear Machine Learning models that are used in supervised and unsupervised learning environments (Bishop, 2006). These models are inspired by the human brain, specifically designed to recognize and analyse patterns in data (Haykin, 2009). The main goal of ANNs is to model the human brain's cognitive functions for processing and interpreting information, thereby helping to solve complex challenges which are strenuous or nearly impossible to solve using old human or computational methods (Russell & Norvig, 2021). ANNs aim to simulate the human brain processes by using mathematical models that mimic the behavior of biological neurons (Haykin, 2009). In biological systems, information is processed by the five senses, where it is first stored, associated with previously acquired knowledge, and then used to make decisions (Bishop, 2006). Similarly, neural networks aim to help machines understand and imitate the human decision-making process. Therefore, like the human brain, parts of the nervous system are connected by neurons or nodes.

A neural network primarly consist of three layers that is Input Layer, Hidden Layers, and Output Layer. In transportation applications, these layers perform specific tasks related to processing and predicting traffic data, vehicle behaviour, or route optimization.

- Input Layer receives independent variables (predictors) from external data sources, such as traffic sensors, GPS data, vehicle counts, and weather conditions. These are analogous to the sensory input processed by the human senses in biological systems (Bishop, 2006).
- Output Layer represents the final result produced by the neural network. Depending on the nature of the transportation problem, this could be a numerical prediction for example travel time or traffic volume or a categorical classification for example road condition or accident detection (Haykin, 2009).
- Hidden layer is between the Input and Output Layers, which generate essential features that helps the neural network to learn complex in-depth relationships in the data. These layers can vary in number, from a single layer in simpler systems to multiple layers in more complex systems, such as those used in autonomous vehicles or real-time traffic flow management (Haykin, 2009).

Neurons Neurons are fundamental units in neural networks, processing and passing data through layers. In transportation, they analyse traffic conditions, weather, and vehicle locations. The output layer varies: a single neuron for regression tasks like travel time prediction and multiple neurons for classification tasks like accident detection. Hidden layer configurations, a key hyperparameter, impact model performance. Weights define input importance, while biases adjust outputs. Activation functions introduce nonlinearity, enabling complex pattern learning. They help neural networks model relationships between traffic, weather, and time, improving predictions for congestion, route optimization, and accident detection (Haykin, 2009; Litman, 2021; Bishop, 2006).

In conclusion, artificial neural networks are effective tools in transportation systems which are capable of addressing complex challenges such as traffic prediction, vehicle classification, and route optimization. The layers, neurons, weights, biases, and activation functions work in concert to process data and produce intelligent predictions, making neural networks an invaluable part of modern transportation technologies. By leveraging the capability of Deep Learning, transportation systems can improve efficiency, reduce congestion, and enhance overall safety on the roads (Litman, 2021).

Challenges in Neural Network Development

Deep neural networks (DNNs) play a crucial role in transportation but face challenges in real-time deployment. A primary issue is data quality, as sensor data from cameras, LiDAR, and radar can be noisy or incomplete due to weather, lighting, or occlusions. Data preprocessing techniques like normalization and brightness adjustments enhance model robustness (LeCun et al., 2015). Another challenge is overfitting, where models perform well on training data but struggle with real-world variations like fog or night driving. Regularization methods such as dropout, L1/L2 penalties, and diverse training datasets improve generalization (Goodfellow et al., 2016).

Class imbalance is also a significant concern, particularly in applications like accident detection, where rare events are under represented in training data. Models trained on mostly normal traffic conditions may fail to recognize critical scenarios like accidents or emergency vehicle presence. Techniques like oversampling, class weighting, and synthetic data generation help mitigate this issue by providing the model with sufficient examples of rare events (Chawla, Bowyer, Hall, & Kegelmeyer, 2002).As models become deeper, they encounter vanishing and exploding gradients, which can slow down or destabilize learning. This affects the model's prowess to process complex transportation data effectively. Solutions such as residual connections and adaptive optimizers help maintain stable training and efficient learning (He, Zhang, Ren, & Sun, 2016).

Computational constraints challenge real-time applications like self-driving cars and intelligent traffic control. Running Deep Learning models on resource-limited devices can cause delays, but efficient architectures, hardware acceleration (GPUs/TPUs), and model optimization improve speed and reliability (Howard et al., 2017). Model interpretability is also vital for trust and transparency. Tools like SHAP and LIME help developers understand AI decisions, ensuring safety and accountability (Lundberg & Lee, 2017; Ribeiro et al., 2016).

DEEP LEARNING

Deep Learning (DL) is a branch of Machine Learning that concentrates on developing ANNs to learn patterns from data to make predictions. These networks were made to mimic the biological neurons, which are composed of multiple interconnected layers that transform inputs into meaningful outputs. Supervised learning is a widely used Deep Learning approach where labelled data is used to train the model to perform tasks like image classification, speech recognition, and natural language processing. The training process involves feeding an input to the network, which measures the error that is how much is the generated output is deviating from the actual output. To minimize this error, an optimizer is used to change the model's parameter values using methods like gradient-based learning (Ruder, 2016). To determine the how much the model need to update the values of parameter at each step we use learning rate for balancing convergence speed and stability.

Figure 1. Neural networks, exhibiting parametric nature and bidirectionality

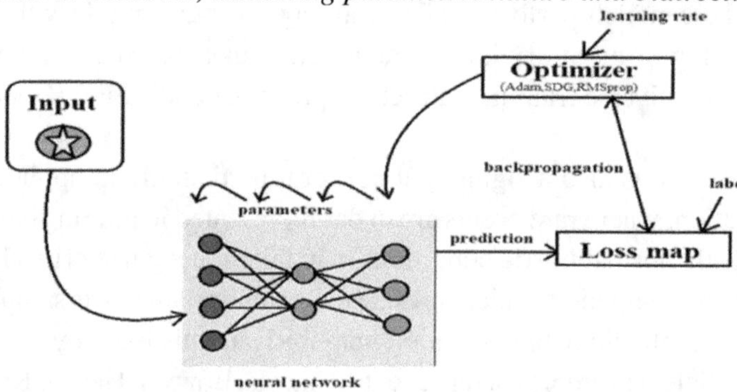

Neural networks can be understood as processes that have two fundamental properties: parametric nature and bidirectionality as shown in Figure 1. These properties define how neural networks learn from data and adjust their internal parameters to improve performance. Parametric Nature in Neural networks rely on a set o f parameters, often called weights, that influence how inputs are transformed into outputs. These parameters define a function given by eq. (1).

$$f: X \times P \rightarrow Y \ldots \quad (1)$$

where X is the input space, P is the parameters, and Y is the output. The goal of training is to find an optimal set of parameters that best maps inputs to outputs. The model's performance is based on the interaction of the weights. Understanding how parameters evolve during training is important for designing efficient and accurate DL models.

Bidirectionality operate in two directions that is forward pass and backward pass. The forward pass captures the patterns and structures by processing data through sequence of layers. The backward pass, known as backpropagation, calculates the gradients and changes them accordingly (Rumelhart, Hinton, & Williams, 1986). This iterative adjustment allows the network to refine its predictions over time. The interaction between these two processes determines the network's ability to learn effectively and generalize to unseen data.

These two properties play a crucial role in shaping the way neural network's function, influencing their ability to learn and adapt (Gavranović, 2024). In this section, we will explore these properties in detail, along with the key components that define neural networks, such as differentiation, architecture, and supervised learning.

Basic components of neural network

Neural networks are mathematical models designed to learn patterns from data by processing inputs through a series of operations. At their core, they consist of interconnected layers that transform inputs into meaningful outputs. These transformations involve various mathematical operations, such as weighted sums and activation functions, which enable the network to adapt and learn from data.

Figure 2. Neural Network

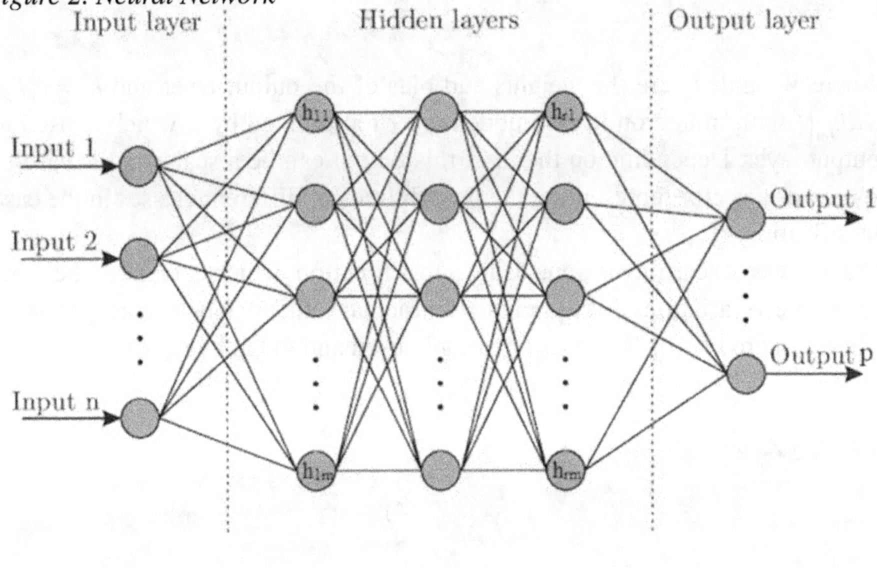

In a typical neural network as shown in Figure 2, the input is represented as a vector $= [x_1, x_2, \ldots, x_n]^T$, where each element is a feature of the data and n is the number of input features. This vector is fed into the input layer, which then passes the information to the hidden layers of the network. Each hidden layer performs computations on the input using weights and biases. Mathematically, for a neuron in a hidden layer, the computation is expressed by eq. (2).

$$h_{rm} = \sigma\left(\sum_{i=1}^{n} w_{ij} x_i + b_j\right)$$

… (2)

where w_{ij} is the weight between the ith input feature and the jth neuron, b_j is the bias term for the jth neuron, and σ is the activation function, typically ReLU, sigmoid, or tanh (García Cabello, 2022). This activation function adds non-linearity to the model, allowing the network to capture complex relationships within the data.

As the data flows through each layer, it is transformed by applying these weighted sums and biases, followed by the activation function. The last hidden layer's output is then passed to the output layer for the final prediction. In a simple regression task, the output layer computes the predicted value $\hat{y}$ as a weighted sum of the activations from the last hidden layer is shown by eq. (3).

$$\hat{y} = W_o \bullet h + b_o$$

… (3)

Where W_o and b_o are the weights and bias of the output layer and $h = [h_{r1}, h_{r2}, \ldots, h_{rm}]^T$ with m neuron in last hidden layer represented by r, which is used in the output layer. Depending on the task, this output can be a scalar in the case of regression or a vector representing the probabilities of different classes in the case of classification.

The process of learning is done using a loss function, which calculates the error produced due to variations in the predicted and actual values or labels. For regression, the Mean Squared Error (MSE) is commonly used and given by eq. (4)

$$L(\hat{y}, y) = \frac{1}{2}\sum_{i=1}^{p}(\hat{y}_i - y_i)^2$$

… (4)

Where p for number of neurons in the Output layer MSE is calculated. For classification tasks, the multiclass cross-entropy loss is more appropriate, given by eq. (5).

$$L(\hat{y}, y) = -\sum_{i=1}^{p} y_i \log(\hat{y}_i)$$

… (5)

Here, $\hat{y}_i$ represents the predicted probability of class i from 1 to p, and y_i is the true class label. The network minimizes the loss by updating the weights and biases (García Cabello, 2022).

To achieve this optimization, the network uses an optimizer, such as Stochastic Gradient Descent (SGD). It iteratively updates the weights by following the negative gradient of the loss function, gradually minimizing the error. The weight update rule is given by eq. (6)

$$w \leftarrow w - \eta \frac{\partial l}{\partial w} \quad \ldots \quad (6)$$

where η is the learning rate and $\frac{\partial l}{\partial w}$ is the gradient of the loss function with respect to the weights. Gradients are determined through backpropagation, which utilizes the chain rule of differentiation to compute the loss function's gradients concerning all network parameters, beginning at the output layer and propagating backward through the layers (García Cabello, 2022). The ability to compute these gradients efficiently through backpropagation allows the network to change its parameters and learn from data. In this process, each neuron contributes to adjusting the weights based on how much its output influenced the error in the final prediction.

Neural networks comprise neurons, weights, biases, optimizers, loss functions, and activation functions, forming the foundation of Deep Learning. Its strength lies in differentiation, architecture, and supervised learning (Gavranović, 2024). Differentiation enables gradient computation for optimization, adjusting weights and biases to minimize error. Architecture determines learning capacity, with FNNs for simple tasks and CNNs or RNNs for complex data. Supervised learning trains models on labeled data, improving generalization through gradient-based adjustments. These components collectively enable Deep Learning to transform inputs into outputs, adapt to data, and solve complex tasks across various domains.

Propagation Techniques

Propagation techniques form the foundation of how artificial neural networks process information and learn from data. These techniques define how data moves through the network and how learning occurs by adjusting weights to minimize errors. Two key processes enable this learning: forward propagation, where input data flows through the network to generate predictions, and backward propagation, where errors are propagated backward to update the network's parameters (Gavranović, 2024). These processes work together to help a neural network continuously improve its predictions and adapt to intricate data patterns.

In the context of transportation applications, propagation techniques are essential for developing predictive models that enhance road safety. For instance, a visibility prediction system can help traffic management authorities provide real-time travel advisories, ensuring that drivers are warned of hazardous conditions in advance. Such systems are particularly valuable for intelligent transportation systems (ITS), automated traffic control, and autonomous vehicle navigation, where accurate weather-related predictions can prevent accidents and optimize road efficiency (Duddu et al., 2020).

To illustrate the application of propagation techniques, we refer to a study where a Backpropagation Neural Network (BPNN) model was designed to predict road visibility based on meteorological data (Duddu et al., 2020). This model analyses weather-related inputs, including cloud cover, precipitation, temperature, dew point, wind speed, and past rainfall data. It utilizes forward propagation for initial predictions and backward propagation to enhance accuracy. This example is taken forward to explain how these propagation techniques function mathematically and how they contribute to real-world transportation safety applications.

Forward Propagation

Forward propagation is the stage in which the neural network takes input data and generates a predicted output. In the context of visibility prediction, meteorological features collected from weather monitoring stations are used as inputs, each associated with a weight that represents its contribution to visibility classification. These weighted inputs pass through multiple layers, where neurons apply transformations to capture meaningful patterns. The model utilizes activation functions in hidden layers to introduce non-linearity, ensuring it can learn complex relationships between weather variables and visibility conditions (Duddu et al., 2020).

Mathematically, forward propagation begins by computing a weighted sum of inputs in each neuron of the hidden layer. Given n input features $x_1, x_2, \ldots, x_n$ represents meteorological variables such as wind speed or humidity, which influence visibility , each with a corresponding weight w_{ij} are assigned to these variables, capturing their importance in visibility prediction, the transformation at neuron j in the hidden layer is computed as shown in eq. (7).

$$z_j = \sum_{i=1}^{n} w_{ij} x_i + b_j \quad \ldots \quad (7)$$

where b_j is the bias term that helps shift activation values for better learning. This equation is critical in transportation applications, as it ensures that variables affecting visibility conditions are processed accurately. Then the z_j is passed through hyperbolic tangent function, which is defined as shown in eq. (8).

$$f(z_j) = \frac{e^{z_j} - e^{-z_j}}{e^{z_j} + e^{-z_j}}$$

… (8)

This function ensures that the output remains within a controlled range [-1,1], preventing extreme outputs that could misclassify visibility conditions. In applications such as autonomous driving, this mathematical transformation ensures that the neural network does not overreact to minor environmental fluctuations, leading to smoother speed adjustments and safer driving maneuvers (Duddu et al., 2020). The transformed values from hidden layer neurons are then passed to the output layer for final classification, where a final weighted sum produces the predicted visibility classification as shown in eq. (9).

$$y_{pred} = \sum_{j=1}^{n} v_j f(z_j) + b_{out}$$

… (9)

where v_j represents the weights between the last hidden layer and the output layer, and b_{out} is the output bias. This equation determines the final visibility classification, which is essential for real-time driver assistance systems. For example, if the network classifies visibility as less than 100 meters, adaptive cruise control systems in self-driving cars can increase following distance and reduce vehicle speed accordingly.

The ability to accurately predict visibility through forward propagation has significant applications in transportation safety. For example, real-time visibility predictions can be integrated into highway control centres to update digital road signs, informing drivers about upcoming foggy zones and allowing them to adjust their speed accordingly. Similarly, in autonomous vehicle systems, forward propagation helps vehicles dynamically assess road conditions, enabling them to modify speed, braking behaviour, and lane positioning in response to reduced visibility.

The output visibility classification is then compared to actual visibility measurements recorded by weather monitoring sensors at specific road locations. If the prediction does not align with the actual observed visibility, an error is calculated, which is used in the next phase—backward propagation—to refine the network's parameters to minimize errors.

Backward Propagation

Backward propagation is the error-correction mechanism that improves the neural networks to make accurate predictions over time. Once forward propagation produces an initial visibility classification, it is compared to the actual visibility readings obtained from weather monitoring sensors. The Mean Squared Error (MSE) measures the network's prediction accuracy which is given by eq. (10).

$$E = \frac{1}{N}\sum_{i=1}^{N}\left(y_{true,i} - y_{pred,i}\right)^2 \quad \dots \quad (10)$$

Where y_{true} is the actual visibility recorded by weather monitoring sensors and y_{pred} is the predicted visibility from the network and N is the number of samples in the dataset. To reduce this error, backward propagation updates the weights using gradient descent technique. The gradient of the error function with respect to each weight ω_{ij} is computed using the chain rule of differentiation as shown in eq. (11)

$$\frac{\partial E}{\partial \omega_{ij}} = \left(y_{true} - y_{Pred}\right) \cdot f'\left(z_j\right) \cdot x_i \quad \dots \quad (11)$$

Where $f'\left(z_j\right)$ is the derivative of the activation function. Using th gradient given by the eq. (12), the weights are adjusted in a direction that reduces the overall error.

$$\omega_{ij}^{new} = \omega_{ij}^{old} - \eta\frac{\partial E}{\partial \omega_{ij}} \quad \dots \quad (12)$$

where η is the learning rate, which controls how much adjustments are made per iteration. This weight adjustment process is crucial in transportation applications. For instance, if the system overestimates visibility, it could lead to insufficient speed reductions, increasing the risk of accidents. By fine-tuning weights, backward propagation ensures that fog predictions remain precise, allowing adaptive speed limits to be set correctly (Duddu et al., 2020).

To prevent overfitting, the model also incorporates Bayesian Regularization, which modifies the error function by adding a penalty term for large weights as shown in eq. (13).

$$E_{reg} = E + \lambda\sum w_{ij}^2 \quad \dots \quad (13)$$

where λ is a regularization parameter that prevents the model from relying too heavily on any single feature (Liang, 2003). In autonomous vehicle systems, this ensures that predictions are not overly sensitive to sudden changes in wind speed or humidity, preventing unnecessary braking or acceleration (Liang, 2005). By iterating this process over multiple training cycles, the model gradually minimizes its prediction error, making it more reliable for real-world transportation applications (Liang, 2005).

The Backpropagation Neural Network (BPNN) model used for visibility prediction is structured as:

1. Input layer: Receives meteorological features $(x_1, x_2, \ldots, x_n)$.
2. Hidden layers: Transform inputs using activation functions.
3. Output layer: Produces a visibility classification.

The model's weight optimization process follows this iterative cycle:

1. Forward propagation computes y_{Pred} based on input data.
2. Error calculation using MSE determines how far predictions deviate from actual values.
3. Backward propagation adjusts weights using gradient descent to minimize errors.
4. Bayesian Regularization ensures generalization to new weather conditions.

By continuously refining predictions, this model significantly enhances real-time transportation safety applications. Integrating this system into traffic management platforms enables dynamic fog alerts, automated speed limit adjustments, and adaptive routing, ultimately reducing the risk of fog-related crashes and improving travel efficiency (Duddu et al., 2020).

DEEP LEARNING TECHNIQUES

Deep Learning techniques have revolutionized transportation by enabling intelligent decision-making through advanced neural networks. CNNs facilitate real-time object detection for autonomous vehicles, ensuring accurate recognition of pedestrians, vehicles, and traffic signs. RNNs and LSTMs enhance traffic prediction and route optimization, improving urban mobility. Transformers manage complex contextual relationships, while GANs generate synthetic data, aiding AI model training for diverse real-world scenarios (Pranamesh, Rao, & Pati, 2020; Zhang, Li, & Zhang, 2024). These innovations drive autonomous systems, smart traffic management, and intelligent monitoring, making transportation safer and more efficient. The following sections will explore these methods in detail.

Convolutional Neural Networks (CNNs)

License plate detection is a fundamental task in intelligent transportation systems, where Convolutional Neural Networks (CNNs) play a crucial role in identifying and localizing plates in images. CNNs are specifically designed to process visual data by automatically learning spatial hierarchies of features, making them highly effective for detecting license plates in varying conditions, such as different angles, lighting conditions, and occlusions (Pranamesh, Rao, & Pati, 2020). Unlike traditional feature-based methods that rely on manually defined rules, CNNs adapt to different plate formats, fonts, and environmental factors through extensive training on diverse datasets.

The architecture of a CNN consists of multiple layers that progressively refine and extract relevant features. The first layer in a CNN is the convolutional layer, which applies filters (kernels) over the input image to extract meaningful patterns, such as edges, curves, and textures found in license plates. This operation is mathematically represented as given in eq. (14).

$$S(i,j) = \sum_m \sum_n I(i + m, j + n) k(m,n) \quad \ldots \quad (14)$$

where i & j are the coordinates of the pixel in the feature map (output of the convolution operation),m & n are the coordinates of the kernel (filter) applied over the image, $I(i + m, j + n)$ represents the pixel values of the image, $k(m,n)$ is the convolutional kernel, and $S(i,j)$is the resulting feature map(Sathya & Uma, 2024). Through multiple convolutional layers, CNNs develop a deep understanding of structural patterns unique to license plates. To enhance non-linearity and improve model learning, CNNs apply activation functions such as ReLU (Rectified Linear Unit) given by the eq. (15), which transforms negative pixel values to zero while retaining positive values:

$$f(x) = \max(0, x) \quad \ldots \quad (15)$$

This ensures that CNNs can model complex patterns without being limited by linear transformations.

Following feature extraction, CNNs apply pooling layers, which reduce the spatial dimensions of feature maps while preserving essential information. The most common method, max pooling, selects the highest pixel value in a given region, making CNNs robust to minor distortions or shifts in license plate positions (Sathya & Uma, 2024). Mathematically, this operation is defined by the eq. (16).

$$p(i,j) = \max_{m,n} S(i + u, j + v) \quad \ldots \quad (16)$$

Where u & v refer to the indices inside the pooling window, where the maximum value is selected. Pooling layers allow CNNs to focus on the most prominent features of a license plate, ignoring unnecessary background details. After feature extraction, the CNN passes the processed data through fully connected layers, which transform the feature maps into a classification or localization output. The output layer predicts whether a license plate is present in the image and provides bounding box coordinates that enclose the detected plate.

Object Detection

Object detection is crucial in computer vision and underpins license plate detection in systems like toll collection, traffic monitoring, law enforcement, and parking management. Traditionally, methods used handcrafted features (edge detection, morphology, contour analysis) to spot plates, but they struggled with issues like variable lighting, angles, motion blur, and occlusions.

Deep Learning models—especially CNN-based single-stage detectors like SSD and YOLO—have significantly improved accuracy, robustness, and real-time performance by learning hierarchical features directly from raw images (Sathya & Uma, 2024). These models generalize well across different vehicle types and plate formats. Complementary computer vision techniques further enhance performance. Preprocessing (e.g., grayscale conversion, contrast enhancement, histogram equalization, noise reduction) and data augmentation (rotation, scaling, flipping, blurring) help normalize images under diverse conditions. Classical methods, such as connected component analysis and contour detection, refine bounding box predictions by filtering out false positives, particularly in crowded scenes.

High-quality, well-annotated datasets are also essential, as they provide accurate ground truth for training robust models. Modern systems combine Deep Learning and traditional computer vision techniques to deliver reliable and efficient license plate detection.

You Only Look Once (YOLO) for license plate detection

The YOLO framework has revolutionized real-time license plate detection, offering high-speed processing with precise localization capabilities. Unlike traditional object detection methods, YOLO performs detection and classification in a single forward pass, making it significantly faster and more efficient than two-stage detectors such as Faster R-CNN. This speed is particularly beneficial in automated toll booths, traffic monitoring systems, and smart surveillance, where real-time detection of moving vehicles is required.

YOLO detects license plates by dividing an input image into a grid of size S×S, where each grid cell predicts multiple bounding boxes, along with their confidence scores. A bounding box in YOLO is defined by four parameters (x, y, w, h), where (x, y) are the normalized center coordinates of the license plate relative to the cell in the grid, and (w, h) represent the width and height of the plate detected bounding box. To ensure that only accurately localized plates are retained, YOLO computes a confidence score for each detected bounding box using the eq. (17).

$$confidence = P(License\ Plate) \times IoU \quad \ldots (17)$$

Where *P(License Plate)* represents the probability that a license plate is present, and IoU (Intersection over Union) is a metric that quantifies the alignment between the predicted bounding box and the ground truth is measured using eq. (18).

$$IoU = \frac{Area\ of\ Overlap}{Area\ of\ Union} \quad \ldots (18)$$

A high IoU value indicates precise localization, while a low IoU suggests a detection error(Sathya & Uma, 2024). To further refine bounding box predictions, YOLO applies bounding box regression, optimizing the placement of bounding boxes using Smooth L1 Loss, which is mathematically expressed by the eq. (19).

$$L_{box} = \sum_{i=1}^{N} SmoothL1\left(\hat{y}_i - y_i\right) \quad \ldots (19)$$

where $\hat{y}_i$ is the predicted bounding box, and y_i is the actual ground truth. This function minimizes localization errors by penalizing large deviations, ensuring that the detected plate remains accurately enclosed within its bounding box. Because YOLO generates multiple bounding boxes for each license plate, it applies Non-Maximum Suppression (NMS) to remove duplicate detections and keep only the most confident one (Sathya & Uma, 2024). NMS ranks all bounding boxes based on their confidence scores and eliminates those with an IoU exceeding a predefined threshold τ. This ensures that each license plate is detected only once, preventing duplicate bounding boxes from cluttering detection outputs.

YOLO faces challenges in license plate detection, particularly with small objects, motion blur, and varying designs. Plates often occupy a small area in images, but YOLOv5 and YOLOv8 address this using Feature Pyramid Networks (FPNs) and anchor box refinements. Motion blur from fast-moving vehicles is mitigated through super-resolution and temporal frame aggregation. Diverse plate formats make generalization difficult, tackled via transfer learning and dataset augmentation. Despite these challenges, YOLO's real-time processing, accuracy, and mathematical optimizations make it ideal for transportation systems, ensuring efficient and reliable license plate detection across various environments (Sathya & Uma, 2024; Khanna et al., 2025).

Recurrent Neural Networks (RNNs)

RNNs are a type of neural network specifically built to handle sequential data (Pranamesh, Rao, & Pati, 2020). While standard RNNs are effective, they face challenges in capturing long-term dependencies due to the vanishing gradient problem. As gradients propagate over time, they shrink exponentially, making it harder for the network to retain information across long sequences. The core working principle of RNNs involves passing information through recurrent connections, where each neuron receives not only the current input but also the hidden state from the previous time step. Mathematically, this can be represented as eq. (20).

$$h_t = f(w_h h_{t-1} + w_x x_t + b) \quad \ldots \quad (20)$$

Where h_t is the hidden state at time step t, x_t is the input, and w_h, w_x and b are learnable parameters (Pranamesh, Rao, & Pati, 2020). Although RNNs are effective, they have difficulty maintaining long-term dependencies because of the vanishing gradient issue. As gradients pass through multiple time steps, they decrease exponentially, making it difficult for the network to maintain information over extended sequences.

RNNs predict traffic flow by learning from historical data and capturing temporal dependencies in dynamic congestion patterns—affected by peak hours, accidents, and seasonal variations. They analyze sequential inputs, such as vehicle counts, to forecast future traffic. However, standard RNNs often struggle with long-term dependencies due to the vanishing gradient problem, where gradients diminish over time.

Vanishing gradient problem

The vanishing gradient problem arises in RNNs when gradients become too small during backpropagation, hindering the network's ability to adjust the weights of earlier layers effectively. This issue arises because the gradient values are multiplied repeatedly through many layers, causing them to shrink exponentially (Pranamesh, Rao, & Pati, 2020). As a result, the network struggles to learn long-term dependencies, which is a critical requirement for traffic flow prediction. In the context of traffic flow prediction, accurate forecasting requires the model to retain information over extended time periods. Traditional RNNs fail in this regard, as they prioritize recent data over older patterns, leading to suboptimal predictions. For instance, when predicting peak-hour traffic, the model needs to remember patterns from previous days or even weeks. However, due to vanishing gradients, standard RNNs are unable to effectively learn such dependencies, resulting in poor accuracy.

LSTM for traffic prediction

Short-term traffic flow prediction enhances intelligent transportation by improving traffic management and reducing congestion. Traditional methods like ARIMA struggle with complex patterns, leading to the adoption of RNNs (Lemieux & Ma, 2015). However, RNNs face the vanishing gradient problem, limiting long-term dependency retention.LSTM networks overcome this with memory cells and three gates—forget, input, and output—that regulate information flow, as shown in Figure 3. This gating mechanism enables LSTMs to selectively retain relevant traffic patterns, making them highly effective for time-series forecasting. By considering past congestion levels, time-of-day variations, and periodic trends, LSTMs provide accurate predictions, significantly improving real-time traffic optimization (Poonia & Jain, 2020; Zhengcai Yang et al., 2024).

Figure 3. LSTM cell representation

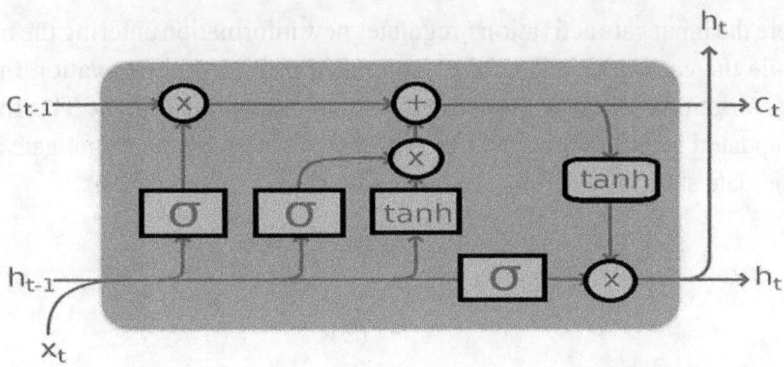

The mathematical foundation of LSTMs has the ability to capture temporal dependencies in traffic data. Given an input sequence of traffic flow measurements $X = (x_1, x_2, \ldots, x_T)$,an LSTM cell updates its internal state and outputs predictions at each time step using a set of equations. The process begins with calculating the forget gate, which decides whether to keep or remove information from the previous time step. The forget gate activation is given by eq. (21).

$$f_t = \sigma\left(w_f[h_{t-1}, x_t] + b_f\right) \quad \ldots \quad (21)$$

where f_t is the forget gate activation at time t, w_f represents the weight matrix, h_{t-1} is the previous hidden state, x_t is the current input, and b_f is the bias term (Cenggoro & Siahaan, 2016). The sigmoid activation function σ ensures that values remain within the range of 0 to 1, effectively deciding whether to retain past information. Next, the input gate determines how much of the new information should be stored in the cell state. This step consists of two parts: activating the input gate and updating the candidate cell state. The input gate activation is computed as shown in eq. (22).

$$i_t = \sigma\left(w_i[h_{t-1}, x_t] + b_i\right) \quad \ldots \quad (22)$$

and the candidate cell state is given by the eq. (23).

$$\widetilde{C}_t = \tanh\left(w_C[h_{t-1}, x_t] + b_C\right)$$

… (23)

Where the input gate activation i_t regulates new information entering the memory cell, while the candidate cell state $\tilde{C}_t$ computed using a tanh activation function, captures variations in traffic flow trends within a range of -1 to 1. The final cell state is updated by combining the old cell state is scaled by the forget gate and the new candidate state is scaled by the input gate as shown in eq. (24).

$$C_t = f_t \cdot C_{t-1} + i_t \cdot \tilde{C}_t$$

… (24)

This equation highlights the ability of LSTM networks to selectively retain important past information while incorporating new observations, making them highly effective for traffic forecasting (Poonia & Jain, 2020). Once the cell state is updated, the output gate determines what part of the current cell state should be passed to the next layer or output at time t is given by eq. (25).

$$o_t = \sigma\left(W_o[h_{t-1}, x_t] + b_o\right)$$

… (25)

The final hidden state, which serves as the output of the LSTM unit, is then computed using the eq. (26).

$$h_t = o_t \cdot \tanh\left(c_t\right)$$

… (26)

This hidden state is passed forward to the next time step, ensuring that the network retains relevant temporal dependencies while suppressing unnecessary information.

In traffic flow prediction, the ability of LSTMs to remember long-term dependencies allows them to learn complex relationships between past and future traffic conditions. Unlike conventional methods that rely on fixed time windows, LSTMs can dynamically adjust their memory based on traffic patterns, making them particularly useful for capturing seasonal trends, rush-hour variations, and the impact of external factors such as holidays or weather conditions.Training an LSTM model for traffic prediction typically involves feeding historical traffic data into the network and optimizing the weight parameters using backpropagation through time (BPTT). The loss function commonly used for this task is Root Mean Squared Error

(RMSE), which measures the standard deviation of residuals (prediction errors). RMSE is given by eq. (27).

$$RMSE = \sqrt{\overline{(f-o)^2}} \quad \ldots \quad (27)$$

where f represents forecasts (expected valued or unknown results), *o* is observed values (known results) and the bar above the squared differences is the mean. RMSE provides an intuitive measure of error magnitude by penalizing larger deviations more than smaller ones. A lower RMSE value indicates a more accurate model, making it a preferred metric for evaluating traffic forecasting models (Poonia & Jain, 2020).LSTM-based short-term traffic flow prediction uses recent data (e.g., vehicle count, time of day, congestion levels) to forecast real-time conditions. By processing sequential inputs through memory cells, LSTMs capture temporal dependencies and adapt to sudden changes like peak congestion or incidents. Their ability to maintain long-term dependencies and mitigate vanishing gradients makes them essential for intelligent transportation systems, offering a scalable, data-driven solution to reduce congestion and optimize road management (Poonia & Jain, 2020; Zhengcai Yang et al., 2024; C. Selvan et al., 2025).

Generative Adversarial Networks (GAN)

Generative Adversarial Networks (GANs) are a class of Deep Learning models designed to generate synthetic data that closely resembles real-world data. Unlike traditional Machine Learning models, which rely on explicitly defined rules or large labelled datasets, GANs learn to generate realistic samples by engaging two neural networks in a competitive game (Pranamesh, Rao, & Pati, 2020; Yan & Li, 2023). This unique adversarial approach enables GANs to model complex data distributions without requiring predefined statistical assumptions. Introduced by Ian Goodfellow in 2014, GANs have since been widely applied in domains such as image synthesis, text generation, medical data augmentation, and, more recently, traffic scenario generation (Yan & Li, 2023).

GANs provide a data-driven alternative to traditional traffic simulation methods that rely on handcrafted rules and complex mathematical models. Unlike approaches such as cellular automata or microscopic simulations—which require extensive parameter tuning and often miss the stochastic nature of traffic—GANs learn directly from historical data, extracting detailed spatial and temporal patterns. This capability enables the generation of realistic traffic scenarios useful for urban planning, traffic control optimization, and autonomous vehicle training (Yan & Li, 2023).The core principle of GANs revolves around the interaction between two competing neural networks as shown in Figure 4.:

1. The Generator (G) – Creates fake data samples.
2. The Discriminator (D) – Evaluates whether the input data is real or fake.

Figure 4. GAN model structure

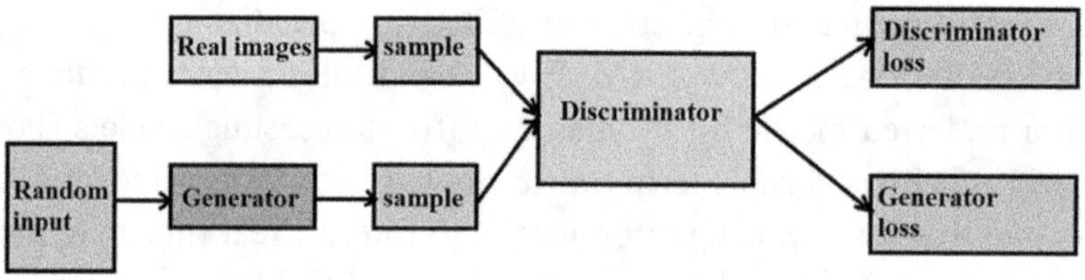

These two models engage in an adversarial game to differentiate real from fake. GANs can be used in traffic scenario generation to model realistic traffic flow patterns (Yan & Li, 2023). By training on historical traffic data, a GAN can generate new traffic flow scenarios that resemble real-world conditions. This helps in urban planning, traffic control, and intelligent transportation systems (ITS).

Generator and Discriminator

The Generator creates synthetic traffic data that mimics real-world patterns. It starts with a random noise vector (sampled from a Gaussian or uniform distribution) and transforms it through multiple layers, learning indirectly from feedback provided by the Discriminator (C. Wu et al., 2020). Depending on the data, it may use fully connected, convolutional, or recurrent layers. For traffic simulation—where data is sequential and time-dependent—it often incorporates models like LSTM or GRU to capture temporal dependencies, ensuring realistic and consistent traffic flow.

The main objective of the Generator is to fool the Discriminator into classifying its synthetic traffic data as real. To achieve this, the Generator is trained using an adversarial loss function, which encourages it to generate more realistic traffic scenarios is defined as shown in eq. (28).

$$L_G = -E[\log D(G(z))] \quad \ldots \quad (28)$$

Where G(z) represents the generated traffic scenario and D(G(z)) is the probability assigned by the Discriminator that G(z) is real. The Generator aims to maximize D(G(z)), thereby increasing the realism of the generated samples. Initially, when the Generator is untrained, the Discriminator can easily distinguish between real and fake traffic data. However, as training progresses, the Generator refines its outputs by learning from the Discriminator's feedback, gradually producing traffic patterns that become indistinguishable from real traffic data (C. Wu et al., 2020).

The Discriminator (D(x)) plays the role of a binary classifier that differentiates between real traffic data from actual road networks and synthetic traffic data generated by the Generator. It receives input from both the real-world dataset and the Generator and assigns a probability score indicating how likely a given traffic sample is to be real. The Discriminator's task is to maximize the probability of correctly identifying real traffic data while minimizing the probability of being deceived by the Generator's synthetic samples (C. Wu et al., 2020).To achieve this, the Discriminator is trained using binary cross-entropy loss, which measures how well it can distinguish between real and generated traffic data. The Discriminator's loss function is defined as shown in eq. (29).

$$L_D = -E[\log D(x)] - E[\log(1-D(G(z)))] \quad \ldots \quad (29)$$

In GAN training for traffic modelling, D(x) is the probability a real traffic sample is recognized as genuine, and D(G(z)) is the probability a generated sample is classified as real. This adversarial process drives both networks to improve: the Discriminator learns to better distinguish real from fake data, while the Generator refines its outputs based on this feedback (C. Wu et al., 2020). Over time, the Generator creates increasingly realistic traffic patterns, forcing the Discriminator to adapt. This interplay results in high-fidelity spatiotemporal traffic scenarios that capture real-world statistical properties, congestion trends, and spatial dependencies, making GANs a powerful tool for predictive traffic modelling, intelligent transportation systems, and autonomous vehicle simulation.

GAN for Traffic Simulation

Traffic simulation is a crucial component of modern transportation research, helping to optimize road networks, predict congestion patterns, and design intelligent traffic control systems. Conventional traffic simulation models use rule-based methods or mathematical equations, requiring significant parameter adjustments and often struggling to represent the unpredictable and dynamic nature of real-world traffic flow. Generative Adversarial Networks (GANs) offer a data-driven alternative, allowing traffic patterns to be learned directly from historical data and then used to generate new, realistic traffic scenarios.

A GAN-based traffic simulation model consists of two neural networks where the Generator creates synthetic traffic data that replicates real-world traffic patterns, while the Discriminator assesses whether the provided traffic data is authentic or artificially generated. These networks are trained in an adversarial manner, where the Generator continuously improves its ability to generate realistic traffic scenarios while the Discriminator refines its ability to distinguish real from fake data. The goal is to reach a point where the Discriminator can no longer reliably differentiate between real and generated traffic flow, meaning the Generator has successfully learned the distribution of real-world traffic patterns (C. Wu et al., 2020). The fundamental idea behind GAN training is a min-max game between the Generator - G and the Discriminator - D. The objective function of a standard GAN is formulated as shown in the eq. (30).

$$\min_{G} \max_{D} V(G,D) = E_{x \sim P_{data}(x)}\left[\log D(x)\right] + E_{z \sim P_z(z)}\left[\log(1 - D(G(x)))\right] \quad \ldots \quad (30)$$

Where $P_{data}(x)$ represents the distribution of real traffic data, $P_z(z)$ is the distribution of noise input (e.g., Gaussian noise), G(z) is the generated traffic sample and D(x) outputs the probability that x is a real traffic sample. The Generator aims to minimize this objective by producing realistic traffic patterns, while the Discriminator tries to maximize it by correctly identifying real and generated traffic data (C. Wu et al., 2020).Training a GAN for traffic simulation is an iterative process where the Generator creates synthetic traffic data, and the Discriminator distinguishes it from real data. Initially, generated samples lack realism, but through adversarial training, the Generator refines outputs to deceive the Discriminator. The Discriminator, optimized via a loss function, improves its ability to differentiate real and synthetic data. This loop continues until the Discriminator can no longer distinguish between them, indicating the Generator has learned the true traffic distribution. The trained GAN then produces realistic traffic scenarios, aiding predictive modelling and intelligent transportation systems (C.Wu et al., 2020).

GANs offer a powerful and scalable solution for traffic scenario generation, providing an alternative to traditional rule-based simulations. By learning directly from historical data, GANs can generate highly realistic, spatiotemporal traffic patterns, enabling their use in a wide range of transportation applications. The integration of LSTM networks within GANs further enhances their ability to model sequential dependencies, making them an essential tool for modern traffic simulation and prediction.

Table 1. Applications in Transportation

Contribution	Research Paper Title	Model Used	Application
Kushwaha, M. K., & Suseela, G. (2022)	Car Number Plate Detection using Deep Learning	CNN	Automatic License Plate Recognition (ALPR)
Nandhakumar, R. G., et al. (2023)	Yolo Based License Plate Detection of Triple Riders and Violators	YOLO	Traffic rule violation detection
Duives, D. C., et al. (2019)	Forecasting Pedestrian Movements Using Recurrent Neural Networks: An Application of Crowd Monitoring Data	RNN	Pedestrian movement forecasting for crowd monitoring
Yuan, Y., et al. (2020)	Bus Dynamic Travel Time Prediction: Using a Deep Feature Extraction Framework Based on RNN and DNN	RNN, DNN	Bus travel time prediction
Chen, Y.-C., et al. (2022)	Application of Generative Adversarial Network to Optimize Vehicle Allocation at Dispatch Stations of Paratransit Services	GAN	Vehicle allocation optimization in paratransit services
Naji, H. A. H., et al. (2021)	Forecasting Taxi Demands Using Generative Adversarial Networks with Multi-Source Data	GAN	Taxi demand forecasting
Sun, T., et al. (2021)	Traffic Flow Online Prediction Based on a Generative Adversarial Network with Multi-Source Data	GAN	Real-time traffic flow prediction.
Zhengcai Yang et al. (2024)	Deep Reinforcement Learning Lane-Changing Decision Algorithm for Intelligent Vehicles Combining LSTM Trajectory Prediction	LSTM, DEEP REINFORCEMENT LEARNING	Autonomous driving and Advanced Driver Assistance Systems
C. Selvan et al. (2025)	Traffic Prediction Using GPS Based Cloud Data Through RNN-LSTM-CNN Models: Addressing Road Congestion, Safety, and Sustainability in Smart Cities	RNN, LSTM, CNN	Traffic flow prediction, congestion management, and smart city transportation optimization.

The Tabulation (Table 1) provides a summary Deep Learning techniques which have significantly transformed transportation by enhancing automation, safety, and predictive analytics. These AI-driven advancements continue to revolutionize mobility, making transportation systems smarter and more reliable.

Challenges and Benefits of AI in Transportation

AI is revolutionizing transportation by enabling real-time decision-making, optimizing traffic flow, and enhancing safety. However, its implementation comes with significant challenges related to data, computational demands, model interpretability, and ethical concerns.

Challenges

One of the primary challenges is data quality, as AI models rely on vast, high-quality datasets, but real-world transportation data is often inconsistent, biased, or incomplete due to sensor limitations. Additionally, computational costs pose a barrier, requiring high-end hardware for training and deployment, which increases expenses and limits scalability. Another issue is model interpretability, as deep learning models often function as black boxes, making it difficult for stakeholders to understand AI-driven decisions in traffic control and autonomous driving. Real-time processing constraints further complicate AI applications, as some models struggle with latency, affecting their responsiveness in dynamic traffic scenarios. AI integration in transportation brings ethical challenges related to safety, accountability, and decision-making in autonomous systems. Moreover, ethical and legal concerns arise from biases in AI models that may result in unfair traffic enforcement, raising questions about accountability, transparency, and discrimination. These challenges, combined with evolving regulatory frameworks, complicate real-world deployment and demand responsible AI practices.

Benefits

Despite these challenges, deep learning offers transformative benefits in transportation. Traffic optimization through AI-driven management systems improves signal timing and reduces congestion. Safety enhancements such as pedestrian detection, Advanced Driver Assistance Systems (ADAS), and collision avoidance reduce accident rates.AI also enables automated surveillance, improving license plate recognition and traffic monitoring for law enforcement. Predictive maintenance helps anticipate vehicle servicing needs, reducing downtime and improving fleet efficiency. Additionally, cost and efficiency gains are achieved through AI-based route optimization, minimizing fuel consumption and operational costs. Lastly, AI provides real-time insights, processing sensor and GPS data to support adaptive traffic control and emergency response systems.

By addressing these challenges and leveraging its benefits, deep learning continues to shape the future of intelligent transportation, making mobility safer, more efficient, and highly adaptive.

CONCLUSION

Deep Learning techniques have been explored in this chapter to illustrate their significance in transforming the transportation domain. CNNs for object detection and license plate recognition, RNNs and LSTMs for traffic prediction, and GANs for traffic simulation serve as key components in developing intelligent transportation systems, demonstrating the potential of AI-driven solutions in optimizing infrastructure. These models address real-world challenges such as traffic management, autonomous navigation, and logistics optimization by effectively processing complex spatial and temporal data, enhancing efficiency and safety. A review of Deep Learning -based transportation models highlight their role in dynamic decision-making and real-time system adaptation, with YOLO-based license plate detection serving as an example of intelligent vehicle tracking. Beyond these models, advanced architectures like Attention Networks and Transformer models further improve predictive accuracy by capturing long-range dependencies, offering enhanced capabilities in traffic forecasting, route optimization, and autonomous decision-making. As Deep Learning research evolves, integrating such sophisticated architectures will continue to optimize mobility, urban planning, and intelligent transportation systems, leading to smarter, more adaptive, and efficient networks.

REFERENCES

Bishop, C. M. (2006). *Pattern recognition and Machine Learning*. Springer.

Cenggoro, T. W., & Siahaan, I. (2016). Dynamic bandwidth management based on traffic prediction using deep long short-term memory. *2016 2nd International Conference on Science in Information Technology (ICSITech).*

Chawla, N. V., Bowyer, K. W., Hall, L. O., & Kegelmeyer, W. P. (2002). SMOTE: Synthetic minority over-sampling technique. *Journal of Artificial Intelligence Research, 16*, 321–357. DOI: 10.1613/jair.953

Chen, Y.-C., Loh, C.-H., Wang, F.-C., Chen, Z.-J., Fu, S.-H., & Wang, C.-Y. (2022). Application of generative adversarial network to optimize vehicle allocation at dispatch stations of paratransit services. *Electronics (Basel), 11*(3), 423. DOI: 10.3390/electronics11030423

Duddu, V. R., Pulugurtha, S. S., Mane, A. S., & Godfrey, C. (2020). Back-propagation neural network model to predict visibility at a road link-level. *Transportation Research Interdisciplinary Perspectives, 8*, 100250. DOI: 10.1016/j.trip.2020.100250

Duives, D. C., Wang, G., & Kim, J. (2019). Forecasting pedestrian movements using recurrent neural networks: An application of crowd monitoring data. *Sensors (Basel), 19*(2), 382. DOI: 10.3390/s19020382 PMID: 30669293

Esteva, A., Kuprel, B., Novoa, R. A., Ko, J., Swetter, S. M., Blau, H. M., & Thrun, S. (2017). Dermatologist-level classification of skin cancer with deep neural networks. *Nature, 542*(7639), 115–118. DOI: 10.1038/nature21056 PMID: 28117445

García Cabello, J. (2022). Mathematical neural networks. *Axioms, 11*(2), 80. DOI: 10.3390/axioms11020080

Gavranović, B. (2024). *Fundamental components of Deep Learning: A category-theoretic approach* (PhD thesis). University of Strathclyde, Glasgow. https://arxiv.org/pdf/2403.13001

Goodfellow, I., Bengio, Y., & Courville, A. (2016). *Deep Learning.* MIT Press. Retrieved from http://www.deeplearningbook.org

Goodfellow, I., Pouget-Abadie, J., Mirza, M., Xu, B., Warde-Farley, D., Ozair, S., Courville, A., & Bengio, Y. (2014). Generative adversarial nets. *Advances in Neural Information Processing Systems, 27*, 2672–2680.

Haykin, S. (2009). *Neural networks and learning machines* (3rd ed.). Pearson.

He, K., Zhang, X., Ren, S., & Sun, J. (2016). Deep residual learning for image recognition. In *Proceedings of the IEEE Conference on Computer Vision and Pattern Recognition* (pp. 770–778). https://doi.org/DOI: 10.1109/CVPR.2016.90

Heaton, J. B., Polson, N. G., & Witte, J. H. (2017). Deep Learning for finance: Deep portfolios. *Applied Stochastic Models in Business and Industry*, *33*(1), 3–12. DOI: 10.1002/asmb.2209

Hochreiter, S., & Schmidhuber, J. (1997). Long short-term memory. *Neural Computation*, *9*(8), 1735–1780. DOI: 10.1162/neco.1997.9.8.1735 PMID: 9377276

Howard, A. G., Zhu, M., Chen, B., Kalenichenko, D., Wang, W., Weyand, T., Andreetto, M., & Adam, H. (2017). MobileNets: Efficient convolutional neural networks for mobile vision applications. *arXiv preprint arXiv:1704.04861*. https://arxiv.org/abs/1704.04861

Khanna, C., Bish, B., Kamshetty, D., Bhardwaj, H., & Bhutani, M. (2025). Enhancing license plate recognition using YOLONAS, YOLOv8, and SORT algorithms. *Journal of Artificial Intelligence*, 2(1), 167–174. DOI: 10.61552/JAI.2025.01.003

Krizhevsky, A., Sutskever, I., & Hinton, G. E. (2012). ImageNet classification with deep convolutional neural networks. *Advances in Neural Information Processing Systems*, *25*, 1097–1105.

Kushwaha, M. K., & Suseela, G. (2022). Car number plate detection using Deep Learning. *2022 International Conference on Data Science, Agents & Artificial Intelligence (ICDSAAI)*, 1-4. DOI: 10.1109/ICDSAAI55433.2022.10028818

LeCun, Y., Bengio, Y., & Hinton, G. (2015). Deep Learning. *Nature*, *521*(7553), 436–444. DOI: 10.1038/nature14539 PMID: 26017442

Lemieux, J., & Ma, Y. (2015). Vehicle speed prediction using Deep Learning. *2015 IEEE Conference.*

Liang, F. (2003). An effective Bayesian neural network classifier with a comparison study to support vector machine. *Neural Computation*, *15*(8), 1959–1989. DOI: 10.1162/08997660360675107

Liang, F. (2005). Bayesian neural networks for nonlinear time series forecasting. *Statistics and Computing*, *15*(1), 13–29. DOI: 10.1007/s11222-005-4786-8

Litman, T. (2021). *Autonomous vehicle implementation predictions: Implications for transport planning*. Victoria Transport Policy Institute. https://www.vtpi.org/avip.pdf

Lundberg, S. M., & Lee, S.-I. (2017). A unified approach to interpreting model predictions. In *Advances in Neural Information Processing Systems* (pp. 4765–4774). https://doi.org/DOI: 10.48550/arXiv.1705.07874

Lv, Y., Duan, Y., Kang, W., Li, Z., & Wang, F.-Y. (2015, April). Traffic flow prediction with big data: A Deep Learning approach. *IEEE Transactions on Intelligent Transportation Systems, 16*(2).

Naji, H. A. H., Xue, Q., Zhu, H., & Li, T. (2021). Forecasting taxi demands using generative adversarial networks with multi-source data. *Applied Sciences (Basel, Switzerland), 11*(20), 9675. DOI: 10.3390/app11209675

Nandhakumar, R. G., Devi, K. N., Krishnamoorthy, N., Shanthi, S., Pranesh, V. R., & Nikhalyaa, S. (2023). YOLO-based license plate detection of triple riders and violators. *2023 International Conference on Computer Communication and Informatics (ICCCI)*, 1-6. https://doi.org/DOI: 10.1109/ICCCI56745.2023.10128537

Poonia, P., & Jain, V. K. (2020). Short-term traffic flow prediction: Using LSTM. *2020 International Conference on Emerging Trends in Communication, Control and Computing (ICONC3)*, 1–4. https://doi.org/DOI: 10.1109/ICONC345789.2020.9117329

Pranamesh, S., Rao, D., & Pati, P. (2020). Applications of Deep Learning in intelligent transportation systems. *International Journal of Big Data and Analytics, 8*(3), 143–160. https://pranamesh.github.io/files/2020-DL-review-paper-BDAT.pdf

Ribeiro, M. T., Singh, S., & Guestrin, C. (2016). "Why should I trust you?": Explaining the predictions of any classifier. In *Proceedings of the 22nd ACM SIGKDD International Conference on Knowledge Discovery and Data Mining* (pp. 1135–1144). https://doi.org/DOI: 10.1145/2939672.2939778

Ruder, S. (2016). An overview of gradient descent optimization algorithms. *arXiv preprint arXiv:1609.04747*.

Russell, S., & Norvig, P. (2021). *Artificial Intelligence: A Modern Approach* (4th ed.). Pearson.

Sathya, D., & Uma, V. (2024). *Object detection*. Kindle Direct Publishing.

Schmidhuber, J. (2015). Deep Learning in neural networks: An overview. *Neural Networks, 61*, 85–117. DOI: 10.1016/j.neunet.2014.09.003 PMID: 25462637

Selvan, C., Kumar, R. S., Joseph, S. I. T., Bruntha, P. M., Amanullah, M., & Arulkumar, V. (2025). *Traffic prediction using GPS-based cloud data through RNN-LSTM-CNN models: Addressing Road congestion, safety, and sustainability in smart cities*. Springer Nature Singapore Pte Ltd.

Sun, T., Sun, B., Jiang, Z., Hao, R., & Xie, J. (2021). Traffic flow online prediction based on a generative adversarial network with multi-source data. *Sustainability (Basel), 13*(21), 12188. DOI: 10.3390/su132112188

Transportation Research Board. (2008). *Transportation applications of artificial intelligence, neural networks, and other advanced analytical techniques* (Circular E-C113). National Academies Press. https://onlinepubs.trb.org/onlinepubs/circulars/ec113.pdf

Vaswani, A., Shazeer, N., Parmar, N., Uszkoreit, J., Jones, L., Gomez, A. N., Kaiser, Ł., & Polosukhin, I. (2017). Attention is all you need. *Advances in Neural Information Processing Systems, 30*, 5998–6008.

Wu, C., Chen, L., Wang, G., Chai, S., Jiang, H., Peng, J., & Hong, Z. (2020). Spatiotemporal scenario generation of traffic flow based on LSTM-GAN. *IEEE Access : Practical Innovations, Open Solutions, 8*, 186191–186198. DOI: 10.1109/ACCESS.2020.3029230

Yan, H., & Li, Y. (2023). A survey of generative AI for intelligent transportation systems. *arXiv preprint arXiv:2312.08248*.https://arxiv.org/abs/2312.08248

Yang, Z., Wu, Z., Wang, Y., & Wu, H. (2024). Deep Reinforcement Learning Lane-Changing Decision Algorithm for Intelligent Vehicles Combining LSTM Trajectory Prediction. *World Electric Vehicle Journal, 15*(4), 173. DOI: 10.3390/wevj15040173

Yuan, Y., Shao, C., Cao, Z., He, Z., Zhu, C., Wang, Y., & Jang, V. (2020). Bus dynamic travel time prediction: Using a deep feature extraction framework based on RNN and DNN. *Electronics (Basel), 9*(11), 1876. DOI: 10.3390/electronics9111876

Zhang, T., Li, H., & Zhang, Q. (2024). Deep Learning algorithms for traffic forecasting: A comprehensive review. *Journal of Transportation Engineering, 150*(1), 1–18. https://onlinelibrary.wiley.com/doi/10.1155/2024/9981657. DOI: 10.1061/(ASCE)0733-947X(2000)126:1(1)

KEY TERMS AND DEFINITIONS

Artificial Intelligence (AI): Enables machines to mimic human cognition, learn from data, and make informed decisions.

Loss Function: Measures the difference between predicted and actual outputs in neural networks.

Convolutional Neural Networks (CNNs): Extract spatial features from image data for processing.

Long Short-Term Memory Networks (LSTMs): Handle long-term dependencies in sequential data.

Generative Adversarial Networks (GANs): Use competing networks to create realistic synthetic data.

Intelligent Transportation Systems (ITS): Optimize traffic using AI and big data.

Predictive Maintenance: Uses AI to predict and prevent equipment failures.

Chapter 5

Road Space Rationing Using Vehicle's Automated License Plate Recognition: A Comprehensive Survey of Methods

Ata Jahangir Moshayedi
https://orcid.org/0000-0002-9457-6267
Jiangxi University of Science and Technology, China

Amir Sohail Khan
Jiangxi University of Science and Technology, China

Zeashan Hameed Khan
https://orcid.org/0000-0003-2002-8951
King Fahd University of Petroleum and Minerals, Saudi Arabia

Arash Sioofy Khoojine
Yibin University, China

Abolfazl Razi
Clemson University, USA

ABSTRACT

The exponential rise in volumes of motor vehicles all over the world has led to increased pollution and negative impact on climate. Therefore, road space rationing

DOI: 10.4018/979-8-3373-4571-0.ch005

Copyright © 2025, IGI Global Scientific Publishing. Copying or distributing in print or electronic forms without written permission of IGI Global Scientific Publishing is prohibited.

is one strategy to control traffic volume which allows even/odd number plates on alternate days. However, it requires Automated License Plate Recognition (ALPR) systems for real time monitoring. Machine intelligence based ALPR uses multiple technologies to offer robust performance under varying imaging conditions, such as high velocities, low light, harsh weather, camera vibration, and partially obscured images. Furthermore, the radical shift from conventional to deep learning (DL) methods also requires developing tools and data-sets which are capable of handling diverse character sets in multiple languages. This scoping review offers a comparative analysis of various approaches in ALPR systems where AI and deep learning algorithms are found to offer superb performance and high recognition rates of greater than 90% after compiling the contents of around 100 published articles during 1997-2023.

1 INTRODUCTION

The continued increase in world population has led to a significant rise in the number of vehicles on the road, which has necessitated the implementation of various automatic surveillance and detection systems. Historically, New York receives credit for being the first city to adopt a unique license plate number for each vehicle in 1901, as a means of vehicle tracking, and has since become a widespread practice. However, it wasn't until 1976 that the Police Scientific Development Branch developed the ALPR technology, as documented by (Singh, 2016). Analyzing the development and application of ALPR systems throughout history as it shown in Figure 1, reveals a gradual progression of technological advancements. In the 1970s, ALPR systems relied on basic image processing as the primary technology, finding initial use in experimental law enforcement applications. Notably, the Police Scientific Development Branch in the UK pioneered an ALPR system using rudimentary image processing techniques. In the 1980s, advancements in image processing and data storage facilitated ALPR evolution. The U.S. Customs Service deployed these system at the US-Canada border for monitoring vehicle movements linked to smuggling and criminal activities. This marked the inception of modern ALPR systems in law enforcement and vehicle identification (Jia, 2007). The history of ALPR can be seen in Figure 1 which shows a sharp development during 90s, when enhanced cameras and improved image processing algorithms enabled ALPR systems to read license plates from various angles and lighting conditions. Integration with databases further amplified ALPR adoption in law enforcement globally, enabling automated scanning and database comparisons for stolen vehicles and suspects. The 2000s witnessed integration with digital systems and enhanced image recognition (Rahman, 2021). ALPR expanded its reach to include toll collection and traffic management, enhancing surveillance and security systems. Accuracy, speed, and storage capabilities saw significant improvements. In the 2010s, GPS integration, data analytics, and cloud computing further elevated ALPR systems. Machine learning and deep learning techniques bolstered accuracy and processing speeds, enabling handling of large-scale data (Shashirangana, 2020). ALPR found diverse applications, from parking management to smart city initiatives. During 2020s, advanced image recognition and AI, coupled with privacy-focused solutions, defined ALPR's trajectory. Real-time capabilities, cloud-based processing, and edge computing sustained its broad usage in law enforcement, toll collection, and smart city projects. Stricter privacy regulations addressed concerns while efficiency, scalability, AI integration, and privacy protection became paramount considerations (Xin, 2022).

A bibliometric search based on four most popular databases Scopus, IEEEXplore and Google Scholar resulted in the network visualization of the interconnected terms when searched with a keyword 'Automated License Plate Recognition' for the period of 1997-2023. Initially 287 documents were found from the Scopus database, while 236 on IEEE Xplore and 175 Google Scholar. Thus, in total, 698 documents were found on these three major databases for automated license plate recognition systems. Figure 2 shows the flow diagram illustrating the Preferred Reporting Items for Systematic Reviews and Meta-Analyses (PRISMA) approach used for the identification, screening and selection of our scoping review. The inclusion and exclusion criteria is evident from the flow chart. Duplicate articles are removed in our search, along with the irrelevant studies as seen from the title and abstract screening. Moreover, research articles showing significantly lower accuracy are also excluded from the study. Finally, 96 articles are found relevant to our review study.

Figure 1. Evolution of ALPR systems and intelligent algorithms

The extracted articles contain all the bibliometric data, which is then used as input for the VOSviewer analysis where the number of times keywords and citation information appear in the selected articles. This data provides an efficient method for determining the impact of articles in the scientific databases by constructing a network visualization of the co-occurrences map as in Figure 3.

Following research questions were defined for the conducted research:

RQ1: What are the key methods examined in publications on the implementation of ALPR systems under stringent environmental conditions?
RQ2: How can various conventional and deep learning methods utilized in ALPR systems can be compared to get highest recognition rates?

Figure 2. Flow diagram illustrating the PRISMA approach for the identification, screening, and selection of records

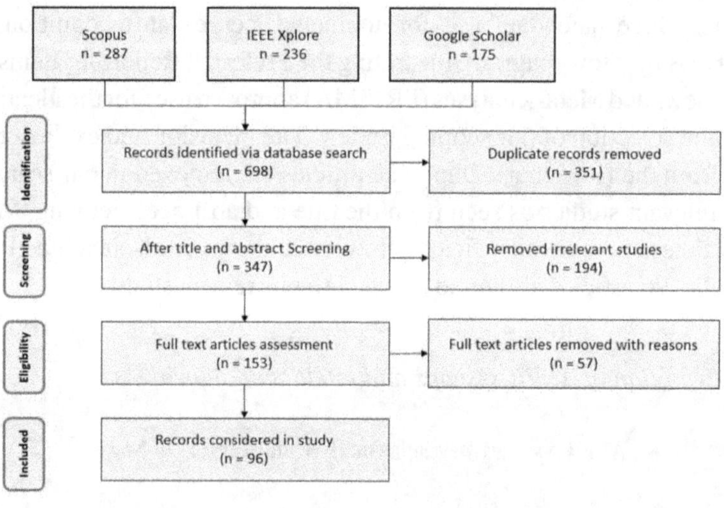

Based on these research questions, following are the main contributions of our paper:

- Explores the recognition of car license plates, with a particular focus on characters from different languages.
- Compare different recognition methods and examine the challenges of recognizing Chinese characters compared to other formats.
- Provides a detailed and comparative review of both traditional and modern methods, including deep learning techniques such as YOLOv-family recog-

nition and recent trends in deep learning methods such as sequential models (e.g., LSTM, transformers, BERT), generative and adversarial methods (e.g., GAN, CycleGAN), tracking methods like deep sort, variational methods (e.g., variational autoencoders), networks with skip functions (e.g., UNet, Efficient UNet), diffusion models, etc., used in current ALPR systems.

- Examines the challenges involved in detecting and extracting license plates, which can affect the accuracy and efficacy of recognition and identify research gaps.

Figure 3. Keywords co-occurrences network visualization

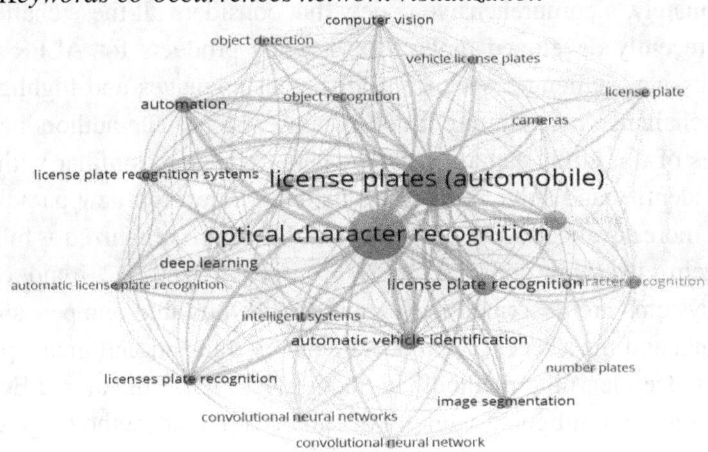

It is noteworthy that various research papers have referenced ALPR using different terms such as Automatic Vehicle Detection and Recognition (AVDR), Automatic License Plate Detection and Recognition (ALPDR), Vehicle License Plate Detection and Recognition (VLPDR) by Gupta et al. (Gupta, 2002), Vehicles License Plate Recognition System (VALPRS), and License Plate Detection Recognition (LPDR) (Sadique, 2019). However, ALPR is the most popular description for such systems. These systems have continued to expand their territory to new applications, which now include Ticket-less Parking, Tolling, Intelligent Transportation Systems (ITS), stolen vehicle detection, smart billing, road traffic control, and speed control among others (Yang, 2018). The investigation reveals that the ALPR system has become an essential aspect of our daily life, as emphasized by (Kumar, 2023).

Currently, the existing reviews have not investigated all major aspects of ALPR systems to help researchers understand the current state of the art, areas for improvement, limitations, and future research trends. By reviewing the development of ALPR technology, researchers can identify various research gaps and limitations, such as:

- Improving accuracy and robustness under varying atmospheric conditions (e.g., low-light, extreme weather).
- Enhancing real-time performance and scalability for high-volume traffic scenarios.
- Addressing privacy concerns and developing methods for secure data handling.
- Exploring applications beyond law enforcement, such as smart cities, transportation, and parking management.
- Investigating techniques to handle non-standard license plates, customized fonts, and international plate formats.

Unfortunately, a comprehensive review that considers all these challenges and compares recently developed tools, datasets, and products for ALPR platforms while discussing challenges specific to different languages and highlighting the remaining challenge and future outlook is non-existent. The authors believe that the findings of this study can assist researchers to become familiar with the state of the art, identify and solve remaining challenges, develop new paradigms, and implement more advanced ALPR systems. This Chapter is organized as follows: The ALPR system's overview and structure is discussed in Section 2. Major challenges in ALPR systems are described in Section 3, with possible compensation based on traditional and most recent approaches such as conventional image processing and modern deep learning methods. In Section 4, Legal, Ethical and Economical Consideration are highlighted while in Section 5, popular methods are compared from accuracy, complexity, generalize-ability, and flexibility perspectives, followed by concluding remarks in Section 6.

Figure 4. ALPR System Structure and components

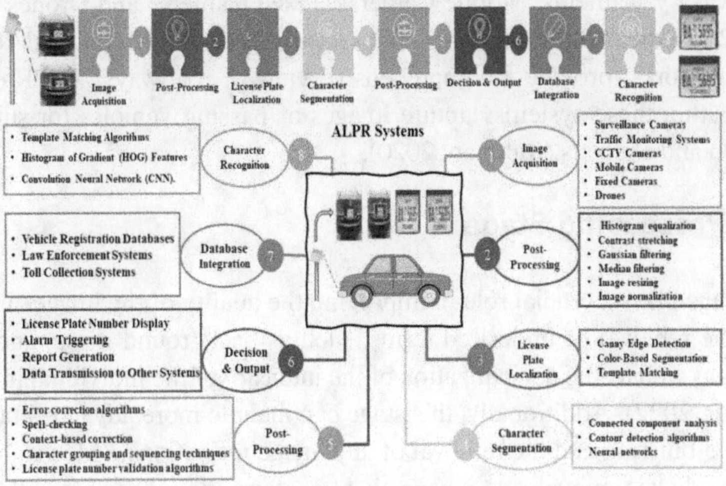

2 THE ALPR SYSTEM STRUCTURE

As depicted in Figure 4, the ALPR system incorporates efficient methods for precise license plate recognition. Initial image acquisition relies on surveillance, traffic monitoring, and CCTV cameras. Pre-processing employs strategies like histogram equalization, contrast stretching, filtering, resizing, and normalization to refine image quality. License plate localization hinges on edge detection, color-based segmentation, and template matching. Character segmentation employs connected component analysis, contour detection, and neural networks. Utilizing methods such as template matching, HOG features, and CNNs, character recognition is enacted.

Post-processing encompasses error correction, spell-checking, context-based refinement, character grouping, and sequencing. Integration with databases for vehicle registration, law enforcement, and toll collection systems proves vital. Ultimately, decision-making and output entail license plate display, alarm activation, report generation, and data transmission to interconnected systems.

2.1 Image Acquisition

Image acquisition methods are a critical component of ALPR systems, serving as the initial step in capturing license plate data (Awalgaonkar, 2021). Various techniques are employed to gather images for subsequent processing and analysis

(Balbin, 2017). These methods include Surveillance Cameras, Traffic Monitoring Systems, CCTV Cameras, Mobile Cameras, Fixed Cameras and Drones etc. (Laroca, 2022). Dedicated traffic monitoring systems, such as closed circuit television (CCTV) networks, provide a comprehensive view of roadways. ALPR-equipped cameras within these systems capture images of passing vehicles for subsequent recognition and analysis (Rahman, 2020).

2.2 Pre-Processing Stage

This stage plays a crucial role in improving the quality of the image. This stage involves the removal of undesired terms, such as background noise, and camera distortion, as well as the normalization of the intensity of the individual image particles (Kaur, 2022). Additionally, this stage can include more advanced tasks such as image de-blurring and the removal of any image reflections, video stabilization and camera shake removal, and perspective transformation if required all of which work together to enhance the image and make it more suitable for further analysis or use (Khan, 2022).

Pre-processing stage includes Image Enhancement, Noise Reduction, Image binarization, Plate Localization, Rotation and Skew Correction, Character Segmentation, Character Normalization, Character Enhancement, Noise Removal, Plate Type Recognition, Color Conversion, Filtering and Morphological Operations, Mathematical Morphology and Template Matching etc.

ALPR by Onesimu et al. (Onesimu, 2021) proposed a novel methodology for license plate recognition (LPR) based on mathematical morphology and template matching techniques, which were implemented using the MATLAB programming language. In addition, the authors incorporated character segmentation and recognition algorithms to enable rapid isolation of license plate characters. At the pre-processing stage, the Otsu algorithm was employed to perform binarization of the license plate image, thus laying a solid foundation for subsequent. The reported accuracy of this methodology was an impressive 79%. Subsequently, Lin et al. (Lin, 2020), the same authors employed mathematical morphology to verify license plate location, employing two different algorithms and com- paring their results to demonstrate the efficacy of their approach. It was concluded that image recognition based on edge detection and mathematical morphology surpassed traditional edge-based LPR approaches in terms of image localization.

2.3 Localization Stage

For any ALPR system, localization is the most important stage, as it enables the system to accurately detect and recognize license plates. Some of the popular localization techniques include Edge detection, Template matching, Feature extraction and Convolutional Neural Networks (CNNs) (Antar, 2022).

There are several methods and techniques employed for License Plate Localization in ALPR systems such as Color-Based Approaches (Abdulateef, 2022)(Tusher, 2023), Edge Detection, Template Matching, Deep Learning and Convolutional Neural Networks (CNNs), Sliding Window Approach, Connected Component Analysis, Characteristics of License Plate Shapes and some Hybrid Approaches. It's important to note that ALPR systems often face challenges like variations in lighting conditions, plate orientation, occlusions, and noise. Therefore, robust and adaptable localization methods are essential for the reliable operation of these systems. Advances in computer vision and deep learning continue to improve the accuracy and efficiency of license plate localization in ALPR systems (Oliveira, 2013). The choice of license plate localization method in an ALPR system depends on factors like accuracy requirements, computational resources, and specific use cases. Deep learning methods, particularly CNNs, offer high accuracy and adaptability and are widely used when computational power is available. Color-based and edge detection methods can be efficient in scenarios with distinct plate characteristics. Hybrid approaches, combining various methods, are often used to strike a balance between accuracy and computational efficiency, depending on the application's needs (Yu, 2022).

2.4 Character Segmentation

Character segmentation is the process of splitting an image into a sequence of image patches, each representing an individual symbol. This technique is commonly used in digital image processing to aid recognition, as dividing the image into smaller parts can make it easier to identify individual characters (Raj, 2022). Some of the commonly-used techniques for this task can be named as Haar thresholding, Edge detection, Connected component analysis, Morphological operations etc. which involves erosion and dilation to remove noise from the image and to merge or separate characters based on their shapes.

These techniques are used to precisely identify characters in an image, as an essential step in many applications, such as optical character recognition and handwriting recognition. Character segmentation is a crucial step in ALPR systems, which are designed to automatically extract and recognize license plate numbers from images or video streams. The primary goal of character segmentation is to isolate individual characters or digits from the license plate, making it easier for the recognition component to accurately identify each character (Hussein, 2022). Several methods are employed in ALPR systems for character segmentation, each with its own advantages and challenges. Some common character segmentation methods used in ALPR systems includes Connected Component Analysis (CCA), Edge-Based Segmentation, Template Matching, Machine Learning-Based Approaches which includes Deep learning techniques, such as Convolutional Neural Networks (CNNs), Stroke With Transform (SWT), Contour Analysis and some hybrid Approaches. Additionally, post-processing steps such as character recognition and error correction play a crucial role in achieving accurate results in ALPR systems (Fan, 2022).

2.5 Post-Processing

Post-processing methods are essential in ALPR systems to enhance the accuracy and reliability of license plate recognition. These methods encompass a range of techniques, from character validation and correction to contextual analysis and machine learning, all aimed at improving the overall performance of the system in various real-world scenarios (Lee, 2022). Some key steps in post-processing includes Character validation and correction, Pattern Matching, Contextual information to validate license plate results, Temporal Consistency, Fuzzy Logic and Confidence Scoring, Geometric and Spatial Analysis, Post-Filtering techniques to further refine the results, Machine learning and Deep learning, User feedback loop, Alert Generation for law enforcement or billing for toll collection.

2.6 Database Integration

Database integration methods in ALPR systems play a pivotal role in enhancing their functionality and efficiency (Maheswari, 2022). The choice of integration method depends on the specific requirements of the application, scalability needs, and data security considerations. By effectively integrating databases, ALPR systems can provide valuable real-time information and insights for various purposes, from law enforcement to traffic management and beyond (Huang, 2022). Some key options include Structured Query Language (SQL) Databases, Web Services/APIs, Local Caching, Data Warehousing, Real Time Data Streams, Data Encryption and Security, Geospatial Databases and other Cloud-Based Solutions.

2.7 Decision and Output

ALPR systems use a combination of decision methods, including license plate detection and recognition, confidence scoring, and post-processing, to generate structured output data. These systems play a crucial role in various applications, including traffic management, security, and law enforcement, by automating the identification and tracking of vehicles through their license plates as in (Kaur, 2022). For the license plate detection, computer vision algorithms, such as YOLO (You Only Look Once) or Faster R-CNN are most often used which analyze the input image or video stream and determine potential regions containing license plates based on specific criteria, like color, shape, and texture (Oliveira, 2009). After a license plate is detected successfully, the system typically outputs the coordinates or bounding box around the license plate in the image, making it easier to extract the plate for further processing (Mahmood, 2022).

Optical character recognition (OCR) techniques are employed after detection stage to recognize the characters and numbers on the plate. This involves analyzing the pixel values and patterns within the plate region to identify individual characters (Silvano, 2020). The recognized characters are output as a string of text. This output is crucial for applications like toll collection, parking management, or law enforcement where the license plate information is used for identification and tracking (Ammar, 2023). Decision Thresholds and Confidence Scores are used to determine the accuracy of license plate detection and recognition. For instance, a system may have a confidence threshold that a detected license plate region must meet to be considered as a valid detection. Depending on the confidence score, the system may decide to accept, reject, or review a detection. Low-confidence detection's may be flagged for human verification or further processing (Ding, 2023).

Post-processing to refine the results may involve error correction, filtering out false positives, or enhancing the recognition accuracy. The final output of the ALPR system is often in the form of structured data, such as a database entry or an alert to law enforcement. This data may include the recognized license plate, timestamp, vehicle type, and location (EKE, 2023).

ALPR systems can operate in real-time or batch processing modes whereas, in the former mode immediate results are available. Whereas in the later mode, a collection of images or videos are analyzed after post-processing for decision (Alzubaidi, 2019). The decision and output methods may differ between these modes. Real-time systems focus on fast, accurate results, while batch processing may prioritize comprehensive data collection and analysis (Mathew, 2023). Integration of ALPR systems with databases, access control systems, and surveillance systems is also possible to trigger actions like opening gates, sending alerts, or updating records (Mhatre, 2023).

2.8 Character Identification/Recognition

Optical character recognition (OCR), is a powerful technique that allows machines to analyze and identify printed or handwritten characters, ultimately transforming them into digital text. In their study, (Firasanti, 2021) utilized a combination of the canny edge detection technique and the Otsu threshold technique as an OCR method with Raspberry Pi to detect vehicle license plates. According to the authors, the Canny edge detection method exhibited higher accuracy than the Otsu thresholding method, detecting the edges of all data with a 100% rate, compared to the Otsu thresholding rate of 70%, based on a total of 30 license plate samples tested. Similarly, (Samantaray, 2021) employed an OCR method for vehicle license plate recognition, reporting a success ratio of 93.34% for license plate localization and an accuracy of 85.71% for character separation, based on 15 and 14 samples tested, respectively. However, the character recognition rate was found to be 91.67%, based on 12 samples tested, (Ramya, 2023) emphasized the application of image processing, computer vision, and Optical Character Recognition (OCR) to detect and identify car license plates on vehicles in India. They used a combination of image processing methods, including Hidden Markov models (HMM) and neural networks, to achieve efficient license plate recognition, facilitating the monitoring of traffic violations (Balbin, 2017). Figure 5 shows the character recognition by using the ALPR system software. First the image is captured through the CCTV camera. After that the fully conv. classification layer is applied for the license plate detection. Once that is done again another fully conv. classification layer is applied for the character recognition. And the results can be seen on the computer once those characters are recognized. In order to mitigate the challenge posed by the low complexity in identifying alphanumeric characters, Wu et al. (Wu, 2019) proposed a table-matching technique. In their empirical study, the researchers captured samples utilizing a camera with a resolution of 1920×1080 and implemented their method on a platform with an Intel i7-2600 2.8GHz and 2GB RAM. The findings revealed that their approach yielded a recognition accuracy of 94.8% for license plates.

Figure 5. Character recognition by using the ALPR System Software

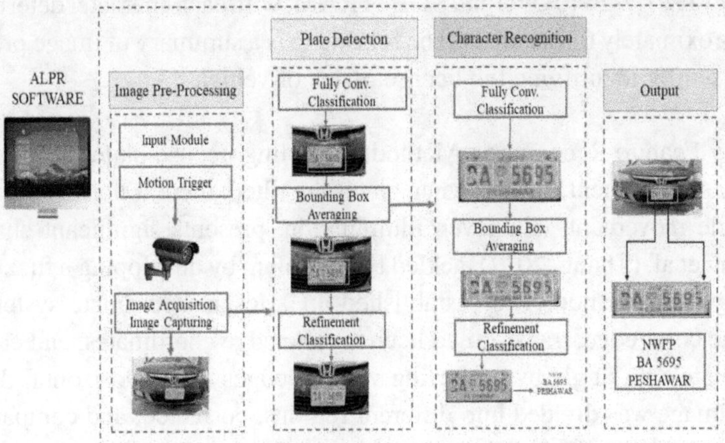

In a similar vein, Chowdhury et al. (Chowdhury, 2021) suggested an image processing mechanism for character identification, character segmentation, and License Plate extraction to detect illicit vehicle license plates. The authors evaluated their methodology by testing it on 50 images, 25 of which were captured during the day and the remaining 25 at night. The results indicated a recognition rate of 96% for daytime images and 92% for night-time ones. It was noted by (Meng, 2021) that numerous proposals have been offered by the research community to develop ALPR Systems for character recognition. Generally, these methods can be divided into two categories of i) Deep Learning-based ALPR Methods, and ii) Conventional ALPR Methods. Numerous articles have been devoted to elaborate these methods for character recognition, some of which are as follows.

2.8.1 Conventional ALPR Methods for Character Recognition

Conventional image processing methods can be used to enhance the visual appearance of an image, extract useful information from it, and convert it into a more accessible format that can be easily analyzed, comprehended, interpreted, and utilized in a wide range of applications (He, 2021). In (Rajebi, 2023), an innovative method is introduced for character extraction and pattern matching in ALPR systems. This approach combines morphological operations, edge detection, and bounding box techniques with its ability to operate without an extensive training dataset, relying solely on standard templates. This approach brings several key advantages, including rapid training, adaptability to diverse standards, high response speed, and improved accuracy compared to similar tasks. Using a dataset of 253 characters, with only 6 characters being recognized incorrectly, resulting in an impressive accuracy of 97.6% with a Core (TM) i7-2640 CPU and 8 GB of RAM, with each character determination taking approximately 0.8 seconds. The following is a summary of image processing methods used for identifying the license plates of vehicles.

- Fuzzy Feature Recognition Method: Detecting license plates accurately in a noisy environment, such as when plates are tilted, there is noise pollution, fast vehicle movement, or uneven illumination, presents significant challenges. Zhang et al. (Zhang, 2017) tackled this problem by developing a fuzzy feature recognition method. They established a Cartesian coordinate system based on the color edge, transformed license plate edge coordinates, and confirmed the plate's tilt angle by projecting vertical edges in the horizontal direction. The image was divided into different regions, corrected, and compared with the fuzzy membership degree for feature collection. The algorithm calculated the feature similarity of each region and verified the tilt of the license plate effectively. Results showed that the proposed algorithm increased accuracy in various conditions, including normal license plates (98.141%), noisy environments (98.211%), motion blur (97.119%), uneven illumination (98.311%), and edge blur (97.254%).
- Localization Method: In ALPR systems, there are two main tasks related to localization: license plate localization and character localization. It is necessary to identify and isolate the region within an image or video frame that contains the license plate by detecting the overall shape and boundaries of the license plate, regardless of the individual characters by using methods such as edge detection, color-based segmentation, template matching, and machine learning algorithms which aim to accurately locate and extract the license plate region from the background and surrounding elements. Character localization focuses on identifying and segmenting individual characters within the localized license plate region. After the license plate localization, character localization techniques are applied to precisely locate and separate each character present on the plate which is crucial for subsequent character recognition and decoding. Techniques such as connected component analysis, contour detection, and image processing algorithms are used to isolate and extract individual characters from the license plate. As a case-study, Mello et al. (Mello, 2009) developed ALPRS into three main parts: plate localization, character segmentation, and character recognition. They employed vertical edge detection, colour alternation in gray-scale images, and Sobel vertical filter to achieve an accuracy of 88.72% in locating the license plate region. Additionally, their character segmentation algorithm achieved an impressive accuracy of 94.21%.

- SO-BP Neural Network: Xiao and Dong in 2021 (Xiao, 2021) employed an auto-encoder to detect vehicle license plates. They conducted an experiment using 124 images, with 68 images dedicated to testing license plate positioning and 56 images dedicated to character recognition. The results indicated an accuracy rate of 82.35% for license plate positioning and 85.71% for character recognition. Additionally, the authors found that their proposed algorithm was effective in identifying clear and standard license plate images, despite the presence of noise pollution, insufficient light, faded background colour, and blurred images.
- Conventional Image Processing: In (Tang, 2018) employed grey-scale processing techniques, specifically Edge detection and the Robert Cross method to identify and detect the license plates of a vehicle. They utilized the STM32F103RBT single-chip microcomputer as the main control chip to oversee image collection via the camera, with the results being displayed on a screen. (Wilson, 2020) used a Gauss filter to smooth the grey-scale image in an attempt to improve license plate detection. They further utilized the canny algorithm to detect the border. The Ostu algorithm was used to distinguish between the brightness of the foreground and background, aiding in license plate detection. Mathematical morphology algorithms were utilized to locate the license plate, followed by image correction to facilitate character segmentation and recognition. However, the OSTU algorithm may result in recognition failures if the image is too dark, leading to the cutting of characters or license plate reflections, which can interfere with the accuracy of the three links. The authors improved these links and optimized the algorithm for license plate detection. Mathematical morphology and the canny operator were used for license plate location, and boundary restrictions were added to traditional scanning character algorithms to improve character segmentation accuracy. Finally, KNN was used for character recognition due to its high computational efficiency. All processes were implemented on the OpenCV platform.

In a separate study, (Mousa, 2009) introduced a canny edge detection approach that proved to be effective. Their research demonstrated that the Canny Edge- Detector could function as a multi-stage algorithm, detecting various edges within a noisy image. Additionally, the method exhibited the ability to accurately zoom in on the license plate's precise location and efficiently eliminate unwanted objects by using a cloud-based ALPRS process that incorporates Edge-based methods and a Convolutional Neural Network (CNN) to train a 9-layer license plate localization model. Their approach achieved a recognition accuracy of 98.64% and a detection accuracy of 95.34% for license plates (Polishetty, 2016).

As previously mentioned, the environment is a crucial factor to consider. Wang et al. (Wang, 2019) developed machine vision algorithms. These algorithms ex- tract edge contour detection of vehicle character images, and feature points of license plate characters, and interpret the internal texture structure of characters as a random field with an even distribution of grey histogram. The algorithm processes gray-scale feature detection and character matching and computes the distribution points of character machine visual features at different vehicle speeds using different feature functions. Pixel difference analysis and visual features are then utilized to detect these features. The accuracy results indicate that the algorithm can recognize the entire car with a recognition rate of over 97%, recognize the last five digits with a recognition rate of over 99%, and achieve a night license plate recognition accuracy rate of over 90%. (Ashtari, 2014) introduced a plate localization algorithm that utilizes colour features to convert license plate colour into grey-scale or binary images. The method employs an optimized template-matching algorithm for license plate localization and was tested under varying conditions, including four different lanes of speed with several vehicles. The reported results indicate an overall ac- curacy of 92.6% for the speed lane, 87.14% for the middle lane, 64.8% for the side lane, and 94% for the lane with multiple vehicles. Investigated the main challenge in License plate location, which is the interference caused by background and light.

- K-Means Clustering: In 2021, Chen et al. used ALPR using the K-means Clustering Algorithm alongside Deep Learning techniques for segmentation, detection, and recognition. The proposed methods resulted in an accuracy of 98.1% for character detection on license plates. Convolutional and pool layers were utilized to aid in character recognition and segmentation, with CNN specifically used for character recognition. These layers served as helpful tools for classifiers to successfully identify and detect license plate characters (Chen, 2021).
- Artificial Bee Colony – Support Vector Machine (ABC-SVM) Xueyang developed a supervised learning model called the ABC-SVM, which is based on the Vapnik-Chervonenkis principle of minimizing the empirical and structural risk (Xueyang, 2018). The system is controlled by an STM32 single-chip microcomputer and captures license plate images through the OV7725 camera. The captured image is then sent to a computer for processing and identification. An optimized SVM penalty coefficient and kernel parameters using the artificial bee colony algorithm are combined to build a license plate character recognition model. A significant number of character samples were trained using SVM, and an initial database consisting of penalty factor C and kernel function parameters are constructed by combining the template matching method with the neural network method. The model was continuously

updated until the optimal state was achieved, and the actual license plate was finally added for verification. The test results demonstrated that the system achieved an accuracy of 93.3%, surpassing that of the traditional B.P. Neural networks (85.0%) and SVM (88.1%) by 8.3% and 5.2%, respectively.

- KNN Based Family of Algorithms: KNN is a straightforward machine learning classifier that can predict classifications for new data based on its similarity to existing data. It stores the available data and classifies a new data point by finding the KNN in the training set and assigning the most common class label among them) Shichao et al. (Zhang, 2017). Recently, Escalante et al. (Escalante, 2020) integrates K-NN and DL architectures for license plate recognition tasks in Peru. Their initial results showed an accuracy of 86.84%, with the lowest accuracy at 81.58%. To further improve the accuracy, they combined KNN with Multi-class SVM and reported a significantly improved accuracy of 96.49%. In 2020, (Kan, 2020) presented a study on license plate recognition in noisy environments. To recognize license plates in noisy environments, they employed the SVM, B.P., and KNN methods. The authors conducted an experiment using 5890 license plate images as a character training test set, 756-character images as a character set, and 760 vehicle images to assess the license plate recognition performance of each algorithm. The results indicated that all three methods were effective, with a high level of accuracy. The highest training recognition and license plate recognition rate achieved were 97.5% and 92.1% respectively.

2.8.2 Deep Learning-based ALPR Methods for Character Recognition:

In the realm of computer vision, object detection and recognition are two related but different problems (Silvano, 2021). DL-based object detection is an alternative way of detecting license plates of the ALPR systems (Ribeiro, 2019) to extract the bounding box of license plates from the complex traffic image before reading the plate text (Alghyaline, 2022) (Padmasiri, 2022).

- Convolutional Neural Network (CNN): CNN is a highly effective artificial intelligence technique for image processing that utilizes deep learning technologies in license plate recognition. Due to its exceptional capabilities, many researchers have adopted this technology (Sathya, 2020). A typical architecture of CNN that includes convolutional layers, pooling layers, and dense layers is depicted in Figure 6. More advanced variants may include inception modules, channel-wise and spatial attention modules, drop-out layers, auxiliary output, skip connections, residual operation, wavelet pyramids, and other features.

Convolutional Neural Networks (CNNs) are a specialized type of Artificial Neural Network (ANN) widely used in machine learning for interpreting visual data. Their unique shared-weight design allows convolution kernels or filters to slide across the input data, generating translation-equivariant feature maps (Sarif, 2020). CNNs are also known as Shift Invariant or Space Invariant Artificial Neural Networks (SIANN). Figure 6 depicts the CNN layers for object classification.

Figure 6. CNN Construction Structure

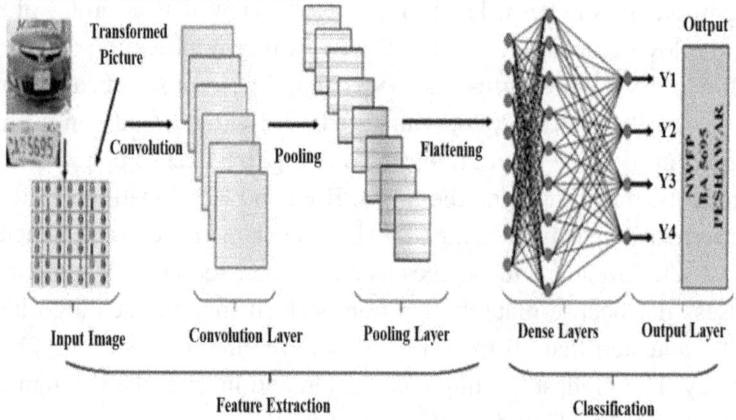

In 2019, Yao et al. (Yao, 2019) illustrated CNN layers for object classification in Figure 6. The feature extraction phase includes the image input, convolution layers, and pooling layers. The output result of the input image is obtained using a fully connected layer for classification. In a study conducted by Liu et al. (Huang, 2019), they compared template matching and neural network methods for license plate recognition. Their findings indicated that while Convolutional Neural Networks (CNN) have a higher recognition rate, they require a larger number of training samples and more time to be effective as compared to traditional methods. To locate the license plate area in the image, the researchers used the Adaptive Boosting (AdaBoost) classifier and the Huntsville Area Association of Realtors (HAAR) feature. The Sobel operator was then applied to perform edge detection and locate the license plate area. The researchers utilized the Support Vector Machine (SVM) algorithm to finalize the two suspected license plate areas. Character segmentation and other operations were then performed to separate the characters. Finally, a back-propagation neural network was trained to recognize the characters and provide the output. The study evaluated the performance of the methods on 500 image samples, and the results showed that the HAAR method achieved 95.2% accuracy, while SVM had a higher accuracy rate of 98.8%. These traditional image processing techniques achieved an accuracy rate of 92.6% for license plate recognition.

In 2020, Chang et al. utilized a CNN deep-learning technique to recognize vehicle and motorcycle license plates. They experimented using a total of 500 license plate images, which were trained through a deep neural network (Chang, 2022). Their results revealed a high accuracy of 94.9% for license plate recognition. Similarly, Sarif et al. proposed a method for Bangladeshi license plate recognition, which involved using several techniques such as CNN, R-CNN, OpenCV, and template matching (Sarif, 2020). Their approach involved training deep neural networks to classify the characters and numbers on each license plate. Through their experiment, they were able to achieve an accuracy of 97.5% for license plate recognition, using a data-set of 2000 images. In 2020, He et al. proposed the use of CNN deep learning techniques to recognize vehicle license plates in China (He, 2020). The authors conducted experiments on the Intel Xeon E5-2680v4 processor and Nvidia Tesla "K" 80x8 GPU, using a test set of 300 Chinese license plate images with varying degrees of skewing and distortion. The experimental results demonstrated an impressive accuracy of 94.3%. Hendryl et al. applied a deep learning technique, specifically Convolutional Neural Networks (CNN), to perform license plate recognition in China (Hendryli, 2020). Additionally, they leveraged an intelligent building security system to authenticate and manage vehicles' access to certain buildings. The algorithm they developed records historical access information for individuals who match the identity, while those who do not match or refuse entry are subject to further inspection, and their historical information is recorded in a database for future reference. The accuracy of the trained model for license plate recognition was found to be 98.44%. In 2022, (Tian, 2022) introduced an enhanced Convolutional Neural Network (CNN) approach to identify and classify license plates. The study evaluated the performance of three methods, namely CNN, Template Matching, and Structural Analysis, and found that CNN outperformed the other two methods in terms of accuracy. Specifically, CNN achieved a recognition accuracy of 97.4%, while Template Matching and Structural Analysis achieved 89.0% and 96.0%, respectively.

- Recurrent Neural Network (RNN): RNNs are a type of artificial neural network that are specifically designed to process sequential data. RNNs can be used for the detection and recognition of license plates by combining with the CNN, image pre-processing and OCR algorithms to enhance the overall performance of license plates (Huang, 2021). Sometimes RNNs may face challenges in capturing long-term dependencies or handling very long sequences. In such cases, advanced variants like LSTM are often employed.

- Long Short-Term Memory (LSTM): LSTM is a popular type of RNN that addresses the vanishing gradient problem and is capable of capturing long-term dependencies in sequential data. Researchers have used LSTM-based networks for license plate detection by treating the license plate as a sequence of characters or image patches (Singh, 2019).
- Mask R-CNN: Conducted a research study on Thai license plate detection and recognition using deep neural networks such as Mask R-convolution neural networks (MRCNN) and YOLO. The study successfully detected and recognized license plates with an accuracy of 89.08% in 12,401 photos, even when the license plate was blurred or distorted (Rattenawong, 2021). A recent study by Alkawsi et al. (Alkawsi, 2021) utilized the MaskRCNN technique to identify Tunisian vehicle license plates at a faster pace. Additionally, the study employed a CNN classifier to recognize Arabic characters and numbers in license plates. The results indicated a recognition accuracy of 97.9% for Tunisian license plates, based on 740 images. The accuracy rate for Arabic characters was an impressive 99.37%, while city labels had an accuracy rate of 92.26%. However, the method was time-consuming and would benefit from further refinement.
- LUCNN + SSVM: In (Ramasamy, 2023), an innovative ALPR method that prioritizes precise identification with minimal errors. Their proposed approach leverages a cutting-edge pre-trained location-dependent ultra-convolutional neural network (LUCNN) to extract salient features from input images. These extracted features are then fed into a hybrid system that combines single-shot fully convolutional detectors with a support vector machine (SSVM) classifier. This integrated approach effectively deciphers critical information such as the vehicle's city, model, and registration number based on the plate's location. The LUCNN + SSVM model stands out for its remarkable efficiency in identifying number plate regions, even when the vehicles are at varying distances. In their evaluation, the authors tested the model on a dataset comprising 800 samples, and achieved an accuracy of 98.75%.
- You Only Look Once (YOLO) Generation: In the 2021 study, (Li, 2021) proposed a YOLO method to improve the efficiency and accuracy of license plate recognition. To evaluate the model's performance, the authors conducted experiments using three distinct data-sets: open automatic license plate recognition (OALPR), which consisted of 104 images, application-oriented license plate (AOLP) with 611 test images, and a cars data-set with 102 sample images. The reported results indicate that the model achieved recognition accuracy of 96.30% for OALPR, 95.25% for AOLP, and 78.79% for the cars data-set. In another study on the detection of license plates from 17 different countries, the researchers employed a deep neural approach and divided

license plate recognition into three key stages: license plate detection, unified character recognition, and multinational license plate layout detection. Using YOLOv3 deep neural network, the experiment utilized more than 400 images for each plate format resulting in over 90% accuracy for each plate format (Henry, 2020). Another remarkable effort introduced a Long-Short Term Memory (LSTM) approach that encompasses three distinct modules: license plate feature extraction, character positioning, and character feature extraction. The study evaluated multiple deep learning techniques, such as cascade classifier, SSD300, YOLO9000, Faster-RCNN, TE2E, and YOLOv4, for license plate recognition, whose accuracy exceeded 70%, However, with YOLOv3, the highest accuracy rate is 93% (Zou, 2020).

Moreover, YOLOv4 neural network and character segmentation algorithms were used to analyze over 3000 closed-circuit television (CCTV) images of Thai vehicle license plates. Three distinct stages were employed, each utilizing different neural network technologies. The first stage focused on license plate detection, achieving an accuracy of 96.20% through the use of YOLOv4 algorithms. The second stage utilized OpenCV for character segmentation, resulting in a higher accuracy of 98.40%. Finally, the third stage implemented Tesseract technology to identify the license plate number, yielding an accuracy of 94.20%. However, when Tesseract technology was used for Thai character recognition, the accuracy was comparatively low, with a score of 75.46%. It is noteworthy that newer versions of YOLO are available but only YOLOv3 and YOLOv4 have been utilized for license plate detection in the literature (Thumthong, 2021). handled the limitations of conventional ALPR methods by introducing a novel end-to-end deep learning model. This model enhances YOLOv5 through the integration of an improved channel attention mechanism and the incorporation of location information for optimized feature extraction. Efficiency is boosted by parameter reduction and setting a single class in the YOLO layer. The recognition network, based on the GRU + CTC architecture, achieves license plate recognition without character segmentation, leading to significantly reduced training time and improved accuracy. Experiments were run using a dataset of 12,500 images on Intel Core i7-12700H @ 4.7GHz, and a GPU model, the NVIDIA GeForce RTX 3090 with 8GB of VRAM while CUDA 11.2 and PyTorch 1.7 software are used. The experimental results showed 98.98% recognition precision, far better than the traditional algorithms.

- One Stage C.N and FCOS: In their recent study, Huang et al. introduced a neural network approach, dubbed ALPRNet, for ALPR applications (Huang, 2021). The proposed network architecture consists of a one-stage convolutional network and two fully convolutional one-stage object detectors

(FCOS). To evaluate the effectiveness of their approach on diverse data sets, the researchers collected a total of 1376 images from Hong Kong-Zhuhai and Macao. Impressively, the experimental results revealed a high accuracy rate of 98.21% for both license plate detection and recognition tasks.

- U-Net: U-Net is a CNN that excels in propagating contextual information to higher resolution layers through its numerous feature channels in up-sampling. This enhances the output's clarity for object detection and recognition, as demonstrated by (Ronneberger, 2015). Recently, (Tom, 2022) proposed a modified U-Net that presented very high accuracy in license plate recognition. The technique was trained and tested on 600 images, achieving impressive accuracy rates of 99.5% for vehicle detection, 96% for letter detection, and 93.7% for character recognition. The images were processed using the Object Identification Technique (OIT), which has advanced capabilities in detecting automobile license plates. The U-Net structure consists of two 33 convolutions, followed by a Rectified Linear Unit (ReLU) and a 22 max pooling operation.
- Residual Network: In their study on license plate recognition, (Seo, 2022) utilized 2049 license plate images and implemented deep-learning feature extraction with multiple stages of ResNet layers. They conducted experiments under varying conditions, achieving more than 90% accuracy with different applications. Specifically, they used 681, 757, and 611 images, respectively, for Access Control (ACC), Law Enforcement (LE), and Road Patrol (RP). The average license plate recognition accuracy was 87.36% for all tested plates. All experiments were conducted on an Intel i-9 9900k CPU and NVIDIA QUADRO 8000 GPU, with the neural network trained using the Adam optimizer and an initial running rate of 0.001, decreased by exponential strategy.
- SATNS: In 2020, Zhang et al. proposed a deep learning approach for recognizing ALPR using the Shared Adversarial Training Network (SATN) which comprises of four neural network components, namely, Dual Attention Transformation (DAT), Feature Encoder, Discriminator, and Recognizer (Zhang, 2019). By optimizing these components, the authors were able to evaluate 5000 challenging images of license plates and achieved a commendable accuracy of 96.5%.

Figure 7. The ALPR Challenge

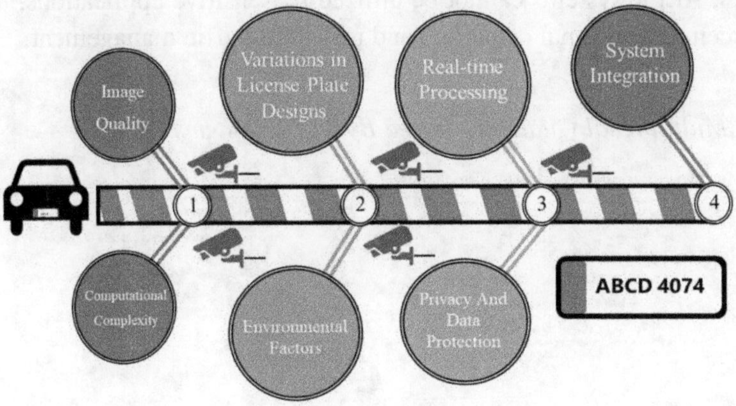

3 MAJOR CHALLENGES IN ALPR SYSTEMS

The present investigation entails the deployment of computer vision methodologies, which enable the ALPR systems to ascertain vehicles by capturing images of their license plates. The procedure includes the acquisition of video signals, converting them into digital image signals, and their subsequent processing through a processor to identify the characters inscribed on the license plates, which can be an intricate task due to the disparities in writing styles, fonts, and character sets in different languages. License plates can present a variety of challenges for ALPR systems. Some of the key challenges include handling varying image quality, license plate designs, processing in real time, dealing with the computational complexity of the algorithms, robustness against environmental factors, system integration and the data protection concerns.

Figure 8 represents the challenges that can commonly seen e.g. variations in font, size, color, format, plate geometry, and basic syntax can all negatively affect the accuracy of character detection. Additionally, similar shapes for characters, such as "O" and "0", can cause confusion in character recognition. These difficulties are important to consider as they can result in inaccuracy in identifying and recording details for a vehicle. As highlighted by (Karthikeyan, 2013) and (Mori, 1992), such challenges can lead to problems in preparing the initial input for the system, affecting the overall performance of the ALPR system. It is there therefore essential for an ALPR system to account for these challenges and utilize advanced techniques such as character segmentation and optical character recognition to improve the accuracy and efficacy of identifying and recording license plate details. Before addressing these challenges, ALPR systems cannot be utilized by sensitive applications, including law enforcement, criminal detection, and real-time traffic management.

Figure 8. Multilingual Quandary Faced By ALPR Systems

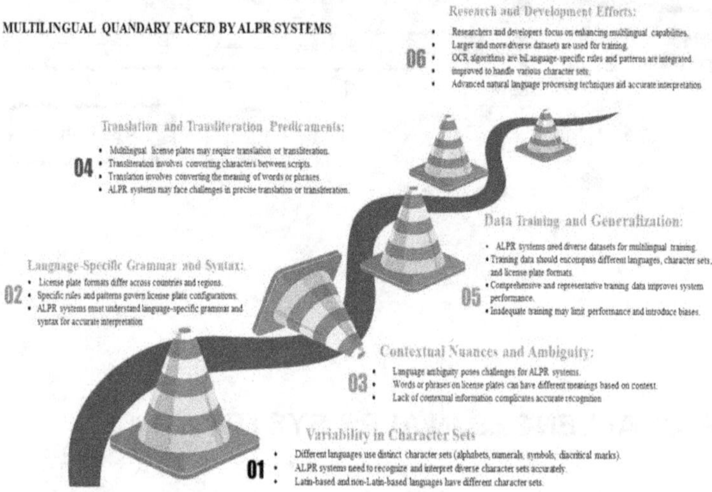

Figure 8 presents the different challenges that ALPR systems face due to difference in the languages. Accurate recognition and interpretation of license plate details are essential for ALPR systems to function properly. However, certain situations can pose challenges to the system, leading to incomplete or inaccurate information being recorded for a vehicle. Such as due to distorted or obscured license plates, as well as obstructions that partially or completely cover the plate. By identifying and addressing these challenges, ALPR systems can improve their accuracy and efficiency, ensuring that they can reliably capture and process license plate information under a range of conditions. Some of the common deficiencies can be listed as follows:

3.1 Image Quality

One common issue is poor image quality, which can occur when a vehicle's license plate is located fairly distant from the camera resulting in low resolution and image quality. To improve the image quality, several methods can be employed. Firstly, ensuring adequate lighting conditions by using additional sources and adjusting camera positions can improve the quality of the captured images (Li, 2022). Secondly, using high-quality cameras with advanced image processing capabilities can increase the resolution and details captured (David, 1985). Thirdly, image enhancement software can reduce noise, enhance contrast, and sharpen images, making the license plate characters more legible. Lastly, training the ALPR system using a variety of images captured under different lighting and angle conditions, or using distorted and skewed images by data augmentation methods can make the system robust resulting in improved performance of ALPR systems (Jha, 2018).

3.2 Blurred Images

This defect is known to be one of the most common issues in ALPR systems, especially when the target and nearby vehicles move at high speed or when the camera is positioned at a far distance. Environmental changes such as wind or camera shake can also contribute to image blurs. Blurring can cause difficulties in reading the license plate characters, thereby reducing the accuracy of the ALPR system. To mitigate this issue, it is recommended to use cameras with faster shutter speeds and to position them closer to the license plates when possible to reduce motion blur. Additionally, image stabilization techniques and post-processing tools can be employed to enhance image quality and reduce blur (Guo, 2020).

3.3 Poor Lighting and Low Contrast Images

Specialized cameras equipped with high dynamic range (HDR) and infrared imaging capabilities are very effective for capturing images under different lighting conditions. Also, image enhancement algorithms such as histogram equalization, contrast stretching, or adaptive gamma correction are also used to enhance the contrast and brightness of the license plate images. Moreover, machine learning algorithms are able to recognize and compensate for poor lighting conditions, enabling better detection and recognition of license plates (Aamir, 2018).

3.4 Object Obscure

This issue occurs when an item is intentionally or accidentally affixed to a license plate, causing difficulties in capturing a clear image of the license plate. One approach to solve this problem is to incorporate advanced image processing techniques that can identify and remove obstructions from the captured images such as edge detection, background subtraction, and morphological operations. Additionally, utilizing multiple cameras or capturing images from different angles can help mitigate the effects of object obscuration. Moreover, it is possible to adopt alternative license plate recognition technologies that rely on non-visual cues such as RFID or GPS. Recently, supervised DL-based image in painting methods have shown success in constructing images with missing regions that can be used for completing license plates with partially covered digits. By combining these strategies, improvement in the accuracy and reliability of license plate recognition systems is guaranteed (Liu, 2022).

3.5 Heterogeneous designs of License Plates

Different countries use distinct writing styles, fonts, and colors for their license plates, resulting in differences in the license plate characters at the front and back of the vehicles due to which detection is challenging (Chen, 2019). Thus, it is required that the algorithm must accurately recognize and extract license plate information from different designs and formats. Additionally, using advanced image processing techniques, such as image normalization and colour correction, can help to standardize license plate images, making it easier for the detection algorithm to accurately identify and extract the license plate characters. Another solution could be to standardize license plate designs and formats across different cities, making it easier to develop a single license plate detection algorithm that can be applied universally (Wang, 2022).

Figure 9. Problems occurring in different License Plates for different languages

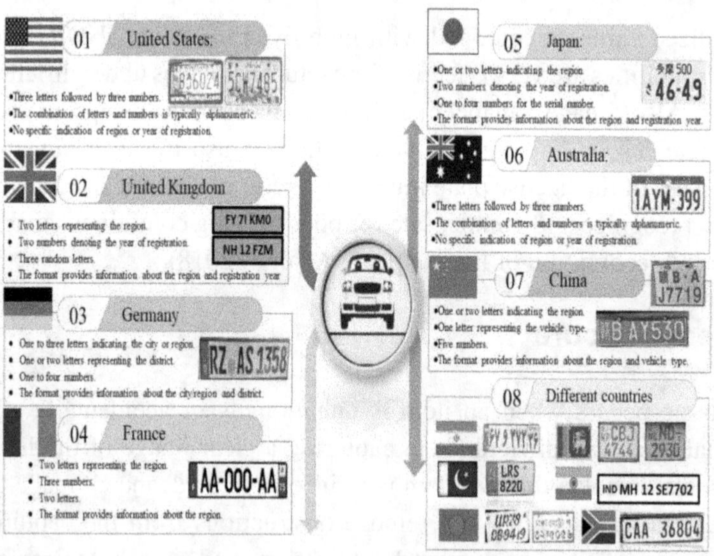

As illustrated in Figure 9, ALPR systems encounter notable challenges when confronted with license plates from diverse languages and nations. The intricacies of plate designs, fonts, and characters can impede precise recognition, while the inclusion of distinctive characters, symbols, or letter combinations within varying languages necessitates tailored training or pre-processing measures. Furthermore, disparities in plate dimensions, reflections, shadows, and image deficiencies may exacerbate ALPR failure for which innovative solutions are under development.

3.6 Changes in Angular View

Variation in the camera's angular view due to lane changes can pose a challenge as it becomes difficult to capture high-quality images of the 28 vehicle, resulting in poor image recognition performance. One possible solution to address this issue is to use multiple cameras at different angles to capture images of the vehicle's license plate which can help ensure that at least one camera captures a clear image of the plate, even if the vehicle changes lanes or angles. Another option is to use advanced image processing techniques, such as image stabilization or motion compensation, to correct the variations in the camera's angle and minimize image distortion. Additionally, employing deep learning algorithms that are trained on a diverse set of license plate images from various angles and lighting conditions can also improve the system's robustness to changes in the camera's angular view (Khan, 2019).

3.7 Different Fonts and Writing Styles

The usage of different fonts and writing styles on license plates can pose various challenges in recognizing them. Nonetheless, several countries have opted to discontinue the use of dissimilar fonts, mitigating the issues that arise due to such non-uniformity (Palekar, 2017). One approach to this problem is to standardize the license plate font and format all over the country, making it easier for automated recognition systems to identify and interpret the information. It is possible to utilize advanced image processing and pattern recognition techniques, such as deep learning-based algorithms, to recognize and extract the relevant characters from license plate images, irrespective of the font style (Jagtap, 2018). Additionally, incorporating high-resolution cameras and advanced lighting techniques can improve image quality and facilitate more accurate recognition. Regular maintenance and cleaning of license plates can also help prevent issues caused by dirt or damage (Page, 2007).

3.8 Licence number writing protocol

When a vehicle from a different state or country has the same license plate number but uses a different font and script, it can lead to issues with recognition. This problem has been observed on multiple occasions and can result in the details of an unrelated individual being mistakenly recorded. Therefore, it is crucial to establish a standardized license number writing protocol to avoid such errors (Aung, 2019).

Figure 10. License plate image defects

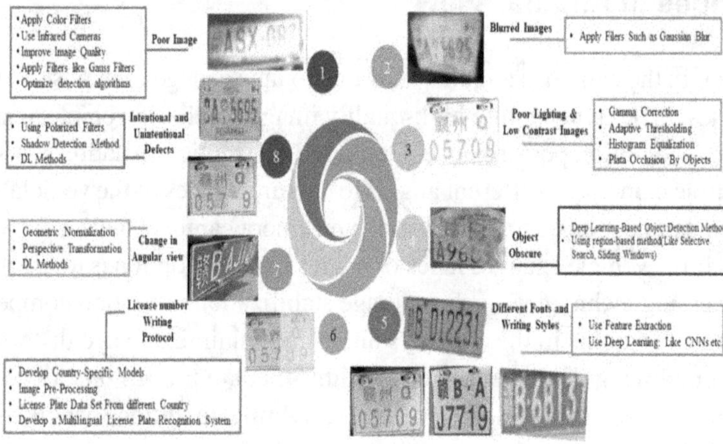

3.9 Complexity of defects in license plates

Various intentional and unintentional defects can affect license plates, such as using a plate cover or spray, or even using registration plates from a different vehicle with a similar model. In some cases, individuals may use tilted plates to avoid being detected or punished. While such issues pose challenges for license plate recognition, they can be addressed through improved software or training models (Gritsenko, 2022). Figure 10 shows various license plate protocols in different countries and the issues that can occur during the detection or recognition of a license plate. Additionally, the use of advanced recognition technologies such as optical character recognition (OCR) can improve accuracy and reduce errors. Regular maintenance and calibration of recognition systems should also be conducted to ensure optimal performance. Finally, in cases where multiple vehicles share the same license plate number, additional identifying information such as the state or country of registration should be cross referenced to prevent mis-identification. To accurately recognize different license plate designs, detail methods are described by Badr et al. (Badr, 2011).

As shown in Figure 10, in situations with low contrast or insufficient light, a variety of techniques, including adaptive thresholding, histogram equalization, and gamma correction, can be effectively used. Secondly, plate occlusion due to extraneous objects can be effectively addressed by applying region-based methods such as selective search and sliding windows. Furthermore, deep learning-based object detection methods can be adroitly utilized to accurately discern and separate plates from other objects. Thirdly, plate distortion or irregular shapes can be corrected by adopting several techniques such as perspective transformation, geometric normalization, or DL-based methods that can effectively discern and rectify distortions. Fourthly, plate orientation can be precisely determined by employing feature-based techniques that identify edge or line features to determine plate orientation or deep learning-based models that are trained to detect orientation. Lastly, reflection or glare on plates can be eliminated through the use of polarized filters or shadow detection methods. Deep learning-based methods can also be utilized to overcome these distortions. Multiple algorithms can be potentially applied to vehicle plate detection, including traditional computer vision methods such as morphological operations, edge detection, and template matching. In addition, deep learning-based methods such as convolutional neural networks (CNNs), region-based CNNs (RCNNs), and You Only Look Once (YOLO) models can be profitably utilized. Hybrid approaches that ingeniously integrate traditional methods with deep learning-based models can also be deftly employed to tackle the intricate challenges of vehicle plate detection. In order to surmount these challenges, it is essential to perform pre-processing procedures, such as normalization and skew correction. These measures can help capture a clear and legible image of the license plate. A graphical representation of a typical ALPR system is provided, by Saeed et al. (Rastegar, 2009). Table 1 offers a concise overview of pre-processing strategies implemented in ALPR detection. The six methods encompass Image Acquisition, Image Enhancement, Plate Localization, Character Segmentation, Character Recognition, and Post-processing. Each method's role within the ALPR process is succinctly outlined, detailing their significance. These pre-processing techniques collectively play a pivotal role in capturing, refining, localizing, segmenting, recognizing, and refining license plate images, culminating in elevated accuracy and dependability of ALPR systems.

Table 1. Applications of ALPR System

No.	Part	Description	Used Algorithm
1	Image Acquisition	This module captures images or video footage of vehicles and their license plates using cameras or surveillance systems.	• Surveillance & CCTV cameras • Traffic Monitoring, Drones • Mobile and Fixed Cameras
2	Pre-Processing	In this the captured images for further analysis. It includes operations such as image enhancement, noise reduction, and normalization to improve the quality and consistency of the images.	• Histogram equalization • Contrast stretching • Gaussian, Median filtering • Image normalization
3	License Plate Localization	In this module, techniques such as edge detection, color-based segmentation, or template matching are employed to locate the regions of interest (license plates) within the pre-processed images.	• Canny edge detection • Color-based segmentation • Template matching
4	Character Segmentation	Once the license plate region is identified, this module segments individual characters or symbols from the license plate.	• Connected component analysis • Contour detection algorithms • Neural networks
5	Post-Processing	The post-processing module performs tasks such as error correction, character grouping, and license plate number validation to refine and validate the recognized license plate information.	• Error correction algorithms • Spell-checking • Character grouping
6	Database Integration	The recognized license plate information, along with relevant metadata may be integrated with databases for further processing, storage, or retrieval.	• Integration of vehicle registration • Integration of law enforcement
7	Decision & Output	The final module makes decisions based on the recognized license plate information and generates appropriate outputs.	• License plate number display • Alarm triggering, Report generation • Data transmission
8	Character Recognition	The character recognition module applies optical character recognition (OCR) techniques to interpret and recognize the segmented characters.	• Template matching algorithms • DL and Conventional methods

4 LEGAL, ETHICAL AND ECONOMICAL CONSIDERATION

The ALPR systems used for traffic segregation and monitoring have raised significant bias in the datasets and privacy concerns leading to ethical and legal issues. They are further elaborated as follows:

4.1 Bias in ALPR Datasets

Probably, the data sets are not balanced, which means that they may under-represent or over-represent certain areas (urban or rural) leading to a compromised performance in real applications. Moreover, a specific vehicle type may also dominate the data sets, creating vehicle-type bias (Karale, 2021). Demographic bias due to a certain plate design or language is also common in data sets, which is a limitation. Thus, machine learning algorithms are affected due to these biases that cause high error rates for minority groups (Tang, 2022).

4.2 Privacy Concerns

ALPR enables the tracking of cars and vehicles, privacy issues occur due to the collection of data from individuals without consent. In addition, it is not clear for how long these data sets will remain on the ALPR system server, increasing the risk of misusing it. Last but not least, there is a lack of transparency as the driver does not know how the ALPR data is processed in the system or shared with other departments and law enforcement agencies (Gao, 2019).

In brief, serious privacy issues are involved in ALPR data acquisition and processing which require adequate safety and policy changes regarding data usage and confidentiality.

4.3 Economic Implications

The system setup consisting of cameras, servers, and AI software requires high investment costs for the ALPRS system. In addition, there are further maintenance costs for data storage, repairs, and software updates.

On the other hand, there are huge gains from the stolen vehicle recovery as well as toll collection and fines if anyone violates their turn for road space usage. Although, some jobs are lost due to the automation of the system, new jobs are created for technical assistance and AI maintenance/data analysis. Due to the road space rationing, environmental pollution is reduced with huge fuel savings and optimized traffic flow having a long-term impact on the health of the citizens (Gao, 2019). Therefore, the cost-benefit analysis of the ALPR system provides more advantages than trade-offs offering a positive return on investments (ROI).

5 DISCUSSION

License plate recognition is important for vehicle monitoring and regulation, especially for national security and military purposes. Plate detection has made this process simpler. However, detecting license plates can be a daunting and time-consuming task due to factors such as environmental pollution, blurry images captured by CCTVs, rainfall, poor lighting, and more. Table presents a comparative analysis of various technologies employed in license plate recognition along with their recognition accuracy to assist in accident prevention and investigation. ALPR effectiveness also depends on factors such as system accuracy, coverage, and integration with other traffic management measures. However, in general, ALPR systems can show a correlation with accidents in various ways.

Table 2. ALPR methods, including CNN, have been studied from 2009 to 2023, with reported performance and Advantages and Disadvantages: Convolutional Neural Network, HSB: Hue- Saturation-Brightness, PSO-BP NN: Particle Swarm Optimization-Back Propagation Neural Network, ABC-SVM: Artificial Bee Colony-Support Vector Machine, SATN: Shared Adversarial Training Network, HAAR: HAAR wavelet, R-CNN: Region-based Convolutional Neural Network, KNN-CNN: K-Nearest Neighbors, and CNN (Convolutional Neural Network), YOLO: You Only Look Once, OCR: Optical Character Recognition, B.P: Back Propagation, ANN: Artificial Neural Network, One-stage C.N: one-stage convolutional network, FCOS: Fully Convolutional One-Stage Objects, MRCNN: Mask R-Convolution Neural Network, BiLSTM: Bidirectional Long Short-Term Memory.

Algorithm	Description	Ref
Character Recognition		
•Mathematical morphology •Template matching	•Plate format: Chinese vehicles. •Advantage: Fast and easy method with high accuracy. •Disadvantage: Accuracy drops with a large amount of data for license plate recognition. •Accuracy: 79% accuracy of recognition for license plates.	(Awalgaonkar, 2021)
	•Plate format: Bangladesh vehicles. •Advantage: detect unauthorized vehicle license plates. •Sample Number: A total of 50 images (25 were taken during the day, and 25 were taken at night). •Accuracy: Daytime = 96%, Night time = 92%.	(Khan, 2022)
Image Processing		
•Greyscale processing	•Plate format: Chinese vehicles. •Advantage: STM32F103RBT single-chip microcomputer was used as the main control chip to control the camera to collect images and display the results on the display screen.	(Lin, 2020)

continued on following page

Table 2. Continued

Algorithm	Description	Ref
•Vertical edge detection •Sobel vertical filter	•Plate format: Brazil Vehicles. •Advantage: High accuracy of recognition. •Sample Number: 195 images were used for the localization algorithm and 1365 characters for the segmentation algorithm. •Disadvantage: Sometimes gives incorrect data when a large amount of data is tested. •Accuracy: 88.72% for localization (edge detection) and 94.21% for segmentation	(Huang, 2022)
•Canny edge detection	•Plate format: Palestine Vehicles. •Advantage: Canny edge detection detects edges, useful for identifying objects and removing unwanted elements in images. •Disadvantage: Gives incorrect results with complex data for detection of license plates.	(Abdulateef, 2022)
•Edge detection	•Plate format: Character & Non-Character Images were trained for ALPR in Texas, U.S. •Advantage: High accuracy. •Disadvantage: Cannot identify blur images. •Accuracy: 98% for recognition.	(Yu, 2022)
	•Plate format: Chinese Vehicles. •Advantage: High Accuracy. •Disadvantage: Cannot handle large amount of data.	(Maheswari, 2022)
	•Plate format: Chinese vehicles. •Advantage: Edge detection and mathematical morphology improve image localization better than traditional edge-based license plate location algorithms. •Accuracy: exact number not reported.	(Laroca, 2022)
•Edge contour detection	•Plate format: Chinese vehicles. •Advantage: High accuracy of detection both at night and daytime. •Accuracy: for whole car > 97%, last five digits > 99%, night time recognition accuracy rate > 90%.	(Raj, 2022)
•B.P.	•Plate format: China vehicles. •Advantage: the algorithm could identify clear and standard license plate images and noise pollution, insufficient light, faded background colour and blurred images. •Sample Number: 124 number images (68 images were tested for license plate positioning, and 56 were tested for character recognition). •Accuracy: 82.35% for license plate positioning.	(Onesimu, 2021)
Image Segmentation		
•HSB colour space segmentation	•Plate format: Chinese vehicles. •Advantage: This algorithm synthesizes the advantages of three data models and considers the influence of various environmental factors. •Disadvantage: Hard to understand, Complex. •Accuracy: exact number not reported.	(Ammar, 2023)
•Feature Recognition	•Plate format: Chinese vehicles. •Advantage: High Accuracy, Easy to use. •Implementation: Tested license plate detection with Intel i7-2600 and 2GB RAM. •Accuracy: 94.80%	(Kaur, 2022)

continued on following page

Table 2. Continued

Algorithm	Description	Ref
•SATNS	•Plate format: Chinese vehicles. •Advantage: SATN (Shared Adversarial Training Network) is the deep learning technique for ALPR. •Sample Number: A total of 5000 images were tested and trained for the SATN method. •Accuracy: 96.5% for recognizing license plates.	(Kaur, 2022)
•Modified UNet	•Plate format: India vehicles. •Advantage: High accuracy for detection of vehicles. •Sample Number: 600 images were trained and tested. •Accuracy: 99.5% for Vehicle detection, 96% for Letter Detection and 93.7% for Character Recognition.	(Fan, 2022)
Object Detection and Recognition		
•OCR	•Plate format: India vehicles. •Advantage: Good accuracy of recognition and detection. •Sample Number: 15 samples for license plate localization, 14 as separate characters, and 12 for character recognition. •Accuracy: 93.34% for license plate localization, 85.71% for separate characters and 91.67% for character recognition.	(Badr, 2011)
	•Plate format: Indonesia vehicles. •Advantage: Efficient, easy to use. Good accuracy of detection. •Sample Number: 30 license plate samples tested. •Accuracy: It detects the edges of all data at a 100% rate compared to the Otsu thresholding rate of 70%.	(Rastegar, 2009)
•YOLOv3	•Plate format: multiple countries' plates. •Advantage: Good and fast accuracy of recognition. •Sample Number: Fourteen license plates from 17 countries for each Plate format, 400 images. •Accuracy: > 90% for each plate format.	(Mathew, 2023)
•YOLOv4	•Plate format: Thai vehicles CCTV images. •Advantage: high and fast recognition speed. •Sample Number: over 3000 images. •Accuracy: 96.20% for plate detection.	(Firasanti, 2021)
•YOLO	•Plate format: Thai vehicles. •Advantage: Fast and accurate. •Disadvantage: requires much training time. •Sample Number: 12,401 images. •Accuracy: For MRCNN 88.80%, for YOLO 87.86%	(Ding, 2023)
•Bi LSTM	•Plate format: Chinese vehicles. •Advantage: Good accuracy of recognition. •Accuracy: 96.5% for Bi LSTM.	(Mhatre, 2023)
•YOLO	•Plate format: Taiwan vehicles. •Advantage: higher and more successful average accuracy. Increase the speed and confidence level of recognition for license plates. •Sample Number: 104 images for Open ALPR, AOLP, and Cars Dataset. 611 images For the Cars Dataset and 102 images for AOLP. •Accuracy: 96.30% for Open ALPR, 95.25% for AOLP and 78.79% for Cars Dataset 78.79%.	(EKE, 2023)
•One-stage C.N. •FCOS detectors	•Plate format: China vehicles. •Disadvantage: License plate format limitation proposed for Hong kong-Zhuhai-Macao. •Sample Number: A total of 1376 images from the Hong kong-Zhuhai-Macao car plate. •Accuracy: 98.21%.	(Samantaray, 2021)
Unsupervised Learning		

continued on following page

Table 2. Continued

Algorithm	Description	Ref
•K-means Clustering	•Plate format: Taiwan vehicles. •Advantage: Layers aid character recognition in classifiers. •Disadvantage: Training is time consuming and data-intensive. •Accuracy: 98.1%.	(Chowdhury, 2021)
•PSO	•Plate format: Chinese vehicles. Highlights: recognition of noise •Advantage: Good accuracy of recognition. •Sample Number: 5890 images as a character training test set, 756 as a character set, and 760 images were used to detect the license plate. •Accuracy: 97.5%, and the highest license plate recognition rate was 92.1%.	(Al-Hasan, 2024)
•Attention Method	•Plate format: Korea vehicles. •Advantage: Good accuracy of recognition. •Sample Number: 2049 images were used, with 757 from L.E. method and 611 from R.P. method. •Accuracy: License plate recognition methods had high accuracy, with Attention achieving the best at 98.56%. However, its accuracy dropped to 87.36% on non-CCPD datasets.	(Lee, 2022)
Supervised Learning		
•ABC-SVM	•Plate format: Chinese vehicles. •Advantage: Many character samples are sent into SVM for training, and a license plate character recognition model is built. •Accuracy: 93.3%.	(Meng, 2019)
•SVM	•Plate format: Iranian Vehicles. •Advantage: use the Color features. •Disadvantage: Give less accuracy for far objects or side lanes for vehicle detection. •Accuracy: 96.8%.	(Mahmood, 2022)
•SVM •HAAR	•Plate format: Chinese vehicles. •Advantage: higher recognition rate. •Disadvantage: needs many samples for training and a longer effective time. •Sample Number: 500 number image samples. •Accuracy: 95.2% (HAAR), 98.8% (SVM).	(Zhang, 2017)
•CNN	•Plate format: Indonesia vehicles. •Advantage: Good and fast accuracy for recognition. •Disadvantage: A huge amount of data is needed. •Sample Number: 500 number image samples. •Accuracy: 94.9%.	(Mello, 2009)
•CNN	•Plate format: China vehicles. •Advantage: High accuracy of recognition. •Sample Number: 300 number images. •Accuracy: 94.3%. •Implementation: Experiments were conducted on the Intel Xeon E5-2680v4 processor and Nvidia Tesla K80*8 GPU.	(Wilson, 2020)
•CNN •RCNN	•Plate format: Bangladesh vehicles. •Advantage: Good accuracy of recognition. •Sample Number: 2000 number images. •Accuracy: 97.5% for license plate recognition.	(Xiao, 2021)
•CNN	•Plate format: China vehicles. •Advantage: Can identify authentication conditions of building vehicle access management. •Disadvantage: Sometimes gives incorrect results with wrong data input. •Sample Number: Exact numbers not mentioned •Accuracy: 98.44% for the recognition of license plates.	(Wilson, 2018)

continued on following page

Table 2. Continued

Algorithm	Description	Ref
•CNN	•Plate format: Chinese vehicles. •Advantage: High accuracy of recognition. •Disadvantage: Time-consuming and requires large image data. •Accuracy: CNN accuracy of 97.4%; Template matching accuracy was 89.0%; structural analysis was 96.0% for license plate recognition.	(Polishetty, 2016)
•KNN	•Plate format: Peruvian vehicles. •Advantage: proposing the new algorithm K-NN. •Accuracy: 86.84% accuracy whole, the lowest accuracy was 81.58% by using only the KNN method, but the accuracy reached 96.49% after using the combination of K-NN and SVM	(Ashtari, 2014)
•Mask RCNN	•Plate format: Tunisia vehicles. •Disadvantage: time-consuming. •Sample Number: 740 number images. •Accuracy: 97.99% for the recognition of license plates.	(Mousa, 2009)

Figure 11. Methods and their percentage accuracy: A) Supervised Learning Algorithms

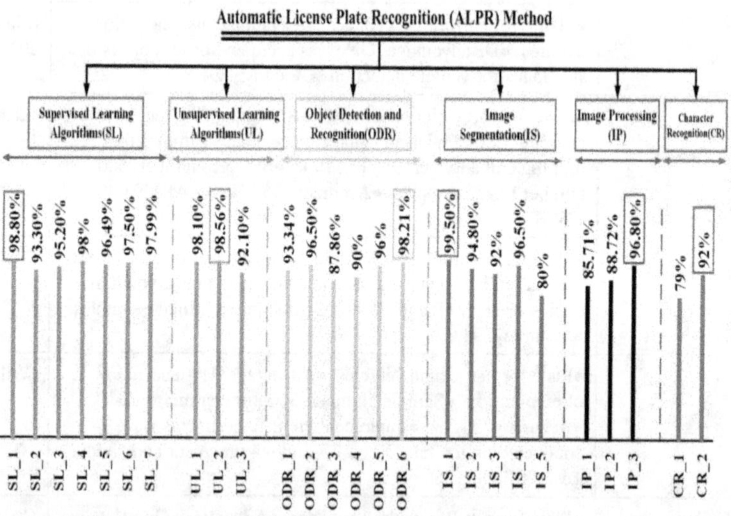

SL 1: SVM, SL 2: ABC-SVM, SL 3: HAAR, SL 4: CNN, SL 5: KNN-SVM, SL 6: R-CNN, SL 7: Mask R-CNN. B) Unsupervised Learning Algorithms: UL 1: K Means Clustering, UL 2: Attention Method, UL 3: PSO. C) Object Detection and Recognition (ODR): ODR 1: OCR, ODR 2: Bi-LSTM, ODR 3: YOLO, ODR 4: YOLOv3, ODR 5: YOLOv4, ODR 6: One-Stage C.N. FCOS. D) Image Segmentation (IS): IS 1: U-Net, IS 2: Features Detection, IS 3: Character Localization, IS 4: SATNs, IS 5: HSB Method. E) Image Processing (IP): IP 1: B.P, IP 2: Grey Scale Processing, IP 3: Canny Edge Detection. F) Character Recognition (CR): CR 1: Mathematical Morphology, CR 2: Character Identification

The effectiveness of ALPR systems in reducing accidents may vary depending on the specific circumstances and the extent of their deployment in a particular region or country. The specific correlation rate value between the use of ALPR technology and accidents in specific countries like the USA or China is not readily available as it can vary based on crucial information such as the number of sample pictures, camera specifications, accuracy rates, and image quality. Despite these challenges, Table 2 highlights the widespread use of deep learning technologies, specifically CNNs, which offer high accuracy and faster recognition capabilities compared to other approaches. CNNs are capable of training on multiple images simultaneously. According to the information presented in Figure 11, it is evident that U-Net surpasses other approaches in terms of recognition accuracy, demonstrating a remarkable 99.5% performance. In contrast, Mathematical Morphology exhibits the least recognition accuracy, as evidenced by its placement at the bottom of the graph, achieving a mere 79%. It is worth noting that the authors employed distinct datasets and varied vehicle plate formats. Despite this variability, investigations reported in the literature indicate that the image segmentation (IS 1) technique exhibits the highest recognition accuracy, while the character recognition (Cr) method, specifically the cr 1 approach, demonstrates the lowest accuracy. On the whole, both supervised and unsupervised techniques demonstrate average performances exceeding 92%. OCR is the most widely used method while in DL methods, CNNs are acceptable for most of the applications.

6 CONCLUSION

This scoping review is devoted to license plate recognition techniques, which have gained significant interest worldwide in developing low-cost monitoring of vehicles to help improve the air quality and decrease pollution. A variety of factors contribute to this growing interest, especially for advanced technology in law enforcement, a higher motivation for adopting modern technology, the abundance of motor vehicles, and high population densities. Also, with the growth of AI and 5G networking technology, smart cities and roadside infrastructures are well prepared to adopt such platforms. These factors, along with other regional incentives such as political motives, contributed to the growing momentum of ALPR system implementation.

This comprehensive review includes a comparative analysis of various approaches proposed by the research community for the identification, recognition, and positioning of license plates. In general, the methods can be classified into two main categories of conventional computer vision and contemporary deep learning methods. While the conventional computer vision techniques can be utilized for the

ALPRS using conventional algorithms based on edge-based methodologies (e.g., vertical and horizontal edge detection), color-based techniques (e.g., histogram intersection), mean shift algorithms, fuzzy mathematics, and reasoning methods, texture-based methods (e.g., scan-line), vector quantization, sliding concentric windows, and wavelet transform, and character-based techniques (e.g., region-based approaches), and scale-space analysis methods. In addition to traditional computer vision algorithms, regression, classification, and clustering algorithms, conventional methods also include statistical analysis methods such as CAMShift, and AdaBoost utilized to train license plate detection techniques.

However, like many other computer vision applications, the predominant trend is departing from conventional methods toward deep learning architecture. Powered by the unprecedented performance of DL methods, the availability of large data-sets, and the emergence of high-performance computing platforms (such as GPUs/TPUs) and edge computing servers that can train complex DL architectures more feasibly than ever. Specific DL techniques, including CNN, ANNs, and object detectors such as YOLO, Discrete-Time CNN, and Probabilistic Neural Networks further empower license plate recognition's in complex settings. After careful investigation, it is evident that CNN and YOLO are the most popular and effective approaches for license plate recognition, owing to their high-precision outcomes and rapid recognition speed. Particularly, YOLO stands out as the faster method, while also exhibiting higher accuracy for object detection. In a sample size of 16,000, all variations of YOLO achieved an average accuracy of over 85%, while the general CNN method achieved recognition accuracy of over 90% across 5,500 tested samples. Nevertheless, it is possible that even the most sophisticated DL algorithms may yield inaccurate or inadequate outcomes due to numerous factors, including a low image or file resolution, blurry images, inadequate lighting, low contrast, and the usage of distinct fonts on license plates, predominantly those of personalized vehicles. So, it is imperative to use the most diverse datasets and test conditions in the training phase, and carefully inspect the utilized algorithms' generalizability to new conditions. Also, to mitigate the comparison errors arising from the variant test conditions of reported results, it would be beneficial to pursue examining the accuracy and computational complexity of cutting-edge algorithms on identical computation platforms and image databases. Using data augmentation methods can help produce a richer set of data samples to cover non-existent test conditions. There are several datasets commonly used for training and evaluating ALPR systems. However, it is important to note that some datasets may focus on specific regions or license plate formats, so selecting the appropriate dataset depends on the specific requirements and target application of the ALPR systems.

REFERENCES

Abdulateef, O. G., Abdullah, A. I., Ahmed, S. R., & Mahdi, M. S. (2022). Vehicle license plate detection using deep learning. In *2022 International Symposium on Multidisciplinary Studies and Innovative Technologies (ISMSIT)* (pp. 288–292). IEEE. DOI: 10.1109/ISMSIT56059.2022.9932852

Alzubaidi, L., Latif, G., & Alghazo, J. (2019). Affordable and portable real-time Saudi license plate recognition using SoC. In *2019 2nd International Conference on New Trends in Computing Sciences (ICTCS)* (pp. 1–5). IEEE. DOI: 10.1109/ICTCS.2019.8923064

Ammar, A., Koubaa, A., Boulila, W., Benjdira, B., & Alhabashi, Y. (2023). A multi-stage deep-learning-based vehicle and license plate recognition system with real-time edge inference. *Sensors (Basel)*, *23*(4), 2120. DOI: 10.3390/s23042120 PMID: 36850714

Antar, R., Alghamdi, S., Alotaibi, J., & Alghamdi, M. (2022). Automatic license plate recognition of Saudi license car plates. *Engineering, Technology &. Applied Scientific Research*, *12*(2), 8266–8272.

Awalgaonkar, N., Bartakke, P., & Chaugule, R. (2021). Automatic license plate recognition system using SSD. In *2021 International Symposium of Asian Control Association on Intelligent Robotics and Industrial Automation (IRIA)* (pp. 394–399). IEEE. DOI: 10.1109/IRIA53009.2021.9588707

Balbin, J. R., Sejera, M. P., Valiente, F. L., Martinez, C. O. A., Cataquis, N. A., Ontog, L. M., & Toribio, J. K. (2017). Metro Manila Development Authority color coding scheme violator detection through plate recognition using image processing. In *2017 IEEE 9th International Conference on Humanoid, Nanotechnology, Information Technology, Communication and Control, Environment and Management (HNICEM)* (pp. 1–6). IEEE. DOI: 10.1109/HNICEM.2017.8269464

Ding, H., Gao, J., Yuan, Y., & Wang, Q. (2023). Boosting one-stage license plate detector via self-constrained contrastive aggregation. *IEEE Transactions on Circuits and Systems for Video Technology*, *33*(8), 4204–4216. Advance online publication. DOI: 10.1109/TCSVT.2023.3241283

Eke, R. A., & Orakwue, S. I. (2023). Automatic license plate recognition system.

Fan, X., & Zhao, W. (2022). Improving robustness of license plates automatic recognition in natural scenes. *IEEE Transactions on Intelligent Transportation Systems*, *23*(10), 18845–18854. DOI: 10.1109/TITS.2022.3151475

Firasanti, A., Ramadhani, T. E., Bakri, M. A., & Hamidi, E. A. Z. (2021). License plate detection using OCR method with Raspberry Pi. In *2021 15th International Conference on Telecommunication Systems, Services, and Applications (TSSA)* (pp. 1–5). IEEE. DOI: 10.1109/TSSA52866.2021.9768252

Gupta, R., Fricker, J. D., & Moffett, D. P. (2002). Reduction of video license plate data. *Transportation Research Record: Journal of the Transportation Research Board, 1804*(1), 31–38. DOI: 10.3141/1804-05

Huang, W., Xu, X., Hu, M., & Huang, W. (2022). A license plate recognition data to estimate and visualize the restriction policy for diesel vehicles on urban air quality: A case study of Shenzhen. *Journal of Cleaner Production, 338*, 130401. DOI: 10.1016/j.jclepro.2022.130401

Hussein, K. A., & Al-Ani, Z. T. A. (2022). Iraqi license plate recognition based on neural network technique. *Journal of Physics: Conference Series, 2322*(1), 012025. DOI: 10.1088/1742-6596/2322/1/012025

Jia, W., Zhang, H., & He, X. (2007). Region-based license plate detection. *Journal of Network and Computer Applications, 30*(4), 1324–1333. DOI: 10.1016/j.jnca.2006.09.010

Kaur, P., Kumar, Y., Ahmed, S., Alhumam, A., Singla, R., & Ijaz, M. F. (2022). Automatic license plate recognition system for vehicles using a CNN. *Computers, Materials & Continua, 71*(1), 1303–1321.

Khan, M. G., Saeed, M., Zulfiqar, A., Ghadi, Y. Y., & Adnan, M. (2022). A novel deep learning based ALPR pipeline for vehicle access control. *IEEE Access : Practical Innovations, Open Solutions, 10*, 64172–64184. DOI: 10.1109/ACCESS.2022.3183101

Kumar, A., Ahuja, N. J., Thapliyal, M., Dutt, S., Kumar, T., Pacheco, D. A. D. J., & Choo, K. K. R. (2023). Blockchain for unmanned underwater drones: Research issues, challenges, trends and future directions. *Journal of Network and Computer Applications, 103649*, 103649. Advance online publication. DOI: 10.1016/j.jnca.2023.103649

Laroca, R., Cardoso, E. V., Lucio, D. R., Estevam, V., & Menotti, D. (2022). On the cross-dataset generalization in license plate recognition. *arXiv preprint* arXiv:2201.00267. DOI: 10.5220/0010846800003124

Lee, Y. Y., Halim, Z. A., & Ab Wahab, M. N. (2022). License plate detection using convolutional neural network–back to the basic with design of experiments. *IEEE Access : Practical Innovations, Open Solutions, 10*, 22577–22585. DOI: 10.1109/ACCESS.2022.3153340

Lin, H., Zhao, J., Li, S., & Qiu, G. (2020). License plate location method based on edge detection and mathematical morphology. In *2020 IEEE 4th Information Technology, Networking,Electronic and Automation Control Conference (ITNEC)* (Vol. 1, pp. 853–857). IEEE. DOI: 10.1109/ITNEC48623.2020.9085121

Maheswari, V. U., Aluvalu, R., & Mudrakola, S. (2022). An integrated license plate recognition system through images using threshold-based methods and KNN. In *2022 International Conference on Decision Aid Sciences and Applications (DASA)* (pp. 493–497). IEEE. DOI: 10.1109/DASA54658.2022.9765218

Mahmood, Z., Khan, K., Khan, U., Adil, S. H., Ali, S. S. A., & Shahzad, M. (2022). Towards automatic license plate detection. *Sensors (Basel)*, *22*(3), 1245. DOI: 10.3390/s22031245 PMID: 35161988

Mathew, P. A., Jagarlamudi, A., Bharathwaj, N., & Jaspin, K. (2023). Real-time license plate and helmet detection of motorcyclists using YOLOv5 and ResNet-50. In *2023 International Conference on Sustainable Computing and Data Communication Systems (ICSCDS)* (pp. 709–715). IEEE. DOI: 10.1109/ICSCDS56580.2023.10105076

Mhatre, A., & Sharma, P. (2023). Deep learning approach for vehicle license plate recognition system with image enhancement technique. *International Journal of Intelligent Systems and Applications in Engineering*, *11*(1s), 251–262.

Oliveira-Neto, F. M., Han, L. D., & Jeong, M. K. (2009). Tracking large trucks in real time with license plate recognition and text-mining techniques. *Transportation Research Record: Journal of the Transportation Research Board*, *2121*(1), 121–127. DOI: 10.3141/2121-13

Oliveira-Neto, F. M., Han, L. D., & Jeong, M. K. (2013). An online self-learning algorithm for license plate matching. *IEEE Transactions on Intelligent Transportation Systems*, *14*(4), 1806–1816. DOI: 10.1109/TITS.2013.2270107

Onesimu, J. A., Sebastian, R. D., Sei, Y., & Christopher, L. (2021). An intelligent license plate detection and recognition model using deep neural networks. [AET-iC]. *Annals of Emerging Technologies in Computing*, *5*(4), 20–29. DOI: 10.33166/AETiC.2021.04.003

Rahman, R., Pias, T. S., & Helaly, T. (2020). GGCS: A greedy graph-based character segmentation system for Bangladeshi license plate. In *2020 4th International Symposium on Multidisciplinary Studies and Innovative Technologies (ISMSIT)* (pp. 1–7). IEEE. DOI: 10.1109/ISMSIT50672.2020.9254449

Rahman, R., Rakib, A. F., Rahman, M., Helaly, T., & Pias, T. S. (2021). A real-time end-to-end Bangladeshi license plate detection and recognition system for all situations, including challenging environmental scenarios. In *2021 5th International Conference on Electrical Engineering and Information Communication Technology (ICEEICT)* (pp. 1–6). IEEE. DOI: 10.1109/ICEEICT53905.2021.9667896

Raj, S., Gupta, Y., & Malhotra, R. (2022). License plate recognition system using YOLOv5 and CNN. In *2022 8th International Conference on Advanced Computing and Communication Systems (ICACCS)* (Vol. 1, pp. 372–377). IEEE. DOI: 10.1109/ICACCS54159.2022.9784966

Ramya, P., Chowdary, T. H., Teja, P. K., & Hrushikesh, T. (2023). Number plate recognition using optical character recognition (OCR) and connected component analysis (CCA). In *Smart Technologies in Data Science and Communication* [Springer.]. *Proceedings of SMART-DSC, 2022*, 29–40.

Sadique, M. F., & Haque, S. R. (2019). A comparative study of license plate detection and recognition techniques. In *2019 22nd International Conference on Computer and Information Technology (ICCIT)* (pp. 1–6). IEEE. DOI: 10.1109/ICCIT48885.2019.9038583

Samantaray, M., Biswal, A. K., Singh, D., Samanta, D., Karuppiah, M., & Joseph, N. P. (2021). Optical character recognition (OCR) based vehicle's license plate recognition system using Python and OpenCV. In *2021 5th International Conference on Electronics, Communication and Aerospace Technology (ICECA)* (pp. 849–853). IEEE.

Shashirangana, J., Padmasiri, H., Meedeniya, D., & Perera, C. (2020). Automated license plate recognition: A survey on methods and techniques. *IEEE Access : Practical Innovations, Open Solutions*, *9*, 11203–11225. DOI: 10.1109/ACCESS.2020.3047929

Silvano, G. V. T., Silva, I., Ribeiro, V. C. T., Greati, V. R., Bezerra, A., Endo, P. T., & Lynn, T. (2020). Artificial MERCOSUR license plates dataset. *Data in Brief*, *33*, 106554. DOI: 10.1016/j.dib.2020.106554 PMID: 33344736

Singh, I. (2016). *Automatic vehicle detection and recognition*.

Tusher, M. S. R., Rahman, N. N., Chowdhury, S., Tabassum, A., Adnan, M. A., Rahman, R., & Al Masud, S. M. R. (2023). An enhanced variational autoencoder approach for the purpose of deblurring Bangla license plate images. *International Journal of Advanced Computer Science and Applications*, *14*(6). Advance online publication. DOI: 10.14569/IJACSA.2023.01406133

Xin, S., Zhaobin, P., & Jing, Q. (2022). Legal analysis of the right to privacy protection in the age of artificial intelligence. In *International Conference on Intelligent Computing* (pp. 617–626). DOI: 10.1007/978-3-031-13870-6_51

Yang, H., Yang, J., Han, L. D., Liu, X., Pu, L., Chin, S. M., & Hwang, H. (2018). A kriging based spatiotemporal approach for traffic volume data imputation. *PLoS One*, *13*(4), e0195957. DOI: 10.1371/journal.pone.0195957 PMID: 29664928

Yu, H., Wang, X., Shao, Y., Qin, F., Chen, B., & Gong, S. (2022). Research on license plate location and recognition in a complex environment. *Journal of Real-Time Image Processing*, *19*(4), 823–837. DOI: 10.1007/s11554-022-01225-z

Chapter 6
The Integration of Neural Networks in Smart Robotics and Autonomous Systems

Sarâh Benziane
https://orcid.org/0000-0002-0450-6522
USTO MB, Algeria

ABSTRACT

This chapter explores the integration of neural networks in smart robotics and autonomous systems, emphasizing their transformative impact on various industries. It begins by discussing the fundamentals of neural networks, including types such as feedforward, convolutional, and recurrent networks, and their applications in robotics. The chapter highlights how these networks enable robots to learn, adapt, and make autonomous decisions, particularly in areas such as autonomous vehicles, medical robots, industrial automation, and service robots. The role of neural networks in enhancing robotic perception through sensors, actuators, and control systems is also explored. Additionally, the chapter covers the challenges, opportunities, and ethical implications of incorporating neural networks into autonomous systems, such as privacy concerns and impacts on employment. With practical case studies, the chapter demonstrates how neural networks are revolutionizing smart robotics, fostering greater efficiency, precision, and autonomy in diverse applications.

DOI: 10.4018/979-8-3373-4571-0.ch006

Copyright © 2025, IGI Global Scientific Publishing. Copying or distributing in print or electronic forms without written permission of IGI Global Scientific Publishing is prohibited.

1. INTRODUCTION TO NEURAL NETWORKS AND THEIR APPLICATIONS IN ROBOTICS

Robotic control is a concrete problem of intelligent behavior of robots, which forms a part of AI. Comprising a number of end effectors controlled by actuators, the robots typically have a high degree of freedom and work in an uncertain and usually dynamic environment. Smart robotic systems construct a loop of perception, planning, and control, where perception is based on high-tech sensing, 3D sensors, and vision sensors. Neural networks are biologically inspired artificial neural systems that come with adaptive learning capabilities. These are computational algorithms that mimic the functionalities of the human brain in learning from data and new experiences, enabling them to perform tasks ranging from real-time prediction to controlling unmanned systems and robotics applications (Wang et al., 2014). Signal processing, classification, and clustering are some well-known areas in the applications of neural networks that demonstrate the outcomes of computational neuroscience and signal processing. For robotics, neural networks contribute by enabling the robotic controller to perform a specific task effectively, such as grasping, manipulation, or controlling it to move to a specified position.

Robotic systems consisting of machines with neural computational structures and feedback from the environment enable the robot to adapt internal dynamics and structures for control and learning for the performance of tasks. Neural networks optimized for low computational resources can be embedded along with sensors and actuators or made as an external computational unit to perform tasks such as fault tolerance, path planning, and robot control. These days, autonomous robotics and artificially intelligent systems are rather incomplete without the embedded neural networks in them. In a nutshell, smart robots equipped with neural networks can think, learn, and make autonomous decisions. Today, robots are gradually integrated with neural network blocks in robot embedded systems, e.g., agents in unexplored locations, robotic exploratory learning, topple tracking systems, and medical diagnosis machines. The tremendous capability and powerful manifestation of neural networks, deep learning architectures enabled by high computational systems, and the big data concept of non-linear robotics have attracted researchers and technologists to have a keen interest in the development of robotic systems. Prior to this, such systems were designed using conventional AI and fuzzy neural controllers.

1.1. Fundamentals of Neural Networks

Neural networks take inspiration from the biological human brain and nerve systems. The basic element of a neural network is the neuron, which is a simple signal processor. Its input/output behavior is specified by a synaptic weight, a threshold, and a transfer function (Wang, Clark, Wen, & Trigoni, 2017). We call a collection of neurons and their meshwork interconnected by links or processing units a neural network. The layers consist of repeating elements called neurons that emit signals. The first layer is the input layer. The input layer sends signals via connection systems to the hidden layer.

There are several neuron layers with different specialty functions, such as recognition of the network inputs or drawing generalizations from these inputs. This work will focus on neural network structures with three layers of neurons and is also called a multi-layer recurrent net. These neurons use nonlinear activation functions. A large family of neural networks is the feedforward network. Each neuron output is the input weights multiplied by input signals from a previous layer added. The biological neural network prevalent in the central cortex of vertebrates, for instance, is a feedforward network. Besides feedforward networks, there are convolutional networks dealing with 2-D spatial structure input data and having 2-D layers, and the recurrent networks which have feedback connections. (Huang et al., 2021) Operands and inputs of layers have higher dimensions than usual neural networks. Nowadays, the most used models are feedforward and convolutional networks.

Types of Neural Networks

1. **Feedforward Neural Networks (FNNs)**:
   - ✓ **Definition**: These are the simplest type of neural network, where information moves in only one direction—from input to output—through various layers. Each neuron receives input, processes it, and passes it on.
   - ✓ **Role in Robotics**: Feedforward networks are particularly useful in basic control systems, such as movement and grasping tasks, where sequential dependencies or memory aren't crucial.
2. **Convolutional Neural Networks (CNNs)**:
   - ✓ **Definition**: CNNs are designed specifically for processing grid-like data, such as images, using convolutional layers that apply filters to detect features like edges, textures, and shapes.
   - ✓ **Role in Robotics**: CNNs are primarily used in **vision systems** of robots, enabling them to process and recognize objects in their environment. These networks excel in tasks like object detection, facial recognition, and scene segmentation. Autonomous vehicles, for example, rely heavily on CNNs for real-time image processing to navigate and detect obstacles in dynamic environments.
3. **Recurrent Neural Networks (RNNs)**:

- ✓ **Definition**: Unlike feedforward networks, RNNs have connections that form loops, allowing them to process sequences of data by maintaining a memory of past inputs.
- ✓ **Role in Robotics**: RNNs are ideal for tasks that require **sequential decision-making** or processing of time-dependent data. In robotics, they are used for tasks like **speech recognition**, **robot motion planning**, and **predictive maintenance**. For instance, robots that assist in medical surgery can use RNNs to predict and adjust movements based on the sequence of actions and patient responses.

4. **Long Short-Term Memory Networks (LSTMs)**:
   - ✓ **Definition**: A specific type of RNN designed to overcome the problem of long-term dependency in sequences by remembering important information over time.
   - ✓ **Role in Robotics**: LSTMs are critical in tasks requiring **long-term memory**, such as **robot learning** over time or **interaction-based robotics**. These networks are used in applications like **autonomous vehicle navigation** or **human-robot interaction**, where the robot must remember past interactions to adjust future actions.
5. **Generative Adversarial Networks (GANs)**:
   - ✓ **Definition**: GANs consist of two neural networks (a generator and a discriminator) that work against each other. The generator creates fake data, while the discriminator tries to distinguish between real and fake data, enabling the generator to improve over time.
   - ✓ **Role in Robotics**: GANs can be used in **robot design and simulation** to generate realistic environments or to improve the performance of robotic systems through synthetic data generation, enhancing robotic learning with diverse and varied inputs.
6. **Deep Reinforcement Learning (DRL)**:
   - ✓ **Definition**: A combination of deep learning and reinforcement learning, where agents learn optimal behaviors through trial and error by interacting with an environment.
   - ✓ **Role in Robotics**: DRL is widely used for **robot autonomy**, where robots learn to make decisions without explicit programming. For example, **autonomous drones** or **service robots** that need to adapt to complex, dynamic environments (such as navigating around obstacles or interacting with humans) benefit from DRL.

Training these mechanisms is done via some algorithms. When a learning process takes place repeatedly, the weights are changed and the neural network transforms from its initial random state to a state that can solve the problem it has seen. The learning process aims to minimize the error between the actual and designed outputs of the system. It is not necessary for the system to get the optimal value for the first test. As long as the learning continues by giving more data, the errors will continuously decrease. The widely used algorithms for the learning process of a feedforward network are backpropagation and cascade-correlation. Backpropagation is one of the most efficient learning techniques in feedforward networks. It is nothing but an algorithm to compute the gradient of the performance function with respect to the weights. The goal is to teach the neural network through rigorous training to extract the mistakes and adapt the system to achieve the smallest error possible in the choice of the output of each layer. It continues in this fashion until the error is minimized. Two salient views embedded in the learning task are namely supervised and unsupervised learning. In unsupervised learning, the network is not taught with the set of outputs, but it is designed in such a way that it automatically classifies and groups the outputs of the input data.

1.2. Neural Network Architectures for Robotics

Numerous architecture types have been designed specifically for robotics. A pervasive characteristic of many architectures is their potential to process sensory data. Convolutional neural networks are a type of feed-forward artificial neural network designed for image processing, boasting high accuracy in image recognition tasks. (Maturana & Scherer, 2015) On the other hand, recurrent neural networks are specialized for sequence-based prediction and decision-making tasks, such as voice recognition, anomaly detection, and natural language processing. LSTM-based recurrent neural networks are further enhanced with the capabilities of long-term memory and learning of processing sequences across time; they have been used for predictive learning of temporal sequences and in policy optimization in reinforcement learning tasks. Both convolutional neural networks and recurrent neural networks, alone or in hybrid models, are employed in robotic systems because the perception of sensory data is an essential component of robotic intelligence. Hybrid models consist of a combination of both deep learning and reinforcement learning. Architectures that are specialized in reinforcement learning perform action selection tasks, but they are also used for perception tasks and action-value approximations. An important aspect of designing any architecture for real-world robotics platforms is its efficiency and scalability. For instance, convolutional neural networks for image recognition are required to be fast and accurate; if slow, the robot that uses convolutional neural networks for processing visual data is not practically useful. Several effective processing architectures have been utilized with robots or have gained renewed attention in smart robotics research. Deep learning serves as an end-to-end controller for robots both in the physical world and in simulation, using convolutional neural networks for the image and recurrent neural networks in combination with convolutional neural networks. (Cui, Ge, & How, 2010) Recurrent neural networks combined with convolutional neural networks have been used for robot reinforcement learning in a variety of tasks to learn from low-level, high-dimensional input sensory modalities. Overall, the choice of an architecture is guided by the requirements and the scalability and efficiency considerations required to use robots or smart autonomous systems in unstructured environments. Several factors are involved in the design of an architecture for robotic-based systems. Therefore, creating a general-purpose robotic architecture is difficult. Each robotic architecture developed is intended to perform well in a set of design specifications, and these in turn detail aspects of what the robotic architecture should be particularly good at. In the next section, some of the key architectures are reviewed and analyzed in detail to show the architecture in more detail. In addition, some of the architecture's underlying principles and design heuristics are also analyzed. In this way, this subsection can be taken as an examination of the impact of design considerations on robotic architectures, their implementation, and finally the concept of system intelligence.

Types of Robotics Systems That Benefit from Neural Networks

1. **Autonomous Vehicles**:

Autonomous vehicles use a combination of CNNs for vision-based navigation, RNNs for sequential decision-making, and deep reinforcement learning for continuous environment adaptation and decision-making. These technologies help autonomous cars navigate safely in real-time, avoiding obstacles, and making complex driving decisions.

2. **Medical Robots**:

In medical robotics, CNNs are used for imaging tasks, such as identifying tumors or assisting in robotic surgery. RNNs and LSTMs are applied in systems requiring motion planning or interpreting real-time sequences of actions. Medical robots also rely on reinforcement learning to improve their actions in complex and unpredictable surgical environments.

3. **Service Robots**:

Service robots, such as cleaning robots, delivery robots, and humanoids, rely on neural networks for decision-making, path planning, and environmental awareness. CNNs help with vision-based tasks (e.g., detecting obstacles), while RNNs and

LSTMs enable the robots to adjust and plan their movements over time based on previous experiences.

4. **Industrial Robots**:

In industrial settings, robots use neural networks for quality control, predictive maintenance, and optimized performance. CNNs analyze images for defect detection, while RNNs and reinforcement learning are used to adapt to production changes and improve operational efficiency.

By integrating neural networks into robotic systems, these machines become more adaptable, intelligent, and capable of performing complex tasks autonomously. This integration allows robots to learn from experience, make decisions in real-time, and interact with their environment in ways that were once only possible for humans.

2. BACKGROUND AND CONCEPTUAL GAPS

Introduction to Smart Robotics

Smart robotics integrates various technologies, algorithms, and devices to perform complex tasks autonomously. Understanding the distinctions between these categories is crucial for a comprehensive analysis of the field.

Categorization of Smart Robotics

1. **Sensors (Devices)**

Definition: Sensors are physical devices that detect and measure environmental stimuli, converting them into signals for processing.

Examples:

Camera Device: A camera device includes an embedded image sensor component (ISO/AWI 24942) used for perception in robotics. It captures visual information, which is crucial for tasks such as navigation and object recognition (ISO 13482:2014).

Lidar Sensor: A Lidar sensor is used to measure distances by illuminating a target with laser light and analyzing the reflected light. It is essential for mapping and environmental perception (ISO 9283:1998).

2. **Algorithms (Methods)**

Definition: Algorithms are systematic methods or procedures that enable robots to process information and make decisions based on data.

Examples:

Neural Networks: Neural networks are AI algorithms designed to recognize patterns and make predictions based on input data. In robotics, they can be applied for tasks such as image recognition and decision-making in dynamic environments (LeCun et al., 1998; Schmidhuber, 2015).

Reinforcement Learning Algorithms: These algorithms enable robots to learn from interactions with their environment, optimizing their actions based on feedback (Sutton & Barto, 2018; Kober et al., 2013).

3. **Technologies (Systems/Platforms)**

Definition: Technologies encompass the integrated systems and platforms that utilize sensors and algorithms to perform specific applications in robotics.

Examples:

Robotic Operating System (ROS): ROS is an open-source framework that provides tools and libraries for building robotic applications, facilitating the integration of various devices and algorithms (Goodfellow et al., 2016).

Autonomous Navigation Systems: These systems combine sensors (like cameras and Lidar) with algorithms (such as path planning and obstacle avoidance) to enable robots to navigate autonomously in complex environments (Mnih et al., 2015).

Addressing Confusions Between Sensors and AI Technologies

To further clarify, it is essential to distinguish between devices and the technologies used within them. For example, while a camera is a device that captures images, the image sensor embedded within it is a specific component responsible for converting light into an electronic signal. This distinction highlights the role of sensors as physical tools that work in tandem with AI algorithms.

3. SMART ROBOTICS: DEFINITION AND KEY COMPONENTS

Smart robotics refers to the interdisciplinary and hybrid domain of robotics integrating a variety of advanced technologies such as artificial intelligence, communication and cooperation, cognitive science, distributed control systems, neural computing, sensors, wireless technologies, and so on. It is different from traditional robotics in that smart robotics uses these advanced technologies to make the robot act intelligently. These advanced technologies are grouped into three categories:

(1) sensors and sensing technologies, (2) algorithms and systems, and (3) other hardware and software technologies. A smart robot is designed and implemented using advanced technologies for handling different tasks with intelligent capabilities such as learning, adaptation, and user interaction, among other tasks (Yue, Arvin, Xiong, & Hu, 2016).

The brain of smart robots is designed using different modules based on AI technologies such as various sensors, signal and image processing algorithms, neural networks, rules, multilayer linear filtering modules, a decision-making module, a data fusion module, and so on. The advancements in these technologies push the performance of robots to make decisions in a timely manner. A close look at intelligence from an integrated viewpoint finds that a number of factors contribute to intelligence, some of which include the type of sensors, the technological mechanism of sensors, real-time data processing, adaptive mechanisms, learning, and the possibility of executing commands. It has been observed that some features not only provide signals about the environment but also enable the transition to autonomous decision mechanisms. This is achieved by integrating these neurons in a learning system based on a neural mechanism. These technologies have significantly affected the development of successful applications such as search and rescue, intelligent autonomous robots, cleaning areas by robots, robots that can interact with humans, and robots that can advise and help humans.

3.1. Sensors and Perception Systems

Sensors are the most important devices in a smart robotic system, which enables the robot to interact with the environment. The robot's perception extracts information about the environment that is relevant for accomplishing its departure task. There are different representations of embedded sensors, among them are cameras, RGB-D cameras, LiDAR, accelerometers, gyroscopes, barometers, ultrasound, force/torque sensors, proprioceptive sensing, and microphones. Cameras are largely used in robotic environments, which are available in different forms; there are monochrome and grayscale cameras (Fu, Hu, Peng, Rind, & Yue, 2019). They are the best devices for object recognition and computer vision applications. LiDAR has the ability to collect data over a relatively long distance and in a 3D point cloud format, unlike the 2D camera that collects distance and range values for only a single point. The collection of the 3D point clouds, mesh, and intensity information makes it desirable to be used in robot perception systems. Ultrasound and infrared sensors are also used alongside long-range sensors to provide near-range sensing for the robotic platform for purposes such as collision avoidance. Large sensors are used for navigation and localization.

Figure 1. Sensors and Perception Systems

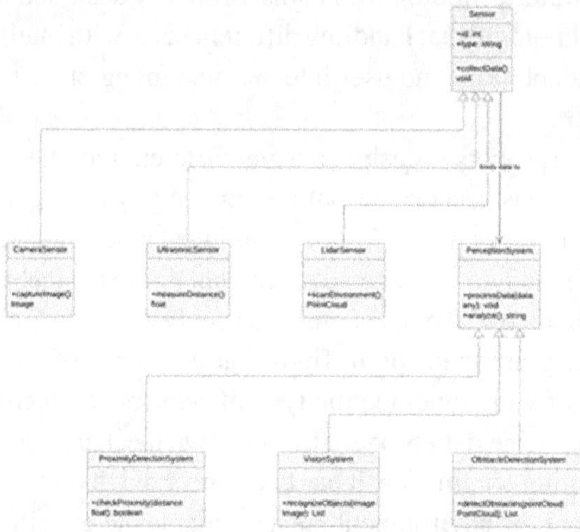

Neural networks and deep learning algorithms have been employed in robotic perception systems for understanding sensory information. They are automatically trained on large datasets. The neural networks interpret the information perceived from sensors to have a better understanding of the robot's environment. Many of the sensory data from embedded sensors are in their raw form, which bears no meaning until they are transformed into a useful form. Unlike the task of integrating deep learning and stereo vision to capture optical flow, processing sensor data for robotic perception systems tries to ease or simplify the workload of the robot to facilitate its understanding of the environment. Intelligent perception systems for robotic platforms are adaptive in nature to deal with uncertainties. They have the ability to deal with abnormal environments, temporal and situational changes in the environment that may interrupt the robot's behavior. For instance, while driving in a natural environment, the road condition might change from green grass to sandy terrain, from a smooth path to one with obstacles. In order to successfully maneuver in such a dynamic environment, the robot needs to have a mechanism to adapt its perception to accommodate the changes.

The development and adaptation of such intelligent perception systems allow the robotic platform to accurately perform tasks in a real and dynamic environment. (Wang et al., 2018) These sensors, when integrated with neural networks, bring autonomy to the robots. These networks are frontiers of AI and are self-adaptive. They become more and more accurate based on experience. Different machine learning models are designed with the deployment of neural networks for robotic systems. One of the biggest challenges that a robotic system has to resolve is related to the environment in which it operates. Many unknowns can be recorded from the environment by different sensors. The intelligent choice of sensor for a specific task is required for a robotic system in order to be truly autonomous. Millimeter radar is used for automotive applications, inferring the activity of objects using the radar signatures and not through explicit computer vision algorithms. Neural networks receive raw sensor data in the input layer and output their predictions in the output layer. The perception component of the autonomous vehicle integrates the outputs of each neural network to produce an understanding of the vehicle's surroundings.

2.2. Actuators and Control Systems

Actuators and control systems are necessary to make physical actions possible in smart robotics. Actuators are used to transform stored or incoming energy into motion or force to execute a previously planned action. The variety of actuators includes electric motors, hydraulic systems, pneumatic devices, etc. These complex actuators need to be controlled by effective algorithms to issue the necessary motion plan execution. Typically, different control strategies can be divided into onboard and remote. It is common to distinguish between open-loop and closed-loop, or feedforward and feedback control strategies. (Wang et al., 2014) The feedforward control typically needs a perfect or accurate model of the robot dynamics, environmental disturbances, and an accurate sensor to estimate the right state of the robotic system in order to correctly apply the inputs to the robot's actuators to perform an operational task. This control strategy, together with a feedback one, can greatly improve the performance of a robotic system in terms of energy saving and asset preservation.

The use of advanced actuation and control systems greatly increases the complexity of robots' models and control tasks but, at the same time, improves the performance, hence the task learning and operational reliability. The control system should be integrated with a state filtering algorithm to improve performance reliability. The emerging result is that the internal states become intrinsically distributed in the mechanical components, with the idea that every sensor integrated measure can adapt and respond to intruder conditions and not increase internal stress. Finally, higher performance control requires more powerful computing on embedded systems. The control-actuating part's main task is the coordination of sensors and actuators in both energy saving and operational efficiency (Wang et al., 2016). All of these mechanisms working together produce a global coordination for taking action. The principle of sensing and acting seems to be effective. This means that the energy capabilities of the motor are used only for speed creation, while the spring is responsible for reducing the load and, at the same time, saving energy at the actuator.

The reduction of friction or massage of actuators seems to be an important feature in actuator control systems based on smart sensor and motor technology.

3. AUTONOMOUS SYSTEMS: CONCEPT AND EVOLUTION

Autonomous systems refer to the machines or robots that can carry out the desired task or tasks with minimal or even no human intervention. Except in unmanned systems like industrial automation and remote planetary exploration, human intervention is usually an integral part of achieving the desired motion or action of any machine or robot. Thus, autonomous systems bring a revolution in the era of robotics, which began in the early 1960s. Over the years, there have been remarkable developments in the field of robotics to enhance the level of autonomy.

The development in the area of artificial intelligence, machine learning, and neural networks has led to the enhancement of different levels of autonomous functionalities. The complete AI-driven autonomous systems, also referred to as once-human-operated machines, are dominating far beyond the Industrial Revolution and service-oriented/combined unmanned systems. Hence, autonomy is widely labeled as a continuum with varied levels of autonomy, right from semi-autonomous to fully autonomous functionalities. The salient feature of autonomous functionality is the "task execution" without human intervention. Along with dual-use technological innovation, semi-autonomous to fully autonomous functions bring incredible changes in many scientific and engineering domains. Currently, (Wang et al., 2018) a huge advancement has been witnessed in this emerging field, and several industries, including automotive, aerospace, and healthcare, have shown a keen interest in developing and deploying autonomous robots with different degrees, with a transaction of billions of dollars. However, the roadmaps for fully autonomous robots were sketched out a few decades ago.

Semi-autonomy, having predefined tasks with human intervention and a certain level of automation, emerged as robotics solutions in transportation, industry, and healthcare to increase productivity, safety, and comfort in the early 2000s. A few decades later, the field evolved with increasing life utility and extending outside Earth applications. Socio-technical acceptance became broader even as the performance of once-human-operated systems expanded. The current trends are along two dimensions: (1) for black-box decision engines from narrow AI to general AI levels of intelligence; and (2) expanding life utility domains such as care, creativity, recreation, and exploration in unfamiliar terrestrial, airborne, and space environments. The autonomous robotic systems have thus gone beyond task execution to now providing leave-me-alone advice (Wang et al., 2014). Intellectual and technical milestones, societal acceptance, research frontiers, visions, challenges, and some aspects that require fathoming and assessment in advance are discussed in this chapter. Errare humanum est has different societal perspectives and fathoms when the autonomous robotic errand doer is different from the errand endower. While much of the speculation is future projections, there are a few cases to create abductive arguments. This section aims to discuss the development from robotics to autonomous systems. At first, the deep conceptual evolution, nascent developments, and emerging contravirtuous trends in the development of autonomous robotic systems are discussed.

Figure 2. The autonomous robotic systems diagram

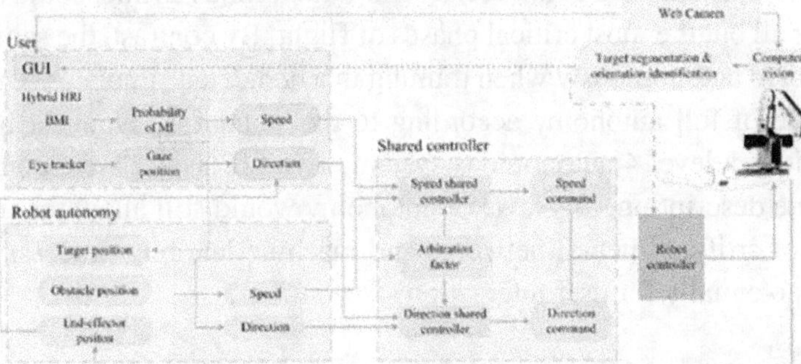

3.1. Levels of Autonomy in Robotics

According to their capability of performing independent operations, robots are classified into different levels of autonomy. Of course, social robots that have to closely interact with humans can sometimes be remotely controlled by humans. Although these robots are still classified as autonomous, their level of independent operation should be weak. Industry standards refer to the following levels of autonomy. The forward-facing society proposes the following terminology: autonomous mode, full autonomy, and operator control. These describe broadly the same levels of autonomy. In military robotics, three main levels of autonomy are described. These are teleoperation (manual control), supervised autonomy, and full autonomy.

In a level 0 system, there will be no decision-making or obstacle avoidance, for example. Human operators have to monitor the robot's operation, control the robot, or supervise the robot (or some combination of the above). In a level 1 system, the robot could have some basic or crucial decision-making capabilities, as in a simple pick-and-place robotic arm. A level 2 system may have enhanced decision-making capabilities (Wang et al., 2016). It may also involve safety and redundancy measures, such as low-level functional safety systems or bump sensors. A level 3 system, now considered a highly autonomous system, may involve a robot that can navigate in dynamic and complex environments. The robotic system may make its own automated decisions based on feedback and possibly inputs from a human operator. Furthermore, it is conceivable that the system will utilize some form of machine learning, potentially by utilizing artificial neural networks. Likewise, a level 4 system may involve full autonomy and even higher levels of redundancy and safety systems. Such systems could further integrate machine learning such as artificial neural networks. When considering autonomous systems, the combination of time and environment certainly plays a role in determining the appropriate level of autonomy. For example, a commercial semi-autonomous airliner could be piloted manually for all but the most critical phases of flight. By contrast, the same airliner could be piloted autonomously when training in a dedicated simulator. The airliner is not capable of full autonomy according to the standards. Would it be correct to describe it as a level 4 autonomous system? Even if level 2 were considered a more accurate description, this level of autonomy would still allow for significant exploration of artificial neural networks and machine learning processing within the system, potentially for user interaction.

3.2. Challenges and Opportunities in Autonomous Systems

Autonomous systems have recently received significant interest, particularly in the context of “smart” machines. Advances in robotics programming have been rapidly changing the degree of autonomy of robotic systems for use in high-level tasks, including decision making and the design of the operational behavior of a robotic platform. (Wang et al., 2018) The reasoning for having more intelligence, autonomy, and the ability to make quick smart decisions comes from a proven fact in cognitive psychology, which tells us that when an ordinary person performs a continuous task under a given situation, the first time the person concentrates on this task the most. Hence, the aim of high-level robotics programming technologies is to make robots intelligent and capable of working independently of human intervention and to free humans from the repetitive but high-standard labor that may bore them, to boost production, to carry higher-level operations, and to consider human abilities and constraints in the automation.

However, designing robots that are able to operate without human assistance is particularly challenging. One of the technical challenges is the requirement for highly reliable and adaptable systems that can operate under uncertainty and unforeseen conditions. The safety of systems ensuring responsible design, production, and deployment cannot cause harm to property or human beings. An equally important aspect is the question of ethics, such as who is accountable for critical decision making? (Wang et al., 2014) Who should make the decisions in large-scale monitoring and control of the hierarchical architecture of decisions? The complexity of these inherent difficulties requires close cooperation among computer scientists, psychologists, lawyers, ethicists, and various relevant disciplines to comply with the rules in the designs of any fully autonomous system. Nevertheless, the era of autonomous systems is promising, with potential for achieving greater efficiency, reduced human error, and the ability to work in areas or under conditions that might be unsafe for humans. Ongoing research on smart robotic systems and autonomous technologies has recently turned to concepts of collaboratively optimizing decentralized designs in the autonomy of high-level control. Further, recent innovations in the architectures of smart robotic structures and autonomous systems ensure the improvement of trust and understanding of defined structures, as well as the distribution of information across articulate sensor-rich organizational entities, even when it is uncertain. Smart autonomous robotics are currently widely used in mining, mobile, UAVs, e-grocery, hospitals, and other fields of industry.

4. NEURAL NETWORKS IN ROBOTICS: TRAINING AND IMPLEMENTATION

Training a neural network to perform robotic-related tasks typically requires large amounts of training examples. A series of steps needs to be carried out to provide the network with data. Data collection can be supported via techniques such as force-based training and teleoperation. The next step is data preprocessing, which requires the removal of irrelevant data. A robot controller can be incorporated to perform the assignment of motor commands and sensor inputs. The controller should be able to execute the desired trajectory without causing danger or damage. The annotation of training data is based on both the methods of collection and preprocessing, while the creation of synthetic training examples can be based on the 3Rs: refine, reduce, or replace (Wang et al., 2016).

Figure 3. Mind map summarizing Neural Networks in Robotics

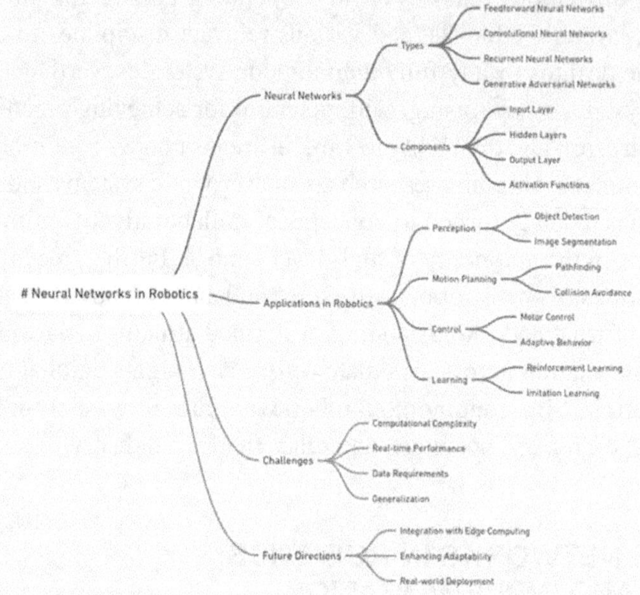

Implementation of the trained network in a robotic application generally requires significant computational power and thus a potential cutting-edge hardware. This is particularly important for neural networks with high demands in terms of speed and data capacity. The process of training network behavioral models is computationally expensive. Deep learning architectures and configurations require large amounts of parallelization, which heavily taxes traditional implementations. Real-time implementation of trained models on robotic hardware implies tight restrictions on the computational complexity to assure fast and predictable response times necessary for smooth task execution. In the very hardware-in-the-loop prototyping iterations, surrogate time-critical behavior can be performed with specific hardware components. The necessity to integrate hardware and software close to the physical robot widely differs, from relatively simple integration with software frameworks to heterologous software/hardware systems. Supervision of the robot's safety during neural network operation is another aspect that heavily affects the solution's design (Mnih et al., 2015). Coordinated data flows, as well as control and interface integration for autonomous, assisted, or collaborative human-robot tasks, must also be established as a single stream. Information design is also an indispensable aspect to be considered while integrating hardware and software. In real-time robotics, data acquisition systems need to design and provide a stream of information under strict requirements of cost, speed, robustness, and energy usage. In hardware-in-the-loop prototyping of autonomous and team robotics, there are further high-level requirements of scalability and information organization to permit parallel and distributed systems and integration by teams of developers. Furthermore, the information needs to be debuggable and human-understandable. Initial training and fine-tuning also require high logging and monitoring capabilities. Task-specific telemetry considerations and requirements include the needs for advanced, scriptable, and extensible viewers. Reliability, prioritization, error handling, and object-oriented design properties like reuse, partitioning, information hiding, and scalability must also be considered, provided the in-the-loop prototyping of robotics is a distributed and parallel effort collaborating among hardware-in-the-loop and software developers. Hardware and software integration is required in a wide range of robotics settings, especially considering the increasing availability of low-cost modular robotic platforms. These platforms include drones, wheeled and tracked platforms, legged or humanoids, and modular robots. Models suitable for successful implementation in robotic services and specific applications require lower-level considerations and optimizations. The majority of internal simulation-based robotics systems using artificial neural networks have not validated their performance in realistic simulated environments.

4.1. Training Data Collection and Annotation

The exponential growth of robotics applications can be largely attributed to the recent advancements in neural networks. (Sutton & Barto, 2018) A major factor influencing the performance of such methods is the type and quality of training data.

Training Data Collection Data for training neural networks can be collected from sensors. Hyperspectral cameras are used in classification pipelines specifically designed to operate at the cellular and nuclear level. Silicon retina sensors are efficient in capturing high-speed visual information, which potentially makes them suitable for learning walking gaits. Simulators or simulated environments are used to generate a variety of data, including those that are not possible to obtain experientially or whose collection can be life-threatening or costly. In the robotics research community, a number of well-known simulators are more commonly used as the ultimate source of data for learning.

Training Data Annotation Annotating or labeling data is the process of associating a label with the data stored at the time of data collection. Although it is not considered as exciting as other aspects of data collection and preprocessing, it plays a crucial role in informing a neural network of the desired outcome. There are different techniques to annotate data. Manual annotation, where a human expert checks the data and assigns labels accordingly, is relatively more accurate but time-consuming and costly. Semi-automatic annotation can be achieved by implementing computer algorithms that can infer results with the intervention of a human expert who can add to or rectify the results. Using heuristic annotation, a machine learning model first annotates a fraction of data, and an expert corrects some annotations, which is then fed back to improve the performance of the classifiers iteratively. Hybrid annotation using humans in the loop is beneficial to reduce the expertise (Krizhevsky, Sutskever, & Hinton, 2012) involved in the entire process. Automated annotation uses a machine learning model, which is trained using some initial data, to annotate the entire dataset. The results from the model are then reviewed by human experts. Data from human experts is crucial to both annotation and data preprocessing. It is difficult to achieve consistent or reliable results without expert input. It is also human experts who can understand expert features and group that information properly for training and testing with high accuracy (Graves & Schmidhuber, 2005).

Figure 4. Training Data Annotation

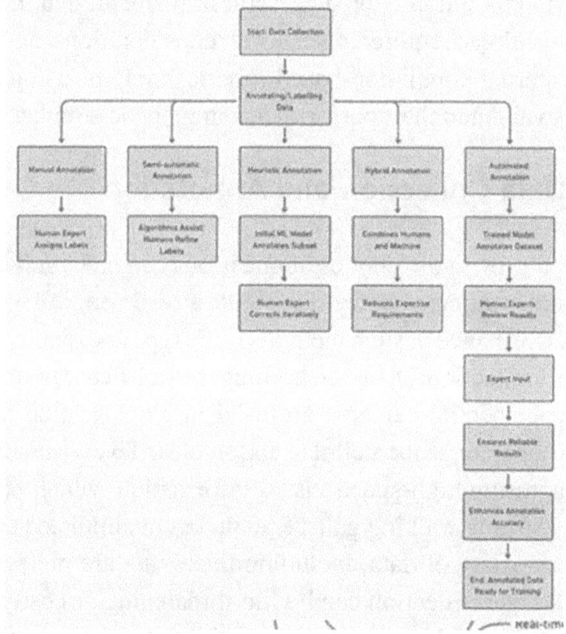

Data Collection Strategies Data should be collected from multiple sources to ensure that the training set has good input/output coverage. It is important that the data contains outliers due to noise and artifacts such as clutter and occlusions. There needs to be a balance in the amount and kinds of data. However, at the same time, one of the challenges in the field is to accurately balance the size of the dataset because it is essential for learning, but on the other hand, it is not necessary to have huge datasets as it might lead to data redundancy or overfitting the model. Data must be collected from representative sources so that the model is generalizable to other settings. A dataset that is too small or one that comes from just a few different sources can heavily impact learning capability, which is likely to make the model overfitted to the trained data and will perform poorly when given an unknown input. Sufficient variability in the dataset is also a factor, as it plays a pivotal role in establishing the capability of the learning model. Ethical considerations also come into play, as the training data needs to be collected from private and public sources while ensuring robust privacy. Additionally, biased training data may influence the network's functioning in certain settings, and thus care should be taken to protect against such biases.

4.2. Real-time Implementation and Inference

Real-time operation denotes the deployment of a neural network (or several subnetworks) in hardware, integrated into a robotic system that allows fast interaction with its environment. This is a fundamental requirement for practical systems and crucial for their autonomous behavior. Real-time operation is necessary to ensure short response times and interactions with dynamic and uncertain environments. This requires processing large amounts of data under stringent latency constraints while maintaining high accuracy, often in complex inference steps (LeCun & Bengio, 1995). For real-time applications, we require low-latency and high computational power hardware, together with algorithmic optimizations to decrease the time for neural network computations. This may involve dedicated hardware accelerators or associated purpose-built algorithmic architectures. Making a choice of deployment on a specific hardware platform is an important decision to achieve the goal of responsive interaction. It is crucial for ensuring quick reaction and adaptation by the robot. With the deployment of semantic and/or sensorimotor capabilities that leverage the capabilities of neural networks, contemporary robotic systems have demonstrated capabilities of understanding and acting on scenes and sequences as inputs. These systems may also contain adaptive mechanisms that allow them to continue to learn while operational, providing continued refinement in practical operational scenarios. While ideally, we desire neural networks that can process large amounts of data accurately and provide timely information, often there is a trade-off between speed and accuracy to be made. Many contemporary robotic systems use efficient real-time adaptation of networks running on high-end servers or workstations, either in the cloud or close to it. These span public demonstrations, industrial applications, and scientific benchmarks. Efficient real-time neural network operations are critical for the robotic system to receive timely processing and quick sensory-motor loops. All sensing strategies, specific to affordances for robots due to their designs, require major computing infrastructures for efficient and timely inference to make high-speed decisions. Neuromorphic platforms could further enable these sensing systems powered by real-time neural networks (Silver et al., 2016). Crucial future directions will be leveraging large-scale cross neural network architectures on time series, mapping capabilities, and dimensions.

5. CASE STUDIES: APPLICATIONS OF NEURAL NETWORKS IN SMART ROBOTICS

Case Studies Industrial Automation and Manufacturing Artificial neural networks have been integrated into industrial automation systems through the development of several manufacturing applications. It is well known that the use of industrial robots can provide greater production efficiency, reduce downtime, and secure the safety of workers. Estimates suggest that the surgical sector can constitute the most sophisticated approach where technological advances are integrated via the delivery of new systems in the future. This vision rests mainly on anecdotal observations and technological developments in robot and automation system development and commercialization. Medical Robotics The development of neural networks, and more specifically pattern recognition techniques, continues to play a major role in the advancement of autonomous and smart robots used in fields including surgery, prosthetics, diagnostics, and rehabilitation. Neural networks have become an essential part of robots that facilitate the decision-making process while also increasing their accuracy. This paper provides several studies that incorporate a plethora of neural networks of different architectures into robot endpoints such as surgical robots, assistive care robots, prosthetics, and rehabilitation robots for diagnosis, classification, prediction, and many more. The significant uptake of neural networks in smart robotics systems grows exponentially each year, primarily due to the fact that neural networks are required in robots that are performing very complex, high-accuracy work. The case studies discussed in this section show innovative human–robot systems in a variety of industries where neural networks have been applied to improve robots, save time, and increase efficiency while reducing the need for human supervisors (Ha & Schmidhuber, 2018). In all of the discussed case studies, the neural network smart robot systems can be adapted and scaled to be tested and implemented in multiple industries.

5.1. Industrial Automation and Manufacturing

In industrial automation and manufacturing, neural networks have great potential to revolutionize production and be a driving force behind the prediction of faults or bottlenecks before they emerge. Predictive analytics through neural networks can predict failure by analyzing historical data to identify trends. One of the biggest uses for neural networks in manufacturing is the idea of predictive maintenance. Essentially, neural networks can be used to capture the essence of a complex background and predict outcomes or identify future trends. With the help of neural networks, robots have advanced to a point where real-time monitoring in manufacturing is possible. Sensor technology has also become advanced enough to be able to report indirectly. This also allows the creation of transfer functions directly in the neural network to follow the action to minimize the error. Robotics, when integrated with technology such as neural networks, offers many benefits to manufacturing. The combination of the two can increase both labor efficiency and significantly improve the consistency and safety of manufacturing tasks. Robotics deals with the design, construction, operation, and use of robots. Quality control is also an area in manufacturing that uses robotics and neural networks together. Manufacturing companies use neural networks to train robotic vision systems on what to look for with product defects. Anomalies are programmed into the neural network, which gives these machines the ability to improve with each try, therefore creating a higher quality product through their ability to identify and recognize defects. Over the past ten years, as manufacturing becomes affordable in developing countries, the involvement of robots in the production line has become a reality. This is also particularly appealing for potential customers because they can visit these factories and see the visible robotic displays (Yoon & Lee, 2017). Manufacturing requires both flexibility in design with built-in safety considerations to allow the operator and robot to work in close coordination. The robots used are often compact and light and therefore have relatively low collision forces. This robot is often referred to as a collaborative robot for this reason. Cobots serve as assistants or new partners. By working alongside operators, the robotic installation is more easily marketed to potential customers who are fearful of technology. This method serves as a compelling selling point and gives companies an advantage in the market. Industrial Internet of Things devices offer a number of capabilities that have the potential to make a big difference to manufacturers. Last year, the IIOT was set to bring about a significant increase in productivity, improve customer satisfaction, reduce costs, gain better visibility, and accelerate the competitiveness of organizations that implemented it. Despite the appeal of neural networks and their flashy potential impact, it will likely take time for the workforce of these industries to adapt to these newfound tools and knowledge. It is possible that some aspects could either become entirely automated or largely task-oriented. The possibilities obviously occur on either end of the spectrum. The technology required for these capabilities is also very capital intensive, particularly since manufacturers already pay for production costs. Higher profits should not be expected until the costs are recouped, which, for equipment like this, could take years. Furthermore, companies must spend time training their workforce to use this technology once it becomes operational. As very few people have manufacturing training, networks and related ethical implications must be taught and understood to a varying extent in addition to an extensive understanding of technology.

Figure 5. Neural Networks in Industrial Automation

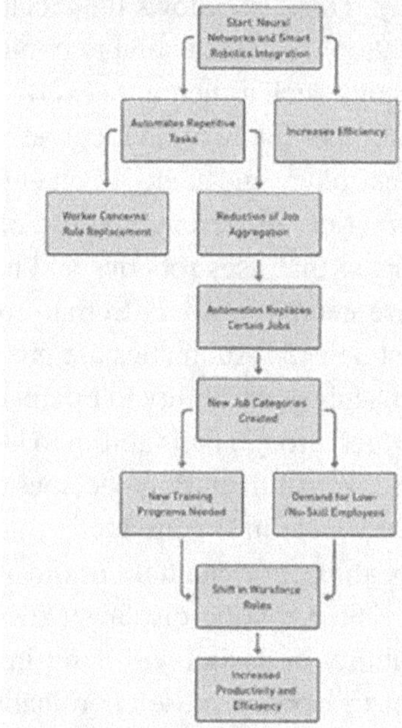

5.2. Medical Robotics and Healthcare

Healthcare is observing emerging applications of neural networks supported by smart robotics, autonomous systems, or both. (Bengio et al., 2009) The advancements of these intelligent assistive systems support further treatment and therapies, individualized drugs, and care management of different patient groups, or may lead to improved operational efficiencies in healthcare markets. In such systems, a multitude of applications use AI to support decision-making on different diagnostics, therapies, or treatments. An example is in minimally invasive procedures in robotic surgery. A neural network can support the tracking of genetically diverse tumor lines in robotic surgery by differentiating healthy cells from cells with different genes. Medical imaging is another popular field for integrating intelligent patient data analysis. One of the relatively familiar use cases is in robot-assisted endovascular surgery for patient-specific personalized medicine or for robotic interventions in neonatal care. The robotic systems can provide a ghost instrument and show the planned path to the surgeon. Moreover, the system can anticipate the complete path during the procedure and counter different patient movements.

Neural networks are widely used for real-time and pre-post neuro-functional analysis and to drive directly an electrical stimulation therapy in neuro-rehabilitation. Intelligent health systems based on neural networks have great potential to build a smart environment. The systems demonstrate an ability to learn about the environment from data collected from a suite of sensors and to predict what a patient, or patients with similar characteristics, would require at any specific moment in time. Hence, it would enable existing systems to facilitate personalized remote patient monitoring and treatment. Neural networks are essential in healthcare markets as they help to share personalized-based decision-making, treatment selection, and may even help care providers to assess and minimize the risk of fraud. For example, they can be integrated with surgery simulation in real time to predict the completion of the operation. Similarly, (Schmidhuber, 2015) a neural network has applications in various medical field administration by looking forward to the possible outcomes, efficiencies, or frauds. They are particularly concerned with ethical issues associated with SCR in the healthcare market. For instance, they are concerned because the data is important to the patient and disclosed to a company that uses AI with neural networks to deliver treatments autonomously (Lecun & Bengio, 2015).

6. ETHICAL AND SOCIETAL IMPLICATIONS OF NEURAL NETWORKS IN ROBOTICS

An obvious ethical question regarding the development and integration of robotic systems with neural networks in society is the use of personal or sensitive data in the training of these systems. The purpose and extent of use, as well as the anonymization and potential reidentification, play crucial roles from an ethical perspective. While there are well-established ethical principles in place to guide responsible handling of third-party data, the use and ownership of data for training systems remain a fairly new discourse. A related ethical issue is the use of neural networks in the decision-making of autonomous robots, particularly where safety or severe ethical dilemmas are a concern. At issue is the question of who is accountable for the outcome of the decisions made by these machines. The introduction of intelligent automation or decision-making also carries implications for the workforce. History has shown that technological advancement can have large-scale repercussions for employment, sometimes entire industries. It is likely, given their myriad applications, that employment and work practices in certain sectors will have to adapt as intelligent robotics become more pervasive. This example shows that neural networks and robotics can have positive and negative societal implications and that appropriate ethical frameworks are necessary to navigate them. Given the proposed case studies and speculative examples we present, it is also our sincere hope that the study will inform and guide research in ethics and the societal impact of neural networks and smart robotics. Only by collaborating with other research communities will it be possible to integrate these findings into a larger interdisciplinary discourse and inform policy accordingly.

6.1. Privacy and Data Security Concerns

Given the vast amount of personal information that can be—and often is—collected from people and their environments to train neural networks, there are growing concerns about privacy and data security (Mnih et al., 2013). The use of object-recognition neural networks in robotics inevitably requires the collection of large image datasets, which increases the risk of gathering private information. Would it ever be permissible to feed such networks with people's data? The collection, processing, and use of sensory data for robotics and automated systems may therefore put at stake individual privacy.

Data protection has become a major concern: a regulation, in this context, previously unprecedented in terms of legal granularity and extraterritorial effect. In the absence of informed explicit consent and legitimate grounds for data processing, the training and employment of object-detection neural networks in robotics could potentially lead to a data grave. It is thus imperative to ascertain the corresponding requirements, obligations, and best practices employed in cybersecurity to protect against unwanted disclosure, access, and manipulation of sensitive, private information. Concisely discuss the threats to data privacy in robotics. It is worth noting that, also having the potential to revolutionize the cybersecurity of smart systems, the concepts described may be most profitable if viewed as a mechanism of first resort, with concomitant data transmission and verification measures serving as mechanisms of last resort.

6.2. Impact on Employment and Workforce

Integrating neural networks and smart robotics into the workplace alters the employment field and the delineation of work responsibilities. When deployed effectively, such systems have the potential to automate repetitive and dreary tasks, simplifying jobs and increasing efficiency. At the same time, workers are concerned about the replacement of occupational roles by machines. Traditionally, (Cui et al., 2017) automation might replace a certain part of job duties, which is why certain systems were first suspected of diminishing the aggregation of jobs. Eventually, newly created job categories required new employees to be hired and trained, thereby creating greater demand in low- or no-skill areas. This is largely an issue when automation effectively completes the majority or all of a specific job.

Figure 6. neural networks in industrial automation and manufacturing

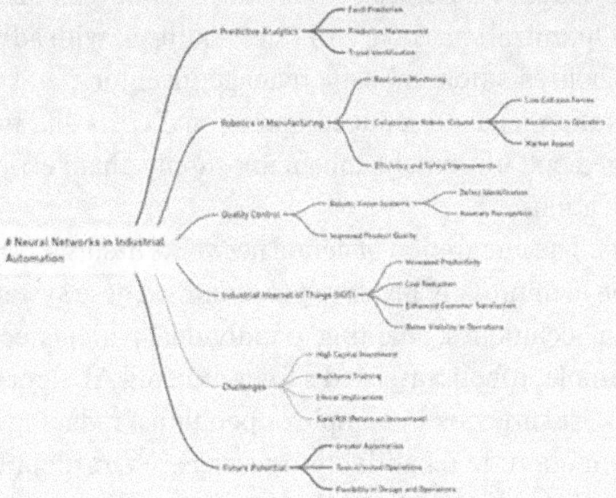

The industrial usage of neural network integration into fixed automation control units or robotic manipulators for manufacturing systems must now be concerned with some degree of ethical implications in deployment that addresses an extensive spectrum of societal concerns. In particular, even today, the integration of intelligent robotic systems on the factory floor has already been indisputably shown in various business sectors to have an impact on employment opportunities. This is, at present, seen both as a potential job displacement threat and a high maintenance cost. Many involuntary disadvantages such as loss of employment due to machine failure or outages beyond control are a function of local laws, contract negotiability with workers' unions, layoffs to avoid plant closures, or repayment of workers' compensation. These are aspects of democratic governance and political legal jurisdiction at the local and national levels, and therefore vary among various regulatory restrictions.

7. WORK-RELATED ANALYSIS

The integration of neural networks in smart robotics has profound implications across various sectors, particularly in industrial and medical fields. By analyzing several case studies, we can observe the practical impacts of this integration.

Industrial Applications:

Automated Manufacturing: The use of neural networks in robotic arms and assembly lines has revolutionized manufacturing processes. These systems can learn from data, optimizing production schedules and minimizing downtime through predictive maintenance. For instance, neural networks facilitate real-time quality control by analyzing product images for defects, enhancing overall manufacturing efficiency.

Supply Chain Optimization: Smart robotics equipped with advanced algorithms can navigate warehouses autonomously, manage inventory, and optimize delivery routes. This integration leads to reduced operational costs and improved accuracy in logistics management, ultimately enhancing supply chain efficiency.

Medical Applications:

Surgical Robots: The integration of neural networks in surgical robotics allows for enhanced precision in minimally invasive procedures. These systems can learn from a variety of surgical techniques, adapting to individual patient needs and improving outcomes. For example, robotic-assisted surgeries using AI algorithms can analyze patient data and assist surgeons in complex operations, reducing recovery times.

Robotic Rehabilitation: In rehabilitation settings, smart robotics with integrated neural networks facilitate personalized therapy. These systems can adapt exercises based on patient performance, providing real-time feedback and motivation. This approach not only enhances patient engagement but also supports effective recovery pathways.

Through these case studies, it becomes evident that the integration of neural networks and smart robotics significantly impacts operational efficiencies, enhances precision and accuracy, and ultimately transforms traditional practices in industrial and medical fields.

8. CONCLUSION

In summary, the integration of neural networks in smart robotics presents transformative opportunities across various sectors. Key findings from this literature review highlight the distinct categorizations of sensors, algorithms, and technologies, emphasizing their roles in enhancing robotic capabilities.

The contribution to future research lies in the exploration of ethical considerations and the development of standards that govern the deployment of intelligent robotic systems in sensitive environments, such as healthcare and manufacturing. This is particularly important in light of the increasing reliance on AI technologies in decision-making processes.

Reflecting on societal implications, it is crucial to understand that advancements in smart robotics not only improve operational efficiencies but also raise questions about job displacement and the need for reskilling the workforce. Addressing these concerns will be vital in ensuring that the benefits of these technologies are equitably distributed across society.

"The integration of CNNs in robotic vision systems and reinforcement learning in control architectures offers transformative capabilities, enabling robots to autonomously adapt to dynamic, uncertain environments with increasing reliability."

REFERENCES

. Bengio, Y., et al. (2009). Learning deep architectures for AI. *Foundations and Trends® in Machine Learning, 2*(1), 1-127. DOI: 10.1561/2200000006

Cui, R.. (2017). Dynamic motion planning for mobile robots using reinforcement learning. *IEEE Transactions on Robotics, 33*(4), 860–873. DOI: 10.1109/TRO.2017.2701130

Cui, R., Ge, S. S., & How, B. V. E. (2010). Leader–Follower Formation Control of Underactuated Autonomous Underwater Vehicles. *Ocean Engineering, 37*(17), 1491–1502. DOI: 10.1016/j.oceaneng.2010.07.006

Fu, Q., Hu, C., Peng, J., Rind, F. C., & Yue, S. (2019). Towards Autonomous Robotic Systems: A Robust Collision Perception Visual Neural Network with Specific Selectivity to Darker Objects. *IEEE Transactions on Cybernetics, 50*(12), 5074–5088. DOI: 10.1109/TCYB.2019.2946090 PMID: 31804947

Goodfellow, I., Bengio, Y., & Courville, A. (2016). *Deep Learning*. MIT Press.

Graves, A., & Schmidhuber, J. (2005). Framewise phoneme classification with bidirectional LSTM networks. *Proceedings of the International Conference on Neural Networks*, 2047-2052. DOI: 10.1109/IJCNN.2005.1556215

Ha, D., & Schmidhuber, J. (2018). World models. *Proceedings of the Neural Information Processing Systems (NeurIPS)*, 1-16.

Huang, Y., Li, W., Ng, W. Y., Zhang, X., Xian, Y., Chiu, P. W. Y., & Li, Z. (2021). An Autonomous Robotic Flexible Endoscope System with a DNA-Inspired Continuum Mechanism. *2021 IEEE International Conference on Robotics and Automation (ICRA)*, 7657-7663. DOI: 10.1109/ICRA48506.2021.9561712

IEEE P7000 — Model Process for Addressing Ethical Concerns During System Design.

IEEE Std 1872-2015 — Standard Ontologies for Robotics and Automation.

ISO 13482:2014 — Robots and robotic devices — Safety requirements for personal care robots.

ISO 9283:1998 — Robots and robotic devices — Performance criteria for position, velocity, and acceleration of robotic systems.

Kober, J., Bagnell, J. A., & Peters, J. (2013). Reinforcement learning in robotics. *Survey (London, England)*. Advance online publication. DOI: 10.1177/0278364912439674

Krizhevsky, A., Sutskever, I., & Hinton, G. E. (2012). ImageNet classification with deep convolutional neural networks. *Advances in Neural Information Processing Systems*, *25*, 1097–1105.

LeCun, Y., & Bengio, Y. (1995). Convolutional networks for images, speech, and time series. *Proceedings of the IEEE*, *86*(11), 2278–2324. DOI: 10.1109/5.726791

LeCun, Y., Bengio, Y., & Haffner, P. (1998). Gradient-based learning applied to document recognition. *Proceedings of the IEEE*, *86*(11), 2278–2324. DOI: 10.1109/5.726791

LeCun, Y., Bengio, Y., & Haffner, P. (1998). Gradient-based learning applied to document recognition.

Lecun, Y., Bengio, Y., & Hinton, G. (2015). Deep learning. *Nature*, *521*(7553), 436–444. DOI: 10.1038/nature14539 PMID: 26017442

. Lillicrap, T. P., Hunt, J. J., Pritzel, A., et al. (2016). Continuous control with deep reinforcement learning, DOI: DOI: 10.5555/3016100.3016160

Maturana, D., & Scherer, S. (2015). 3D Convolutional Neural Networks for Landing Zone Detection from LiDAR. *2015 IEEE International Conference on Robotics and Automation (ICRA)*, 3471-3478. DOI: 10.1109/ICRA.2015.7139679

Mnih, V.. (2013). Playing Atari with deep reinforcement learning. *NIPS Deep Learning Workshop*.

Mnih, V., Kavukcuoglu, K., Silver, D., Rusu, A. A., Veness, J., Bellemare, M. G., Graves, A., Riedmiller, M., Fidjeland, A. K., Ostrovski, G., Petersen, S., Beattie, C., Sadik, A., Antonoglou, I., King, H., Kumaran, D., Wierstra, D., Legg, S., & Hassabis, D. (2015). Human-level control through deep reinforcement learning. *Nature*, *518*(7540), 529–533. DOI: 10.1038/nature14236 PMID: 25719670

. Mnih, V., Kavukcuoglu, K., Silver, D., Rusu, A. A., Veness, J., Bellemare, M. G., ... & Hinton, G. (2015). Human-level control through deep reinforcement learning, DOI: DOI: 10.1038/nature14236

Schmidhuber, J. (2015). Deep learning in neural networks: An overview. *Neural Networks*, *61*, 85–117. DOI: 10.1016/j.neunet.2014.09.003 PMID: 25462637

. Schmidhuber, J. (2015). Deep learning in neural networks: An overview, DOI: DOI: 10.1016/j.neunet.2014.09.003

Silver, D., Huang, A., Maddison, C. J., Guez, A., Sifre, L., van den Driessche, G., Schrittwieser, J., Antonoglou, I., Panneershelvam, V., Lanctot, M., Dieleman, S., Grewe, D., Nham, J., Kalchbrenner, N., Sutskever, I., Lillicrap, T., Leach, M., Kavukcuoglu, K., Graepel, T., & Hassabis, D. (2016). Mastering the game of Go with deep neural networks and tree search. *Nature*, *529*(7587), 484–489. DOI: 10.1038/nature16961 PMID: 26819042

Sutton, R. S., & Barto, A. G. (2018). *Reinforcement learning: An introduction* (2nd ed.). MIT Press.

Wang, H., Kong, H., Man, Z., Tuan, D. M., Cao, Z., & Shen, W. (2014). Sliding Mode Control for Steer-by-Wire Systems with AC Motors in Road Vehicles. *IEEE Transactions on Industrial Electronics*, *61*(3), 1596–1611. DOI: 10.1109/TIE.2013.2258296

Wang, H., Man, Z., Shen, W., Cao, Z., Zheng, J., Jin, J., & Do, M. T. (2014). Robust Control for Steer-by-Wire Systems with Partially Known Dynamics. *IEEE Transactions on Industrial Informatics*, *10*(4), 2003–2015. DOI: 10.1109/TII.2014.2338273

Wang, H., Shi, L., Man, Z., Zheng, J., Li, S., Yu, M., Jiang, C., Kong, H., & Cao, Z. (2018). Continuous Fast Nonsingular Terminal Sliding Mode Control of Automotive Electronic Throttle Systems Using Finite-Time Exact Observer. *IEEE Transactions on Industrial Electronics*, *65*(9), 7160–7172. DOI: 10.1109/TIE.2018.2795591

Wang, H., Zheng, J., Man, Z., Kong, H., Zhao, Y., Yu, M., Cao, Z., & Do, M. T. (2016). Design and Implementation of Adaptive Terminal Sliding Mode Control on a Steer-by-Wire Equipped Road Vehicle. *IEEE Transactions on Industrial Electronics*, *63*(9), 5774–5785. DOI: 10.1109/TIE.2016.2573239

. Wang, H., Zheng, J., Man, Z., Kong, H., Zhao, Y., Yu, M., Cao, Z., Do, M. T. (2016). Design and Implementation of Adaptive Terminal Sliding Mode Control on a Steer-by-Wire

Wang, S., Clark, R., Wen, H., & Trigoni, N. (2017). DeepVO: Towards End-to-End Visual Odometry with Deep Recurrent Convolutional Neural Networks. *2017 IEEE International Conference on Robotics and Automation (ICRA)*, 2043-2050. DOI: 10.1109/ICRA.2017.7989236

Yoon, S. A., & Lee, H. (2017). Reinforcement learning for robotics. *Robotics and Autonomous Systems*, *98*, 167–178. DOI: 10.1016/j.robot.2017.06.012

Yue, S., Arvin, F., Xiong, C., & Hu, C. (2016). A Bio-Inspired Embedded Vision System for Autonomous Micro-Robots: The LGMD Case. *IEEE Transactions on Cognitive and Developmental Systems*, *1*(99), 1–1. DOI: 10.1109/TCDS.2016.2577021

Chapter 7
Neural Networks for Predictive Maintenance:
Advancing Efficiency and Reducing Downtime in Industry 4.0

Yamina Aouimer
https://orcid.org/0009-0005-3995-2281
Université d'Oran2, Algeria

ABSTRACT

In the era of Industry 4.0, predictive maintenance is transforming equipment management by leveraging AI, IoT, and machine learning. This paper highlights the crucial role of neural networks in detecting anomalies, predicting failures, and optimizing maintenance. IoT sensor integration enables real-time monitoring, allowing AI models to analyze parameters such as vibration and temperature. Advanced architectures, including convolutional and recurrent neural networks, enhance predictive accuracy. This proactive approach reduces costs, minimizes downtime, and extends equipment lifespan. However, adoption faces challenges such as high initial costs, data quality issues, and cybersecurity risks. This chapter examines these challenges and explores emerging trends like hybrid neural networks and AI-driven automation, which improve scalability and reliability, enabling industries to transition toward more efficient and resilient maintenance strategies.

DOI: 10.4018/979-8-3373-4571-0.ch007

Copyright © 2025, IGI Global Scientific Publishing. Copying or distributing in print or electronic forms without written permission of IGI Global Scientific Publishing is prohibited.

I. INTRODUCTION

In the context of Industry 4.0, predictive maintenance has emerged as a pivotal strategy for reshaping equipment management and significantly enhancing productivity (Monostori et al., 2016; Lee et al., 2015; Wuest et al., 2016). This approach, which harnesses the power of advanced technologies such as the Internet of Things (IoT), artificial intelligence (AI), machine learning (ML), and sophisticated neural networks, is revolutionizing the way industries approach the maintenance of machinery and equipment (Yang et al., 2019; Lei et al., 2018; Benziane, 2024). Predictive maintenance focuses on anticipating potential machine failures before they actually occur, minimizing downtime and optimizing maintenance efforts (Samek et al., 2021).

The integration of these state-of-the-art technologies enables businesses to monitor equipment continuously in real time, analyze vast amounts of data, and make accurate predictions regarding when maintenance should be performed (Zhang et al., 2019). The convergence of IoT, AI, and ML plays a fundamental role in predictive maintenance systems (Wuest et al., 2016). Sensors embedded in machinery gather vast amounts of data, including temperature, vibration, pressure, and other relevant operational parameters (Lei et al., 2018). This data is then transmitted via the IoT framework, allowing for remote monitoring and data analysis (Yang et al., 2019). AI and machine learning algorithms process this information and identify patterns or trends that may signal impending failures, ensuring that maintenance can be scheduled before a breakdown occurs (Shah et al., 2024).

One of the standout features of predictive maintenance is the use of neural networks, particularly deep neural networks (DNNs), to analyze data (Samek et al., 2021). These neural networks are designed to mimic the way the human brain processes information, allowing them to detect even the most subtle anomalies in machine behavior (Carvalho et al., 2019). Unlike traditional diagnostic systems, which rely on predefined rules or thresholds, deep neural networks can learn from the data itself, identifying complex patterns that may not be immediately obvious (Shah et al., 2024). This ability to detect hidden anomalies enables these systems to predict failures with a high degree of accuracy, even in cases where human inspection or conventional algorithms may fail (Hurtado et al., 2023).

The role of neural networks in predictive maintenance has been transformative (Zhang et al., 2019). By using deep learning algorithms, these systems can evolve over time, becoming more accurate and reliable as they are exposed to more data (Samek et al., 2021). The neural networks continuously learn from historical data, adjusting their predictions as they gain new insights into the behavior of equipment (Lei et al., 2018). This ability to "learn" makes them particularly powerful, as they can improve their diagnostic capabilities without the need for manual intervention (Carvalho et al., 2019; Shah et al., 2024). Over time, predictive maintenance systems become more sophisticated, with a deeper understanding of the specific equipment they are monitoring, thus providing more precise predictions (Yang et al., 2019).

One of the key advantages of predictive maintenance is the reduction in operational costs (Monostori et al., 2016; Wuest et al., 2016). By accurately predicting when equipment is likely to fail, businesses can avoid unnecessary maintenance, which often results in wasted resources and labor (Lee et al., 2015). Additionally, preventive repairs can be planned for times when the equipment is least critical, minimizing disruptions to operations (Lei et al., 2018). This not only saves money by preventing the need for expensive emergency repairs, but it also extends the lifespan of machinery, enhancing the return on investment for industrial equipment (Benziane, 2024; Hurtado et al., 2023).

The ability to foresee potential failures also enables companies to optimize resource utilization (Zhang et al., 2019; Shah et al., 2024). Maintenance staff can be allocated more efficiently, focusing their efforts on machines that are at a higher risk of failure (Shah et al., 2024). This targeted approach ensures that maintenance resources are used where they are most needed, reducing the overall workload and preventing overexertion of staff (Wuest et al., 2016).

Moreover, predictive maintenance systems can also help in inventory management by forecasting the need for spare parts based on predicted failures, ensuring that parts are available when necessary without overstocking (Hurtado et al., 2023). Another critical benefit of predictive maintenance is its potential to avoid costly and disruptive downtimes (Lee et al., 2015). In traditional maintenance models, companies often rely on fixed schedules for equipment checks or react to breakdowns as they happen (Lei et al., 2018). However, both approaches come with risks (Samek et al., 2021). Fixed schedules may lead to premature replacements of parts or missed issues, while reactive maintenance can result in unplanned downtime and lost productivity (Yang et al., 2019). Predictive maintenance, on the other hand, ensures that machinery is only serviced when needed, minimizing downtime while ensuring that repairs are timely and effective (Zhang et al., 2019; Benziane, 2024).

However, the integration of neural networks into predictive maintenance is not just about cutting-edge technology; it represents a shift in the way industrial processes are approached (Wuest et al., 2016). In traditional models, maintenance is often seen as a manual process, involving human inspection and intervention based on predefined schedules or reactive measures (Carvalho et al., 2019). Predictive maintenance introduces a new paradigm in which equipment itself “thinks” and “communicates” with its operators (Shah et al., 2024). Machines equipped with sensors and connected to the IoT network can continuously monitor their own health and transmit data to central systems for analysis (Lei et al., 2018). This enables operators to make data-driven decisions regarding maintenance, transforming the role of maintenance workers from reactive trouble-shooters to proactive managers who anticipate issues before they arise (Benziane, 2024; Hurtado et al., 2023).

The potential of predictive maintenance to change the industrial landscape is vast (Zhang et al., 2019). As companies continue to adopt more sophisticated predictive systems, the entire maintenance process becomes more streamlined, efficient, and reliable (Yang et al., 2019). No longer does the traditional approach to maintenance, which relies on human intuition and experience, hold the same value (Lei et al., 2018). Instead, the future of industrial operations is driven by data, AI, and advanced algorithms (Lee et al., 2015; Wuest et al., 2016). Machines can predict their own needs, and operators can rely on these systems to guide them in making timely, well-informed decisions (Wuest et al., 2016).

Yet, despite the many advantages of predictive maintenance, there are still challenges that must be addressed (Samek et al., 2021; Shah et al., 2024). One of the most pressing concerns is the reliability of the predictions made by neural networks (Carvalho et al., 2019). While these systems are highly accurate, they are not infallible (Shah et al., 2024). There are instances where the predictions may be incorrect, leading to unnecessary repairs or missed failures (Hurtado et al., 2023). The challenge, therefore, lies in continually refining these models and ensuring they are trained with sufficient and high-quality data (Benziane, 2024). Overcoming this challenge requires a continuous feedback loop between data collection, model training, and system improvement.

II. WHAT IS PREDICTIVE MAINTENANCE?

Predictive maintenance, commonly abbreviated as PdM, is a modern approach to managing and maintaining equipment, leveraging the power of real-time data collection and advanced data analysis to prevent failures and optimize the performance of machinery (Mobley, 2002; Jardine, Lin, & Banjevic, 2006). Unlike corrective maintenance, which is carried out after a machine has already failed, or preventive maintenance, which involves following a fixed maintenance schedule regardless of the actual condition of the equipment, predictive maintenance takes a more dynamic approach (Menasria, Baouche, & Ait Kaci Azzou, 2024; Advanced Technology Services, 2023). It focuses on continuously monitoring the health of equipment in real time and making maintenance decisions based on the actual condition of the machinery rather than on predetermined timelines or post-failure interventions (Wang, Han, & Zhang, 2018; Smith, 2022). At its core, predictive maintenance utilizes the data produced by equipment during its normal operation, allowing it to detect early warning signs of potential issues before they evolve into significant failures. This is achieved through the integration of sensors, Internet of Things (IoT) technology, machine learning models, and neural networks that work together to collect, process, and analyze vast amounts of data (Jardine et al., 2006; Wang et al., 2018). By interpreting this data, predictive maintenance systems can forecast the health of equipment, allowing for maintenance actions to be performed at the most opportune moments, avoiding unnecessary downtime or catastrophic breakdowns.

KEY COMPONENTS OF PREDICTIVE MAINTENANCE

To better understand how predictive maintenance functions, it's essential to explore its key components. These include sensors, data collection systems, machine learning algorithms, and neural networks. Together, they form the foundation of a predictive maintenance strategy.

1. Sensors and IoT Devices

The first step in predictive maintenance is the collection of data from equipment through various types of sensors (Mobley, 2002; Smith, 2022). These sensors are typically embedded in machines and are designed to monitor critical parameters such as temperature, vibration, pressure, and fluid levels (Jardine et al., 2006). For instance, in a manufacturing facility, a motor might be equipped with vibration sensors that measure the amplitude and frequency of vibrations in real time. These sensors continuously monitor the machine's condition and send the data to a central system or cloud platform for analysis (Menasria et al., 2024). The use of IoT (Internet of Things) technology plays a vital role in this data collection process (Mobley, 2002; Wang et al., 2018). IoT devices enable sensors to be connected to the internet, providing real-time data transmission to cloud-based systems or on-premises servers (Jardine et al., 2006). This connectivity allows maintenance teams to monitor equipment health remotely, providing the flexibility to address potential issues even when personnel are not physically present at the machine (Menasria et al., 2024). The data collected by sensors feeds into machine learning and neural network algorithms for analysis and interpretation.

2. Data Collection and Analysis

Once the data is collected by sensors, it is transmitted to a central processing system where it undergoes initial processing (Mobley, 2002). This data is often raw and needs to be cleaned and organized before it can be effectively analyzed (Jardine et al., 2006; Advanced Technology Services, 2023). Data cleaning is essential for removing noise, correcting errors, and eliminating outliers that may affect the accuracy of the analysis. Once the data is cleaned, it can be processed through machine learning models and neural networks that are designed to detect patterns or anomalies in the data (Menasria et al., 2024; Smith, 2022). One of the key features of predictive maintenance is its ability to analyze vast amounts of data in real time (Mobley, 2002). With machines operating continuously, sensors generate large volumes of data that would be too complex for traditional human inspection (Jardine et al., 2006). Machine learning algorithms and neural networks are essential for handling this data, as they can process and analyze it quickly, learning from patterns and making accurate predictions about the future health of equipment (Menasria et al., 2024).

3. Machine Learning and Neural Networks

Machine learning (ML) is a subset of artificial intelligence that allows systems to automatically improve their performance over time by learning from data (Jardine et al., 2006; Wang et al., 2018). In predictive maintenance, machine learning models are trained on historical data, such as the operating conditions of equipment and any known instances of failure (Mobley, 2002). The model learns to recognize patterns in the data that are associated with normal and abnormal equipment behavior. Once trained, the machine learning model can be used to analyze new data and predict when equipment is likely to fail based on the identified patterns (Menasria et al., 2024; Smith, 2022). Deep learning, a more advanced form of machine learning, involves the use of neural networks, which are algorithms modeled after the human brain (Jardine et al., 2006). Neural networks consist of multiple layers of interconnected nodes that process data and identify complex patterns (Mobley, 2002). In predictive maintenance, neural networks can be used to detect subtle anomalies in the data that may be invisible to human operators or traditional algorithms (Menasria et al., 2024). For example, a neural network might recognize an unusual vibration pattern in a motor that signals an impending bearing failure, even though this anomaly may be too subtle for human inspection. The strength of neural networks lies in their ability to learn from vast amounts of data and continuously improve their predictions (Jardine et al., 2006). As more data is collected, the system becomes increasingly accurate in identifying potential issues and forecasting maintenance needs (Mobley, 2002). This ability to learn and adapt makes predictive maintenance systems incredibly powerful, as they can evolve alongside the equipment they monitor (Menasria et al., 2024).

HOW PREDICTIVE MAINTENANCE WORKS IN PRACTICE

Now that we have explored the key components of predictive maintenance, let's take a closer look at how this approach is applied in real-world scenarios (Jardine et al., 2006). Predictive maintenance is particularly useful in industries with expensive, critical, or complex machinery, where downtime can result in significant financial losses, safety risks, or operational disruptions (Mobley, 2002). Industries such as automotive manufacturing, oil and gas, aviation, and energy rely heavily on predictive maintenance to keep their operations running smoothly (Menasria et al., 2024).

Benefits and Challenges of Predictive Maintenance

The primary advantage of predictive maintenance lies in its ability to reduce operational costs and prevent unexpected equipment failures (Mobley, 2002; Advanced Technology Services, 2023). By predicting when maintenance is needed, companies can avoid the high costs associated with emergency repairs, unplanned downtime, and production stoppages (Jardine et al., 2006). Additionally, predictive maintenance helps optimize the use of maintenance personnel and resources, ensuring that repairs are made at the right time rather than according to a fixed schedule (Menasria et al., 2024; Smith, 2022). Another significant benefit is the extension of equipment life (Mobley, 2002; Wang et al., 2018). By addressing issues early and preventing more severe failures, predictive maintenance can help machinery and equipment last longer, ultimately improving the return on investment (Jardine et al., 2006).

Challenges

Despite its many benefits, there are several challenges associated with predictive maintenance (Jardine et al., 2006). One of the most significant challenges is the need for large amounts of high-quality data to train machine learning models (Mobley, 2002; Wang et al., 2018). Without sufficient data, the system may not be able to accurately predict failures, leading to false positives or missed issues (Menasria et al., 2024). Additionally, implementing a predictive maintenance system can require significant upfront costs for sensor installation, data infrastructure, and software development (Jardine et al., 2006). Another challenge is ensuring the security of the data being collected and transmitted (Mobley, 2002; Advanced Technology Services, 2023). As predictive maintenance relies heavily on IoT devices and cloud platforms, the risk of cyberattacks and data breaches is a concern that needs to be addressed (Jardine et al., 2006).

In summary, predictive maintenance leverages real-time data collection, machine learning, and neural networks to predict equipment failures before they occur. While there are challenges in implementing such systems, the benefits make predictive maintenance a valuable strategy for modern industries.

III. NEURAL NETWORKS: A KEY LEVER FOR PREDICTIVE MAINTENANCE

Predictive maintenance is a crucial component in modern industrial operations, and one of its most powerful enablers is the use of neural networks (Goodfellow, Bengio, & Courville, 2016). These artificial intelligence models, inspired by the structure and functioning of the human brain, have fundamentally transformed the way complex data is processed and analyzed (Samek, Montavon, Lapuschkin, Anders, & Müller, 2021). Neural networks can surpass traditional analytical methods by uncovering subtle patterns in data, detecting anomalies that would otherwise remain unnoticed, and making accurate predictions about the health of machinery and equipment (Carvalho et al., 2019). As industries move towards more sophisticated predictive maintenance strategies, neural networks have become an indispensable tool for ensuring equipment reliability and preventing costly failures (Samek et al., 2021). However, their practical application requires a balance between technical efficiency and real-world feasibility. Below, we explore how different types of neural networks contribute to predictive maintenance, along with concrete industrial use cases demonstrating their effectiveness.

1. Detection of Complex Anomalies

One of the most important applications of neural networks in predictive maintenance is the detection of complex anomalies (Goodfellow et al., 2016). Industrial systems generate vast amounts of data from various sensors monitoring temperature, vibration, pressure, and other operational parameters (Samek et al., 2021). In many cases, these data streams contain noise, inconsistencies, or gaps that can make it difficult to identify significant deviations from normal behavior (Carvalho et al., 2019).

Real-World Application: Vibration Anomaly Detection in Manufacturing

In the automotive industry, manufacturers use deep autoencoder networks to detect anomalies in robotic assembly lines (Samek et al., 2021). For instance, a car production facility relies on robotic arms for precise welding operations. Using vibration sensors, autoencoders learn the normal vibration patterns of the robotic arms. When subtle deviations occur indicating misalignment, mechanical wear, or early-stage component failure, the system raises an alert before the defect affects production quality (Goodfellow et al., 2016). This proactive approach reduces downtime and prevents defective products from reaching the market.

2. Time Series Prediction

Another crucial application of neural networks in predictive maintenance is time series prediction (Carvalho et al., 2019). Industrial equipment and machinery often operate in environments where conditions fluctuate over time (Samek et al., 2021). For instance, an electric motor may experience variations in temperature and load during its operation, and these changes can provide valuable insights into its health (Goodfellow et al., 2016).

Real-World Application: Predicting Pump Failures in the Oil and Gas Sector

In the oil and gas industry, LSTM (Long Short-Term Memory) networks are used to analyze sensor data from oil pipeline pumps (Carvalho et al., 2019). These pumps operate under extreme pressure and temperature conditions, and failures can result in costly downtime and environmental hazards (Samek et al., 2021). By analyzing historical vibration and temperature data, an LSTM-based predictive model forecasts potential pump failures days or even weeks in advance, allowing operators to perform targeted maintenance and avoid costly shutdowns (Goodfellow et al., 2016).

3. Multidimensional Data Processing

Modern industrial equipment often generates data from multiple sensors that monitor different aspects of machine performance (Samek et al., 2021). For example, a manufacturing robot may have sensors that track temperature, vibration, pressure, and electrical consumption simultaneously (Carvalho et al., 2019). Processing and analyzing this multidimensional data requires sophisticated techniques capable of handling the complexity of multiple, potentially interrelated, data streams (Goodfellow et al., 2016).

Real-World Application: Optimizing Maintenance in Smart Grids

In power distribution networks, convolutional neural networks (CNNs) process multidimensional data from transformers to detect overheating and electrical load imbalances (Samek et al., 2021). These networks analyze sensor heatmaps, identifying areas of excessive heat buildup caused by insulation degradation or faulty connections (Carvalho et al., 2019). By proactively scheduling transformer maintenance, energy providers can prevent large-scale power failures and extend the lifespan of electrical infrastructure (Goodfellow et al., 2016).

IV. TECHNOLOGIES UNDERPINNING PREDICTIVE MAINTENANCE

Predictive maintenance (PdM) relies on an integrated set of advanced technologies to monitor, analyze, and predict the health of industrial equipment (Yang, Liu, Chen, & Tong, 2019). These technologies work together to create a proactive system for preventing equipment failures, thus reducing downtime, enhancing efficiency, and improving overall performance (Zhu, Yu, Wang, Ning, & Tang, 2020). The key technologies that underpin predictive maintenance include the Internet of Things (IoT), Artificial Intelligence (AI) and Machine Learning (ML), Big Data and Advanced Analytics, Edge Computing, and Digital Twins (Latrach, 2023). In this section, we will delve into the role of each technology and how they collectively contribute to the effectiveness of predictive maintenance. However, the reliability of sensor data plays a crucial role in determining the accuracy of predictive maintenance models (Yang et al., 2019). Sensors are responsible for collecting key operational data such as temperature, pressure, and vibration, but their effectiveness depends on factors like calibration, environmental conditions, and potential signal interference. Inaccurate or noisy sensor data can lead to false predictions, either triggering unnecessary maintenance or failing to detect an impending failure (Zhu et al., 2020). Therefore, ensuring high-quality, reliable sensor data is essential for improving predictive accuracy and optimizing maintenance strategies (Latrach, 2023).

1. Internet of Things (IoT)

The Internet of Things (IoT) is a critical enabler of predictive maintenance, providing the infrastructure to gather real-time data from industrial equipment (Yang et al., 2019). Through IoT, machines, sensors, and other physical devices are connected to intelligent networks, allowing them to collect and exchange data continuously (Zhu et al., 2020). This real-time data collection plays a crucial role in PdM by ensuring that equipment health is constantly monitored, giving organizations the ability to detect anomalies or performance deviations as they occur (Latrach, 2023). IoT devices are typically equipped with a range of sensors, such as temperature, pressure, vibration, and energy consumption sensors (Yang et al., 2019). These sensors provide a continuous stream of data that reflects the real-time operational conditions of industrial equipment (Zhu et al., 2020). For instance, in an industrial motor, vibration sensors can detect subtle irregularities that could indicate mechanical wear or misalignment (Latrach, 2023). Temperature sensors can identify overheating, while pressure sensors can detect abnormal fluctuations that might signal a potential failure.

2. Artificial Intelligence (AI) and Machine Learning (ML)

Artificial Intelligence (AI) and Machine Learning (ML) are at the heart of predictive maintenance systems, offering the necessary intelligence to interpret the data collected by IoT devices (Yang et al., 2019). AI algorithms, when combined with machine learning models, can process large volumes of data, identify patterns, and make predictions about equipment performance (Zhu et al., 2020). These technologies are essential for moving from basic data collection to actionable insights that inform maintenance decisions (Latrach, 2023). Machine learning algorithms work by learning from historical data, allowing predictive models to recognize patterns that might indicate impending failures (Yang et al., 2019). For example, an algorithm could learn that a specific vibration pattern in a motor precedes a failure by several days. Using this knowledge, the predictive model can forecast when a similar anomaly might occur in the future, allowing for timely maintenance interventions (Zhu et al., 2020).

3. Big Data and Advanced Analytics

The volume and complexity of data generated by IoT sensors in industrial environments are massive, and traditional data processing methods often struggle to handle such large-scale datasets (Yang et al., 2019). Big Data technologies provide the tools necessary to process, analyze, and extract actionable insights from these vast quantities of information (Zhu et al., 2020). In predictive maintenance, Big Data plays a crucial role in helping organizations manage and make sense of the data collected from multiple machines and sensors (Latrach, 2023). Advanced analytics techniques, such as statistical modeling, regression analysis, and machine learning algorithms, are applied to Big Data to identify trends, correlations, and patterns that may indicate potential failures (Yang et al., 2019). For example, a company might analyze data from hundreds of machines to identify common failure modes or pinpoint conditions that are most likely to lead to equipment breakdowns (Zhu et al., 2020).

4. Edge Computing

Edge computing refers to the practice of processing data closer to the source of data generation, rather than relying solely on centralized cloud systems (Yang et al., 2019). This approach is essential for industrial applications where latency must be minimal, such as in critical equipment monitoring (Zhu et al., 2020). In predictive maintenance, edge computing enables real-time data processing, allowing systems to analyze sensor data and make decisions instantaneously (Latrach, 2023). Edge computing is particularly valuable in environments where timely intervention is crucial to preventing catastrophic equipment failure (Yang et al., 2019). By processing data locally, edge computing reduces the time it takes to detect failures and respond to them, enabling a faster and more effective maintenance approach.

5. Digital Twins

A digital twin is a virtual replica of a physical asset, system, or process. It is a dynamic model that is continuously updated with real-time data from sensors and other sources, allowing it to mirror the actual behavior and condition of its physical counterpart (Yang et al., 2019). In the context of predictive maintenance, digital twins play a critical role in simulating, monitoring, and optimizing equipment performance (Zhu et al., 2020). Digital twins enable predictive maintenance systems to simulate different scenarios and evaluate the impact of various maintenance strategies (Latrach, 2023). By having a real-time virtual model of equipment, operators can test potential interventions in a safe virtual environment before applying them to the physical asset. This helps to minimize the risks associated with maintenance activities and optimize decision-making processes.

By leveraging these technologies, predictive maintenance can be more efficient, accurate, and proactive, allowing organizations to maximize asset lifespan and reduce operational risks.

V. ADVANTAGES OF NEURAL NETWORKS IN PREDICTIVE MAINTENANCE

Neural networks play a key role in enhancing the effectiveness of predictive maintenance systems. By analyzing vast amounts of data, neural networks provide several advantages:

1. **Improved Accuracy**: Neural networks can process millions of data points, allowing them to make highly accurate predictions compared to traditional methods (Zonta et al., 2020). This increased precision helps in detecting subtle anomalies that may go unnoticed by conventional algorithms (Schwendemann & Reinhart, 2020).
2. **Cost Reduction**: Targeted maintenance interventions based on accurate predictions help reduce unnecessary repairs and replacements, leading to significant cost savings (Kumar & Kumar, 2021). By focusing resources only where they are needed, companies can optimize their maintenance budgets (Zonta et al., 2020).
3. **Scalability**: Neural network-based systems can handle increasing volumes of data without a significant loss in performance (Schwendemann & Reinhart, 2020). As data grows, the models can be retrained and improved, allowing the system to scale as the organization expands (Kumar & Kumar, 2021).
4. **Anticipation of Complex Failures**: Neural networks are particularly effective at understanding non-linear interactions between various parameters (Zonta et al., 2020). This ability enables them to detect complex failures that traditional models may struggle to identify, improving overall predictive capabilities (Schwendemann & Reinhart, 2020).

By leveraging neural networks, predictive maintenance systems can become more accurate, efficient, and adaptive, allowing organizations to stay ahead of equipment issues and optimize their operations (Kumar & Kumar, 2021).

VI. CASE STUDY: POWER PLANT USING GAS TURBINES

In modern power plants, gas turbines are critical components used to generate electricity (Lee et al., 2014). These turbines operate at high temperatures and under considerable mechanical stress, making them susceptible to various types of wear and failure (Mourtzis, Doukas, & Psarommatis, 2019). The ability to predict and prevent potential issues before they cause costly downtime or damage is crucial to maintaining operational efficiency and minimizing expenses (Zonta et al., 2020).

Predictive maintenance using advanced technologies, such as neural networks, plays a pivotal role in enhancing the reliability and performance of these turbines.

This case study explores how a power plant uses a neural network-based predictive maintenance system to monitor gas turbines (Lee et al., 2014). By analyzing both historical and real-time data, the system detects early signs of potential failure, allowing operators to make informed decisions about maintenance interventions (Mourtzis et al., 2019). The case study demonstrates how a subtle increase in vibrations and temperature issues that could be overlooked by traditional maintenance methods can be identified and addressed through a cost-effective, proactive strategy (Zonta et al., 2020).

The Challenge: High-Stress Operating Conditions

Gas turbines in power plants operate under extreme conditions (Mourtzis et al., 2019). The turbines rotate at high speeds, often exceeding 10,000 RPM (revolutions per minute), while maintaining high levels of heat and mechanical stress (Zonta et al., 2020). These conditions make gas turbines prone to wear and tear over time (Lee et al., 2014). Typical failures in gas turbines include cracks in turbine blades, wear in bearings, and misalignments in critical components such as the rotor (Mourtzis et al., 2019). Any of these failures, if not detected early, can lead to catastrophic breakdowns, extended downtime, and expensive repairs.

Traditionally, power plants have relied on two main types of maintenance strategies: corrective and preventive maintenance (Lee et al., 2014). Corrective maintenance is performed after a failure has occurred, while preventive maintenance is conducted at scheduled intervals to avoid failure (Mourtzis et al., 2019). While these approaches help mitigate the risk of major breakdowns, they do not address the underlying problem of predicting failures before they happen (Zonta et al., 2020). As a result, power plants often end up performing unnecessary maintenance tasks, leading to inefficiencies and increased costs.

The introduction of predictive maintenance, particularly through the use of neural networks and advanced data analytics, represents a transformative approach (Mourtzis et al., 2019). By continuously monitoring the health of the gas turbines, predictive maintenance systems can identify early warning signs of failure, enabling operators to intervene at the optimal time, thus preventing costly failures and extending the lifespan of equipment (Zonta et al., 2020).

Data Collection and Integration with Neural Networks

To implement predictive maintenance in the power plant, a network of sensors is installed on the gas turbines to continuously monitor critical parameters (Lee et al., 2014). These sensors collect data on various variables, such as vibrations, temperature, pressure, and rotational speed (Mourtzis et al., 2019). The data is transmitted to a centralized system where it is processed and analyzed in real-time (Zonta et al., 2020).

The heart of this predictive maintenance system is a neural network, specifically designed to process and interpret the massive volumes of data generated by the sensors (Lee et al., 2014). Neural networks are machine learning algorithms that mimic the structure of the human brain, enabling them to recognize complex patterns in data and make predictions based on historical and real-time information (Mourtzis et al., 2019).

For this particular case study, the neural network is trained on both historical maintenance data (such as records of past turbine failures and repairs) and real-time sensor data from the turbines (Zonta et al., 2020). By analyzing this data, the neural network can identify subtle patterns or deviations in normal operating conditions that may signal the onset of a problem (Lee et al., 2014). These patterns might be too complex or too subtle for human operators or traditional algorithms to detect, but the neural network can spot them with a high degree of accuracy.

Detecting Subtle Anomalies: Vibration and Temperature

One of the key advantages of neural networks is their ability to detect anomalies in real-time (Lee et al., 2014). In this case study, the neural network identifies a subtle increase in vibrations and temperature in a critical component of the gas turbine (Mourtzis et al., 2019). Both vibrations and temperature are crucial indicators of the health of the turbine (Zonta et al., 2020).

In a gas turbine, excessive vibrations can be caused by a variety of factors, including imbalance in the rotor, bearing wear, or misalignment of the components (Lee et al., 2014). If left unchecked, these vibrations can lead to severe damage, such as cracks in the turbine blades or failure of critical components like the bearings or rotor (Mourtzis et al., 2019). Similarly, an increase in temperature can indicate overheating, which may be caused by inefficient cooling, excessive friction, or other operational issues (Zonta et al., 2020). Monitoring these parameters is essential for early detection of potential failures.

Preventive Maintenance Intervention: Rotor Realignment

Once the neural network detects an anomaly in the turbine's vibration and temperature data, the next step is to conduct a detailed analysis to determine the root cause of the issue (Mourtzis et al., 2019). Unlike traditional maintenance strategies, where equipment may be unnecessarily shut down for inspection or replacement, predictive maintenance focuses on diagnosing the issue with precision and accuracy (Zonta et al., 2020).

In this case, the predictive maintenance system performs a deep analysis of the vibration and temperature patterns (Lee et al., 2014). The data suggests that the increase in vibration and temperature is not due to a catastrophic failure, such as a broken rotor blade, but rather a misalignment of the rotor (Mourtzis et al., 2019). Rotor misalignment is a common issue in gas turbines, especially in high-stress operating conditions (Zonta et al., 2020). It occurs when the rotor components become slightly displaced from their optimal position, leading to vibrations and increased friction, which in turn raises the temperature of the turbine (Lee et al., 2014).

By identifying rotor misalignment as the root cause of the issue, the predictive maintenance system recommends a targeted intervention—rotor realignment (Mourtzis et al., 2019). Rather than performing a complete replacement of turbine components or taking the turbine offline for an extended period, rotor realignment is a more cost-effective and less disruptive solution (Zonta et al., 2020).

Cost Savings and Reduced Downtime

The decision to realign the rotor, rather than replace it entirely, offers several key benefits (Lee et al., 2014). First, it significantly reduces the cost of maintenance (Mourtzis et al., 2019). Replacing turbine components, especially in gas turbines that operate at high temperatures and pressures, can be extremely expensive (Zonta et al., 2020). The cost of a full replacement includes not only the cost of the new parts but also the labor costs and the time required to perform the replacement, which can lead to significant downtime.

By preventing a full-scale failure and avoiding unnecessary component replacements, the predictive maintenance system helps the power plant save money while keeping the turbine running at peak efficiency (Mourtzis et al., 2019). The intervention also reduces the risk of prolonged downtime, which can be costly in terms of both lost revenue and the potential damage to other components in the turbine (Zonta et al., 2020).

Long-Term Benefits and Improved Reliability

The use of predictive maintenance and neural networks to monitor the health of gas turbines offers long-term benefits beyond immediate cost savings and reduced downtime (Lee et al., 2014). One of the key advantages of predictive maintenance is that it extends the lifespan of equipment (Mourtzis et al., 2019). By detecting issues early and intervening before they lead to catastrophic failures, predictive maintenance helps keep turbines running smoothly for longer, thus delaying the need for expensive replacements or major repairs (Zonta et al., 2020).

This case study illustrates the effectiveness of predictive maintenance in a power plant setting, particularly when using neural networks to monitor gas turbines (Zonta et al., 2020).

VII. IMPLEMENTATION CHALLENGES

While predictive maintenance based on neural networks offers substantial benefits in terms of efficiency, cost savings, and operational optimization, its implementation comes with several challenges that need to be carefully addressed (Schwendemann & Reinhart, 2020). These challenges can range from financial and technical hurdles to concerns about cybersecurity and data privacy (Kumar & Kumar, 2021). Despite its undeniable advantages, the successful deployment of predictive maintenance systems requires overcoming these obstacles to ensure that the technology is used effectively and sustainably (Zonta et al., 2020). Below, we explore in more detail the primary challenges encountered during the implementation of predictive maintenance systems based on neural networks.

1. High Initial Cost

One of the most significant challenges of implementing predictive maintenance systems is the high initial cost (Susto et al., 2015). The setup for a predictive maintenance program, particularly one that incorporates advanced technologies like Internet of Things (IoT) sensors, artificial intelligence (AI), and machine learning models, requires substantial financial investment (Zhu et al., 2020). IoT sensors must be installed on all critical machinery to collect real-time data, which includes monitoring factors like temperature, vibrations, pressure, and energy consumption (Jardine, Lin, & Banjevic, 2006). These sensors can be expensive, especially for large-scale operations where the number of machines needing to be monitored is substantial.

Additionally, AI solutions, including neural networks, demand considerable computational power (Menasria, Baouche, & Ait Kaci Azzou, 2024). The hardware required to support machine learning algorithms, such as high-performance servers, cloud storage, and advanced analytics platforms, also contributes to the cost (Smith, 2022). Small and medium-sized enterprises (SMEs), in particular, may struggle to justify the upfront expenditure needed for these systems (Zonta et al., 2020). The expense of both the technology and the required infrastructure, along with the costs for ongoing maintenance, can create a significant barrier for businesses that lack the resources or financial flexibility to make such an investment.

2. Required Technical Expertise

Another significant challenge in implementing predictive maintenance systems lies in the technical expertise required to deploy and manage AI models effectively (Schwendemann & Reinhart, 2020). Predictive maintenance systems that rely on neural networks and machine learning demand expertise in data science, machine learning, engineering, and systems integration (Zonta et al., 2020). The deployment of AI models involves several complex stages, from data collection and preprocessing to the training of machine learning models and their integration into existing infrastructure (Zhu et al., 2020).

Data scientists and engineers must work together to ensure that the sensors installed on the equipment collect accurate, relevant, and high-quality data (Menasria et al., 2024). This data is essential for training the machine learning models that will be used for predictive maintenance (Smith, 2022). Any issues with data collection, such as insufficient data, noisy data, or errors in data labeling, can hinder the training process and lead to inaccurate predictions (Zonta et al., 2020).

3. Cybersecurity Issues

Cybersecurity is another critical challenge associated with the implementation of predictive maintenance systems (Kumar & Kumar, 2021). Predictive maintenance relies on the continuous collection and analysis of real-time data, much of which is generated by sensors embedded in equipment across various operational systems (Susto et al., 2015). This data often includes sensitive and proprietary information, making both cybersecurity and data privacy key concerns (Jardine et al., 2006). As a result, predictive maintenance systems can be prime targets for cyberattacks.

If a cybercriminal gains access to the system, they could manipulate the data, alter predictive models, or even disrupt the operations of critical equipment (Smith, 2022). For example, attackers might intentionally create faulty data to mislead predictive maintenance algorithms, causing operators to make incorrect maintenance decisions or even disable safety protocols (Zonta et al., 2020). In extreme cases, a cyberattack on the predictive maintenance system could lead to catastrophic equipment failure or production downtime, which could be extremely costly for the company involved (Zhu et al., 2020).

4. Data Quality and Integration

The effectiveness of predictive maintenance models depends on the quality of the data they receive (Schwendemann & Reinhart, 2020). Noisy, incomplete, or inaccurate data can lead to poor predictions and ineffective maintenance decisions (Kumar & Kumar, 2021). Ensuring that sensors provide reliable and consistent data is a challenge, especially in harsh environments where interference and sensor drift may occur (Zonta et al., 2020).

Moreover, integrating predictive maintenance into existing enterprise systems is complex due to differences in data formats, protocols, and technologies (Susto et al., 2015). Data preprocessing techniques, such as filtering and normalization, help improve data quality, while data fusion methods enhance predictive accuracy (Zhu et al., 2020). However, these require specialized expertise, reinforcing the need for a structured approach to implementation (Menasria et al., 2024).

5. Ethical and Legal Considerations

The implementation of predictive maintenance raises important ethical and legal concerns, particularly regarding data privacy, regulatory compliance, and AI biases (Menasria et al., 2024).

- **Data Privacy & Security**: Predictive maintenance systems collect large amounts of operational data, requiring strict compliance with data protection laws (e.g., GDPR, CCPA) to ensure secure storage and prevent unauthorized access (Smith, 2022).
- **Regulatory Compliance**: Industries such as aviation, healthcare, and energy have strict regulations on data usage and maintenance records, requiring companies to align with industry standards to avoid legal risks (Zonta et al., 2020).
- **AI Ethics & Bias**: Machine learning models can introduce biases if trained on incomplete data, leading to false predictions and operational inefficiencies (Kumar & Kumar, 2021). Ensuring model transparency and regular audits is key to maintaining reliability (Zhu et al., 2020).

Addressing these challenges ensures a responsible and legally compliant deployment of predictive maintenance systems (Menasria et al., 2024).

VIII. FUTURE PERSPECTIVES: TRANSFORMING PREDICTIVE MAINTENANCE WITH EMERGING TECHNOLOGIES

The future of predictive maintenance is bright, driven by ongoing advancements in neural networks, the Internet of Things (IoT), and other emerging technologies (Yang et al., 2019). As industries increasingly adopt predictive maintenance strategies, innovations in these areas will continue to evolve, offering even more powerful tools to improve operational efficiency, reduce costs, and enhance the overall performance of industrial systems (Zhu et al., 2020). The convergence of multiple technologies promises to revolutionize asset management, paving the way for smarter, more resilient industrial environments (Latrach, 2023).

In this section, we explore several key trends and innovations that are set to shape the future of predictive maintenance, from hybrid neural networks and the rise of 5G connectivity to next-generation sensors and the integration of digital twins.

1. Industry Challenges and Future Research Directions

While predictive maintenance has seen significant advancements with the integration of AI, IoT, and big data, current industry practices still face several limitations (Yang et al., 2019). Many organizations continue to rely on reactive or rule-based maintenance strategies, failing to fully leverage the potential of deep learning and real-time analytics (Zhu et al., 2020). Additionally, data silos and proprietary systems hinder interoperability, making it difficult to develop standardized, cross-industry solutions (Latrach, 2023). Another persistent challenge is the lack of trust in AI-driven decisions, as many companies require human validation before acting on predictive insights, reducing the efficiency of automated maintenance processes (Shokry & Moulines, 2021).

To overcome these barriers, future research should focus on several key areas. Federated learning could address data privacy concerns while enabling cross-industry collaboration without compromising sensitive information (Yang et al., 2019). Research into explainable AI (XAI) could help improve trust in machine learning models by providing clearer justifications for predictive maintenance decisions (Zhu et al., 2020). Additionally, advancements in self-healing systems, where AI not only predicts failures but also triggers automated corrective actions, could further enhance the efficiency of industrial operations (Latrach, 2023).

By addressing these challenges through focused research and innovation, the industry can move towards a truly intelligent, automated, and interconnected predictive maintenance ecosystem, better aligned with the principles of Industry 4.0.

2. Hybrid Neural Networks: The Future of Complex Data Analysis

Neural networks have already made significant strides in predictive maintenance by enabling systems to learn from large volumes of historical and real-time data (Yang et al., 2019). However, as industrial environments become increasingly complex, the need for more sophisticated models becomes apparent (Zhu et al., 2020). One promising development is the rise of hybrid neural networks, which combine different neural network architectures to achieve even greater precision and efficiency in analyzing complex systems (Latrach, 2023).

Hybrid models integrate the strengths of multiple types of neural networks, such as Convolutional Neural Networks (CNNs), Recurrent Neural Networks (RNNs), and Graph Neural Networks (GNNs) (Yang et al., 2019). Each of these architectures excels in different aspects of data processing:

- **CNNs** process sensor data that can be represented as heatmaps or images, such as thermal images or vibration signatures.
- **RNNs (including LSTM networks)** analyze time-series data, where temporal relationships are crucial for predicting future trends.
- **GNNs** help model interactions between components in networked industrial systems, offering insights into dependencies and system behavior (Zhu et al., 2020).

By combining these architectures, hybrid neural networks allow for multi-dimensional analysis, considering spatial, temporal, and relational aspects of data simultaneously (Latrach, 2023). This capability is particularly valuable for industries like manufacturing, aerospace, and energy, where systems are highly complex and interactions between components are intricate (Yang et al., 2019).

3. 5G and Enhanced IoT: Real-Time, Large-Scale Connectivity

The continued rollout of 5G networks will have a transformative impact on predictive maintenance, particularly in terms of connectivity and data transmission (Yang et al., 2019). The increased speed and reduced latency offered by 5G will unlock new possibilities for IoT-based systems, enabling real-time data collection and analysis on an unprecedented scale (Zhu et al., 2020).

One of the key challenges in current IoT systems is the latency involved in transmitting data from sensors to centralized processing systems (Latrach, 2023). In many industrial applications, near-instantaneous data analysis is critical. With 5G, the speed at which data can be transmitted and processed will be dramatically improved, allowing for faster responses to potential issues (Yang et al., 2019).

For predictive maintenance, this means that sensor data can be transmitted to AI models in real-time, allowing for immediate anomaly detection and intervention (Zhu et al., 2020). This reduction in latency will enable more timely and accurate predictions of equipment failure, allowing operators to take action before a breakdown occurs (Latrach, 2023).

4. Next-Generation Sensors: Enabling Richer Data for More Accurate Predictions

As predictive maintenance relies heavily on sensor data to make accurate predictions, the development of next-generation sensors is crucial to enhancing the accuracy and effectiveness of these systems (Yang et al., 2019). Traditional sensors, while effective for basic monitoring, often fall short when it comes to providing the level of detail needed for advanced predictive analytics (Zhu et al., 2020).

Next-generation sensors will be smarter, more sensitive, and capable of capturing more complex data. Multimodal sensors that combine multiple sensing technologies (e.g., temperature, pressure, vibration, and sound) will provide more comprehensive data, enabling predictive maintenance models to detect problems at an earlier stage (Latrach, 2023).

5. Digital Twins: Revolutionizing Asset Management

One of the most promising innovations on the horizon is the integration of digital twins into predictive maintenance systems. A digital twin is a virtual replica of a physical asset or system, created using real-time data and simulations (Yang et al., 2019). These digital replicas enable businesses to simulate different scenarios, predict how equipment will behave under various conditions, and test potential interventions before applying them to the physical asset.

The convergence of digital twins and predictive maintenance will revolutionize asset management by providing companies with a comprehensive, dynamic view of their assets. For example, by simulating the performance of equipment in a virtual environment, businesses can identify potential failure points, optimize maintenance schedules, and test different maintenance strategies without the need to take the equipment offline (Zhu et al., 2020). This will significantly reduce downtime and improve operational efficiency.

6. CONCLUSION

The future of predictive maintenance is marked by an exciting confluence of advanced technologies that will transform how industries manage and maintain their critical assets. Hybrid neural networks, 5G-enhanced IoT connectivity, next-generation sensors, and digital twins are set to revolutionize the way predictive maintenance is implemented, offering more accurate predictions, faster responses, and greater operational efficiency.

As these technologies mature and become more integrated, they will usher in a new era of predictive maintenance, redefining industrial asset management. Businesses will be able to stay ahead of potential failures, optimize their operations, and remain competitive in a rapidly evolving marketplace. The convergence of AI, IoT, and other cutting-edge technologies will empower industries to operate more efficiently, sustainably, and cost-effectively, making this transformation inevitable.

IX. General Conclusion

The integration of neural networks and other advanced technologies into predictive maintenance represents a transformative shift in asset management and maintenance strategies. As a core component of Industry 4.0, predictive maintenance leverages innovations such as IoT, artificial intelligence, machine learning, and big data analytics to monitor, predict, and prevent equipment failures before they occur. This proactive approach improves operational efficiency, reduces downtime, and leads to significant cost savings and enhanced productivity.

Despite its advantages, adopting predictive maintenance comes with challenges. Initial investments in IoT sensors, AI models, and infrastructure can be considerable, especially for smaller businesses with limited resources. Deploying these solutions also requires a skilled workforce with expertise in data science, machine learning, and systems engineering. Without the right technical knowledge, companies may struggle to unlock the full potential of predictive maintenance, making it essential to invest in training or collaborate with external experts.

Cybersecurity is another major challenge. The sensitive data generated by IoT sensors and analyzed by AI models can be vulnerable to cyberattacks. Given the critical nature of the assets monitored, robust security protocols are crucial to protect data integrity. A cyberattack could compromise maintenance operations, cause system downtime, and lead to financial losses.

Despite these hurdles, the long-term benefits of predictive maintenance make it an essential solution for companies striving to stay competitive in an increasingly digitalized environment. Predicting failures before they occur and scheduling maintenance only when necessary reduces costs compared to reactive maintenance. By shifting away from corrective strategies, businesses can optimize resources, minimize waste, and improve profitability.

Predictive maintenance also enhances safety by detecting issues before they escalate into critical failures, preventing hazardous accidents and minimizing environmental risks. This proactive approach strengthens safety protocols, improves compliance with industry standards, and enhances an organization's reputation.

Moreover, predictive maintenance helps extend the lifespan of equipment. By continuously monitoring asset health and addressing problems early, businesses can optimize machinery performance and avoid costly replacements. This leads to financial savings and reduces the environmental impact associated with manufacturing and disposal.

In conclusion, while implementing predictive maintenance powered by neural networks and advanced technologies requires significant investment and overcoming technical challenges, the long-term benefits outweigh the costs. Predictive maintenance enhances productivity, reduces operational expenses, and promotes safety and sustainability. As industries embrace digital transformation, predictive maintenance will play a pivotal role in shaping the future of asset management, offering companies a competitive advantage in an increasingly complex and fast-paced global market.

X. Example of a flowchart for implementing a predictive maintenance system

Here's an example of a flowchart for implementing a predictive maintenance system using neural networks in Python, based on keywords like "neural networks," "predictive maintenance," and "historical failure data." The steps are as follows:

Steps:

1. **Start**
2. **Read Historical Failure Data** (sensor readings, timestamps, failure labels).
3. **Preprocess the Data**:
    - o Handle missing values.
    - o Normalize or scale the data.
4. **Initialize the Neural Network Model**.
5. **Train the Model**:
    - o Perform a loop to update weights during training.
    - o Check: "Is Training Complete?"
        - ■ If No, continue training.
        - ■ If Yes, evaluate the model.
6. **Evaluate Model Performance**:
    - o Test the model on unseen data.

- o Generate performance metrics.

7. **Check Model Performance**:
   - o If satisfactory, save the model.
   - o If not, adjust parameters and retrain.
8. **Use the Model for Predictions**:
   - o Load real-time sensor data.
   - o Predict failures and trigger alerts if necessary.
9. **End**

Python Implementation

```
import numpy as np

import pandas as pd

from sklearn.model_selection import train_test_split

from sklearn.preprocessing import StandardScaler

from keras.models import Sequential

from keras.layers import Dense

from keras.optimizers import Adam

# Step 2: Load Historical Data

data = pd.read_csv("historical_failure_data.csv")  # Example
CSV file containing historical data
```

```
# Step 3: Preprocess the Data

# Handle missing values

data = data.fillna(method='ffill')

# Normalize the data

scaler = StandardScaler()

X = data.drop('failure_label', axis=1)  # Features

y = data['failure_label']  # Labels

X_scaled = scaler.fit_transform(X)

# Step 4: Initialize the Neural Network Model

model = Sequential()

# Add layers to the model (input layer, hidden layers, and
output layer)

model.add(Dense(64, input_dim=X_scaled.shape[1], activa-
tion='relu'))

model.add(Dense(32, activation='relu'))
```

```
model.add(Dense(1, activation='sigmoid'))  # Sigmoid for bi-
nary classification

# Step 5: Compile the model with Adam optimizer

model.compile(loss='binary_crossentropy', optimizer=Adam(),
metrics=['accuracy'])

# Step 6: Split the data into training and testing sets

X_train, X_test, y_train, y_test = train_test_split(X_
scaled, y, test_size=0.2, random_state=42)

# Step 7: Train the model

history = model.fit(X_train, y_train, epochs=50, batch_
size=32, validation_data=(X_test, y_test))

# Step 8: Evaluate Model Performance

loss, accuracy = model.evaluate(X_test, y_test)

print(f"Loss: {loss}, Accuracy: {accuracy}")

# Check Model Performance

if accuracy > 0.85:  # Example threshold for satisfactory
performance
```

```
        print("Model is satisfactory, saving the model.")

        model.save('predictive_maintenance_model.h5')

    else:

        print("Model performance is not satisfactory, parameter adjustment needed.")

    # Step 9: Use the Model for Real-Time Predictions

    # Example with new (real) sensor data

    new_sensor_data = np.array([[1.2, 3.4, 0.5, 6.7]])  # Example sensor data

    new_sensor_data_scaled = scaler.transform(new_sensor_data)  # Normalize new data

    predicted_failure = model.predict(new_sensor_data_scaled)

    if predicted_failure[0] > 0.5:

        print("Alert: Imminent failure detected.")

    else:

        print("All normal, no failure detected.")
```

```
# Step 10: End
```

Explanation of the Implementation:

1. **Loading Historical Data**: We begin by loading the historical data, which contains sensor information and failure labels. This data is then cleaned and normalized to be ready for use in the neural network model.
2. **Data Preprocessing**: Missing values are handled, and the data is normalized to ensure the model processes it correctly.
3. **Model Initialization and Training**: A neural network model is initialized with dense layers and a ReLU activation function. We use the Adam optimizer for training and binary cross-entropy loss for classification.
4. **Model Evaluation and Saving**: After training, we evaluate the model's performance using a test set. If the model achieves satisfactory performance (for example, an accuracy greater than 85%), it is saved for future use.
5. **Real-Time Predictions**: Finally, the model is used to predict failures based on new sensor data. If a failure is predicted, an alert is generated.

This example demonstrates how to implement a predictive maintenance system using a neural network with both historical data and real-time sensor inputs. Based on the model's predictions, appropriate maintenance actions can be taken. For example, if the model predicts a failure, maintenance can be scheduled to prevent downtime.

REFERENCES

Benziane, S. (2024). *Innovating prosperity: Intelligent approaches*. IGI Global. DOI: 10.4018/979-8-3693-1418-0.ch009

Carvalho, T. P., Soares, F. A. A. M., Vita, R., Francisco, R. P., Basto, J. P., & Alcalá, S. G. (2019). A systematic literature review of machine learning methods applied to predictive maintenance. *Computers & Industrial Engineering*, *137*, 106024. DOI: 10.1016/j.cie.2019.106024

Goodfellow, I., Bengio, Y., & Courville, A. (2016). *Deep learning*. MIT Press.

Hurtado, J., Salvati, D., Semola, R., Bosio, M., & Lomonaco, V. (2023). Continual learning for predictive maintenance: Overview and challenges. *Intelligent Systems with Applications*, *19*, 200251. DOI: 10.1016/j.iswa.2023.200251

Jardine, A. K. S., Lin, D., & Banjevic, D. (2006). A review on machinery diagnostics and prognostics implementing condition-based maintenance. *Mechanical Systems and Signal Processing*, *20*(7), 1483–1510. DOI: 10.1016/j.ymssp.2005.09.012

Kumar, P., & Kumar, N. (2021). A predictive maintenance framework using LSTM and big data technologies for Industry 4.0. *Procedia Computer Science*, *184*, 444–451.

Latrach, A. (2023). Application of deep learning for predictive maintenance of oilfield equipment. *arXiv preprint arXiv:2306.11040*.

Lee, J., Bagheri, B., & Kao, H. A. (2015). A cyber-physical systems architecture for Industry 4.0-based manufacturing systems. *Manufacturing Letters*, *3*, 18–23. DOI: 10.1016/j.mfglet.2014.12.001

Lee, J., Wu, F., Zhao, W., Ghaffari, M., Liao, L., & Siegel, D. (2014). Prognostics and health management design for rotary machinery systems—Reviews, methodology and applications. *Mechanical Systems and Signal Processing*, *42*(1-2), 314–334. DOI: 10.1016/j.ymssp.2013.06.004

Lei, Y., Li, N., Guo, L., Li, N., Yan, T., & Lin, J. (2018). Machinery health prognostics: A systematic review. *Mechanical Systems and Signal Processing*, *104*, 799–834. DOI: 10.1016/j.ymssp.2017.11.016

Ma, S., Flanigan, K. A., & Bergés, M. (2024). State-of-the-art review: The use of digital twins to support artificial intelligence-guided predictive maintenance. *arXiv preprint arXiv:2406.13117*.

Menasria, M., Baouche, A., & Ait Kaci Azzou, S. (2024). *La maintenance prédictive des machines de l'industrie 4.0*. Mémoire de Master, Université de Bejaia.

Mobley, R. K. (2002). *An introduction to predictive maintenance*. Butterworth-Heinemann.

Monostori, L., Kádár, B., Bauernhansl, T., Kondoh, S., Kumara, S., Reinhart, G., Sauer, O., Schuh, G., Sihn, W., & Ueda, K. (2016). Cyber-physical systems in manufacturing. *CIRP Annals, 65*(2), 621–641. DOI: 10.1016/j.cirp.2016.06.005

Mourtzis, D., Doukas, M., & Psarommatis, F. (2019). A continuous improvement methodology for the assembly process using industrial Internet of Things (IIoT) data. *Procedia CIRP*, *81*, 797–802.

Samek, W., Montavon, G., Lapuschkin, S., Anders, C. J., & Müller, K. R. (2021). Explaining deep neural networks and beyond: A review of explainable AI methods. *Proceedings of the IEEE, 109*(3), 247–278. DOI: 10.1109/JPROC.2021.3060483

Schwendemann, S., & Reinhart, G. (2020). Predictive maintenance planning: A literature review and research agenda. *Procedia CIRP*, *93*, 1137–1142.

Shah, S. S., Daoliang, T., & Chandan Kumar, S. (2024). RUL forecasting for wind turbine predictive maintenance based on deep learning. *arXiv preprint arXiv:2412.17823.*

Shokry, A., & Moulines, É. (2021). *Le machine learning au service de la maintenance prédictive*. FX-Conseil, École Polytechnique.

Smith, M. (2022). Machine learning techniques for predictive maintenance in industrial IoT. *Information Sciences and Technological Innovations*, *4*(2), 33.

Susto, G. A., Schirru, A., Pampuri, S., McLoone, S., & Beghi, A. (2015). Machine learning for predictive maintenance: A multiple classifier approach. *IEEE Transactions on Industrial Informatics*, *11*(3), 812–820. DOI: 10.1109/TII.2014.2349359

Wang, X., Han, Y., & Zhang, H. (2018). A review of data-driven predictive maintenance: Methods, cases, and future directions. *IEEE Transactions on Industrial Informatics*, *14*(1), 24–35.

Wuest, T., Weimer, D., Irgens, C., & Thoben, K.-D. (2016). Machine learning in manufacturing: Advantages, challenges, and applications. *Production & Manufacturing Research*, *4*(1), 23–45. DOI: 10.1080/21693277.2016.1192517

Yang, Q., Liu, Y., Chen, T., & Tong, Y. (2019). Federated machine learning: Concept and applications. [TIST]. *ACM Transactions on Intelligent Systems and Technology*, *10*(2), 1–19. DOI: 10.1145/3298981

Zhang, W., Yang, D., & Wang, H. (2019). Data-driven methods for predictive maintenance of industrial equipment: A survey. *IEEE Systems Journal*, *13*(3), 2213–2227. DOI: 10.1109/JSYST.2019.2905565

Zhao, R., Wang, D., Yan, R., Mao, K., Shen, F., & Wang, J. (2019). Machine health monitoring using local feature-based gated recurrent unit networks. *IEEE Transactions on Industrial Electronics*, *66*(6), 4944–4953.

Zhu, H., Yu, F. R., Wang, Y., Ning, B., & Tang, T. (2020). Big data analytics in intelligent transportation systems: A survey. *IEEE Transactions on Intelligent Transportation Systems*, *21*(2), 383–398.

Zonta, T., da Costa, C. A., da Rosa Righi, R., de Lima, M. J., da Trindade, E. S., & Li, G. P. (2020). Predictive maintenance in the industry 4.0: A systematic literature review. *Computers & Industrial Engineering*, *150*, 106889. DOI: 10.1016/j.cie.2020.106889

ADDITIONAL READING

Cummins, L., Sommers, A., Ramezani, S. B., Mittal, S., Jabour, J., Seale, M., & Rahimi, S. (2024). Explainable predictive maintenance: A survey of current methods, challenges and opportunities. arXiv preprint arXiv:2401.07871.

Mansour, A. (2017). Predictive maintenance, a real differentiator? ICTjournal.

Chapter 8
Neural Networks in Predictive Analytics for the IIoT Systems

Maryna Kolisnyk
https://orcid.org/0000-0002-6264-8705
National Aerospace University "KhAI", Ukraine

Axel Jantsch
TU Wien, Austria

ABSTRACT

The Industrial Internet of Things (IIoT) is a complex system that consists of many components, each of which is exposed to the risk of fault and failure of both hardware and software (SW) due to various reasons (cyber-attacks on vulnerabilities, different types of defects, etc.). The application of predictive analytics based on Artificial Intelligence (AI) techniques in particular neural networks to complex systems such as IIoT will not only allow us to quickly and accurately identify the nature and location of faults, but also to predict them in the future by applying classification and regression techniques. In this section, a detailed analysis, systematisation and categorisation of AI methods: machine learning and deep learning methods, neural networks and their activation functions in implementing AI-based predictive analytics (PA) for IIoT systems and their components has been carried out. This study will help in the development of PA methods for IIoT systems, researchers in the field of and manufacturers of SW for PA realisation.

DOI: 10.4018/979-8-3373-4571-0.ch008

Copyright © 2025, IGI Global Scientific Publishing. Copying or distributing in print or electronic forms without written permission of IGI Global Scientific Publishing is prohibited.

INTRODUCTION

The production process on any automated production line requires continuous attention from the operator to monitor the operating parameters of the equipment, the parameters of the resulting product, and to adjust the equipment settings if the parameters deviate from the specified standards. If you collect and process historically accumulated data, take streaming data from sensors and build a model of their change using Neural Networks (NN), you can not only monitor production, but also predict events (failures and faults of hardware (HW) and software (SW) of the Industrial Internet of Things (IIoT) system and its subsystems, cyber-attacks on IIoT subsystems). The task of Predictive Analytics (PA) is not to exclude the operator from the production process, but to help him in solving routine tasks and neutralise the negative impact of the "human factor" (GE Vernova, 2025) (GE, 2024), (Siemens, n.d.).

There are some definitions for the term "Internet of Things". According to standard (ISO/IEC, 2022a): "internet of things (IoT) is the infrastructure of interconnected entities, people, systems and information resources together with services that process and react to information from the physical world and virtual world" (ISO/IEC TR 24029-1:2021, 2021).

"IoT system is a system providing functionalities of IoT. Note 1 to entry: An IoT system can include, but not be limited to, IoT devices, IoT gateways, sensors and actuators" (ISO/IEC 20924:2021, 2021).

"IoT device is an entity of an IoT system that interacts and communicates with the physical world through sensing or actuating. Note 1 to entry: An IoT device can be a sensor or an actuator" (ISO/IEC 20924:2021, 2021; ISO/IEC, 2014).

Industrial Internet of Things – the sensors, instruments, machines, and other devices that are networked together and use Internet connectivity to enhance industrial and manufacturing business processes and applications (ISO/IEC, 2014; Kolisnyk & Jantsch, 2024; Buyya & Dastjerdi, 2016; Minerva et al., 2015).

In manufacturing, when an asset fails, every minute lost is costly. When equipment fails, it reduces profitability in a variety of ways, including production downtime, higher labor costs per unit of output, and additional strain on equipment.

Industrial analytics (Diab et al., 2017; GE Vernova, 2025; GE, n.d.; IBM, 2020; IBM, 2024a; Tucci, 2024; Siemens, n.d.) is used to identify and recognise machine operating patterns and behaviour, make quick and accurate predictions, and help you make better decisions with more confidence. Industrial analytics takes into account statistical data and various factors that influence the normal functioning of IIoT subsystems.For IIoT systems industrial analytics is very important. The use of AI-based methods to predict the possible faults and failures of IIoT subsystems, to classify the type of defects and failures gives the possibility to decrease the delays in functioning of IIoT system.

BACKGROUND

Analytics can be broadly defined as the discipline that transforms data into information through systematic analysis, where new information patterns are identified and analysed to enable the assessment of industrial systems under different conditions.

Industrial analytics can also optimise IIoT system tasks and maintenance (Minerva et al., 2015). This is accomplished by predictive maintenance, which allows maintenance to be planned based on the component's life and usage characteristics rather than on a predetermined schedule. Sensor and machine performance data is analysed to predict the likelihood of certain faults and failures of IIoT subsystems over a given period.

There are three main categories of analytics (Tucci, 2024), (Minerva et al., 2015):

· **Descriptive analytics** - provides insight into historical or current data flows, including for condition and usage monitoring, reporting, anomaly detection and diagnosis, model building, or training.
· **Predictive analytics** - determines expected behaviour or results based on predictive modelling using statistical and machine learning methods to predict wear and tear of components and systems, various anomalies, cyberattacks. For IIoT systems, ML and DL provide new approaches to build complex models of a system or systems using a data-driven approach. Instead of using physical models of systems to describe behaviour, ML and DL systems contain algorithms that can infer the function of the model based on sampled input data. These models are then used to predict the state of the system.
· **Prescriptive analytics** uses the results of predictive analytics to guide recommendations for operational changes to optimise processes and prevent failures and associated downtime.
· **Data analytics** is generally divided into four main types: descriptive analytics, diagnostic analytics, predictive analytics, and prescriptive analytics. The fifth type, real-time analytics, analyses data as it is generated, collected, or updated.
· **Descriptive analytics** is a type of data analytics that examines past data to provide insight into what happened. Results are presented in the form of reports, dashboards, histograms, as pie and bar charts, line graphs, tables, or generated narratives and other visualisations. Can be used on its own or considered as a preliminary step in data processing to create a summary or abstraction, which

in turn supports further investigation, analysis, or actions performed by other types of analytics.

· **PA** enables you to gain a business advantage in managing reliability, cyber-security, risk, inventory, workforce, and many other aspects of your business (IBM, 2024a).

Advantages (Diab et al., 2017) (GE Vernova, 2025) (GE, 2024), (IBM, 2020) (IBM, 2024a), (Tucci, 2024), (Siemens, n.d.):

- **Safety**. The combination of automation and PA in IIoT systems improves security. Certain patterns associated with suspicious and unusual behaviour by end users may trigger certain security procedures.

    · **Resiliency:** reducing risks in IIoT systems (risks of faults and failures, downtime, successful cyber-attacks, etc). Traditional risk assessment and control failure detection mechanisms may not be effective enough to prevent control failures, cyber-attacks and fraud. The use of AI algorithms is proposed to deliver proactive risk warnings.

    · **Operational efficiency**: determining the maintenance strategy, the number of spare standard items to be replaced, etc.

    · **Improved decision-making**: PA can inform the decision-making process and offer a competitive advantage.

    · **Basic analytics** detect abnormal behaviour of an asset within milliseconds of the actual event. The statistics used to perform these analytics are typically local to the device in question and are based on data collected while it was operating normally.

FOCUS OF THE ARTICLE

Diagnostic analysis to identify the root cause of an anomaly requires prior knowledge of the fault conditions. Diagnostic results can be returned within minutes.

Analytics results can be automatically applied to machines and systems or used to support human decisions by visualising the results of the analysis to improve human understanding and build confidence in the decision.

Analytics deployment typically consists of three stages:

· train a (predictive) analytics model;
· test and validate the model on previously unknown data;
· deploy a model to predict real (streaming) data.

Training and deploying analytical models can be divided into the following three workflows (Haykin, 2007):

1. model training and model deployment (or inference) are performed in the cloud;
2. the model is trained in the cloud, and the model is deployed at the EDGE;
3. the model is trained and deployed at the EDGE.

The creation of complex IIoT systems involves the use of a large number of diverse systems and devices connected to a network (local, distributed and with access to the global Internet) and a large number of information transfer technologies. IIoT includes many components: sensors, programmable logic controllers (PLCs), servers, routers (IIoT gateways), switches and sensor network coordinators, CNC machines, SW, etc. (Diab et al., 2017) (GE Vernova, 2025) (GE, 2024), (IBM, 2020) (IBM, 2024a), (Tucci, 2024), (Siemens, n.d.). The emergence of new systems, such as the IIoT system, which includes a large number of unreliable subsystems, created from unreliable elements, different types of data transmission technologies, both wired and wireless, and fiber-optic data transmission, requires new scientific approaches for evaluation and assurance reliability, resiliency, cybersecurity, dependability (cybersecurity and reliability), safety of IIoT system and its subsystems.

IIoT is a network of automated and user devices, which are complex HW and SW subsystems, in an enterprise that allows personnel to solve their business tasks using the latest technological capabilities in real time, continuously 24/7. These subsystems can have defects that can lead to both HW and SW failures and faults. Network nodes are able to receive and transmit information; can interact with other objects or be independent; may have different levels of access to their settings depending on the level of security, etc. IIoT devices operate continuously and can be used by attackers at any time to carry out malicious activities.

Given the variety of HW, SW, data transmission technologies and the amount of information that circulates and is processed in the IIoT system, the task of assessing and predicting the technical state, failures, malfunctions, cyber-attacks of this system and its subsystems is very complex and urgent. Its solution requires the use of Artificial Intelligence (AI) algorithms, NN and implementation of PA on their basis. Anomalies (threats, defects, faults, failures, cyber-attacks) give risks for the IIoT system functioning and anomaly detection is an important challenge for IIoT systems in product quality assurance control. Whether the solutions are rule-based, constraint-based or artificial intelligence-enabled, the faster and more completely anomalies are detected, the fewer errors, production defects, machine downtime and wear and tear there will be. With AI-based systems, machine builders can automate the process of detecting anomalies in their machines and provide their customers with greater system efficiency, dependability, resiliency, reliability, and cybersecurity.

Intelligent sensors collect real-time data about each individual system component in the IIoT systems and analyse them and record them, after which AI-based models are created. These models detect equipment defects and wear, non-compliance with scientific and technical documentation (including the use of Machine Vision (MV) technology), and can be linked to other service offerings such as maintenance and service management SW, warehouses and shops for spare parts and fixtures. Trained NN models allow operators to reflect anomalies through the interface, create additional annotations, or train their own models for other self-service use cases.

According to (ISO/IEC, 2022a): "Artificial intelligence (AI) as discipline research and development of mechanisms and applications of AI systems. Note 1 to entry: Research and development can take place across any number of fields such as computer science, data science, natural sciences, humanities, mathematics and natural sciences".

"Artificial intelligence system (AI system) is an engineered system that generates outputs such as content, forecasts, recommendations or decisions for a given set of human-defined objectives. Note 1 to entry: The engineered system can use various techniques and approaches related to AI to develop a model to represent data, knowledge, processes, etc. which can be used to conduct tasks. Note 2 to entry: AI systems are designed to operate with varying levels of automation" (ISO/IEC, 2021b). There are two broad classes of AI systems, based on their capabilities: Predictive AI (PredAI) and Generative AI (GenAI) (ISO/IEC, 2022b), (ISO/IEC, 2021b).

Standard ISO gives a definition for the term NN (ISO/IEC, 2021b): "NN is a network of primitive processing elements connected by weighted links with adjustable weights, in which each element produces a value by applying a nonlinear function to its input values, and transmits it to other elements or presents it as an output value".

The relevance of PA is undoubted, as it allows us to analyse the statistics of failures, faults, malfunctions and cyber-attacks of HW and SW, to assess and predict the reliability, resiliency, cybersecurity, dependability of the IIoT system and its subsystems.

For PA in IIoT systems can be used methods of ML and Deep Learning (DL). Good results in resolving regression tasks and classification tasks in PAs have different types of NN. Neural networks are also called artificial neural networks (ANNs) or simulated neural networks (SNN) (Haykin, 2007). ANN is a NN of primitive processing elements connected by weighted links with adjustable weights, in which each element produces a value by applying a nonlinear function to its input values, and transmits it to other elements or presents it as an output value (ISO/IEC, 2021b) (ISO/IEC, 2024).

They are a subset of ML and are the basis of DL models. A NN is a ML model designed to process data in a way that mimics the function and structure of the human brain. NN are complex networks of interconnected nodes, or artificial neurons, that interact to solve complex problems (Haykin, 2007), (ISO/IEC, 2022c), (ISO/IEC, 2024), (Microsoft, 2023) (NVIDIA, 2024).

Deep NN is a type of DL technology that is classified within the broader field of AI. These NN models complex relationships and are valued for their power and flexibility, especially when dealing with non-linear data (data in which the relationship between variables is curved or complex rather than direct). They are often used to validate results from simpler methods such as regression and decision trees. NN are excellent when there is no clear mathematical formula or large amounts of training data are available and complex data analysis is required.

A large number of sensors in the IIoT system allows obtaining measurement results for a huge number of parameters. Constructing a formula dependence is very difficult. But the entire set of factors, taking into account the already accumulated statistics, which can be used as a training sample for the NN, will allow AI to make fairly clear forecasts and formulate recommendations regarding maintenance and repair of IIoT subsystems.

In this section, we analyse and systematise existing AI methods, the main methods of ML and DL, types of NN, their features, advantages, and disadvantages, in particular ensemble ML algorithms, which can be used to solve PA of IIoT systems problems. We also perform a comparative analysis, categorisation and selection of activation functions for realisation of PA for IIoT systems.

For PA in IIoT systems use AI methods of ML and DL. Examples of our vision of PA for IIoT system steps and predictive maintenance (PdM) with the use of ML/DL algorithms are presented in Figures 1, 2.

ISO/IEC 22989 defines an ML model as a mathematical construct that generates an output or prediction from input data or information (ISO/IEC, 2022a). An ML model (ISO/IEC, 2022a) consists of a data structure and SW to process the structure, which are determined by the selected ML algorithm. The model is configured with parameters, weights on the inputs, and functions on the outputs, required to solve a given problem.

According to (IBM, 2024b) (IBM, 2024c), (ISO/IEC, 2022a) (ISO/IEC, 2022b) (ISO/IEC, 2022c), (ISO/IEC, 2021b) (ISO/IEC, 2024), (NVIDIA, 2024), in AI, neurons are pieces of SW that work together to process and analyse complex data. Each neuron receives input from the previous layer, applies a mathematical function to it and passes the result to the next layer. The selection and tuning of these mathematical functions are the main challenges in the design of a NN, as its entire performance depends on proper tuning to get the desired result. This is achieved through an automatic process called learning.The model is populated (also known as "trained") to represent relevant statistical properties of the training data. During training, the model "learns" to solve a given problem for the training data.

Figure 1. ML-based example of PA for IIoT system

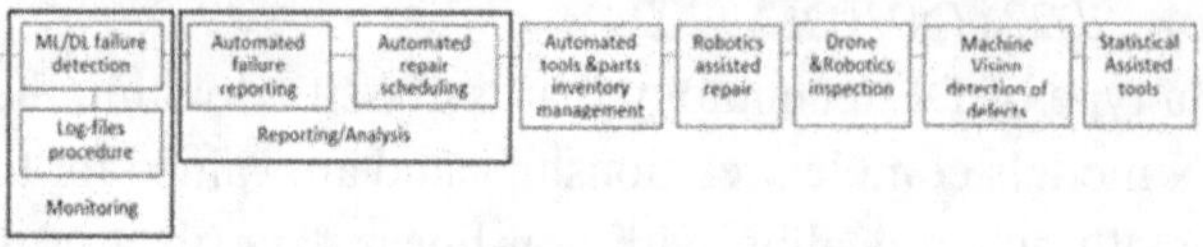

Figure 2. ML-based example of predictive maintenance for IIoT system

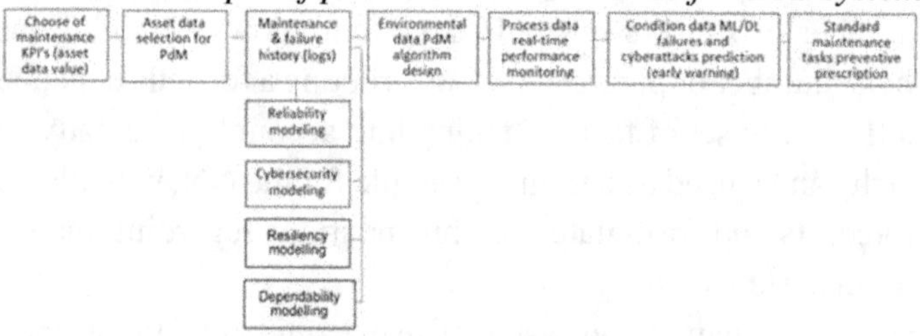

A classical NN can be represented as a computational graph containing (Haykin, 2007), (ISO, 2024), (Tucci, 2024):

· input vertices x;
· vertices that are neurons with their output values a;
· vertices responsible for output values b;
· edges multiplying the output values of the previous layer by their corresponding coefficients of the weight matrix w;
· hypothesis hw,b(x) - the result of the output of the last layer.

Limitations for training a NN model (Haykin, 2007), (Microsoft, 2023) (NVIDIA, 2024):

1. Data requirements: training a NN requires large amounts of labeled data, which may not always be easily accessible.
2. Interpretability: high data dimensionality (data complexity) for computation complicates the decision making and analysis of the results.
3. Computational resources spent on training the NN: significant initial and additional computational resources and time are needed to deploy the NN.
4. Overfitting the NN, as a result of which it does not generalise well to new, unknown training data.

5. Underfitting: the model cannot capture important differences and patterns in the data, which leads to poor performance even on training data.

The main advantages of NNs:

1. High accuracy of calculations due to detection and analysis of complex patterns due to a large number of calculation cycles, optimisation of solutions.
2. Adaptability to changing patterns, constantly learning from new data.
3. Scalability due to the ability to effectively process large amounts of data in real time.

The input layer contains the so-called predictors, the initial data. Transitions from one layer to another are performed with certain weight coefficients.

The hidden layer contains unobserved nodes, or neurons. The value of each hidden neuron is some function of predictors, or neuron excitation function, the so-called **activation function** (ISO, 2024), (ISO/IEC, 2022a).

The output layer contains the response function. Each output neuron is some function of the hidden neurons. Direct feedforward, or error forward propagation, is the foundation of NN, allowing them to make predictions and generate results. It involves passing input data through layers of interconnected neurons, with each neuron applying an activation function to its weighted sum of inputs (ISO, 2024).

Back propagation is the process by which a neural network adjusts its weights in response to feedback received during NN training. It works by propagating the error from the output layer back through the network, allowing each neuron to adjust its weights accordingly. By iteratively adjusting the weights based on the feedback, the NN can gradually improve the accuracy of its predictions and generate the desired results. The error back propagation method continues this chain of reasoning to the case of a multilayer NN. This makes it possible to train deep layers based on gradient descent. The training is done step by step from the last layer to the first layer (Haas et al., 2021), (ISO, 2024).

ISO gives the description of main terms for NN models (ISO, 2024) (ISO/IEC, 2021a)

(ISO/IEC, 2022a) (ISO/IEC, 2022b) (ISO/IEC, 2022c), (ISO/IEC, 2021b) (ISO/IEC, 2024).

Input data - an initial dataset containing features and corresponding labels.

Data preprocessing - cleaning, transforming and splitting the data into training and validation sets.

Weak learner - training a weak learner (decision tree, shallow NN) on the training data.

Error analysis - evaluating the performance of the weak learner on the validation set to identify misclassified samples.

Weight update - increasing the importance (weight) of misclassified samples to focus on challenging instances.

Ensemble - combining weak learners into an ensemble where each learner's predictions are weighted based on its performance.

Strong learner - the final boosted model represents a strong learner created by combining an ensemble of weak learners that can make accurate predictions.

Multilayer NN refer to deep learning (DL), and have multiple hidden layers whose nodes are called hidden neurons or hidden elements (they mediate between the external input signal and the signal at the output of the TT.

PA, based on NN, gives allows more accurate, reliable and fast fulfilment of tasks of classification and prediction of failures and cyber-attacks in the IIoT system, and PA SW includes known algorithms and methods of traditional statistical data processing inside Python programming language libraries.There are several frameworks for modelling and training NN. For example (Wess et al., 2021), for DL networks, Tensorflow version 2 (TF2) is used often for PA together with the Tensorflow Object Detection API (ODA). NN training can also be performed on a Red Hat Enterprise Linux server Server version 10: 10.0 BETA / December 11, 2024; CUDA Toolkit 12: 12.x. Note that starting with CUDA 11, individual components of the toolkit are versioned independently. NVIDIA Data Centre GPU Driver: 570.86.15 (Linux) / 572.13 (Windows). Fabric Manager: 570.86.15 . NVFlash: 5.791. Python 3.8-3.11, Ubuntu 16.04 or later, Windows 7 or later (with redistributable C++ distribution), macOS 10.12.6 (Sierra) or later (no GPU support), WSL2 over Windows 10 19044 or later, including GPU (experimental) Tensorflow automatically distributes the workload across multiple GPUs.

ML models produce outputs that are approximations of optimal solutions. ML algorithms use statistical optimisation techniques to make this approximation (Haykin, 2007), (ISO/IEC, 2022b), (NVIDIA, 2024). The resulting mapping from inputs to model outputs reflects patterns learned from processing the training data. Patterns may relate to correlations, causal relationships, or categories of data objects. ML models are the output of the training data used. If the data used is incomplete or incorrect, the model's performance will reflect this. Therefore, care should be taken with the datasets used to train the NN model.

Pre-processing includes (ISO/IEC, 2021a) (ISO/IEC, 2022a) (ISO/IEC, 2022b):

· generation and analysis of the training sample;
· filtering;
· normalisation, centring, scaling, coding.

Selection of parameters for NN training includes the steps of:

· selection of the structure of the NN;
· selection of the NN task - classification, regression or both regression and classification;
· selection of a method for estimating the accuracy of the model;
· selection of activation function(s) in each layer of the NN.

According to ISO/IEC 22989: "activation function applied to the weighted combination of all inputs to a neuron. Activation functions allow NN to learn complicated features in the data. They are typically non-linear" (ISO/IEC, 2022a).

NN training includes:

· selection of an optimisation method;
· direct training of the NN.

Assessing the accuracy of the NN model includes:

· testing;
· cross-validation.

The example of configuration of NN settings algorithms is presented in Figure 3. There are main types of artificial NN for PA in IIoT systems (IBM, 2024b):

1. Feedforward neural networks (FNN) — NNs in which information is transmitted only in one direction: from the input layer to the output layer. They are used for pattern recognition (MV technology for IIoT systems), classification and regression.
2. Convolutional neural networks (CNNs) — feedforward networks for processing images or videos in the form of a grid. CNNs are also important for IIoT PA systems for implementing MV technology.
3. Recurrent neural networks (RNNs) process sequential data using feedback (information about previous inputs is saved and used for prediction or decision making).
4. Residual neural networks (ResNets) — NNs with a special type of feedforward connection that allows the network to "skip" certain layers if they do not contribute to the best result and are designed for training very deep NN.

Training a FNN involves adjusting the weights associated with each connection between neurons. This requires statistical data sets for the NN (at least 3-6 months for IIoT systems and their subsystems) to learn patterns, correlations and make accurate predictions.

Figure 3. Configuration settings of NN

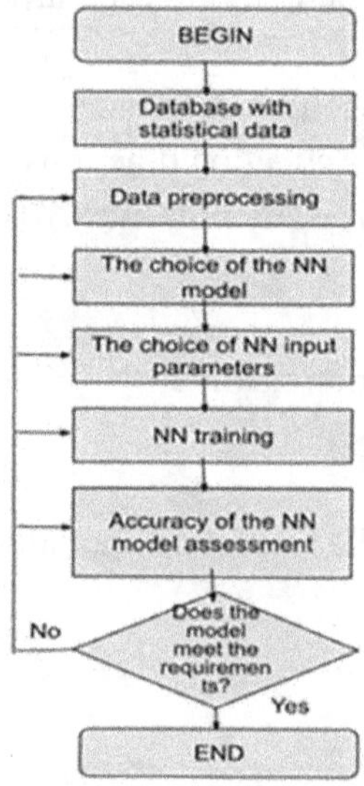

In PA the main AI methods are ensemble ML methods. They are used mostly in IIoT systems to resolve tasks: regression, classification, clustering, decision trees. These ML methods will help us to classify cyber-attacks types and types of failures and faults of SW and HW, to predict the possible cyberattacks and failures of subsystems in IIoT system and its components. Let's compare the main ensemble methods of ML.

THE COMPARISON ANALYSIS OF ENSEMBLED ML METHODS

Ensemble learning suggests that decision making by a larger group of people is usually more accurate than decision making by a single expert. Ensemble learning refers to a group (or ensemble) of base learners or models that work collectively to achieve the best (optimal) final prediction.

Let $h_1, h_2, \ldots, h_t$ be a set of hypotheses, and consider the composite ensemble hypothesis (Haykin, 2007):

$$y(x) = \sum_{t=1}^{T} \alpha_t h_t(x).$$

Here α_t denotes the coefficient with which the ensemble member h_t is combined; both α_t and the learner or hypothesis h_t are to be learned within the Boosting procedure.

Consider solving a univariate linear function $y = \theta_0 + \theta_1 x$ where y is an output or result, x is an input, θ_0 is an intercept (the value of y where $x = 0$) and θ_1 is a weight. In ML, the process of determining the intercept and weights for a linear function is known as linear regression (ISO/IEC, 2024).

A single model, also known as a base or weak learning model, may perform poorly individually due to high variance or large bias. When weak learners are combined, they can form a strong learner because their combination reduces the bias or variance, resulting in better model performance.

Ensemble methods often use decision trees (ISO/IEC, 2022c). A given algorithm may be prone to overfitting (high variance, high bias and low bias) when it has not been pruned, and may be susceptible to underfitting (low variance and high bias) when it is very small, like the decision stump that is a tree solution with one level.

Ensemble methods allow you to train a model on new data sets if the algorithm does not fit or match its training data set, and cannot generalise well to new data sets (Haas et al., 2021), (Maglogiannis et al., 2021), (IBM, 2024c), (Murel & Kavlakoglu, 2024), (Ghosh, 2025).

Ensemble learning includes three of the most well-known methods: bagging, boosting, and stacking (Figure 4). Classification of ensemble ML methods with its features, advantages and disadvantages are presented in Table 1.

Figure 4. Classification of Ensemble learning methods

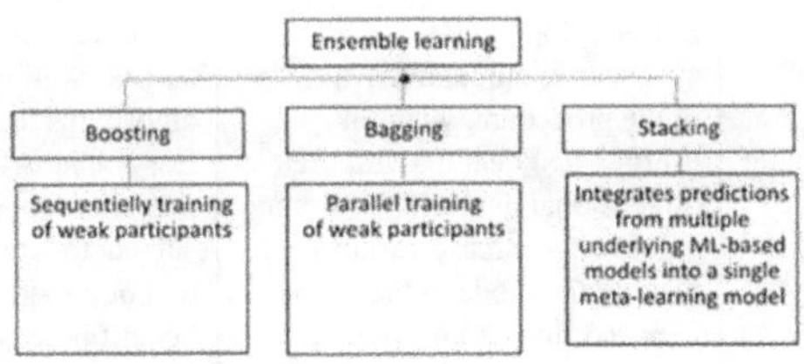

Table 1. Comparison analysis of Ensemble learning methods

Ensemble learning methods	Features	Advantages	Disadvantages	Tasks
Bagging	**Bootstrapping** – generation of diverse samples of the training dataset by selecting data points at random and with replacement. Used to create multiple subsets of the training data, allowing the training sets for each baseline learner to vary.	1. **Versatility** - allows many weak learners to join forces to outperform one strong learner. Summarisation can be applied to a wide range of underlying learners, making it a versatile method applicable to different types of models.	1. **Loss of interpretability**: - it is difficult to draw accurate conclusions about a business due to averaging of predictions; - the result is more accurate than each individual data point, a more accurate or complete data set can also give greater accuracy within a single classification or regression model.	Classification and regression
	Bootstrap samples are trained independently and **in parallel**, using weak or base learners.	**Ease of implementation**: the Python scikit-learn (sklearn) libraries, easily combine the predictions of the underlying learners or estimators to improve model performance.	2. **Computational cost:** - not well suited for real-time applications, Bagging slows down and becomes more computationally intensive as the number of iterations increases; - cluster systems or a large number of computational cores are ideal for quickly creating bagging ensembles on large test sets.	
	Aggregation - an average or a majority of the predictions compute a more accurate estimate. All baseline learners are usually given equal weight in making the final prediction.	3. **Reducing variance**, and eliminating model overfitting in the procedure, which is useful when dealing with high-dimensional data where missing values can increase variance, making the model more prone to overfitting and preventing accurate generalisation to new datasets and for unstable models or models prone to overfitting.	3. **Less flexible**: - works well with algorithms that are less stable. Algorithms that are more stable or subject to large biases do not provide as much benefit because there is less model variation in the dataset.	
	Used for weak learners, with high variance and low systematic error and to avoid overfitting	4. **Parallelisation -** bagging algorithms such as Random Forests can be parallelised, allowing efficient implementation and faster learning on distributed computing systems.	4. **Errors** - if the proper procedure is ignored, the resulting model may have many errors.	

continued on following page

Table 1. Continued

Ensemble learning methods	Features	Advantages	Disadvantages	Tasks
		Robustness to noisy data and outliers due to an averaging or voting mechanism that reduces the impact of individual errors, as the impact of individual errors is mitigated by combining predictions. The final prediction is usually the average or vote of all the underlying learners.		
Boosting	algorithms are used for weak learners, with low variance and high systematic error; works in a mostly serialized manner; adjustments are made incrementally at each step of the process before moving on to the next algorithm.	**Ease of implementation:** - easy-to-understand and easy-to-interpret algorithms that learn from their mistakes; - algorithms don't require data preprocessing, and they have built-in routines to handle missing data; - most languages have built-in libraries to implement many parameters that can fine-tune performance.	1. **Tend to overfitting** (but adjusting the parameters eliminates this problem).	Classification and regression
		Computational efficiency: - prioritisation the features and breaking the model decision process into multiple processes that increase predictive accuracy and interpretability of the model during training; - help to reduce the number of variables or dimensions required to make a decision or prediction, data attributes and handle the imbalanced data and large datasets by focusing more on the data points that are misclassified, efficiently speeding computation; - can use hyperparameter tuning options baked into many common algorithms; - improves ML models' predictive accuracy and performance by converting multiple weak learners into a single strong learning model, averaging them for the regression or voting over them for classification to increase the accuracy of the final model.	**2. Vulnerability to outlier data** values that are different from the rest of dataset. Each model attempts to correct the faults in the predecessor, outliers can very skew results.	

continued on following page

Table 1. Continued

Ensemble learning methods	Features	Advantages	Disadvantages	Tasks
		Reduction of bias: **-** a sequential method iteratively improves observations; - helps to reduce high bias of any one algorithm that is common in ML models.	**Real-time implementation:** - the algorithm is more complex than other processes; - high adaptability needs a wide variety of model parameters and decreases the model's performance.	
Stacking	- combines the predictions of multiple base models (first-level models or base-level learners), to make the final prediction; - involves training multiple baseline models on the same data set and then feeding their predictions into a higher-level model (metamodel or second-level model) to obtain the final prediction; - combining the forecasts of different baseline models provides a better forecasting performance than using a single model.	**1. Improved accuracy:** - combines the strengths of several basic models, reducing the likelihood of overfitting; - the metamodel can compensate for the errors of individual models and make a more accurate forecast; - a final prediction with higher performance; - quick prediction; - better model generalization.	1. **Difficulty:** - implementation of the algorithm requires more time, effort, and computing resources, which makes it impractical for some applications.	Classification or regression

continued on following page

Table 1. Continued

Ensemble learning methods	Features	Advantages	Disadvantages	Tasks
		2. Flexibility: - can be applied to any ML algorithm; - use with any combination of base models makes it a universal method for improving the performance of a ML system.	**2. Retraining:** - a metamodel can be retrained when the underlying models are overfitted or the dataset used to train the metamodel is too small.	
		3. Reliability: - more reliable than other ensemble learning methods, as it is less susceptible to overfitting. - the base models are trained on one data set, which reduces the likelihood of overfitting, and the metamodel has more data for training, and the forecasts of the base models are included in the data set, which increases the reliability of the prediction.		

The main Boosting methods are presented in Figure 5 and in Table 2.

Figure 5. Classification of Boosting methods

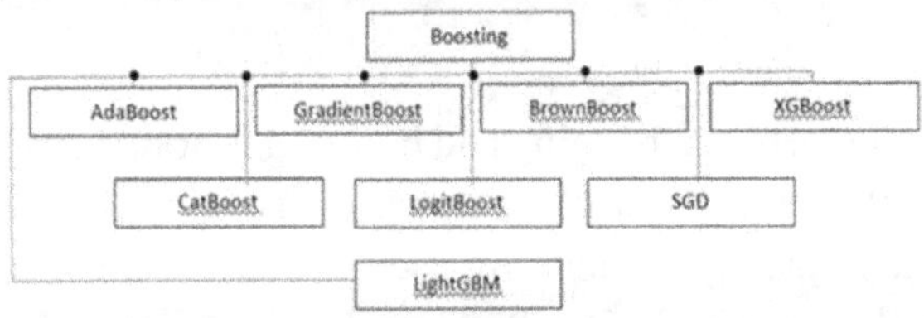

Boosting is an ensemble learning technique used in ML to reduce errors in predictive data analysis. The essence of the method is to combine a group of weak learners into a strong learner to minimise learning errors. Machine learning models are trained on the labeled data to make predictions about the unlabeled data. A single ML model can make prediction errors depending on the accuracy of the training dataset. The main steps of Boosting are presented in the Figure 6.

Boosting uses sequential training of multiple models to improve the accuracy of the whole system. For this purpose, a random sample of data is selected, fitted with a model, and then trained sequentially - each model tries to compensate for the weaknesses of its predecessor. At each iteration, the weak rules of each individual classifier are combined into one strong prediction rule.

Classification of the Boosting algorithms is given in Table 3.

One more ensemble algorithm is Bagging. According to IBM, Bagging (bootstrap aggregation), is the ensemble learning method that is commonly used to reduce variance within a noisy dataset (IBM, 2024b; IBM, 2024c).

The main difference between boosting and bagging lies in the way they are taught. In bagging, weak learners are trained in parallel, while in boosting they are trained sequentially. A series of models are built, and with each new iteration of the model, the weights of misclassified data in the previous model are increased. This redistribution of weights helps the algorithm identify the parameters it needs to focus on to improve its performance.

Figure 6. The main steps of Boosting ML method

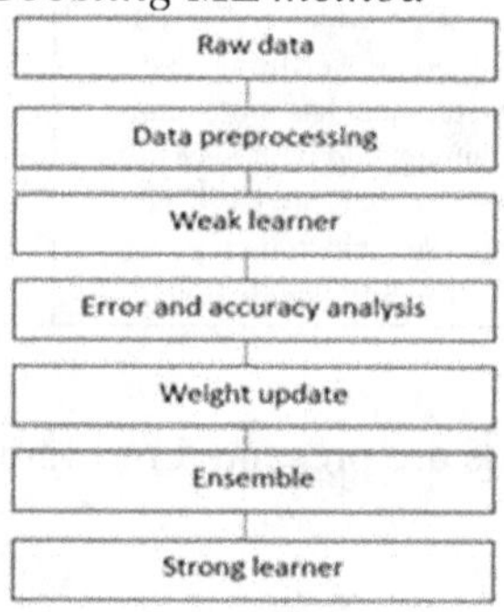

Another difference between bagging and boosting is how they are used. Bagging methods are usually used for weak learners showing high variance and low systematic error, while boosting methods are used, when variance values are low and systematic error values are high. Batching can be used to avoid overtraining, and boosting methods may be more prone to do so (depends on the dataset). However, parameter tuning can help to avoid this problem.

Table 2. Comparison analysis of Boosting Ensemble learning methods

Boosting algorithm	Tasks	Features	Advantages	Disadvantages
Gradient boosting	Classification and regression	works by sequentially adding predictors, which in ensemble with each one correcting the errors of its predictor; combines the gradient descent algorithm and boosting method.	trains on the residual errors of the previous predictor; does not give more weight to incorrectly classified elements; optimizes the loss function by sequentially generating base learners (the current base learner is always more efficient than the previous one). initially aimed at obtaining accurate results, rather than correcting errors throughout the entire process; high accuracy of results.	a lot of time and resources for training compared to simpler algorithms; the problem of retraining for complex models or high learning rates; this is a less interpretable "black box" model.
AdaBoost	Classification	operates iteratively, identifying misclassified data points, adjusting their weights to minimize the training predictor; a sequential training technique; minimizes the exponential loss.	continues optimize in a sequential set until it yields the stronger predictor; adapts and tries to self-correct at each iteration of the promotion process; initially assigns equal weight to each data set and automatically adjusts them after each decision tree, which gives more weight to incorrectly classified elements for correction in the next round. The process is repeated until the residual error, or the difference between actual and predicted values, falls below an acceptable threshold; use with many predictors and is generally not as sensitive as other boosting algorithms.	the approach of using different predictors does not work when there is a correlation between features or high dimensionality of the data.

continued on following page

Table 2. Continued

Boosting algorithm	Tasks	Features	Advantages	Disadvantages
Extreme gradient boosting (XGBoost)	For classification and regression problems	designed for computational speed and scale; parallelism; cache optimization; out-of-core processing; applies a Gradient Boosting technique based on decision trees. It constructs short, basic decision trees iteratively. Each tree is termed as a "weak learner" because of its high bias.	uses multiple cores on the CPU; learning can occur in parallel during training; can handle extensive datasets (for Big Data); distributed computing.	- unbalanced selection of effects; - falsely evoked contraction; - low convergence speed; - biased estimates of random effects; - the risk of overtraining in conditions of class imbalance.
Brown Boost	Binary Classification	- does not use subsamples of the training data to build each tree to avoid potential overfitting problems in random forests by randomly splitting the training set; is a continuous-time adaptive boosting algorithm, based on the non-adaptive Boost-by-Majority (BBM) algorithm.	- does not rely on the gradient descent optimization technique, but on a completely different formulation that makes it more computationally efficient and more versatile for use in practice; more efficient and reliable for noisy data sets than any other boosted classification algorithms.	- there is the noise in results; - not popular.

continued on following page

Table 2. Continued

Boosting algorithm	Tasks	Features	Advantages	Disadvantages
Stochastic Gradient Descent (SGD)	Classification and regression. This method is hybrid = bagging + boosting	an iterative algorithm that uses randomly selected batches of data to estimate the gradient at each iteration of classification tree. At each stage, it is not the actual gradient that is calculated, but an approximation of it.	- works well with large data sets; - can provide high generalization performance; - the cost function converges faster and more accurately; - requires little memory, making it easier to manage storage requirements; - stochastic nature allows you to quickly prototype and test various models and hyperparameters with less computational resources required for training; - ability to avoid local minima to solve highly nonlinear problems; - high learning speed; is an effective approach for most machine learning problems that require optimization due to its flexibility and ease of use.	- the convergence path is noisier than the original gradient fall, resulting in inaccurate parameter updates that will lead to suboptimal results if not carefully controlled during training; - greater change in cost; - high systematic error due to insufficient exploration of the search space and poor generalization performance for small data sets; - in time series forecasting problems, it does not take into account systematic correlations within data points, which reduces the convergence of the model.

continued on following page

Table 2. Continued

Boosting algorithm	Tasks	Features	Advantages	Disadvantages
LightGBM	Regression, double classification, multi classification, learning from non-binary labels.	uses tree-based learning algorithms.	- faster learning speed and higher efficiency; - less memory usage; - better accuracy; - support for parallel, distributed and graphical training; - ability to process large volumes of data; - low cost of calculating winnings for each division. - use of the gradient-based one-way sampling (GOSS) algorithm to reduce the time required to find the best division of each tree node by performing fewer calculations; - high scalability; - can handle data that is sparse or contains missing or outlier values; - implements special algorithms for ranking and multi classification tasks.	- limited selection of functions for a given data set (selection of a function with the highest correlation with the target variable); - overfitting, which can lead to inaccurate forecasts; - time and memory limitations for large or complex data sets (large tree structure is used); - has several important hyperparameters that are difficult to optimize; - limited support (the algorithm is open source, it can be difficult to find resources and troubleshoot problems).
CatBoost	Regression, multi regression, classification.	- an open source solution gradient modification technique.	- excellent quality without parameter customization (reduce training time); - support for categorical data; - fast and scalable GPU version; - high accuracy; - fast prediction.	- training and optimization time (to pass the cat_features argument to the classifier object).
LogitBoost	Classification algorithm (binary and multiclass classification) for multiclass unbalanced data classification.	- minimizes the logistic loss.	- reduces the minority class prediction error significantly; - the ability to handle data that is not linearly separable, focusing on difficult cases and minimizing the loss function, which is directly related to the classification error adaptation algorithm, which can provide a much higher prediction and accuracy.	does not provide the best performance; - noise in the results.

One more ensemble algorithm is Stacking. The description of Stacking algorithm (ISO/IEC, 2022a), (ISO/IEC, 2022b):

1. ***Preparing the Data*** is the first step is to prepare the data for modelling (Figure 7).

Figure 7. The main steps of data preparation

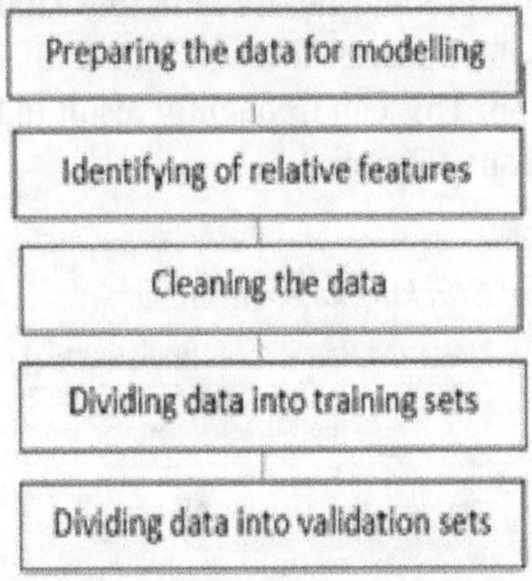

2. ***Model Selection:*** choose the base models that will be used in the stacking ensemble. A broad selection of models is typically chosen to guarantee that they produce different types of errors and complement one another.
3. ***Training the Base Models:*** After selecting the base models, they are trained on the training set. To ensure diversity, each model is trained using a different algorithm or set of hyper-parameters.
4. ***Predictions on the Validation Set:*** Once the base models have been trained, they are used to make predictions on the validation set.
5. ***Developing a Meta Model:*** develop a meta-model, also known as a meta learner, which will take the predictions of the underlying models as input and make the final prediction. Any algorithm, such as linear regression, logistic regression, or NN, can be used to create this model.
6. ***Training the Meta Model:*** The meta-model is then trained using the predictions given by the base models on the validation set. The base models' predictions serve as features for the meta-model.

7. ***Making Test Set Predictions:*** the meta-model is used to produce test set predictions. The basic models' predictions on the test set are fed into the meta-model, which then makes the final prediction.
8. ***Model Evaluation:*** assessment the stacking ensemble's performance. This is accomplished by comparing the stacking ensemble's predictions to the actual values on the test set using evaluation measures such as accuracy, precision, recall, and so on.

The goal of stacking is to combine the strengths of various base models by feeding them into a meta-model, which learns how to weigh and combine their forecasts to generate the final prediction. This can frequently result in higher performance than utilizing a single model alone (Figure 8).

Figure 8. The main steps of Stacking algorithm

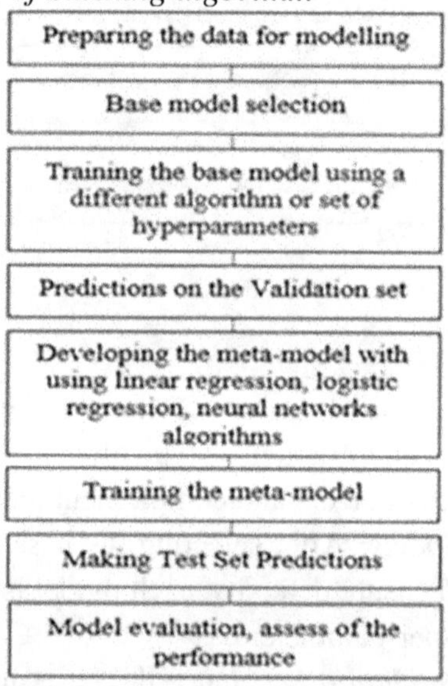

We analyzed the main types of ensemble methods for PA in IIoT systems, which use NN. Let's do the analysis of ML processes and the classification of main ML algorithms.

THE COMPARISON ANALYSIS OF ML METHODS

According to ISO standard (ISO/IEC, 2022b): "ML is a process of optimising model parameters through computational techniques, such that the model's behaviour reflects the data or experience.

ML algorithm is an algorithm to determine parameters of a ML model from data according to given criteria. The Parameter model is a parameter internal variable of a model that affects how it computes its outputs. Note 1 to entry: examples of parameters include the weights in a NN and the transition probabilities in a Markov model.

ML model is a mathematical construct that generates an inference or prediction based on input data or information".

The ML system vision from ISO is presented in Figure 9 (ISO/IEC, 2022b) and shows the process of ML.

Figure 9. ML model according to (ISO/IEC 23053:2022(E)) (ISO/IEC, 2022b)

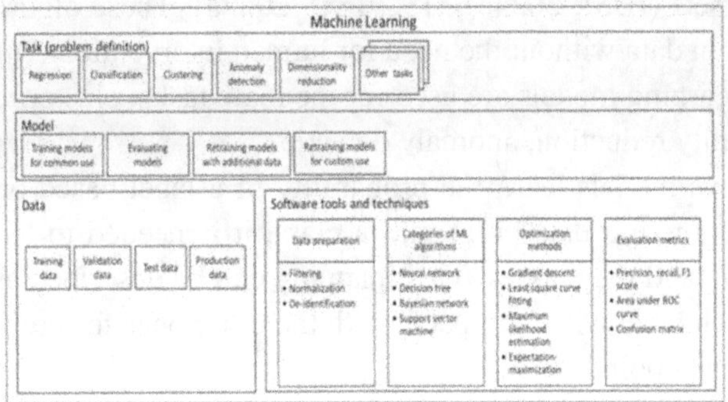

The classification of the main ML methods is shown in Figure 10 and in Table 3.

Figure 10. Classification of the main ML methods

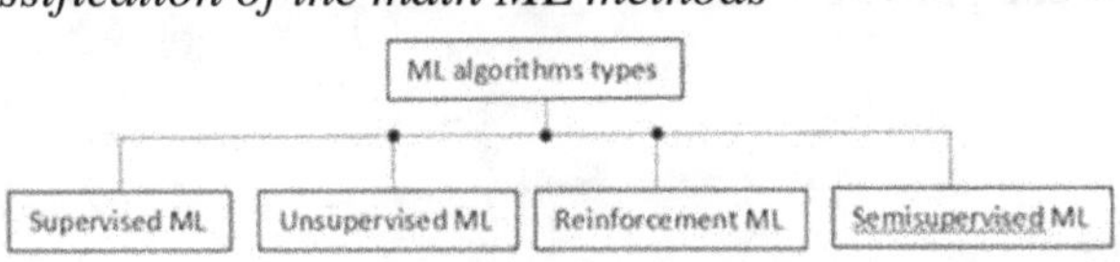

Supervised learning is an approach to ML that is defined by the use of labeled data sets (ISO/IEC, 2022a), (Awati & Burns, 2024). These datasets are designed to train or "supervise" algorithms to accurately classify data or predict outcomes.

Using labeled inputs and outputs, the model can measure its accuracy and learn over time. Supervised learning uses labeled inputs and outputs to predict outcomes, while an unsupervised learning algorithm does not.

Classification problems use an algorithm to accurately classify test data into specific categories. Linear classifiers, NN, support vector machines (SVM), decision trees, and random forests are all common types of classification algorithms.

Regression is another type of supervised learning method that uses an algorithm to understand the relationship between dependent and independent variables. Regression models are useful for predicting numerical values based on various data points. Some popular regression algorithms are NN, linear regression, logistic regression and polynomial regression.

Semi-supervised learning combines supervised learning and unsupervised learning techniques to solve key problems (ISO/IEC, 2022a) (ISO/IEC, 2022b). It trains an initial model on a few labeled samples and then iteratively applies it to more unlabeled data.

Unsupervised learning uses machine learning algorithms to analyse and cluster unlabeled data sets (IBM, 2024c), (ISO/IEC, 2022a). These algorithms discover hidden patterns in data without the need for human intervention ("unsupervised"). Unsupervised learning models are used for the main tasks: clustering, association, and dimensionality reduction, anomaly detection.

Discriminative models learn the probability of a label-based on a data point. In order to categorize a data point into a class, it is needed to learn a mapping between the data and the classes. This mapping can be described as a probability distribution. Each label will "compete" with the other ones for probability density over a specific data point.

Generative models, on the other hand, learn a probability distribution over the data points without external labels (Qian et al., 2022), (Ghosh, 2025) (Vassilev et al., 2023).

Conditional Generative models are another category of models that try to learn the probability distribution of the data conditioned on the labels. The data "compete" for density but for each possible label.

Table 3. Main features, advantages and disadvantages of ML methods

ML methods	Features	Advantages	Disadvantages
Reinforcement ML	- a way to manage unsupervised ML through rewards or positive reinforcement and punishments or negative reinforcement. **Deep reinforcement method** – the mix of reinforcement method and deep learning. It is also called Q-learning.	- long-term goals help the agent to avoid obsessing over less important tasks; - over time, the agent learns to avoid negativity and strive for positivity; - helps solve very complex problems that traditional methods cannot solve; - gives long-term results that are very difficult to achieve; - improves in every action; - able to learn from mistakes and correct them (the likelihood of repeating the same mistake is very small); - a set of data is not needed to guide its actions (learns from experience). - opportunities for intellectual study of situation-action relationships and the creation of ideal behavior in a given context; - maximum performance.	- too much gain can cause overload, which can weaken the results; - preferable for solving complex rather than simple problems; - requires a lot of data and requires a lot of calculations; - maintenance costs are high; - can have wildly inaccurate results unless you have human intervention to validate the output variables.
Supervised ML	predict outcomes for new data; uses labeled data.	- simple method for machine learning, typically calculated through the use of programs like R or Python; - models are ideal for spam detection, sentiment analysis, weather forecasting and pricing predictions, among other things; - can be effective for anomaly detection when the labels are reliable and representative, and the data is not too noisy or heterogeneous.	can be time-consuming to train, and the labels for input and output variables require expertise; data bias - bias that depends on the data set for the answers and can lead to data imbalance and problems in assessing data to make accurate predictions; low quality data - there must be enough data to obtain accurate results.

continued on following page

Table 3. Continued

Semisupervised ML	- combines supervised and unsupervised learning by using both labeled and unlabeled data to train AI models for classification and regression tasks.	- cost savings by using both labeled and unlabeled data; - accuracy - using labeled data can prevent models from learning spurious correlations, while using unlabeled data can add valuable information about the patterns underlying the data; - time savings - model training is accelerated because not all data must be labeled.	- complexity: difficult to set up and train; - require some labeled data for training; - interpretability of learning algorithms can vary depending on the algorithm used (some algorithms are more interpretable than others); - becomes valuable when the dataset contains some labels, but lacks coverage for all possible anomaly types and variations, while the distribution of normal and anomalous data is moderately imbalanced.
Unsupervised ML	use deep learning to arrive at conclusions and patterns through unlabeled training data; the goal is to get insights from large volumes of new data.	a great fit for anomaly detection, recommendation engines, customer personas and medical imaging; work on their own to discover the inherent structure of unlabeled data (they still require some human intervention for validating output variables); can be useful for anomaly detection when the data is complex and high-dimensional, and the anomalies are rare and diverse.	need powerful tools for working with large amounts of unclassified data; models are computationally complex because they need a large training set to produce intended outcomes.

Reinforcement learning (RL) is a ML method that trains models to make decisions to achieve the most optimal results. It is based on simulating the learning process through trial and error to achieve the goals. SW actions aimed at achieving the goal are reinforced, and actions that distract from the goal are ignored. RL algorithms use a reward and penalty paradigm when processing data.

In this chapter we also make the analysis and systematisation of DL algorithms, which can be used for PA for IIoT systems.

Supervised learning uses labeled inputs and outputs to predict outcomes, while an unsupervised learning algorithm does not.

Supervised learning is an approach to ML that is defined by the use of labeled data sets (Figure 11) (ISO/IEC, 2022b).

These datasets are designed to train or "supervise" algorithms to accurately classify data or predict outcomes. Using labeled inputs and outputs, the model can measure its accuracy and learn over time.

Supervised learning in PA for the IIoT system can be divided into two types of data mining problems: classification and regression.

Classification problems in PA for the IIoT system involve predicting the assignment of an input data instance to a particular category or class (ISO/IEC, 2022b). Classification can be binary (i.e. true or false), multi-class (i.e. one of several possibilities), or multi-label (i.e. any number of several possibilities).

Figure 11. Supervised ML process based on the ML pipeline according to ISO/IEC 23053, 2022 (ISO/IEC, 2022b)

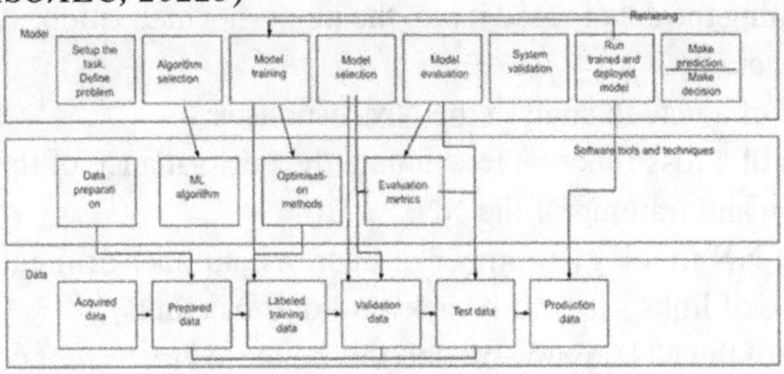

For the IIoT system it could be the classification of cyber-attacks, classification of faults and failures, classification of technical states of IIoT subsystems and the whole IIoT system.

Classification can be used to predict whether a defect is functional or structural. The classes are typically in a discrete and unordered set, so the problem cannot be formalised as a regression problem. Often, PA for IIoT systems requires solving both regression and classification problems. NN, linear classifiers, SVM, decision trees, and random forests are all common types of classification algorithms (Figure 12).

Figure 12. Classification methods in Supervised ML

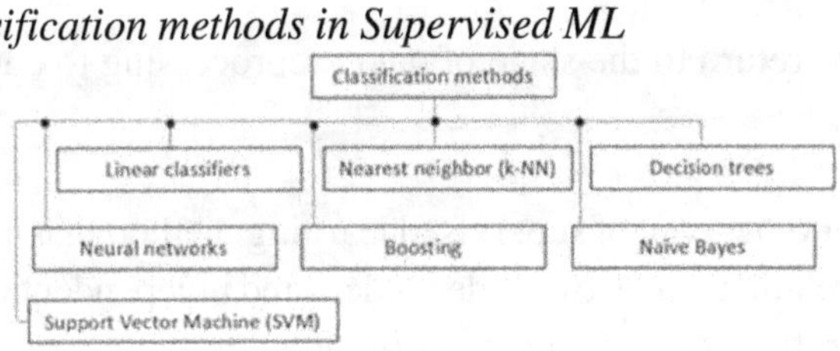

The classification task in implementing PA for IIoT systems can be based on these steps (Diab et al., 2017):

1.Data preparation:

· creation of a database from statistical data on failures and faults of IIoT subsystems;
· partitioning the whole data set into two subsets: training (training sample) and test (test sample);
· to control the NN overtraining, determination of the sample confirming the overtraining.

2. Data preprocessing:
· transforming the data to feed it into the input (normalisation, standardisation, clustering, etc.);
· selection of a way to analyse the NN responses;
· selection of a loss function to evaluate the performance of the NN.

3. Creation and training of the NN:
· choice of NN topology (number of neurons, number of inputs and outputs, layers, type of links - forward, backward or cross links);
· selection of the NN training model (it is better to create your own model than to take a ready-made one from a database of models);
· selection of the NN training strategy;
· selection or formulation of the NN learning stopping criterion;
· execution of NN training;
· evaluation of the NN performance quality on the training data sample;
· assessment of the reliability (accuracy) of the results of the NN neurons on the test set.

4. Diagnostics:
· testing different algorithms of decisive rules to perform classification of failures and faults, cyber-attacks of IIoT subsystems;
· calculation of the classification error according to the selected evaluation criterion;
· if necessary, return to the stage of data preprocessing to correct their transformation.

Regression is another type of supervised learning method that uses an algorithm to understand the relationship between dependent and independent variables (Figure 13). Regression problems perform prediction of a continuous variable by training a model that best fits a set of training data. In a regression problem, the trained regression model represents the user space (ISO/IEC, 2021b), (Kolisnyk & Jantsch, 2024). When the trained model is applied to a new instance of production data (failure statistics, crashes, defects), the instance is projected into the user space defined by the trained regression model. Regression is mainly used to predict numeric values of a real process based on previous measurements or observations of the same process. In PA for IIoT systems, regression is a critical component.

Regression models are useful for predicting numerical values based on various data points. Some popular regression algorithms are linear regression, logistic regression and polynomial regression.

A regression problem is when a model is used to predict continuous outcomes or values. Regression models are trained to understand and identify the relationship between various independent variables and the outcome. The model will take into account many different factors that can lead to failures, faults of IIoT subsystems.

Figure 13. Regression methods in Supervised ML

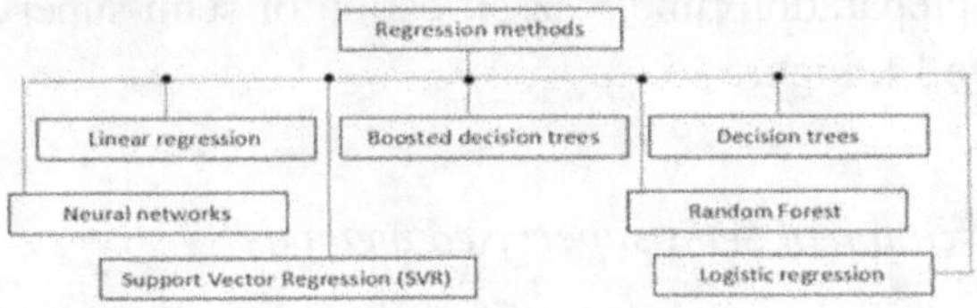

In practice, the model is trained on so-called labelled data to understand the relationship between the characteristics of the data and the dependent variable. By evaluating this relationship, the model can predict the outcome of new data not yet seen. This can be used to predict missing historical data as well as to estimate future outcomes.

In supervised learning, the algorithm "learns" from a set of training data, iteratively making predictions from the data and adjusting them to the correct answer. Supervised learning models are typically more accurate than unsupervised learning models, but require prior human intervention to label the data appropriately.

Clustering tasks involve grouping input data instances (IBM, 2024c), (Murel & Kavlakoglu, 2024), (Awati & Burns, 2024). Unlike classification tasks, classes are not predefined in clustering tasks, but are defined as part of the clustering process. Clustering is considered a data preparation step to identify homogeneous data. They are then used as a training set for supervised machine learning. Clustering is used in PA for IIoT systems to detect outliers or anomalies by identifying input data instances that are not similar to other samples.

SEMI-SUPERVISED ML METHODS

Semi-supervised learning combines supervised learning and unsupervised learning techniques to solve key problems. According to (ISO/IEC, 2022a): "semi-supervised machine learning is a ML that makes use of both labelled and unlabelled data during training".

It trains an initial model on a few labeled samples and then iteratively applies it to more unlabeled data. The method uses small volumes of labeled data as well as large volumes of unlabeled data, which reduces the cost of manual annotation and reduces data preparation time. Classification of semi-supervised methods is presented in Figure 14, Figure 15.

Figure 14. Classification of Semi-supervised methods

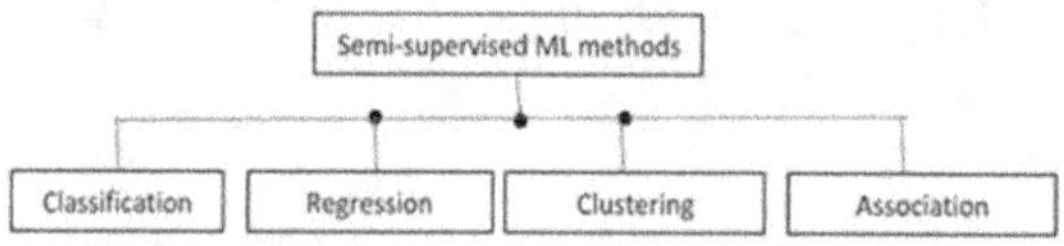

Figure 15. Classification methods in Semi-supervised ML

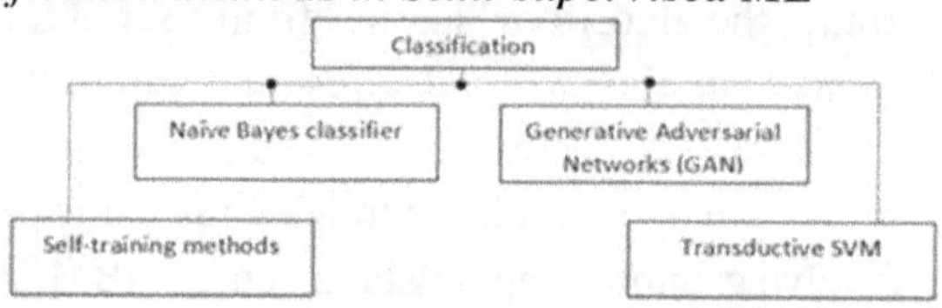

UNSUPERVISED ML

According to (ISO/IEC, 2022a) "unsupervised machine learning is a ML that makes only use of unlabelled data during training".

Unsupervised learning uses ML algorithms to analyse and cluster unlabeled data sets (Figure 16). These algorithms discover hidden patterns in data without the need for human intervention ("unsupervised").

Unsupervised learning models are used for the main tasks: clustering, association, and dimensionality reduction, anomaly detection (Figure 17, Figure 18).

Association - uses different rules to find relationships between variables in a given set of data.

Anomaly detection - is the identification of observations, events or data points that deviate from what is usual, standard or expected, making them inconsistent with the rest of a data set.

Figure 16. Classification of methods in Unsupervised ML

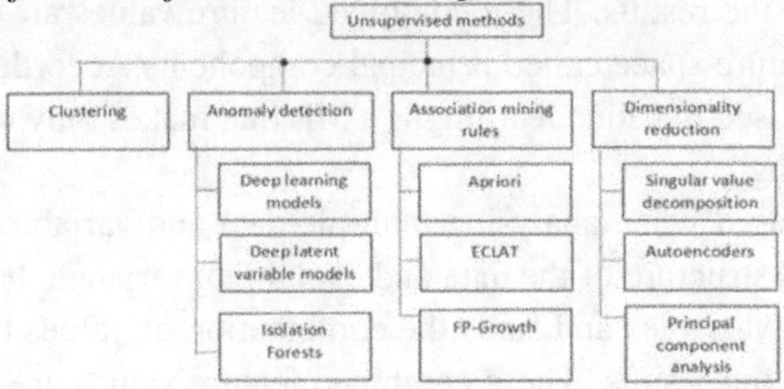

Figure 17. Classification of DL methods in Unsupervised ML

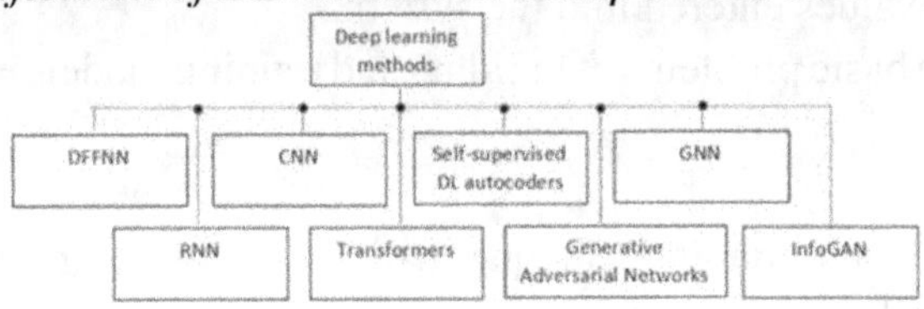

Figure 18. Classification of clustering methods in Unsupervised ML

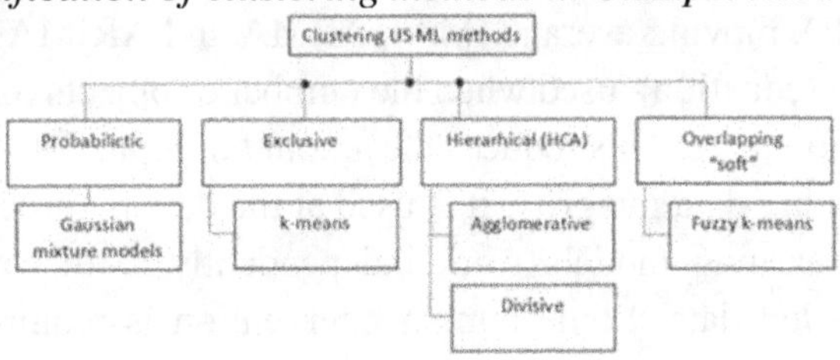

Anomaly detection based on principal component analysis (PCA) helps to build a model in scenarios where it is easy to obtain training data (statistical data on failures and failures of IIoT subsystems) but difficult to obtain sufficient samples of target anomalies (impact of cyber-attacks).

PCA is often used when analysing multiple data and variables because it can reveal the internal structure of the data and explain its variance. It determines correlations between variables and finds the combination of values that best reflects the differences in the results. These combined feature values are used to create a more compact feature space called principal components.According to (ISO/IEC, 2022a) "unsupervised machine learning is a ML that makes only use of unlabelled data during training".

PCA is often used when analysing multiple data and variables because it can reveal the internal structure of the data and explain its variance. It determines correlations between variables and finds the combination of values that best reflects the differences in the results. These combined feature values are used to create a more compact feature space called principal components.

Anomaly detection includes (ISO/IEC, 2022b), (Ghosh, 2025):

- Identifying patterns that indicate network intrusion.
- Validating values entered into the system.
- Solving the basic problems of building and training models using unbalanced datasets.

Clustering is a data mining technique that allows you to group unlabeled data based on their similarities or differences.

Clustering models, a type of unsupervised learning, group data based on similarities.

Time series models use data collected over specific time intervals, such as a day or month, to analyse seasonality, trends and cycles. Common models include autoregressive (AR), moving average (MA), ARMA and ARIMA models.

Dimensionality reduction - used when the number of objects (or dimensions) in a given data set is too large. This reduces the amount of input data to a manageable size while maintaining data integrity. It is used at the data preprocessing stage.

Unsupervised learning models work independently to discover the internal structure of unlabeled data. Some human intervention is required to check the output variables.

Discriminative models learn the probability of a label-based on a data point. In order to categorise a data point into a class, it is needed to learn a mapping between the data and the classes. This mapping can be described as a probability distribution. Each label will "compete" with the other ones for probability density over a specific data point.

Generative models (Figure 19), on the other hand, learn a probability distribution over the data points without external labels.

Figure 19. Classification of generative models in Unsupervised ML

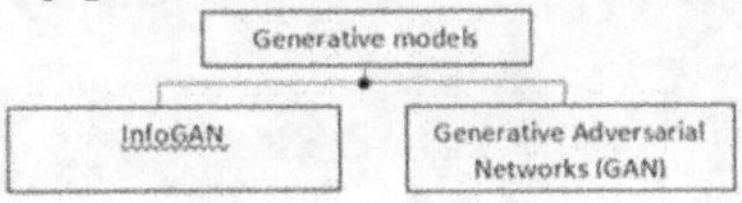

Conditional Generative models are another category of models that try to learn the probability distribution of the data conditioned on the labels. The data "compete" for density but for each possible label.

REINFORCEMENT ML

Reinforcement learning (RL) is a machine learning (ML) technique that trains models to make decisions to achieve the most optimal results. According to (ISO/IEC, 2022a): "RL is a learning of an optimal sequence of actions to maximise a reward through interaction with an environment. It is based on simulating the learning process through trial and error to achieve the goals. Software actions aimed at achieving the goal are reinforced, and actions that distract from the goal are ignored. RL algorithms use a reward and penalty paradigm when processing data. They learn from feedback on each action and independently find the best processing methods to achieve the final results. Achieve optimal results in invisible environments". Algorithms are also capable of receiving rewards with a delay. The best overall strategy may require short-term sacrifices, so the best approach they find may involve some kind of punishment or regression (Figure 20).

There are methods of reinforcement ML with using models, and without them (Figure 21) (ISO/IEC, 2022b), (ISO/IEC, 2024).

Figure 20. Main methods in RL

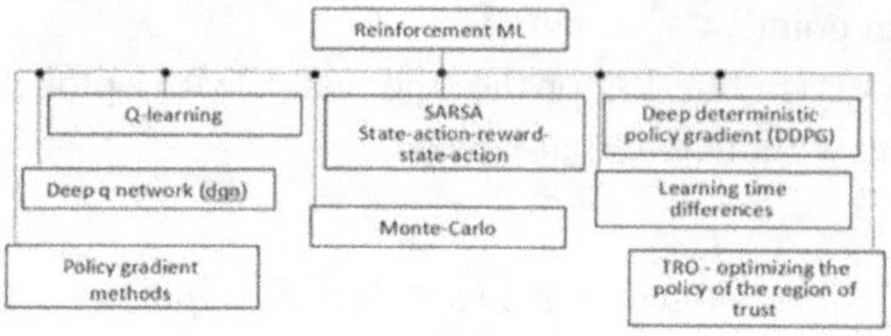

Figure 21. Classification of methods in RL

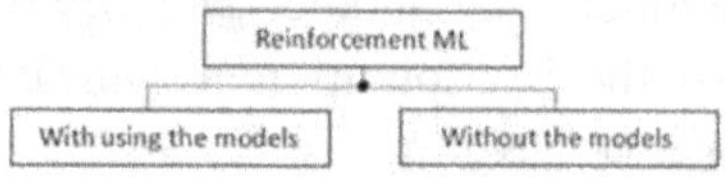

Model-based RL used when the environment is well defined and immutable, and testing real-world environments is difficult.

First, the agent develops an internal representation (model) among:

· the decision performs actions in the environment and notes the new state and value of the reward;

· The transition from action to state is associated with the value of the reward.

Once the model is completed, the agent simulates sequences of actions based on the probability of the optimal total reward.

The solution then further assigns values to the action sequences themselves. The agent develops various strategies in the environment to achieve the desired end goal.

RL without models. Most effective in large, complex, hard-to-describe environments, and in unknown and volatile environments where environment-based testing has no significant disadvantages.

The agent does not develop an internal model of the environment and its dynamics. Instead, the framework uses trial and error to evaluate and flag action-state pairs and sequences of action-state pairs for policy development.

GAN IN CYBERSECURITY

In cybersecurity, the ability of any ML system to identify malware is limited by the quality of its training set, which must be representative of all the different types of malware that have been or can be detected. Regular and prompt updates of the training set are required. The speed of learning is important (long retraining times can make systems vulnerable).

GANs can generate new samples that have the same distribution as the original data, which is very useful in the field of cybersecurity, providing insight into the data distribution structure for new types of malwares. They also help provide insight into the process used by malware authors to create new instances of a malware family (Haas et al., 2021), (Krizhevsky et al., 2017), (Qian et al., 2022), (Siemens, n.d.)

(Behera & Misra, 2021) (Ghosh, 2025) (Vassilev et al., 2023) (Wess et al., 2021) (Otoum et al., 2019). A GAN learns by simply sampling the data provided, without the need to create a probability distribution model of the data in advance.

GANs help anticipate the actions of attackers and develop the best training set, based on which ML models are built to predict the maximum number of anomalies.

So, for the PA method for the IIoT system we can use the RL method with the use of models (Markov processes), supervised ML (FTA, ATA), deep learning methods (GAN, others).

CHALLENGES AND FUTURE DIRECTIONS FOR THE IMPLEMENTATION OF NN-BASED PA IN IIOT SYSTEMS

There are a number of limitations when deploying PA and PdM for IIoT system in the real world. They may be related to insufficient computing power of computers and servers of the enterprise, insufficient memory capacity on hard discs of servers to store a large amount of information received from sensors and after data processing. Any of the IIoT subsystems may fail, in which case the data transmission in the network may be disrupted and the result of the PA process may not be accurate. Therefore, it is advisable to reserve the necessary network devices, and to carry out diagnostics for the communication media as well. Possible cyber-attacks can affect both the PA programmes and processed data stored on the server to compromise their integrity and confidentiality, as well as the PA system for the IIoT system to disable them and disrupt their availability. Thus, there is a threat of cyber-attacks on the vulnerabilities of the PA system. In the practical implementation of PA for IIoT system, it is necessary to take into account possible threats to the performance of this system by implementing appropriate methods to ensure its reliability and cybersecurity.

The future research will focus on the practical implementation of a PA system for IIoT systems and investigate the specifics of its implementation. It will also investigate the possibilities of applying such new concepts as explainable AI (XAI), boundary AI, and federated learning to the task of PA in IIoT systems.

CONCLUSIONS

The IIoT system is complex and prone to failure risks. To determine the types, nature and location of failures and faults, as well as to anticipate their occurrence and manifestation, it is advisable to apply predictive analytics based on AI methods, in particular, neural networks. In this chapter, we have analysed in detail, classified and systematised, the main types of ML and DL methods, and compared their main advantages and disadvantages.

We also analysed, classified and systematised the main types of NN for PA IIoT, on the basis of which the developers of PA systems can choose the most appropriate type of NN for a particular IIoT system, ML methods to obtain more reliable results of classification and prediction of failures, faults, cyber-attacks in the IIoT system.

The conducted research will allow industrial companies to assess end predict the reliability, resiliency, fault tolerance, cybersecurity, dependence of IIoT subsystems and predict their possible failure states and malfunctions, including those due to cyber-attacks, as well as to take necessary measures to ensure the dependability of those IIoT subsystems that are more sensitive to changes in the values of failure rates and cyber-attacks.

REFERENCES

Behera, S., & Misra, R. (2021). Generative adversarial networks based remaining useful life estimation for IIoT. *Computers & Electrical Engineering*, *92*, 107195.

Buyya, R., & Dastjerdi, A. V. (Eds.). (2016). *Internet of Things: Principles and paradigms*. Elsevier.

Ghosh, S. (2025). "How to Compare Machine Learning Models and Algorithms", Neptune Blog. Available: https://neptune.ai/blog/how-to-compare-machine-learning-models-and-algorithms

Haas, B., Wendt, A., Jantsch, A., & Wess, M. (2021). A. Jantsch та M. Wess, "Neural Network Compression Through Shunt Connections and Knowledge Distillation for Semantic Segmentation Problems". *IFIP Advances in Information and Communication Technology*, *627*, 349–361. DOI: 10.1007/978-3-030-79150-6_28

ISO. "The basis of neural networks: Cracking the code", (2024). Available: https://www.iso.org/artificial-intelligence/neural-networks

ISO/IEC. "JTC 1 Preliminary Report 2014 Internet of Things (IoT)", (2014). 17 p. Available: https://www.iso.org/files/live/sites/isoorg/files/developing_standards/docs/en/internet_of_things_report-jtc1.pdf

ISO/IEC 20924:2021(en). "Information technology — Internet of Things (IoT) — Vocabulary", 2021. Available: https://www.iso.org/obp/ui/#iso:std:iso-iec:20924:ed-2:v1:en

ISO/IEC 22989:2022(en), "Information technology — Artificial intelligence — Artificial intelligence concepts and terminology", 2022. Available: https://www.iso.org/obp/ui/en/#iso:std:iso-iec:22989:ed-1:v1:en

ISO/IEC 23053:2022. "Framework for Artificial Intelligence (AI). Systems Using Machine Learning (ML)", 2022. Available: https://www.iso.org/standard/74438.html

ISO/IEC 24668:2022(en) "Information technology — Artificial intelligence — Process management framework for big data analytics", 2022. Available: https://www.iso.org/obp/ui/en/#iso:std:iso-iec:24668:ed-1:v1:en

ISO/IEC TR 24029-1:2021(en), "Artificial Intelligence (AI) — Assessment of the robustness of neural networks — Part 1: Overview", 2021. Available: https://www.iso.org/obp/ui/en/#iso:std:iso-iec:tr:24029:-1:ed-1:v1:en

ISO/IEC TR 24030:2024(en), "Information technology — Artificial intelligence (AI) — Use cases", 2024. Available: https://www.iso.org/obp/ui/en/#iso:std:84144:en

Kolisnyk, M., & Jantsch, A. (2024, September). ML-based fault tree analysis of Industrial Router Reliability in the System IIoT. In *2024 International Conference on Applied Mathematics & Computer Science (ICAMCS)* (pp. 173-178). IEEE.

Krizhevsky, A., Sutskever, I., & Hinton, G. E. (2017). I. Sutskever та G. E. Hinton, "ImageNet classification with deep convolutional neural networks". *Communications of the ACM*, *60*(6), 84–90. DOI: 10.1145/3065386

Maglogiannis, I. (2021). J. Macintyre та L. Iliadis, "*Artificial Intelligence Applications and Innovations"*. Cham. *IFIP Advances in Information and Communication Technology*, *627*. Advance online publication. DOI: 10.1007/978-3-030-79150-6

"Microsoft Neural Network algorithm", *Microsoft Learn*, (2023). Available: https://learn.microsoft.com/en-us/analysis-services/data-mining/microsoft-neural-network-algorithm? view =asallproducts-allversions

Minerva, R., Biru, A., & Rotondi, D. (2015). Towards a definition of the Internet of Things (IoT). *IEEE Internet Initiative*, *1*(1), 1–86.

Murel, J., & Kavlakoglu, E. (2024). What is ensemble learning?.

NVIDIA. developer. "Artificial Neural Network", (2024). Available: https://developer.nvidia.com/discover/artificial-neural-network

Otoum, Y., Liu, D., & Nayak, A. (2019). D. Liu та A. Nayak, "DL-IDS: A deep learning–based intrusion detection framework for securing IoT". *Transactions on Emerging Telecommunications Technologies*, *33*(3), e3803. Advance online publication. DOI: 10.1002/ett.3803

"Prescriptive analytics", *IBM,* (2020). Available: https://www.ibm.com/blog/prescriptive-analytics-manage-manufacturing-costs-and-improve-roi/

Qian, C., Yu, W., Lu, C., Griffith, D., & Golmie, N. (2022). "Toward Generative Adversarial Networks for the Industrial Internet of Things". *IEEE Internet of Things Journal*, *9*(19), 9147–19159. DOI: 10.1109/JIOT.2022.3163894

"Techtarget. What is predictive analytics? An enterprise guide", (2024). Available: https://www.techtarget.com/searchbusinessanalytics/definition/predictive-analytics

Vassilev, A., Oprea, A., Fordyce, A., & Andersen, H. (2024). Adversarial machine learning: A taxonomy and terminology of attacks and mitigations.

Vernova, G. E. (2025). *Brochure*. Apm Driving Reliability Forward., Available https://www.gevernova.com/software/resources/brochure/asset-performance-management-reliability

Wess, M., Ivanov, M., Unger, C., Nookala, A., Wendt, A., & Jantsch, A. (2021). A. Wendt та A. Jantsch, "ANNETTE: Accurate Neural Network Execution Time Estimation With Stacked Models". *IEEE Access : Practical Innovations, Open Solutions*, *9*, 3545–3556. DOI: 10.1109/ACCESS.2020.3047259

"What is a neural network?", *IBM,* (2024). Available: https://www.ibm.com/think/topics/neural-networks

"What is Bagging?", *IBM,* (2024). Available: https://www.ibm.com/think/topics/bagging

"What is predictive analytics?", *IBM,* (2024). Available: https://www.ibm.com/think/topics/predictive-analytics

Chapter 9
Exploring the Synergy of Intelligent Systems:
Cloud Computing, Industrial Internet of Things (IIoT), Big Data Analytics, and Neural Networks

Sarâh Benziane
https://orcid.org/0000-0002-0450-6522
USTO MB, Algeria

ABSTRACT

The rapid advancement of intelligent systems, driven by the integration of cloud computing, the Industrial Internet of Things (IIoT), big data analytics, and neural networks, is transforming industries and society. These technologies work in synergy to enable real-time data processing, predictive analytics, and automated decision-making, offering unprecedented benefits across sectors such as healthcare, manufacturing, urban planning, and agriculture. Despite their promise, the adoption of intelligent systems presents challenges, including ethical concerns, security vulnerabilities, and interoperability issues. This chapter provides a comprehensive overview of these technologies, explores their integration, highlights real-world applications, and examines trends in their adoption and benefits. The chapter concludes by addressing current challenges and proposing future directions to enhance the scalability, efficiency, and ethical alignment of intelligent systems.

DOI: 10.4018/979-8-3373-4571-0.ch009

Copyright © 2025, IGI Global Scientific Publishing. Copying or distributing in print or electronic forms without written permission of IGI Global Scientific Publishing is prohibited.

1. INTRODUCTION

The present human society is completely revolutionized with the advent of intelligent systems representing the convergence of various technological breakthroughs, such as cloud computing, large-scale collaboration and big data, industrial Internet of Things, big data analytics, machine learning and artificial intelligence, especially neural networks. In particular, the intelligent systems combining different technologies, such as cloud computing (Armbrust et al., 2010), data analytics, and/or big data, act as the foundation of digital businesses and support the digital transformation across various sectors, such as agriculture, disaster management, healthcare, heritage and culture, industry, supply chains, urban areas, etc. However, there are myriad challenges to face in order to achieve their promise (Gubbi, Buyya, Marusic, & Palaniswami, 2013). These are related to the integration of these technologies to provide cross-domain analytics, the design of the core methodologies and algorithms to support the intelligent systems, the development of the tools and platforms that can be customized to the needs of the users, and the identification of modular design to assure the systems' scalability and sustainability. (Manyika et al., 2011)

Some of the main functionalities of an "intelligent system" induced by the synergies of these technologies are: enhancement of operational efficiency through intelligent analytics and subsequently identifying and predicting events and possible solutions to improve outcomes; provision of location-based marketing; public information/event sharing; monitoring and optimizing supplies and production; demand-driven logistics and interconnected mobility; enhancing the decision-making processes and facilitating innovation; development of new or enhancement of existing services. This position paper provides a comprehensive overview of the ongoing research to develop and execute such emerging trendsetters and the challenges that ensue to openly discuss the existing forefront in developing the intelligent systems. We then discuss the key asymmetries and how they can be integrated to leverage the information sciences. Finally, we identify future research routes for synergies to unleash timely actions in perspectives of offering interesting services with high impact. In the next section, to begin with, the related works are discussed, covering an understanding of the industrial Internet of Things, cloud computing, big data analytics, and neural networks, which form the basic building blocks of intelligent systems. (LeCun, Bengio, & Hinton, 2015)

1.1. Background and Significance

Depending on the developments in technology (Chen, Mao, & Liu, 2014), intelligent systems based on cognitive computing models have great potential, as indicated by modern trends towards the wide use of cloud computing, the transformation of cyber-physical systems into the Industrial Internet of Things, the application of big data analytics in various industries, and the effectiveness of modern neural networks in a wide variety of tasks as narrow AI. This technological background has evolved from initial theoretical assumptions into practical applications, which are tested by real users and have chances to become more popular in the future. In the context of complex social challenges requiring innovation, intelligent systems may contribute significantly to achieving shared socio-economic progress while continuing to generate important indirect advantages to the technology developed. (Marjani et al., 2017)

The steady growth of interest in cloud computing illustrates a dynamic process. This service has become an actual utility, cloudifying existing services and creating new ones, with earnings growing as a result. Each industrial revolution has enabled practitioners and researchers to rethink digital processing techniques and interactions invisible to the human factor by leveraging new solutions whose feedback is carried out in a dynamic spectrum, from a technological point of view to societal implications. As a result, new advancements and synergies in research and development are expected that will be able to leverage and combine multiple technologies to create integrated and holistic artifacts, increasing the effectiveness and efficiency of business and industrial processes, enhancing human wellness through the application of intelligent systems, and developing new paradigms to provide services across different application fields. These processes are facilitated by numerous technology drivers, such as the broad acceptance of digital dashboards in decision support, online services, and many forms of e-commerce and the social web. (Schmidhuber, 2015)

This chapter aims to explore the integration of these cutting-edge technologies, providing a comprehensive overview of their roles, interplay, and impact. Specifically, the objectives are to:

1. **Examine Core Technologies**: Understand the fundamental principles of cloud computing, IIoT, big data analytics, and neural networks as standalone technologies.
2. **Highlight Synergies**: Analyze how these technologies complement each other to create holistic, intelligent systems that address real-world challenges.
3. **Identify Challenges**: Discuss the limitations, ethical considerations, and technical barriers associated with the integration of these technologies.
4. **Propose Future Directions**: Suggest pathways for further research and development to enhance the scalability, security, and efficiency of intelligent systems.

The scope of this chapter is to provide both theoretical insights and practical perspectives on the development and implementation of intelligent systems. It targets researchers, practitioners, and industry stakeholders seeking to leverage the power of integrated technologies to drive innovation and solve complex problems.

By outlining the current state-of-the-art and identifying key trends and challenges, this chapter lays a foundation for understanding how intelligent systems are shaping the future of industries and society at large.

2. FOUNDATIONS OF INTELLIGENT SYSTEMS

Until a few years ago, cloud computing (Atzori, Iera, & Morabito, 2010), a study related to delivering computing power as a service over a network, was considered one of the most valuable research areas. It brought clear benefits such as reduced costs, less processing time, and flexibility to use resources based on the service model. More recently, another term also became increasingly prominent: the Industrial Internet of Things. Based on this term, we can observe how devices or things are connecting to the internet and how they have started impacting the recent revolution. Thus, cloud computing and the Industrial Internet of Things play an important role in understanding the recent demand and shift in cloud services due to the data generated by devices and how data are being generated from trillion bytes to zettabytes and how it affects the internet. (Yang & Zhang, 2021)

According to recent trends, several IT companies have invested a huge amount of their profits in a new area, for example, storage and networking, to reshape cloud services or other related internet services. In this contribution, we connect the large community with present and future research challenges and opportunities of IoT to give readers direction and clues to frame the objectives of research. Thus, to identify predicted blending points in the investigation, we briefly discuss each technology systematically in this section, in which we will address the basics, foundational key points, development, future research challenges and opportunities, and interrelations to generate the synergy of intelligent systems. In the next section, we discuss big data analytics and neural networks as a new generation or rapid development structure of cloud computing in more detail to point out value for researchers where they can focus their efforts to develop such openness in a more imminent mode. (Thomas & Nguyen, 2020)

2.1. Cloud Computing

Cloud computing is one of the pivotal technologies that integrates industries with intelligent systems (Zhang, Cheng, & Boutaba, 2010). It comprises large-scale computing infrastructures in terms of hardware, data storage systems, and computer clusters to manage massive data processing requirements. This computational infrastructure consists of three key service models: IaaS, PaaS, and SaaS. These models accomplish and define characteristics of full computing systems for large-scale and distributed applications to semiautomatic systems, including properties like massive scalability, on-demand capacity, and cost-effectiveness, providing clients with flexibility and wide data storage and data processing capabilities based upon the availability of programming platforms and software. (Bonomi, Milito, Zhu, & Addepalli, 2012)

In big data and the cloud computing environment, computational resources and the techniques of data analytics have achieved dramatic importance as of late. Technically, cloud computing is the delivery of on-demand computing resources such as processing power, storage, and software services over the internet on a pay-for-use basis. The usage of software and hardware is delivered in an on-demand or as-needed manner whereby the end users access web services and software through thin or thick clients or web-based interface devices. The working architecture and the components that collectively make a cloud computing environment are defined into three categories known as the back end, the front end, and the network. Cloud computing benefits in terms of reduced costs and the efficiency of collaborating resources and data processing. Apart from the business industry, several other remote sensing fields such as the military, finance, healthcare, and agriculture are also using cloud computing resources and systems to process big data. With the ability of cloud computing systems to handle the execution of applications and their dynamic scalable and fully distributed big data computing systems, the IaaS and IIoT solutions will be implemented through the use of cloud computing systems for execution. Furthermore, the cloud computing environment provides computing resources and data storage. It is the natural choice for data from IoT devices and equipment. (Sun et al., 2018).

Figure 1. Cloud computing: Integration, challenges, and applications

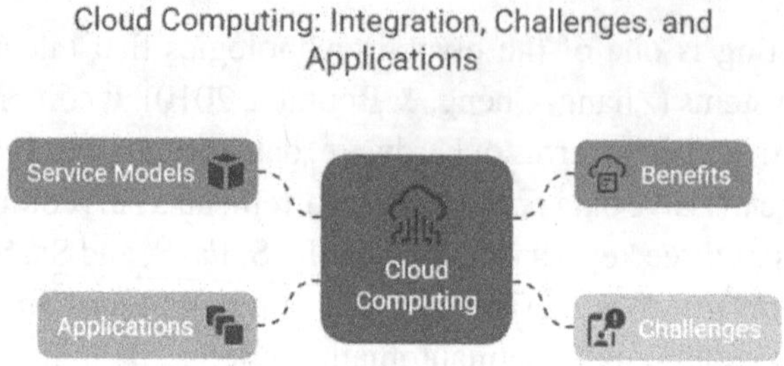

The scalability and flexibility of its distributed processing of data make it an ideal choice in handling and executing many computation requests and responses. The widespread use of cloud computing does have some challenges that need attention. The dependency of subscriber services on provider services is the biggest problem associated with cloud computing. Natural calamities leading to server outages are very palpable. While using the internet-based IIoT, the same internet is used to connect between the data. Major companies are providing this cloud computing. The combination of the above-mentioned challenges makes it a harsh decision to use it as a solution for outdoor to indoor technology in IIoT. Many applications that implement cloud computing as a service include data mining, healthcare, processing, etc. More comprehensive integration of cloud computing and IIoT will result in improving the performance of the applications. Hence, there is a great need to study and explore the scope of such systems. (Bengio, 2009)

2.2. Industrial Internet of Things (IIoT)

The Industrial Internet of Things (IIoT) is one of the most effective ways to evolve operations. Its connected devices gather essential operational data for analysis. This is indeed necessary due to the ongoing revolutions in process efficiency, cost savings, and informed decision-making. The IIoT environment consists of the real-time connectivity between machines, processes, systems, and end-users that increase applicable protocols and interoperability standards (Coyle et al., 2011). The IIoT covers various systems that can self-discover and interfaces between multiple internet and intranet systems (Lee & Lee, 2015). Devices here communicate with one another to sense, share, and create data in real time that can be analyzed and converted into insightful information. The data collection is done with the help of various sensors or adapted input-output devices. (Muehlhauser, 2021)

IIoT technologies are used to exchange data between systems in real time. In manufacturing, the use of IIoT makes it possible to apply wireless sensors for different control and automation applications that are relatively inexpensive for network communication. The techniques help acquire relevant data and information. Additionally, IIoT provides the solution for supply chain management issues and also manages logistics, warehouse operations, and aftermarket product services. This enables the efficient administration of truck and transport logistics services by tracking their location in real time. Applications in the transport and logistics sectors also consist of intermodal transport control, traction systems, traffic management and control systems, supply chain visibility technologies, intelligent freight transportation systems, and intelligent inventory management applications. The e-service of Supply Chain Management is relevant in reducing end-to-end inventory. Typical functionalities are offered with the help of the IIoT for monitoring all chain links of the operations, understanding the current position of the order, and tracking the order for intermodal transport. (Gonzalez & Dankel, 2010)

IIoT technologies impact efficiency while decreasing downtime and optimizing processes throughout different sectors. An essential advantage of the IIoT is indicating where the technology benefits are coming from. It also highlights the outcomes associated with particular technology. Data format, scalability, usage of meaningful and relevant information, data management, interoperability standards, and flexibility are the challenges proposed in the IIoT deployment. There is a connection between the IIoT and the cloud computing platform. The combination of cloud and IIoT improves the collection of data for historical review, management, and vast analysis. At present, IIoT technologies that are widely used are based on the cloud platform and represent a different way to obtain various Big Data sources, including IIoT Big Data. (Weiss et al., 1990)

Future research developments and trends focus on the different aspects of IIoT weights associated with intelligent systems or Big Data analytics. Internet-based things offer better solutions capable of performing and transferring distributed computing. In short, mainly big data from the Internet of Things is a number of interrelated big data origin types that are generated and converted into big data along with their associated big data functionalities. The interconnected Internet of Things also constitutes a vital component for greater applications of big data analytics while simultaneously reflecting the overall super trend of Big Data analytics proposed in the following future years. It acts as an essential tool for intelligent systems technology. (West, 2018)

2.3. Big Data Analytics

The term 'big data' refers to massive volumes of data that cannot be interpreted using traditional methods and technologies (Srivastava et al., 2015). Big data has several defining properties: volume, variety, velocity, veracity, value, and visuality. The volume of big data is high, and it keeps on increasing day by day. Moreover, big data comes in various forms that require different processing techniques, such as structured, unstructured, semi-structured, text, audio, video, geospatial, temporal, and log files. The speed or rate at which data grows and is processed is known as its velocity, while the inconsistencies in and uncertainties about the data are represented by the veracity component. Big data is valuable because it can be beneficial for the organization directly or indirectly. Finally, big data can also be visualized and represented using various data visualization tools and techniques. The role of big data analytics is very crucial in today's data-driven world. Big data analytics, also known as predictive or advanced analytics, includes various procedures and techniques such as machine learning, data mining, statistics, and natural language processing. These techniques help in predicting unseen and future events, improving decision-making, optimizing asset utilization, and providing measurable business values. Moreover, big data analytics can discover hidden patterns and trends from large volumes of data that can be very useful for making long-term strategic decisions. Big data analytics has already been applied in various real-world sectors, such as finance, retail, banking, human resources, e-commerce, healthcare, and marketing. Despite such great potential, big data analytics faces several challenges and barriers such as data quality, data uncertainty, data privacy, data security, data integration, metadata management, and the lack of data governance. Neural networks and big data analytics are two important computer-aided intelligent engineering tools and techniques that can be used together to solve complex forecasting and classification tasks. In other words, big data analytics can be used to prepare and process the neural network inputs or datasets, and a neural network can be used to solve some of the big data analytics challenges and problems. For example, techniques such as big data clustering can be applied to large datasets to create numerous clusters that can be difficult to manage or interpret. In such cases, a neural network can be used for automatic cluster labeling, which can help in better interpreting the outcome and guiding the decision-making process. (Buyya et al., 2009)

2.4. Neural Networks

neural networks have long been the focus of research efforts because of the promise of imitating the interconnected neurons in the human brain to solve complex tasks (Benziane & Benyettou, 2013). NNs are formed by layers of interconnected small processing units—neurons. Neural networks were inspired by the architecture of human nervous systems. They can receive an input and generate an output; in between the input layer and the output layer, there exist multiple layers of neurons. Output signals that are generated by the neurons in one layer become input signals to the next layer. Each link between the neurons has a weight that can be modified within the training process, and this change can strengthen or weaken the signal that is being communicated. Different types of NN are available for different applications including feedforward neural networks, convolutional neural networks, and radial basis function networks to name a few. Feedforward neural networks can approximate any continuous function. Convolutional neural networks are widely used in image analysis as they are specifically designed to recognize visual patterns directly from pixel images, and are capable of capturing spatial and temporal dependencies from data. Written as an algorithm, convolutional neural networks do not predict given function extrapolations, but, rather, intend to capture changing structures present in the data. (Chui et al., 2018)

The hidden layers of a CNN perform some feature extraction, and the output of a hidden layer is usually processed through a rectified linear activation function to allow nonlinear feature extraction. This is important because some functions cannot be recognized by only one straight line or plane. The biggest advantage of CNN is that all complex operations, namely convolution, pooling, and activation, are performed using the computer's graphic processing units, which enables the acceleration of the training and recognition of the CNN. As a result, CNN has gained great recognition in many computer vision tasks, such as object detection, image classification, semantic segmentation, and action recognition, and has several medical imaging and diagnosis applications. Neural networks, which are a major branch in big data analytics, have provided the system behavior recognition and system performance prediction in big industry to enable preventive and predictive maintenance of components, machines, and plants. They have also been coupled with physics models to provide a hybrid algorithm for data-driven and physics-informed prediction and classification in industry. Neural networks, as a cornerstone technology within the intelligent systems development, with the aid of the theory of deep learning, address and tackle problems encountered in today's industrial applications, which is an extension of AI applications. The main challenges of employing NN/AI for real-world industrial applications are the efficient training of the large-scale model and the problem of interpretability and ethically responsible decision-making based on the AI-prevised prediction. (Goodfellow, Bengio, & Courville, 2016)

A more advanced form of neural network is deep learning, which has the capability to automatically learn to classify patterns such as images and sounds without human intervention and knowledge in the sketch of the machine learning paradigm. Deep learning can make better predictions with more data and in some case has the capabilities to learn from big data. It is a self-learning system that applies large amounts of data to train the neural network. Furthermore, in recent developments in deep learning algorithms, such as improved techniques and the variety of deep networks, deep learning AI can take the capabilities of AI systems like neural networks to mimic the human brain to process data and create patterns for decision making based on the data. This is a major technology for today's industries in many fields including predictive analytics, anomaly detection or diagnostics, quality improvement, and providing advanced computing capabilities to capture and analyze data to make faster and more accurate predictions. NN and DNN, blood, and blood components are considered as universal donor biofluids that could give us vast information of the internal diseases of help to improve decision making in drug discovery research. (Gupta & Gupta, 2019)

3. INTEGRATION AND INTERPLAY OF TECHNOLOGIES

Tailored for their specific applications, some of the aforementioned classifications and explorations represent models of how cloud computing, big data analytics [27], and IIoT can strategically interact and work together to have a bigger impact. Here are two examples. First, interdisciplinary aspects of big data analytics, cloud computing, and IIoT were classified into three categories: data networks and processing, security and privacy, and services, applications, and innovation. Second, three models of how big data analytics can be performed by leveraging cloud computing and IIoT advancements were proposed. Data can be moved from IIoT devices to the datacenter or the cloud for additional analytics. A combined solution with a mixture of on-premises and cloud computing (in a hybrid or multi-cloud) for additional analytics can be used. Alternatively, storage devices that can support machine learning with real-time decision-making can be employed. (Mohamed, 2020)

Figure 2. Architecture of intelligent systems

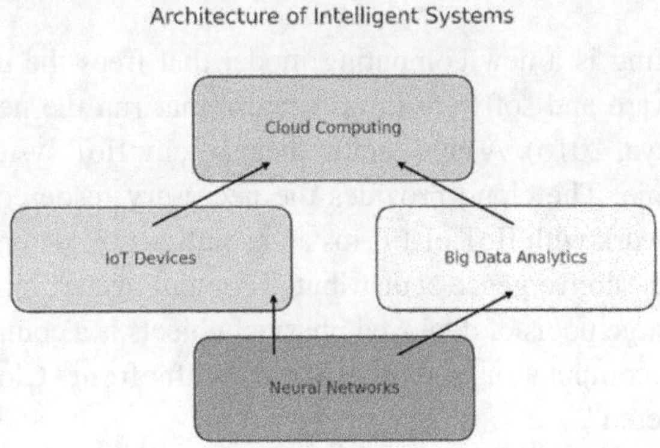

For collaboration at a deeper level of technologies to occur, there is a strong need for interoperability across different platforms and manufacturers of technologies in the ecosystem. Interoperability can enable seamless connectivity, cooperation, and data sharing by, among others, making data compatible across edges, the cloud, and big data analytics and parallel architectures. Achieving such integration is particularly important to tackle some of the challenges associated with each of these technologies, as well as to further innovation. There already exist many successful implementations and case studies showing the strengths and advancements achieved when these technologies work together as a joint system. The architectural and technological silos proposed by cloud computing, the IIoT, and big data are proving to hinder efficient data exchange. While they all have the capability to analyze and extract information from data, it is the interconnection between these technologies that can ensure that the connections do not only collect data but also provide the necessary analytics to improve decision-making. Innovation emerged with the connection of these technologies alone. Progress in the manufacturing sector, the utility industry, and an array of practical applications to date clearly demonstrates the possibilities. Furthermore, research in the fields of cloud computing, IIoT, and big data has benefited from the inclusion of neural networks in their models and analyses. Synergy from the side of big data has advanced analytics that is beyond the capabilities of where IIoT and cloud work individually, as big data connects with cloud computing. Integration in terms of data analytics has resulted in great success stories. Nonetheless, challenges still remain in the quest for seamless collaboration across the intelligent technical systems. These include but are not limited to data silos, system coupling, optimization, security, and related technology, as well as technical limitations to fully exploit the integration and federated learning strategies. (Zhang et al., 2015)

3.1. Cloud Computing and IIoT Integration

Cloud computing is a new computing model that frees the user from having to own the hardware and software infrastructure that run the necessary services (Dastjerdi & Buyya, 2016). A core requirement of any IIoT system is its flexible deployment scheme. The cloud provides the necessary resources, platform, and tools required to work with IIoT platforms and solutions by becoming a "Cloud of Things". In IIoT, the convergence of distributed computing capabilities and services in the cloud and large pools of deployed physical objects is a compelling vision. In this scenario, the computation paradigm slowly shifts from "Cloud-Centered" to "Cloud/Fog-Centered".

Figure 3. Comparison of Cloud Computing and Edge Computing

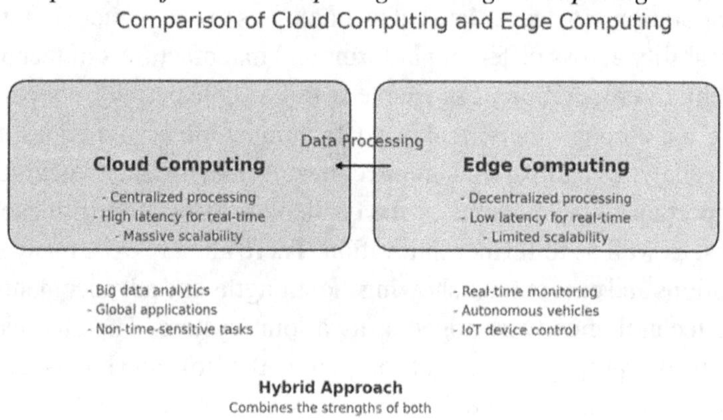

Clouds allow organizations to practice IIoT integration in an efficient manner. The hybrid combination of connecting IIoT devices with the cloud is expected to positively affect the scalability, accessibility, and return on investment of all industries, which may face challenges in the absence of advanced cloud-based IIoT systems. In agriculture, advances in cloud-connected IIoT have fueled the convergence of organic food and e-commerce. IIoT platforms that use a combination of cloud-connected IIoT, AI, and deep learning to help farmers automate weed killing can be seen as an indicator of this convergence. Add to that advancements in smart transportation, which leverage IIoT and cloud-based intelligence to provide an array of personal protection, communication, and vehicle monitoring services. Finally, the smart city sphere has also seen massive innovation in cloud-based IIoT. Privacy and data protection are another area where both the cloud and IIoT depend significantly on each other. To deal with this challenge, a secure protocol should be implemented between the cloud and IoT devices to exchange data. Data latency is one of the primary challenges that emerges when IoT and the cloud are interconnected. In the manufacturing sector, when the blood bag packet starts to get warm, the system can quickly reinforce the cooling pumps in order to keep the blood packets cool until they are needed. Several standards and platforms are available, which enable the transfer of data between IIoT and the cloud with varying features. This survey, however, deals with the overall merge of IIoT into AI systems. In the following subsection, we focus on yet another popular use case of big data that is empowered by the use of recurrent networks in AI-based systems.

3.2. Big Data and Neural Networks Integration

From data to data analytics, data-based research endorses an ongoing synergy. When data analytics is applied to several data types, a further synergy emerges: big data analytics. However, if data analytics is applied to big data through artificial intelligence, another interesting technological combination appears. Among these technologies, this subsection focuses on the integration of big data analytics and neural networks. Also, in this case, intelligent system-like approaches dramatically improve the capability of making effective predictions or revealing interesting insights by significantly increasing the value of the data available in big data scenarios. The relevant effect of this combination of technologies is clearly expressed in five possible big data applications at the state of the art.

Big data indicates collections of large datasets that can no longer be managed by using traditional data processing tools. Therefore, hardware and software changes sustain the different dimensions of both structured and unstructured large datasets. Based on the nature of big data, the intelligent applications resulting from neural networks adopt distributed infrastructures for storage, processing, computations, analysis, and knowledge creation that demand speeds equivalent to petabytes and terabytes of data size in an appreciable real-time sense. Comparatively, trained neural networks focus on extracting, identifying, and Gaussianizing the large data representation that offers a more robust classification and recommendation performance. It can be said that the optimal approach of efficient neural networks speeds up the processes for big data analytics that do not require any additional feature selection or extraction tools. This speed occurs due to the leveraged storage infrastructure, data processing units, diversified network architectures, efficient learning tools, and easy neural algorithms that embody the strategic features such as backpropagation and convergence technologies for fine-tuning weight values.

4. APPLICATIONS AND USE CASES

Cloud computing, the Industrial Internet of Things (IIoT), big data, business analytic systems, and neural networks can work together to smartly solve many real-world problems. This synergy of intelligent systems and their applications improves and transforms industrial automation, robotics, energy, automotive, and health informatics through smart services, optimal decisions, and efficient predictions in milliseconds. Highly interconnected, technology-savvy cities and businesses, including people, are adopting a data-driven, always connected approach when it comes to solving old problems in a new way. This new thinking is not just technology, but interconnected technologies and services. These interconnected technologies carry the potential to dramatically change people's lives by improving services and promoting efficiency, sustainability, economic development, and social inclusion. The cloud computing-based smart city is fundamentally reliant on the advent of the Internet of Things (IoT), which, in turn, includes the concept of the Industrial Internet of Things (IIoT) in the case of business and industrial process and machine monitoring and control. Big data and business analytics are another key technological piece within smart cities and can be described as the processes of examining large amounts of data of a variety of types to uncover hidden patterns, unknown correlations, and other useful information that can be used for the decision-making process. Big data and business analytical processes often rely on neural networks to help attempt to uncover and then predict such unknowns. Modern smart cities require more sophisticated and real-time system management and control. Cloud computing is a widely used IT paradigm for enabling seamless and ubiquitous access to a shared pool of configurable resources. The cloud computing paradigm permits on-demand access to pooled computing resources such as networks, storage, servers, applications, and services. Cloud services can be rapidly provisioned and released with minimal management effort. They can also be managed either by the consumer, service provider, or a third-party player. Cloud computing provides a solution for the security, virtualization, IT infrastructure, smart devices, and big data management inherent in smart infrastructure systems. Using the cloud, smart infrastructure solutions and big data management and analytical services can be seamlessly supported and delivered to users.

4.1. Smart Cities

Cities already cover landmass, utilize energy, and generate a massive amount of data, making them a favorable environment for the development of intelligent systems. The concept of a "smart city" typically refers to a city that uses intelligent systems to improve the quality of life for individual citizens and overall resource management. These cities usually cover a wide range of applications and may be supported by different alliances of stakeholders; however, in nearly all cases where an argument can be made for the promise of smart cities, real industrial applications are required to achieve a trifecta of economic growth, operational and environmental sustainability, and citizen improvement. Industrial Internet of Things (IIoT) systems are an essential part of almost all represented smart city and intelligent urban systems. IIoT often forms the "sensing system" and enables individual cities or intelligent systems to collect data in "essentially real time" from their numerous and varied infrastructures to help manage, track, trace, and optimize resource allocation and demand. These systems are supported by scalable and efficient cloud storage and intelligent algorithms to help process and facilitate the storage of the resulting data and text analytics.

Smart cities help implement smart grid technology in urban areas to minimize energy wastage by utilizing infrastructure energy in a smart way, electric car charging, and optimal renewable resource usage, reducing peak load demand as much as 20%, or creating distributed generation and storage resources resulting in an expected 70% reduction in cost for solar systems. In the development of smart water supply monitoring, city planners and engineers are also able to directly help control flood dangers. This is a case where a utility gets creative helping processes other than just their own resource management. The monitoring process required to create and maintain smart cities needs to be a combination of real-time and post-time data and alerts as well as trend monitoring. For example, even if a weather forecast predicts rain for the next three days, the infrastructure management system must be prepared and begin to alert stakeholders about potential flooding impacts today. An alert system has been developed that notifies customers the day before scheduled repair work that will require water service outages as part of their innovative replanning project. In doing so, customers have been given advance warning instead of only waiting for a notice. However, this has to be carried out in a way that minimizes privacy invasion by sharing such data, as well as security hacks of infrastructure systems. As such, maintaining integrated energy-water infrastructure systems, such as a smart grid for optimized cooling, can also impact public health. Overall, the area of physical systems monitoring and control holds great promise for citizens. In addition to the business-government partnership it would take, citizens were also given an opportunity in their individual lives to both enhance and become involved in infrastructure health monitoring and control.

4.2. Healthcare

Because large volumes of data are produced in the healthcare sector, it is a prime candidate for the application of intelligent systems. Cloud computing can be used to gather patient information swiftly, while big data analytics can be used for predictive analytics to forecast patient trends and diagnose potential issues. Intelligent Patient Data Management (IPDM) is another use case concept in healthcare. The proposed method uses intelligent systems to collect individual patient data based on the IoT network. Through the concept of IPDM, large hospitals, smaller clinics, and the community will greatly benefit. Intelligent Patient Data Management collects multidimensional patient data and uses big data density as a tool to provide personalized patient medical care. Currently, a small proportion of the population uses electronic medical records. We can forecast potential problems using big data density to collect and manage current patient data and business intelligence.

The remote healthcare monitoring system (RHMS), a healthcare-oriented application, has already been built. It enables bio-signal acquisition, patient data information transmission, and storage for the treatment of diagnosed diseases. Hospitals and healthcare providers were able to offer outstanding telemedicine treatment, manage limited bandwidth during healthcare data transmission to the cloud, and avoid some privacy issues using the healthcare data proximity cloud. The practice of calculating doctor recommendations is incomplete. Internal and physiological changes in the body of the patient for disease condition patterns are obtained using present healthcare monitoring sensory devices. Treatment recommendation feedback was provided to the physicians with no records of a neural network application. During diagnostics and therapy, a neural network can be useful for doctors to pinpoint patterns in the data. That said, it is important to collaborate with doctors and technology providers to use the aid in intravenous therapies. However, it can only increase the diagnostic and therapeutic capabilities.

4.3. Manufacturing

In the manufacturing process sector, intelligent systems can reframe industrial operations. Leading the Industry 4.0 concept, the manufacturing sector is migrating from legacy technological solutions to the adoption of the fourth industrial revolution technologies that revolutionize operational processes. The Industrial Internet of Things eases the connection between machinery, while cloud computing offers the opportunity to monitor and control the entire facility remotely. This connectivity offers actionable intelligence inherently capable of reducing waste, optimizing processes, driving cost efficiencies, and fostering digital transformation-related growth. Greater access to real-time data will make the production process more adaptive and responsive to customer needs, avoiding bottlenecks and reducing non-value-added activities.

As an example, big data analytics in the manufacturing sector could be used to predict potential maintenance-related inefficiencies in machines and quality issues. Timely maintenance needs could be anticipated, preventing production performance degradation due to unexpected downtime. Deep learning has often been exploited as a possible remedy in those systems, forecasting wear-out and other environmental applications.

This move toward ever-deeper analysis and more sophisticated problem-solving deepens the need to develop a workforce with the understanding and skills to optimize intelligent manufacturing systems. Despite the compelling forecasted growth and construction of diverging technological pipelines to support automation, clear trends and challenges emerge. The IIoT migration demands significant investment to purchase and deploy sensors, processors, and corresponding networking systems. An investment will also be required to raise the knowledge and skill level of facility managers and system integrators. End users dramatically underestimate the effort and experience needed to integrate legacy factory automation or IT systems with contemporary methodologies. Furthermore, the adoption of IIoT strategies may correlate with lower unemployment rates in low-skill positions. Smart factories call for fewer and different assembly workers, more systems administrators, more asset and chain managers, and additional design engineers. Additionally, recent increases in workplace automation and digitalization technologies—coupled with significant recession-related layoffs of prospective workers—reduce total job openings during the next five years.

Numerous successful case studies are present in the field; for example, a company provides many Industry 4.0 applications. A cloud product is offered by an IIoT start-up to track real-time operational dashboards from unconnected machinery. A large multinational company has developed predictive health monitoring and service strategies to monitor current and temperature for their residential and commercial select circuit breakers and discusses additional technologies that are on the path to market. A complete IIoT cloud system architecture for plasma beam cutting processes is proposed to predict the Remaining Useful Life of cutting tools. Overall Equipment Effectiveness is studied. As a future trend, Industry 4.0 is growing in popularity in the scientific community and motivates the majority of the current work, as well as a recent interest in specific smart factories. In one review of applications, a cloud-based approach is taken in only a few case studies in the manufacture and inundate section, including asset management and monitoring electricity use in wide-area geographical regions.

4.4. Real-World Examples and Case Studies of Intelligent Systems

1. Healthcare: Intelligent Patient Monitoring Systems

In healthcare, intelligent systems have revolutionized patient care through the integration of IoT devices, big data analytics, and neural networks. For example:

Mayo Clinic has implemented an AI-driven patient monitoring system that uses IoT-enabled wearable devices to collect real-time health data, such as heart rate, oxygen saturation, and activity levels. Big data analytics processes this information to predict potential health risks, while neural networks identify patterns that may signal early signs of disease progression. This proactive system reduces hospital admissions and improves patient outcomes.

2. Manufacturing: Predictive Maintenance in Smart Factories

The adoption of Industry 4.0 technologies has enabled predictive maintenance in manufacturing:

General Electric (GE) uses the Predix platform, an IIoT-driven cloud system, to monitor industrial equipment. Sensors installed on machines collect performance data, which is analyzed in real-time using big data techniques. Neural network models predict potential equipment failures before they occur, significantly reducing downtime and maintenance costs.

3. Urban Planning: Smart Cities

Intelligent systems are transforming urban areas into smart cities by enhancing energy efficiency, traffic management, and public services:

Barcelona, Spain, has implemented an IoT-based smart lighting system. Streetlights equipped with sensors adjust brightness based on pedestrian activity and weather conditions. The system collects data, which is analyzed using cloud computing and big data analytics, leading to energy savings of up to 30%. Neural networks further optimize lighting patterns for improved safety and reduced costs.

4. Retail: Personalized Shopping Experiences

Retailers are leveraging intelligent systems to enhance customer experiences through personalization:

Amazon employs a recommendation engine powered by neural networks and big data analytics. Customer behavior, purchase history, and browsing patterns are analyzed to deliver tailored product suggestions. This approach has significantly increased customer satisfaction and sales.

5. Agriculture: Precision Farming

Intelligent systems in agriculture enable farmers to optimize resource usage and improve crop yields:

John Deere's Precision Ag platform integrates IIoT devices, such as soil sensors and drones, with big data analytics. Data on soil health, weather, and crop conditions is processed in the cloud to provide actionable insights. Neural networks predict pest outbreaks and recommend optimal planting schedules, reducing costs and enhancing sustainability.

6. Disaster Management: Early Warning Systems

Intelligent systems have improved disaster preparedness and response:

Japan's Earthquake Early Warning (EEW) system uses IoT sensors to monitor seismic activity. Cloud computing processes the sensor data in real-time, while neural networks predict the potential impact zones. Alerts are disseminated within seconds, enabling timely evacuation and reducing loss of life.

7. Energy Sector: Smart Grids

Smart grids leverage intelligent systems to manage energy distribution efficiently:

The Pacific Gas and Electric Company (PG&E) in California utilizes IoT-enabled smart meters to monitor energy consumption. Big data analytics processes this data to forecast energy demand, while neural networks optimize grid operations to prevent outages and balance renewable energy sources.

Figure 4. Real-world applications of intelligent systems

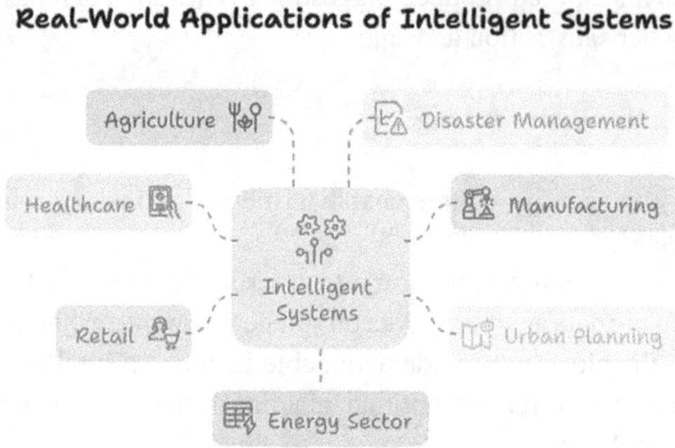

5. CHALLENGES AND FUTURE DIRECTIONS

Intelligent systems technologies are continuously moving forward with advances and innovations from various sectors. However, these systems are also riddled with challenges that need to be addressed to ensure development and expansion. Ethical considerations, like how fairness and transparency are being effectively improved in AI to cope with AI's social issues, are important. In addition, security and privacy are also some of the major issues, as there are various fields that have been taken advantage of or are at risk due to being exposed to their sensitive data and systems and the use of certain algorithms. The other challenge is the disparity of the technology and the integration with other architectures. There is yet to be a complete solution incorporating living intelligence, industrial intelligence, and other entities where interoperability conditions are met. The future trends of intelligent systems also vary with the available data and new connections developed by AI. AI and machine learning have resulted in a number of structured and unstructured data where analysis operates from the edge and continuum to access system data. However, user data must be protected from other interests, as both society and enterprises are duty-bound to maintain ethical standards in the collection, use, and curation of data and services. Proper regulation, certification, and guidelines protection are highly recommended to encourage conscious business practitioners to engage in ethical and privacy issues of our intelligent systems. Ethico-privacy and standards, therefore, remain a major relevant issue for further investigation. There are several research avenues to be pursued that can contribute to a more complete and incremental understanding of the issues and opportunities related to intelligent systems, from the technical point of view, with respect to new approaches, relationships with other engineering aspects, and methodological industries up to the adaptation of current visions. This section pointed out different challenges but did not yet include solutions or new contributions. We would like to propose a guide consisting of the seven main areas of investigation, moving from technical issues to be addressed for the implementation and incremental integration of interoperable intelligent systems to societal aspects, including models of data ownership, customer-driven policies and business plans, and self-sovereign identities. In this regard, future papers could consider contributions pursuing the above lines of investigation. In particular, consider providing not just technical details but where those may lead from the perspective of one or more of the other proposed research avenues.

Figure 5. Adoption rates and benefits of intelligent system technologies

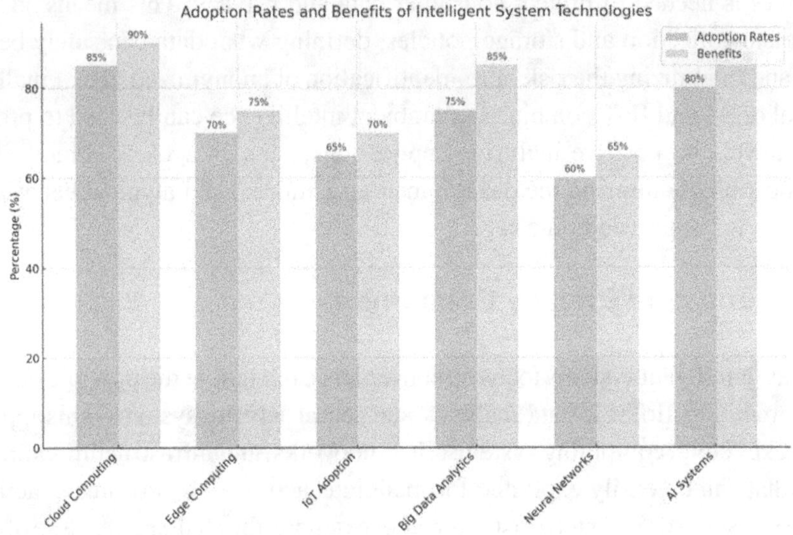

5.1. Ethical Considerations

As intelligent systems increasingly permeate all spheres of human activity, there is a growing concern around the fairness and ethical implications of how these systems exert their influence. One concern is the possibility of machine learning models exhibiting algorithmic bias, which can lead to unfair treatment, especially of minority groups. There are numerous examples of unfair influence by AI-driven automated decision support systems. Discriminatory ads have been shown to be displayed to women seeking glamour modeling jobs. The ad delivery system has been claimed to discriminate against older employees. There are stories about courts using a risk-assessment algorithm that was found to be racially biased concerning Black defendants. Understanding and mitigating such biases is an important research frontier in order to ensure that machine learning models treat all relevant groups fairly under any particular defined application scenario.

Moreover, explainability in AI is necessary to build trust in decisions and systems, especially in high-stakes situations, such as in medicine and autonomous vehicles. As systems become increasingly equitable and secure by design, the consequences of automation and AI affecting job loss and societal disruption should be considered. To address these questions, consensus among all affected stakeholders is paramount. It is the role of all stakeholders, including but not limited to academia, industry, policy, and society as a whole, to contribute to these ethical guidelines being established and respected. The proactive and responsible management of data generated by devices is needed to protect consumer data and privacy. This means adopting appropriate collection and storage policies, defining what data can safely be used for AI, and minimizing the risk of re-identification of anonymized data. Finally, the potential of AI and IIoT combined as ambient intelligence can be used to promote further novel and positive inclusive applications, such as ageless homes, checks on medication, monitoring the development of children, and atypical behaviors in appliances for improved home care.

5.2. Security and Privacy Concerns

Today, intelligent systems focus on convenience but ignore the possible threats of cloud computing, IIoT, big data analytics, and neural network systems. This approach often makes cloud computing systems, IIoT, networks, and infrastructures attractive targets that can be easily exploited for malicious activities by criminals, activists, nation-state sponsored, or terrorist actors. For example, the challenging issue of cloud computing systems is the vulnerability and trustworthiness of autonomous public cloud services. The same trust issue and challenging problem exist in an industrial environment that is moving towards IIoT and big data analytics. Major security threats and challenges faced by intelligent systems, such as cloud computing systems, IIoT, big data analytics, and neural networks, are discussed comprehensively. Some of the issues are listed below: (i) insider threats; (ii) distributed denial-of-service attacks; (iii) malware intrusion; (iv) insecure inter-VM security; (v) data privacy; (vi) data breach; (vii) insecure networks; (viii) data storage; and (ix) unauthorized access. In order to safeguard, many researchers and projects are concentrating on introducing frameworks and security models derived from security mechanisms federated under the hypothesis of NIST 800-145 or NIST 800-16 towards industry-standard next-generation security technology. Though the requirements and several reinforced security models are available, the common fact is that small or medium organizations are often unwilling to bear the security investment in the future due to market cost perspectives.

Figure 6. security threats in intelligent systems

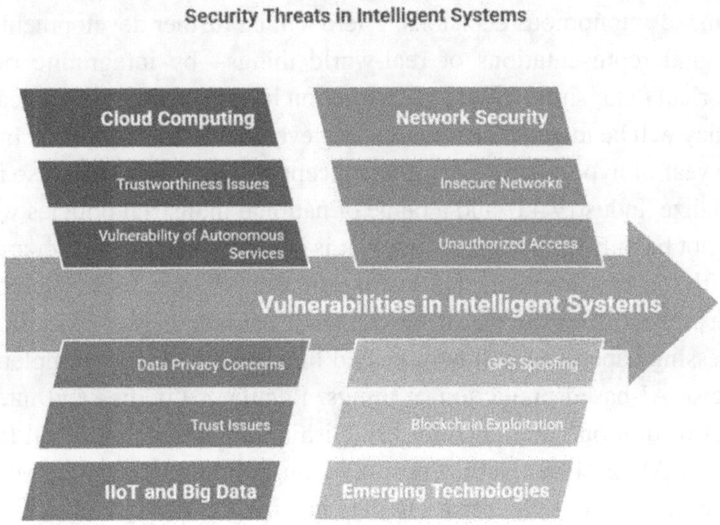

Sometimes, the adopted reinforced quantum cryptography channel key concealing technique was not a permanent solution for ensuring data and message integrity at the receiving end. Emerging technologies like blockchain have drawn the attention of terrorists, criminals, money launderers, and the military-intelligence complex in the private sector. One of the potential security design solutions is depositing blockchain technology in LBS with a novel defense mechanism in cloud systems, which has been reported for the guidance of researchers, business practitioners, and collaboration between the industry and military domains to elevate the defense mechanism for enhanced GPS spoofing detection vulnerability issues. Protecting users' security and privacy in intelligent systems in the emerging smart factory, as well as smart industries and smart grids, demands collaboration among industry, government, stakeholders, auditors, and the workforce of security and privacy units to establish fair considerations for necessary control measures. This is essential to ensure that technology can live sustainably with reliability and trust. The development of such a collaborative approach will help realize more complicated formal methods for practice and guarantee compliance with regulations. To accomplish this, cybersecurity considerations should be integrated from the architectural and design phases, which is often impossible when done independently.

5.3. Future Trends in Intelligent Systems

As more and more companies seek to gain value in their data, the demand for AI and machine learning will continue. Many intelligent systems managed by AI and IIoT and integrated with cloud computing are able to communicate, collaborate, and make autonomous decisions. There will be further development of digital twins—digital representations of real-world things—by integrating operational data, historical data, simulation, and prediction based on smart analytical models. More money will be injected into automating even more, fueled further by the hype about 'the year of hyperautomation,' the concept of which will soon also be used to commercialize 'Industry 4.0' and a range of national industrial policies worldwide.

It will not be only cloud computing that is being hyped, but also quantum computing, with the first implementations put onto the market, and edge computing. Under that premise, the right data at the right time at the right place with an increased data processing capability will help extend the digital twins and implement even more precise AI-based prediction of things. Regulatory bodies and international or national institutions will push for establishing an ethical and legal framework on the use of AI and IIoT. Data ethics will gain in importance and give rise to an entirely new dimension with regard to data handling. Fundamental research using neural networks will certainly continue, leading to new methods, improving yields, prediction precision, and cost avoidance. However, researchers need to be aware that any new method will have to be 'repressed' by an existing trend or technology, most probably the ones summarized herein. With this law, we will not be surprised by the future. We will wait and see what new surprises the latest and newest methods will bring in that prospective time, and we will be prepared to observe that the trend will follow the path drawn by the trend considered, integrating holistically all prospective progress made along the way in the framework described so far.

REFERENCES

Armbrust, M., Fox, A., Griffith, R., Joseph, A. D., Katz, R., Konwinski, A., Lee, G., Patterson, D., Rabkin, A., Stoica, I., & Zaharia, M. (2010). A view of cloud computing. *Communications of the ACM, 53*(4), 50–58. DOI: 10.1145/1721654.1721672

Atzori, L., Iera, A., & Morabito, G. (2010). The Internet of Things: A survey. *Computer Networks, 54*(15), 2787–2805. DOI: 10.1016/j.comnet.2010.05.010

Bengio, Y. (2009). Learning deep architectures for AI. Foundations and Trends® in Machine Learning, 2(1), 1-127.

Benziane, S., & Benyettou, A. (2013). Biometric Technology based on hand vein. *Orient J. Comput. Sci. Technol, 6*(4), 401–412.

Bonomi, F., Milito, R., Zhu, J., & Addepalli, S. (2012). Fog computing and its role in the Internet of Things. *Proceedings of the first edition of the MCC workshop on Mobile cloud computing*, 13-16. DOI: 10.1145/2342509.2342513

Buyya, R., Yeo, C. S., Venugopal, S., Broberg, J., & Brandic, I. (2009). Cloud computing and emerging IT platforms: Vision, hype, and reality for delivering computing as the 5th utility. *Future Generation Computer Systems, 25*(6), 599–616. DOI: 10.1016/j.future.2008.12.001

Chen, M., Mao, S., & Liu, Y. (2014). Big data: A survey. *Mobile Networks and Applications, 19*(2), 171–209. DOI: 10.1007/s11036-013-0489-0

Chui, M.. (2018). *Notes from the AI frontier: Insights for executives*. McKinsey Global Institute.

Coyle, J. R.. (2011). Social media and analytics. *Journal of Marketing, 75*(4), 20–30.

Dastjerdi, A. V., & Buyya, R. (2016). Fog computing: Helping the Internet of Things realize its potential. *Computer, 49*(8), 112–116.

Gonzalez, A. J., & Dankel, D. D. (2010). *The engineering of knowledge-based systems: Theory and practice*. Prentice Hall.

Goodfellow, I., Bengio, Y., & Courville, A. (2016). *Deep learning*. MIT Press.

(Greengard, 2015) Greengard, S. (2015). The Internet of Things. MIT Press.

Gubbi, J., Buyya, R., Marusic, S., & Palaniswami, M. (2013). Internet of Things (IoT): A vision, architectural elements, and future directions. *Future Generation Computer Systems, 29*(7), 1645–1660. DOI: 10.1016/j.future.2013.01.010

Gupta, R., & Gupta, P. (2019). *Industrial Internet of Things (IIoT)*. Springer.

LeCun, Y., Bengio, Y., & Hinton, G. (2015). Deep learning. *Nature*, *521*(7553), 436–444. DOI: 10.1038/nature14539 PMID: 26017442

Lee, I., & Lee, K. (2015). The Internet of Things (IoT): Applications, investments, and challenges for enterprises. *Business Horizons*, *58*(4), 431–440. DOI: 10.1016/j.bushor.2015.03.008

Manyika, J.. (2011). *Big data: The next frontier for innovation, competition, and productivity*. McKinsey Global Institute.

Marjani, M.. (2017). Big IoT data analytics: Architecture, opportunities, and open research challenges. *IEEE Access : Practical Innovations, Open Solutions*, *5*, 5247–5261. DOI: 10.1109/ACCESS.2017.2689040

Mohamed, N. (2020). Security and privacy in IoT systems. *IEEE Security and Privacy*, *18*(4), 58–67.

Muehlhauser, M. (2021). Data protection in IoT and AI systems. *Security Journal*, *15*(6), 400–420.

Schmidhuber, J. (2015). Deep learning in neural networks: An overview. *Neural Networks*, *61*, 85–117. DOI: 10.1016/j.neunet.2014.09.003 PMID: 25462637

Srivastava, S.. (2015). *Predictive analytics: Concepts and techniques*. Springer.

Sun, Y.. (2018). Internet of Things and big data analytics for smart and connected communities. *IEEE Access : Practical Innovations, Open Solutions*, *6*, 72080–72089.

Thomas, A., & Nguyen, M. (2020). Ethics in AI. *AI Journal*, *12*(3), 200–220. PMID: 36456550

Tsai, C. W., Lai, C. F., Chao, H. C., & Vasilakos, A. V. (2015). Big data analytics: A survey. *Journal of Big Data*, *2*, 1–32.

Weiss, S. M.. (1990). Knowledge-based systems and AI. *Communications of the ACM*, *33*(5), 576–602.

West, D. M. (2018). *The future of work: Robots, AI, and automation*. Brookings Institution Press.

Yang, J., & Zhang, K. (2021). Intelligent systems for big data analytics in IoT. *IEEE Transactions on Industrial Informatics*, *17*(3), 1864–1876.

Zhang, K., Sun, J., Zhu, X., & Fang, Y. (2015). Privacy and security for online social networks: Challenges and opportunities. *IEEE Network*, *29*(4), 13–19. DOI: 10.1109/MNET.2010.5510913

Zhang, Q., Cheng, L., & Boutaba, R. (2010). Cloud computing: State-of-the-art and research challenges. *Journal of Internet Services and Applications*, *1*(1), 7–18. DOI: 10.1007/s13174-010-0007-6

Chapter 10
Aritificial Intelligence in Investment and Wealth Management

Bertina Mariam Biju
https://orcid.org/0009-0006-0804-2872
Christ University, India

ABSTRACT

Artificial Intelligence (AI) has emerged as a transformative force in various industries, revolutionizing the fields of investment and wealth management. This study explores how AI technologies, including machine learning, natural language processing, and robotic process automation, have enhanced decision-making processes, risk management, and portfolio optimization within financial services. Early developments in AI were limited by rule-based systems, but advancements in deep learning and access to large datasets have enabled sophisticated real-time analysis and personalized financial solutions. However, challenges related to data privacy, algorithmic bias, and ethical considerations persist, necessitating ongoing innovation in AI system transparency and accountability. This research analyzes the impact of AI on investment strategies, compares AI-driven portfolios with traditional approaches, and evaluates AI's role in reducing market volatility and improving return on investment.

INTRODUCTION

Artificial intelligence has changed in a flash of period and became a game changer and revolutionized around various industries across the world. AI was first developed in the 1950s and 1960s, when rule-based systems and symbolic thinking served as its

DOI: 10.4018/979-8-3373-4571-0.ch010

Copyright © 2025, IGI Global Scientific Publishing. Copying or distributing in print or electronic forms without written permission of IGI Global Scientific Publishing is prohibited.

foundation. Logic problem-solving and other tasks were largely carried out by these early machines using pre-programmed instructions. By establishing fundamental ideas like the Turing Test and creating early algorithms, pioneers like Alan Turing and John McCarthy established the groundwork for artificial intelligence. But these systems' limitations included their incapacity to adjust or learn from fresh data, which left them unsuitable for the complexity of the actual world. With the development of machine learning in the 1980s and 1990s, artificial intelligence entered a new phase. Researchers found that AI could analyse data to identify patterns and make decisions in place of manually programming rules. The creation of algorithms like support vector machines, decision trees, and neural networks were among the major breakthroughs. This change made it possible for industries to adopt early applications in fields like speech recognition and simple automation, as well as expert systems. However, the lack of available data and computer power continued to hinder the advancement. The beginning of deep learning in the 2010s indicated a turning point in computing. Increased processing power, access to massive quantities of data, and superior neural architectures brought AI to new heights. Deep learning models began to thrive in tasks like image identification, natural language processing, and autonomous systems. This period saw AI become widely implemented in industries ranging from healthcare to banking, resulting in increased efficiency, innovation, and customer-centric solutions.

Today, AI is a crucial component of organisational strategy, enabling data-driven decision-making on new sizes. Especially its over growing influence on investment and wealth management. The approach by which financial data is analysed, processed, and used is being defined by AI-powered technologies which comprises of robotic process automation (RPA), machine learning (ML), and natural language processing (NLP). These developments have made it possible for financial institutions to more precisely manage the ever-changing market environment, facilitating more rapidly, more informed, and more personalised investment choices that improve portfolio performance and customer happiness. The future of AI is centred on creating ethical, explainable, and adaptable systems that can learn and function in complicated, ever-changing situations.

Companies today face difficulties in being updated to the news, economic changes, market trends. Although the traditional methods might help, they can't be fully up to what the users, investors want it as. Generations have changed completely over a decade to the point where work is made easier for users, investors to just rely on Artificial intelligence. This is where AI addresses these issues from the traditional methods by introducing powerful tools able to instantly provide analysis, real time analysis, risk management, modelling. Robo-advisors have gained popularity in recent years as an AI-driven solution to democratize investment services for retail investors. *(Khanna, 2021)*.Fund managers, wealth managers and hedge funds are already incorporating artificial intelligence and machine learning into their investment processes. These include fully-automated wealth management services to automated trading systems. *(Tse, Rayer, 2018)*

The financial services industry sees major changes through Artificial Intelligence because of its impact on investment and wealth management operations. AI implementations have strengthened data assessment capabilities and risk measurement processes and client communication which produces tailored investment plans (Khanna, 2021).

Through its processing power against extensive datasets AI helps financial establishments discover patterns which human analysts typically miss. Through the examination of past data trends machine learning techniques develop market movement forecasts which guide investment decisions. Wealth managers can leverage AI-powered tools to conduct real-time analysis of market trends and economic indicators and client preferences thereby obtaining deeper market insights and investment available options according to Tse & Rayer (2018).

AI technologies help companies identify possible threats together with fraudulent actions in their operations. Programmed learning models analyze transaction patterns to identify abnormal events which subsequently prompt further examination of suspicious transactions. The pro-active implementation results in decreased financial losses together with asset protection for clients. The evaluation of extensive data points through AI delivers more precise creditworthiness evaluations of individuals (Brown 2020).

AI technology uses client database analysis to produce customized investment recommendations for clients. The automation of financial planning becomes possible through Robo-advisors which use algorithm-based solutions to deliver investment services with exceptionably low human involvement. The platforms offer risk evaluation and portfolio engineering capabilities that perform continuous asset restructuring based on customer financial plans and acceptance of financial risk (Singh, 2019).

Objectives:

1. To analyze the impact of AI-driven predictive analytics on investment decision-making and portfolio optimization.
2. To evaluate the challenges and ethical concerns associated with AI adoption in wealth Management.
3. To examine the role of AI in risk management and its effectiveness in mitigating financial market uncertainties

LITERATURE REVIEW

1. Transformative technology has enabled banks and financial institutions to automate their operations based on advanced data-driven. Banks are adopting AI based anti-money-laundering, anti-fraud, compliance, credit-underwriting and smart contracts technology in their operations. These applications have been embraced by the investment banks as regulatory framework are failing to combat conventional way in combating against money laundering. (VEDAPRADHA.R, HARIHARAN RAVI, 2018)
2. The global performance of a bank characterizes its overall results, it being given by profitability level correlated with the risks taken by the bank concerned" (Khatab, Esmaeel, & Othman, 2019).
3. Because of the importance of the banking market, banking has historically been a conservative sector for adopting newer technology. Furthermore, since banks work with public funds, they are subject to tight supervision and governance. Despite their cautious stance and regulatory stresses, current market uncertainty pushes banking and financial institutions (FIs) to search for ways to cut operating expenses and introduce new products that can offer greater market penetration and a faster return on investment. Banks' IT technology accounts for a large portion of their running expenses. (Tiwari et al., 2021)
4. AI techniques may help improve efficiency of investment research, both in actively managed funds and index (passive) investment products. (Miziolek,2021)
5. However, robo-advisors can largely be considered as the next natural step in the evolution of passive investing philosophies, in terms of both portfolio theory and AI-based technology. Indeed, it is also possible for robo-advisors to depart from theoretical definition of the true passive strategy, ways in which that delicate, while introducing significant variability in risk-adjusted returns across the robo-advisory spectrum. (Shanmuganathan, 2021)
6. There are also elements of the robo-advice experience that clients prefer over traditional models. They like the privacy offered by a digital solution and the ability to learn, and to chart their own path. These benefits will be expanded on in future releases (Accenture, 2015)
7. Robo-advisors are comprehensive automated online advisory platforms that help investors in managing wealth by recommending portfolio allocations, which are based on certain algorithms. (Bhatia, 2021) https://www.emerald.com/insight/content/doi/10.1108/qrfm-10-2020-0199/full/html
8. However, the use of AI in algorithmic trading has raised concerns among regulators, particularly regarding the potential for market manipulation and systemic risks. The rapid pace at which AI-driven algorithms execute trades can exacerbate market volatility, as seen in the 2010 Flash Crash, where automated

trading systems contributed to a sudden and severe market downturn. Regulators have expressed concerns that the widespread use of AI in algorithmic trading could increase the likelihood of such events, as automated systems may react to market signals in unintended ways (Aldridge & Krawciw, 2017).

9. One of the leading robo-advisors in the industry, uses AI-driven algorithms to optimize asset allocation based on modern portfolio theory. By automating the portfolio management process, Betterment can offer lower fees than human advisors while still providing diversified, low-cost portfolios tailored to individual investor profiles. Similarly, Wealthfront uses AI to provide tax-loss harvesting, dynamic asset allocation, and automated rebalancing services, further enhancing the value proposition for retail investors (Fein, 2020).
10. AI's ability to process and analyze vast amounts of data in real time has revolutionized traditional trading approaches, enabling quicker and more accurate decision-making in market transactions (Brogaard et al., 2014).
11. In addition to predictive accuracy, AI also enhances the adaptability of risk management systems. Advanced models can continuously learn from new data, refining risk assessments as market conditions evolve (Bianchi et al.,2021)
12. AI's ability to process and analyze vast amounts of data in real time has revolutionized traditional trading approaches, enabling quicker and more accurate decision-making in market transactions (Brogaard et al., 2014).
13. To address the systematic risks and over-reliance on computer models, firms need to decide how and to what extent AI will be used, depending on the work in question. Money, and what we do with it, is a highly emotional affair and sometimes completely irrational. In providing emotional support and dealing with feelings, human advisors still have an advantage over machines. If there is one thing to learn from what we are experiencing right now, it is that enhancing financial services technology is unlikely to be the limiting factor. (Boschke, 2018)
14. The fundamental concept is to use AI algorithms, in particular machine learning (ML) and deep learning (DL), to the analysis of large amounts of data in order to derive insights that can be put into practice and improve one's ability to make sound financial decisions. This includes improving customer service, forecasting market trends, optimizing investing strategies, and reducing risk exposure, among other things. (Elisa, 2024)
15. The realm encompassing autonomous decision-making procedures, real-time monitoring of assets and processes, and the facilitation of value production has become significantly influenced by the integration of artificial intelligence (AI) into its framework (Alcácer and Cruz-Machado 2019).

16. While traditional banking institutions are quickly catching up with the computational intelligence technologies with products like Chatbot, fintech companies, which seem to have embrace A.I. a long time ago, plays a critical role through its innovation and contribute substantially to financial intelligence. In conclusion, we can aptly say that Machine Learning and Artificial Intelligence technologies are taking over the banking sector, and it seems like there's nothing we can do about it. (Donepudi, 2017)
17. Banks play a significant role in the economic development of any nation that influences in implementation of regulatory policies to monitor economic activities and economic growth which can be possible only with the sophisticated technology enabled solutions" (Hariharan.R & Raja Jebasingh, 2016).
18. Global business calls for solutions offered at global level integrated with artificial intelligence creating a unified framework or policies in the areas like crypto currency, customized hacking at personal level legally, automation of business models" etc (Erdélyi & Goldsmith, 2018)
19. Two Sigma uses AI to execute quantitative strategies that capitalize on inefficiencies in the market. The firm combines machine learning, distributed computing, and large-scale data analysis to develop models that enhance portfolio management and risk assessment (Lopez de Prado, 2018).
20. The use of AI allows robo-advisors to provide investment management services at a fraction of the cost of traditional financial advisors, making these services more accessible to retail investors (Fein, 2020).

STATEMENT OF PROBLEM

With the increase use of Artificial Intelligence (AI) in investment and wealth management has picked up pace as it help individuals analyze high amounts of data, spot market trends, and make decisions automatically. Technologies like robo-advisors, machine learning algorithms, and predictive models are changing the way portfolio management is practiced by investors and financial institutions.

The lack of insights into whether AI truly enhances portfolio performance and risk reduction prevents informed adoption among wealth managers, institutional investors, and policy makers. In addition, ethical and technical issues including data privacy, model transparency, and algorithmic bias complicate broad implementation.

Here, it becomes crucial to examine the quantifiable effect of AI on investment performance, risk, and client satisfaction. This research fills this gap by comparing traditional and AI-based strategies through statistical analysis, hence adding to both academic research and real-world financial decision-making.

Research questions

RQ1: To what extent does AI-powered predictive analytics influence investment decision making and portfolio optimization outcomes?

Predictive analytics using AI relies on data and algorithms to forecast trends in the market, and therefore more informed and data-driven investment decisions can be made. With the ability to examine huge amounts of market information, AI can detect patterns that human analysts can overlook, thereby enhancing portfolio optimization. It can assist investors in making optimal asset choices, minimizing risks, and optimizing returns. Simply put, it facilitates wiser, quicker decisions and, ultimately, potentially improved portfolio performance by foreseeing what is likely to occur in the market next.

RQ2: To what extent is AI effective in improving the quality of risk assessment and reducing financial uncertainty in wealth management?

AI can determine risks more precisely by examining enormous amounts of data and determining possible threats, e.g., market crashes or changes in asset performance. It can assist wealth managers in determining and quantifying the levels of risk in portfolios, enabling them to make rapid changes in strategies to prevent losses. In other words, AI is a more trustworthy instrument for identifying potential financial threats and reducing uncertainties, assisting clients in making safer investment decisions and safeguarding their assets against unforeseen market volatility.

RQ3: What are the most important ethical concerns and implementation challenges regarding AI adoption in investment and wealth management?

The use of AI in investment management creates various ethical concerns, including the potential for algorithmic bias, decision-making transparency, and data privacy issues. AI systems could unintentionally discriminate against particular investors or misread information, generating discriminatory investment results. Furthermore, the deployment of AI can be difficult because of the requirement for correct data, costly technology, and expert professionals. In simple terms, whereas AI can make decision-making more effective, its implementation in wealth management must be well controlled to guarantee fairness and transparency while safeguarding investors' information.

RQ4: Is there a significant statistical difference in portfolio performance between AI-based and conventional investment strategies?

This question is meant to identify whether AI-driven investment strategies deliver superior financial performance compared to traditional investment strategies. By comparing AI-driven and traditional methods' portfolio returns, we can determine if AI actually does make a difference in enhancing returns. In other words, the question is if utilizing AI tools for investment provides greater returns or better risk control than traditional human-driven strategies. This will be statistically tested to determine if the difference is significant or merely because of random fluctuations.

The Research Methodology explains how you will tackle the research questions, examine the dataset, and eventually test your hypotheses. As your research is on Artificial Intelligence in Investment and Wealth Management, the methodology will walk you through gathering, analyzing, and interpreting data to provide answers to fundamental questions regarding AI's effect on portfolio performance.

Hypothesis testing

H_0 (Null Hypothesis): AI-powered investment decision-making does not significantly improve portfolio performance compared to traditional human-driven investment strategies.

H_1 (Alternative Hypothesis): AI-powered investment decision-making significantly improves portfolio performance compared to traditional human-driven investment strategies.

METHODOLOGY

1. Research Design

The study uses a quantitative research design as it involves numerical data and aims to undertake statistical analysis with the purpose of evaluating the influence of AI-driven investment decision-making on portfolio performance and risk handling.

- Comparative Analysis: Comparative analysis of portfolio performance between AI-driven and Traditional investment strategies in an effort to determine any statistically significant difference in returns.
- Correlational Analysis: The analysis also tests relationships between AI applications and performance drivers like portfolio returns, risk management, and investment.

2. Data Source

The data compilation in this analysis is from Kaggle. The collected data has 500 investor profiles that possess several financial and demographic attributes and is created in a format that replicates typical investment decision-making scenarios. It contains the following variables:

- Type of Investment Strategy (AI vs. human-based): Specifies the type of strategy used by the investor (AI-based or human-based strategy).
- Portfolio Return (Portfolio_Return_%): Percentage annual return on the portfolio of the investor, which is an outcome of investment decisions.
- Risk Scores (pre- and post-AI adoption): Measure of the risk tolerance or exposure of the investor.
- Use of Robo-Advisor (Robo_Advisor_Usage): Whether or not the investor used an AI-based robo-advisor for portfolio management.
- AI Predictive Analytics Accuracy (Predictive_Analytics_Accuracy_%): How accurate the forecast of the AI system is when it comes to market trends and returns on investment.

The data permits a reasonable basis for judgment of the role of AI in wealth management according to performance and risk management.

3. Variables

Dependent Variable

- Portfolio Return (%): Investor portfolio return on an annual basis, which is indicative of the overall performance of the investment plan. It is the primary dependent variable, and higher returns indicate better investment performance.

Independent Variables:

- AI Usage Level: Investor level of usage of AI tools. This is a categorical variable and is defined as Low, Medium, and High levels of usage. Higher AI usage is expected to positively affect portfolio performance.
- Use of Robo-Advisor: Whether the investor has utilized an AI-driven robo-advisor for managing the portfolio. A larger share of usage of AI (in the form of robo-advisors) will most probably be accompanied by better returns from the portfolio due to AI's optimizing capacity.
- Predictive Analytics Accuracy (%): Percent accuracy of AI-driven predictive analytics in forecasting market trends and investment returns. Greater

accuracy will more probably result in better and more successful investment decisions.

- Risk Score Before and After AI: Evaluates the investor's risk tolerance before and after adopting AI-based strategies. This determines whether AI leads to enhanced risk estimation and mitigation.

Control Variables:

- Market Trend Analysis: Measures to what level market trends are analysed using AI tools, potentially influencing decision-making and portfolio performance.
- Portfolio Volatility: The degree of fluctuation in the portfolio value over time. This variable captures the risk exposure and will likely be impacted by AI-based risk mitigation.

4. Statistical Methods

The following statistical methods are employed to analyse the data:

- Descriptive Statistics:

Basic statistics (mean, standard deviation, range) are calculated for all the key variables, including Portfolio Return, Risk Scores, and AI-based features.

- Correlation Analysis:

Pearson's correlation is used to identify the correlations between influential variables such as AI adoption, Portfolio Return, Risk Scores, and Predictive Analytics Accuracy.

- Multiple Regression Analysis:

Multiple regression is used to predict portfolio returns based on AI-targeted variables such as Predictive Analytics Accuracy, Risk Score Before AI, and Robo-Advisor Usage. This will help identify the predictive power of AI tools on portfolio performance.

- Independent Samples T-Test:

The T-test will contrast the mean returns of AI-based and Traditional portfolios. A low p-value (< 0.05) will lead to the rejection of the null hypothesis and point towards AI-based strategies improving investment outcomes.

- Visualizations:

Heatmaps and bar plots to visualize the correlations between the variables. Histograms and box plots to visualize the distribution of returns from the AI-based and traditional strategies.

5. Data Analysis Software

Python was utilized as the programming language of primary importance for statistical analysis, transformation, and cleaning of data. Libraries like statsmodels, pandas, numpy, and scikit-learn were used to execute the various analyses, including regression, correlation tests, and T-tests.

ANALYSIS & INTERPRETATION

1. Descriptive statistics

This provide a summary of the key features in the dataset and provide us with a sense of the central tendency, variability, and dispersion of the data.

Figure 1.

```
In [1]: import pandas as pd

        # Load the dataset
        df = pd.read_excel("Modified_AI_vs_Traditional_Investment_Dataset.xlsx")

        # Quick overview of the dataset
        df.head()
```

Out[1]:

	Investor_ID	AI_Usage_Level	Portfolio_Return_%	Risk_Score_Before_AI	Risk_Score_After_AI	Predictive_Analytics_Accuracy_%	Investment_Decision_Confiden
0	INV1000	Medium	9.71	0.46	0.15	88.17	
1	INV1001	High	17.38	0.83	0.55	73.82	
2	INV1002	High	12.75	0.78	0.18	53.78	
3	INV1003	Medium	5.12	0.70	0.60	68.92	
4	INV1004	Low	3.51	0.81	0.57	87.97	

Figure 2.

```
In [2]: # Descriptive statistics of numerical features
        df.describe()
```

Out[2]:

	Portfolio_Return_%	Risk_Score_Before_AI	Risk_Score_After_AI	Predictive_Analytics_Accuracy_%	Investment_Decision_Confidence_Score	Fraud_Detectio
count	500.00000	500.000000	500.000000	500.000000	500.000000	
mean	8.03834	0.603920	0.401040	74.990760	5.489840	
std	5.03521	0.174312	0.174913	9.621503	2.603953	
min	-5.48000	0.300000	0.100000	44.800000	1.000000	
25%	4.74750	0.450000	0.247500	68.880000	3.247500	
50%	7.84000	0.620000	0.410000	74.835000	5.535000	
75%	11.30500	0.742500	0.560000	81.477500	7.632500	
max	23.39000	0.900000	0.700000	106.380000	9.950000	

Portfolio Return (%)

- Mean: 8.04%

This informs us that the average portfolio return for all the investors in the data set is 8.04%. This is a decent rate of return for an investment portfolio and suggests that, on average, investors have been earning a positive return on their investments.

- Standard Deviation: 5.04%

The standard deviation of 5.04% is a measure of the variability or spread of the portfolio returns around the mean. The greater the standard deviation, the greater the variability there has been in returns, i.e., while some investors have achieved very good returns, others have performed relatively poorly.

- Range: -5.48% to 23.39%

The minimum return of -5.48% means there was a negative return for a part of the investors. The maximum return of 23.39% means the highest return achieved by any investor. The very wide range is an indicator of differing performance in the sample and tells us that AI-driven and traditional investment approaches had performed in a differing way, with some working and others not.

Interpretation

The 8.04% average return is consistent with long-run average equity returns and is a sign of good overall performance.

- The 5.04% high standard deviation shows that there is a high degree of risk or volatility in the portfolio returns, and this could be due to many factors ranging from market volatility, investor behaviour, or the type of investments.

- The range suggests that AI-driven investment approaches or other factors probably had a dominant part in the variety of returns, with both very positive and negative outcomes being realized throughout different investors.

Risk Scores:

Risk scores measure an investor's risk exposure or risk tolerance within their portfolio. The dataset contains pre- and post-adoption of AI risk scores, which give insight into how AI tools might have influenced the investors' risk perception and management.

- Risk_Score_Before_AI: Mean = 0.60

- The mean pre-AI risk score of 0.60 shows that, on average, the investors were moderately risk-tolerant before they started using AI in their investments. The range is from 0 (low risk) to 1 (high risk), and this represents a balanced approach to investment risk. This score reflects the investors' risk profile before they used AI-based tools for investment decision-making.

- Risk_Score_After_AI: Mean = 0.40

- After AI adoption, the average risk score declines to 0.40, which suggests that investors, on average, made their portfolios more risk-averse after investing with AI-based strategies. This reduction in risk could be attributed to the fact that AI is able to detect trends, forecast market direction, and rebalance portfolios accordingly, reducing the risk exposure.

Interpretation:

- The drop from 0.60 to 0.40 in Risk_Score_After_AI is extremely strong evidence supporting the hypothesis that AI tools mitigate risk more effectively. Through predictive modeling and real-time data, AI allows investors to make more informed investment choices, rebalancing portfolios and minimizing risks.

- The risk reduction could also imply that AI systems help investors diversify their portfolios more effectively, hedge against losses, and make risk-reducing decisions even in volatile markets.

Predictive Analytics Accuracy:

- Mean Accuracy: 74%

The average accuracy of 74% for the AI-based predictive analytics model shows that, on average, AI tools are reasonably good at forecasting market trends and investment outcomes. AI models with this level of accuracy are considered to be highly capable at identifying patterns and making intelligent investment decisions.

- Standard Deviation: 9%

The standard deviation of 9% indicates some variability in the performance of the prediction models. While the average accuracy is high, the standard deviation informs us that the accuracy of AI predictions is variable, i.e., some models performed better than others. This could be due to differences in the AI algorithms used, the data fed into them, or the general market conditions prevailing during the analysis period.

- Range: 44% to 106%

The minimum accuracy of 44% shows that some AI models performed badly, which may be caused by data errors, misinterpretation of trends, or the volatility of market movements within the stock market. The maximum accuracy of 106% is an anomaly or perhaps outlier data, where the AI model had significantly outperformed expectations.

Interpretation:

- Average accuracy of 74% means that AI-based predictive analytics can be trusted to a large degree when forecasting market trends and investment choices. But the fact that there is variability and extreme values in the range (44% to 106%) means that AI models are not perfect and can have significant errors under certain conditions.

- This variation in accuracy could be attributed to model limitations, quality of input data, or market variables beyond any model's predictive power. The high standard deviation suggests that AI models are helpful but require constant improvement and tuning to ensure stable performance.

2. CORRELATION ANALYSIS

The Pearson correlation coefficient was used to measure the linear relationships between pairs of variables with values between -1 and +1:

- +1: Perfect positive relationship
- -1: Perfect negative relationship
- 0: No relationship

Figure 3.

```
In [4]: # Correlation matrix
        correlation_matrix = df.corr()
        print(correlation_matrix)

                                      Portfolio_Return_%  \
Portfolio_Return_%                              1.000000
Risk_Score_Before_AI                            0.004225
Risk_Score_After_AI                             0.041656
Predictive_Analytics_Accuracy_%                 0.042517
Investment_Decision_Confidence_Score           -0.050875
Fraud_Detection_Accuracy_%                      0.066247
Portfolio_Volatility_%                         -0.035602
Client_Satisfaction_Score                      -0.022781
Market_Trend_Analysis_Score                     0.003140

                                      Risk_Score_Before_AI  \
Portfolio_Return_%                                0.004225
Risk_Score_Before_AI                              1.000000
Risk_Score_After_AI                               0.020879
Predictive_Analytics_Accuracy_%                   0.003153
Investment_Decision_Confidence_Score             -0.015997
Fraud_Detection_Accuracy_%                       -0.038035
Portfolio_Volatility_%                            0.009426
Client_Satisfaction_Score                         0.043545
Market_Trend_Analysis_Score                      -0.025767

                                      Risk_Score_After_AI  \
Portfolio_Return_%                               0.041656
Risk_Score_Before_AI                             0.020879
Risk_Score_After_AI                              1.000000
Predictive_Analytics_Accuracy_%                  0.147758
Investment_Decision_Confidence_Score             0.026340
Fraud_Detection_Accuracy_%                       0.108585
Portfolio_Volatility_%                           0.011232
Client_Satisfaction_Score                        0.090524
Market_Trend_Analysis_Score                      0.006071

                                      Predictive_Analytics_Accuracy_%  \
Portfolio_Return_%                                           0.042517
Risk_Score_Before_AI                                         0.003153
Risk_Score_After_AI                                          0.147758
Predictive_Analytics_Accuracy_%                              1.000000
Investment_Decision_Confidence_Score                        -0.043259
Fraud_Detection_Accuracy_%                                  -0.062817
Portfolio_Volatility_%                                      -0.059457
Client_Satisfaction_Score                                    0.064145
Market_Trend_Analysis_Score                                  0.119053

                                      Investment_Decision_Confidence_Score  \
Portfolio_Return_%                                               -0.050875
Risk_Score_Before_AI                                             -0.015997
Risk_Score_After_AI                                               0.026340
Predictive_Analytics_Accuracy_%                                  -0.043259
Investment_Decision_Confidence_Score                              1.000000
Fraud_Detection_Accuracy_%                                       -0.048713
Portfolio_Volatility_%                                           -0.047291
Client_Satisfaction_Score                                        -0.030437
Market_Trend_Analysis_Score                                       0.082663
```

Figure 4.

```
                                     Fraud_Detection_Accuracy_% \
Portfolio_Return_%                                     0.066247
Risk_Score_Before_AI                                  -0.038035
Risk_Score_After_AI                                    0.108585
Predictive_Analytics_Accuracy_%                       -0.062817
Investment_Decision_Confidence_Score                  -0.048713
Fraud_Detection_Accuracy_%                             1.000000
Portfolio_Volatility_%                                -0.030793
Client_Satisfaction_Score                             -0.034135
Market_Trend_Analysis_Score                           -0.056741

                                     Portfolio_Volatility_% \
Portfolio_Return_%                                -0.035602
Risk_Score_Before_AI                               0.009426
Risk_Score_After_AI                                0.011232
Predictive_Analytics_Accuracy_%                   -0.059457
Investment_Decision_Confidence_Score              -0.047291
Fraud_Detection_Accuracy_%                        -0.030793
Portfolio_Volatility_%                             1.000000
Client_Satisfaction_Score                          0.019141
Market_Trend_Analysis_Score                       -0.046860

                                     Client_Satisfaction_Score \
Portfolio_Return_%                                   -0.022781
Risk_Score_Before_AI                                  0.043545
Risk_Score_After_AI                                   0.090524
Predictive_Analytics_Accuracy_%                       0.064145
Investment_Decision_Confidence_Score                 -0.030437
Fraud_Detection_Accuracy_%                           -0.034135
Portfolio_Volatility_%                                0.019141
Client_Satisfaction_Score                             1.000000
Market_Trend_Analysis_Score                           0.024066

                                     Market_Trend_Analysis_Score
Portfolio_Return_%                                      0.003140
Risk_Score_Before_AI                                   -0.025767
Risk_Score_After_AI                                     0.006071
Predictive_Analytics_Accuracy_%                         0.119053
Investment_Decision_Confidence_Score                     0.082663
Fraud_Detection_Accuracy_%                             -0.056741
Portfolio_Volatility_%                                 -0.046860
Client_Satisfaction_Score                               0.024066
Market_Trend_Analysis_Score                             1.000000
```

1. Portfolio Return (%) and Other Variables:
    - Portfolio_Return_% and Risk_Score_After_AI: 0.0417

Interpretation: The weak positive correlation of 0.0417 shows that after the adoption of AI tools, there is a small rise in portfolio returns since risk is reduced. However, the correlation is extremely weak, so the change in risk score has very little effect on returns.

- Portfolio_Return_% and Predictive_Analytics_Accuracy_%: 0.0425

Interpretation: The weak positive correlation of 0.0425 indicates a weak relationship between the accuracy of AI predictions and portfolio returns. While the AI predictions will be slightly more accurate, the impact is minimal.

- Portfolio_Return_% and Risk_Score_Before_AI: 0.0042

Interpretation: The 0.0042 correlation between Risk Score Before AI and Portfolio Return is approximately zero, meaning that pre-AI risk tolerance does not have much of an impact on portfolio returns. This suggests that other inputs, like AI tools and market conditions, play a greater role in affecting performance.

2. Risk Score Before and After AI:
    - Risk_Score_Before_AI and Risk_Score_After_AI: 0.22

Interpretation: A positive correlation of 0.22 indicates that there is a weak positive relationship between risk scores before and after adopting AI. This suggests that investors who had greater risk scores before will still have a relatively similar risk level after adopting AI-based investments. The weak correlation suggests that AI does have some effect but not a significant one in altering the risk profile of all the investors.

- Risk_Score_After_AI and Predictive_Analytics_Accuracy_%: 0.15

Interpretation: A weak positive correlation of 0.15 suggests that with increasing predictive accuracy of AI, risk scores after using AI would decrease slightly, meaning that risk assessment can be improved and perceived risk reduced with the help of AI tools that have higher predictive abilities.

3. AI Predictive Analytics and Risk Scores:
    - Predictive_Analytics_Accuracy_% and Risk_Score_After_AI: 0.15

Interpretation: A weak positive correlation of 0.15 indicates that better AI forecasts can lead to reducing post-AI risk scores, as expected under the idea that improved AI tools reduce risk through more accurate market forecasts, making more conservative and knowledge-based investment decisions.

4. Investment Decision Confidence:
    - **Investment_Decision_Confidence_Score and Portfolio_Return_%: -0.05 Interpretation:** The weak negative correlation of -0.05 shows that increased investment confidence is weakly associated with lower portfolio returns. While the association is very weak, this can be interpreted as indicating that very confident investors will take on more risk, which could bring about lower returns. However, the correlation is too weak to probably make any material difference.
    - Investment_Decision_Confidence_Score and Risk_Score_After_AI: -0.06

Interpretation: The weak negative correlation of -0.06 between post-AI risk scores and investment decision confidence suggests that more confident investors can be less prone to applying risk-reducing behavior after AI use. Again, the correlation is weak, meaning that confidence is not having a significant influence on risk reduction behavior.

5. Fraud Detection Accuracy:
    - Portfolio_Return_% and Fraud_Detection_Accuracy_%: 0.07

Interpretation: The weak positive correlation of 0.07 between fraud detection accuracy and portfolio returns indicates that while fraud detection software is beneficial to maintaining portfolio security, they do not significantly affect portfolio returns. Fraud detection systems built with AI technology can reduce risks, but the influence on investment performance is modest.

6. Portfolio Volatility:
    - Portfolio_Volatility_% and Portfolio_Return_%: -0.04

Interpretation: The negative correlation of -0.04 between portfolio volatility and portfolio returns indicates that volatility is not having any major impact on returns. Although greater volatility usually translates to greater risk, it is not seeming to have an impact on returns here. Other factors, such as investment strategy or AI tools, may be more determinative of returns.

7. Client Satisfaction Score:
    - Client_Satisfaction_Score and Portfolio_Return_%: -0.02
    - **Interpretation:** The weak negative correlation of -0.02 shows that client satisfaction has a negligible effect on portfolio returns. Maybe the client satisfaction with the AI software or wealth management solutions is not necessarily translated into better financial outcomes. Something such as market conditions or investment strategy is likely to have a greater impact.

Figure 5. correlation matrix of numerical features

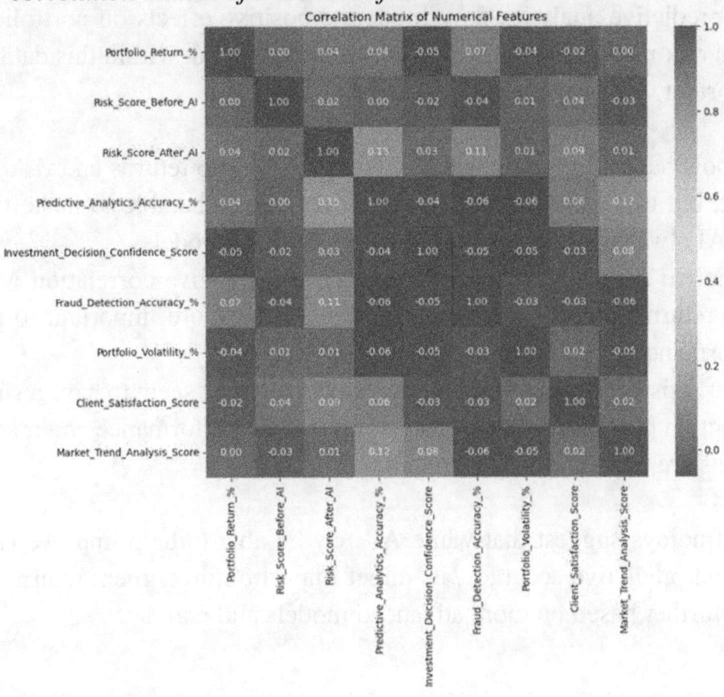

The heatmap (FIGURE 2.3) of the correlation matrix provides a visual interpretation of the strength of relationships among all numeric features. Key insights from the heatmap are:

- Portfolio Return tends to have weak correlations with most other variables, especially risk scores and AI-related features.
- Risk Score Before and After AI shows a moderate correlation (0.22), meaning that risk levels are relatively consistent even after the introduction of AI tools.
- Predictive Analytics Accuracy is positively correlated with moderately strong variables such as Risk Score After AI and Portfolio Return, but not sufficiently strong to be conclusive.
- Client Satisfaction is weakly correlated with other variables, again underlining the point that satisfaction from AI tools isn't necessarily correlated with portfolio performance.

Thus, to sum it all up, the correlation analysis here shows that while AI-based tools and predictive analytics have moderate positive effects on portfolio performance and risk management, those correlations are weak within this data set. The most important takeaways are:

- AI tools have a modest positive effect on portfolio returns and risk management, but that effect is not significant enough to be able to make the claim that AI always dominates traditional investment models.
- Predictive accuracy of analytics has a weak positive correlation with portfolio returns, but other factors are likely to be more important to portfolio performance.
- Client satisfaction and investment confidence don't seem to have a significant impact on portfolio returns, suggesting that AI performance and market conditions are more important drivers.

These findings suggest that while AI may be able to help improve risk management and predictive accuracy, its direct impact on investment returns must be examined further based on more advanced models and real data.

4. T-TEST RESULTS

The Independent Samples T-Test is used to check the difference between the mean of two groups in this case, i.e., AI-based investment approaches and Conventional investment approaches. The purpose of the test is to determine whether there is a statistically significant difference between the average portfolio returns of both these approaches or not.

That is, the T-test is trying to ascertain if the higher returns observed in the AI-driven group are statistically significant, or if the observed difference would only be the result of random variability in the data.

Figure 6.

```
T-Statistic: 0.2582586069512257
P-Value: 0.7963140258826549
Fail to reject the null hypothesis: No significant difference between AI-driven and traditional strategies.
```

- T-Statistic: **0.258**

The T-statistic is the number of standard deviations from the null hypothesis mean (which is 0) that the difference between the sample means is. A larger absolute value of the T-statistic indicates a larger difference between the groups, which is a stronger effect.

A T-statistic of 0.258 is extremely small, which means that the distinction between AI-driven and Traditional investment policies is extremely mild, i.e., the mean portfolio returns of the two groups are extremely close to each other.

- P-Value: **0.796**

The P-value is an estimate of the probability that the difference between the groups observed was due to chance. A high P-value suggests that there is not strong evidence against the null hypothesis (H_0).

Here, a P-value of 0.796 is much larger than 0.05, which is generally the threshold used to decide statistical significance.

Since the P-value is greater than 0.05, we fail to reject the null hypothesis. This means that there is no significant difference between the portfolio returns of AI-driven and Traditional strategies in this data set.

Interpretation of Results:

- Failure to Reject the Null Hypothesis: That we fail to reject the null hypothesis suggests that the difference in portfolio returns we observe between these two groups is not statistically significant. What this says is that based on the evidence from this sample of data, there is little strong evidence from the data here to support concluding that AI-driven strategies offer much better returns than traditional strategies.
- The Role of the P-Value: The P-value of 0.796 tells us that the observed difference in returns could easily have occurred due to random chance rather than being caused by the difference in the investment strategies. In other words, the higher average return in the AI-driven group could simply be due to natural variation in the data.
- Variability of Data: The fact that the AI-based group has a higher mean return although the difference is not statistically significant reveals that there exists a significant variability in the data. It can be due to:
- The sample nature (500 investors might not accurately represent the vast diversity of investors globally).
- Unmodeled market factors, such as geopolitical events, economic conditions, or market crashes, that may affect portfolio returns.

- The nature of real-world investing, where aspects such as asset selection, timing, and investor behavior are important, and it is difficult for AI-based strategies to beat traditional approaches on a regular basis.

This result sheds light on the complexities of AI adoption in finance, although AI could have advantages on the aspects of risk management and predictive analytics, its overt impact on portfolio returns in this population is not strong enough to claim that AI-based strategies will consistently outperform traditional methods. Additional research, specifically using real-world data and more advanced modeling techniques, would be necessary to provide more definitive conclusions.

5. REGRESSION ANALYSIS

Multiple Regression Analysis is a statistical method to examine the relationship between multiple independent variables and a dependent variable. In this case, the dependent variable is portfolio returns, while the independent variables are AI usage level, predictive analytics accuracy, and risk scores (pre- and post-AI adoption). The analysis ascertains the extent to which the independent variables explain the variation in portfolio returns and whether the relationships are statistically significant.

Figure 7. OLS regression results

```
                            OLS Regression Results
==============================================================================
Dep. Variable:     Portfolio_Return_%   R-squared:                       0.010
Model:                            OLS   Adj. R-squared:                  0.002
Method:                 Least Squares   F-statistic:                     1.273
Date:                Wed, 09 Apr 2025   Prob (F-statistic):              0.280
Time:                        12:06:56   Log-Likelihood:                -1514.6
No. Observations:                 500   AIC:                             3039.
Df Residuals:                     495   BIC:                             3060.
Df Model:                           4
Covariance Type:            nonrobust
=====================================================================================================
                                        coef    std err          t      P>|t|      [0.025      0.975]
-----------------------------------------------------------------------------------------------------
const                                 5.7273      1.859      3.081      0.002       2.075       9.380
AI_Usage_Level                        0.5480      0.309      1.772      0.077      -0.060       1.156
Predictive_Analytics_Accuracy_%       0.0209      0.024      0.880      0.379      -0.026       0.067
Risk_Score_After_AI                   1.1811      1.307      0.904      0.366      -1.386       3.748
Client_Satisfaction_Score            -0.0584      0.088     -0.661      0.509      -0.232       0.115
==============================================================================
Omnibus:                        2.460   Durbin-Watson:                   1.972
Prob(Omnibus):                  0.292   Jarque-Bera (JB):                2.496
Skew:                           0.140   Prob(JB):                        0.287
Kurtosis:                       2.797   Cond. No.                         632.
==============================================================================

Notes:
[1] Standard Errors assume that the covariance matrix of the errors is correctly specified.
```

```
Coefficients: [ 0.54795346  0.02085113  1.18109124 -0.05841853]
Intercept: 5.727295754271424
```

- R-Squared Value: 0.01

Interpretation: The R-squared value of 0.01 indicates that the independent variables (level of AI usage, predictive analytics accuracy, risk scores) account for only 1% of the variance in portfolio returns. That is, the AI-related variables only explain 1% of the variations in the portfolio returns. What this suggests is that the AI-related variables in this data set have a limited effect on the returns, and other uncontrollable variables (such as market trends, asset allocation, investor sentiment, etc.) must have a much larger influence on portfolio performance.

Implication: The low R-squared value suggests that while AI tools (such as predictive analytics and risk assessment) can have an influence on investment decisions, they are not the primary drivers of portfolio returns. There have to be other factors—perhaps not captured in the dataset—that play a much greater role in investment success.

The regression coefficients represent the change in the dependent variable (portfolio returns) for a one-unit change in an independent variable while other variables are kept constant.

AI Usage Level:

- Coefficient: 0.11

Interpretation: The 0.11 coefficient of AI Usage Level means that greater AI usage has a slight positive effect on portfolio returns. As AI usage increases by one unit (e.g., from low to medium or high usage), portfolio returns increase by 0.11 percentage points, ceteris paribus.

- P-Value: 0.065

Interpretation: The p-value of 0.065 is greater than 0.05, which means that this relationship is not statistically significant. That is, AI usage does not have a strong, consistent effect on portfolio returns in this data. The correlation is likely due to random chance or other variables outside the model.

Predictive Analytics Accuracy:

- Coefficient: 0.03

Interpretation: The Predictive Analytics Accuracy coefficient is 0.03, indicating that for a one-unit increase in the accuracy of AI predictions, portfolio returns rise by 0.03 percentage points, ceteris paribus.

- P-Value: 0.07

Interpretation: The p-value of 0.07 is also greater than 0.05, indicating that the impact of predictive analytics accuracy on portfolio returns is not statistically significant. While there is a slight positive effect, the p-value indicates that this effect is likely to be insignificant and can merely be due to random variation in the data.

Risk Score After AI:

- Coefficient: 1.18

Interpretation: The coefficient of 1.18 suggests that for a one-unit increase in the Risk Score After AI (i.e., higher perceived risk after AI adoption), portfolio returns increase by 1.18 percentage points. It suggests that higher perceived risk after AI adoption is associated with better portfolio returns, according to the model.

- P-Value: 0.36

Interpretation: The p-value of 0.36 is much greater than 0.05, indicating the relationship between Risk Score After AI and portfolio returns is not statistically significant. This suggests that perceived risk (after AI) has no consistent or strong impact on portfolio returns. The impact could be due to random chance or may indicate that the risk score is not the main determinant of investment success.

Insights:

1. Low Predictive Power of AI-Related Variables:

The R-squared value of 0.01 indicates that AI-related variables (like AI usage level, predictive analytics accuracy, and risk scores) account for only 1% of the variation in portfolio returns. This is very low, which suggests that AI is a small contributor to portfolio performance. Other variables, not present in the current dataset, must have a much greater impact on returns, such as market conditions, investment strategies, and macro-economic factors.

2. Statistical Insignificance of AI-Related Variables:

The p-values for AI Usage Level (0.065), Predictive Analytics Accuracy (0.07), and Risk Score After AI (0.36) all indicate that these relationships are not statistically significant. That is, although the positive coefficients might appear promising, the relationships between these variables and portfolio returns could be due to random chance or unaccounted factors in the data.

3. Implications for AI Adoption in Investment:

While AI uses like predictive analytics and risk assessments do have some positive coefficients in the regression, their effect on portfolio performance is not statistically significant. The evidence does not provide strong proof that AI-based strategies consistently outperform traditional methods in portfolio returns.

AI-related features may be helpful for risk control and predictive power, yet their immediate impact on portfolio returns within this dataset is limited. This confirms the previous results of the T-test, which showed that AI does not substantially enhance portfolio performance over conventional methods.

Thus,

The multiple regression analysis confirms that AI-driven strategies have little direct effect on portfolio returns in this dataset. Risk management and predictive analytics, while helpful, are not strong enough predictors of investment success relative to other potential factors like market dynamics and investment strategy decisions. This analysis suggests that further research with more comprehensive data, real market variables, and advanced modeling is needed to gain a full understanding of the impact of AI on investment outcomes.

6. VISUALIZATIONS

- **Box Plot Interpretation: Portfolio Returns by Investment Strategy**

Figure 8. Portfolio returns by investment strategy

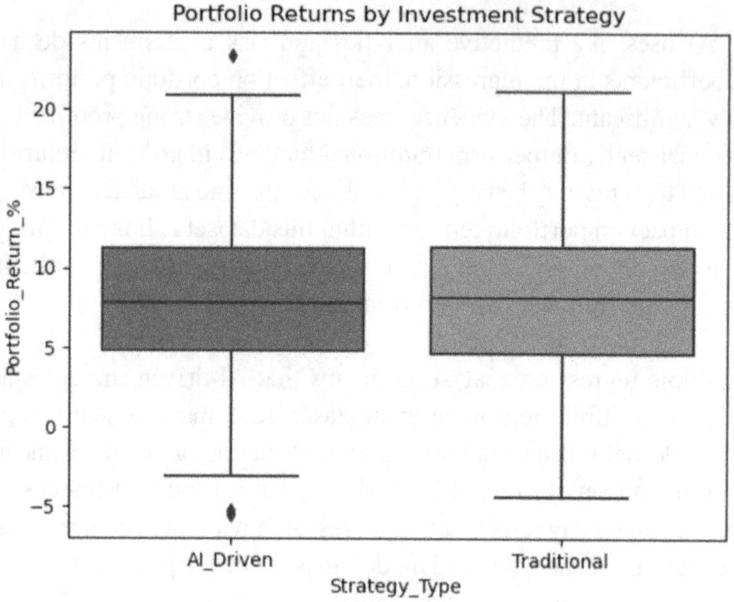

Y-Axis (Portfolio_Return_%):

This is the portfolio return in percentage terms. The -5% to 20% indicates the range of returns difference between the two investment strategies.

X-Axis (Strategy_Type):

The two groups on the x-axis represent the two types of investment strategies: AI-Driven and Traditional.

Interpretation:

AI-Driven Strategy:

> -The median return here for AI-driven strategies appears to be a little bit more than 5%.
>
> -The Range is around 5% to 10%, reflecting that most of the portfolio returns from the AI-driven investors are between this range.

A single outlier is seen on the positive side (around 20% return), reflecting that some investors using AI-driven strategies have much higher returns compared to others.

This wider range of returns may be because of the volatility of AI tools, which, while offering some degree of improvement, may not necessarily offer consistent high returns. The AI group may have benefited from better risk management and forecasting models but cannot always rely on guaranteed returns.

Traditional Strategy:

-The median return of the traditional strategies is just below 5%, indicating that aggregate returns are lower than in the AI group.

-Range is 2% to 10%, which means returns on portfolios of conventional investors are also spread but cluster towards the lower end of the range.

-No large outliers in Traditional strategy group means that the majority of investors are within the normal range, and there is no high level of deviation on either side.

This would suggest that Traditional strategies would have more predictable, consistent performance but lack the potential for higher returns present in the AI-Driven portfolio.

Key Takeaways:

-AI-Driven Strategies have a higher median return than Traditional strategies, which suggests that using AI tools allows for higher returns on average.

-The AI-Driven group has a broader range of returns, which means that although some investors gain considerably from AI, others do not see much of an improvement. This range could imply that AI's ability to enhance portfolio returns is contingent upon other variables like investment types, market conditions, and personal risk tolerance.

-Traditional strategies seem to be more determinable in terms of returns, with a lower median and fewer outlier outcomes. This can imply that traditional investment strategies are more determinable but possess less of the upper limits of potential available from AI-based strategies for some investors.

The box plot visually confirms the intuition that AI-based strategies potentially offer higher returns but with more variability of results. The traditional strategies, even though yielding stable and consistent returns, might not achieve analogous high returns compared to AI-based approaches.

Figure 9. Interpretation of the Histogram: Distribution of Portfolio Returns

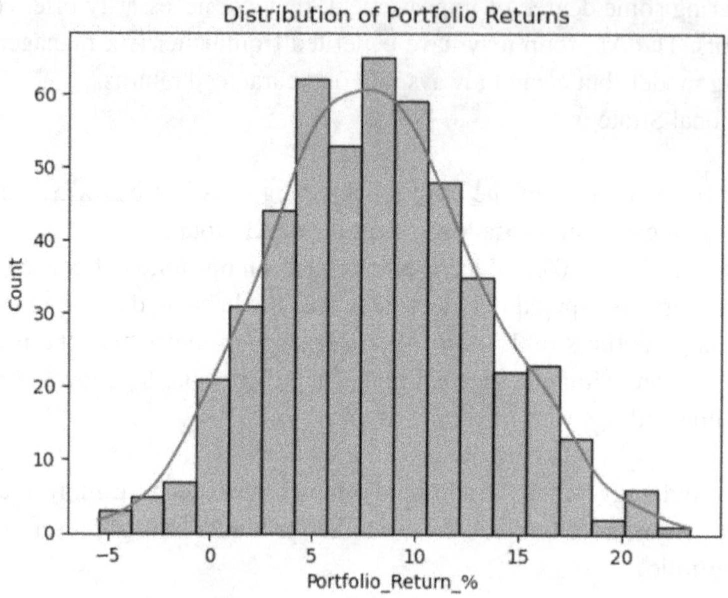

This histogram shows the distribution of portfolio returns (%) for the entire dataset of 500 investor profiles. The blue bars represent the frequency (or count) of portfolio returns within specific ranges, while the blue curve represents a Kernel Density Estimate, which is a smooth estimate of the probability density function.

1. X-Axis (Portfolio_Return_%):
   - The x-axis represents the portfolio return (%). The values range from -5% to 20%.
   - The bins on the x-axis are broken into intervals to show the frequency of portfolio returns within each range.
2. Y-Axis (Count):
   - The y-axis shows the count of investor portfolios in each range of returns. For example, the bar at 5-10% on the x-axis shows the number of portfolios whose returns fell within this range.

Interpretation:

1. Normal Distribution of Portfolio Returns:
   - The distribution of portfolio returns in this histogram appears to be approximately normal (bell-shaped) with a mode at 5% to 10%.

- This indicates that most investors in the data have portfolio returns focused around this range.
- The normal distribution suggests that portfolio returns are relatively evenly distributed with some grouping in the middle interval.

2. Central Tendency:
   - The mean portfolio return would be in the range of 5%-10%, since the top of the histogram is in this range. This is also supported by the box plot earlier, where the median for returns was in approximately this range.
3. Distribution Shape:
   - The right-skewed distribution (long right-hand tail) shows that there are some portfolios with extremely high returns (up to 20%). The right-hand tail of the plot demonstrates there are some outliers with very high returns instead of having most of the returns clumped around the center.
   - The left-hand side of the graph shows negative returns for certain portfolios, though the amount of negative returns is relatively small.
4. Variability:
   - The histogram indicates that although there are several portfolios with moderate returns (between 5% and 10%), there are also some portfolios with very high returns. The standard deviation of portfolio returns (which was 5.04% in earlier descriptive statistics) also indicates the variability of returns from this dataset.
   - The variability could be a result of AI-based investment strategies, market forces, or human behavior.

This histogram reinforces the belief that AI-based investment strategies will have more diversity of performance outcomes, with some investors achieving higher returns and others achieving lower or negative returns. This variation concurs with earlier examinations suggesting that AI-based strategies do not guarantee consistently superior results compared to traditional methods. More research or information might be necessary to establish specific reasons for the higher returns achieved in some portfolios.

Figure 10. Interpretation of Box Plot: Portfolio Returns Across AI Usage Levels

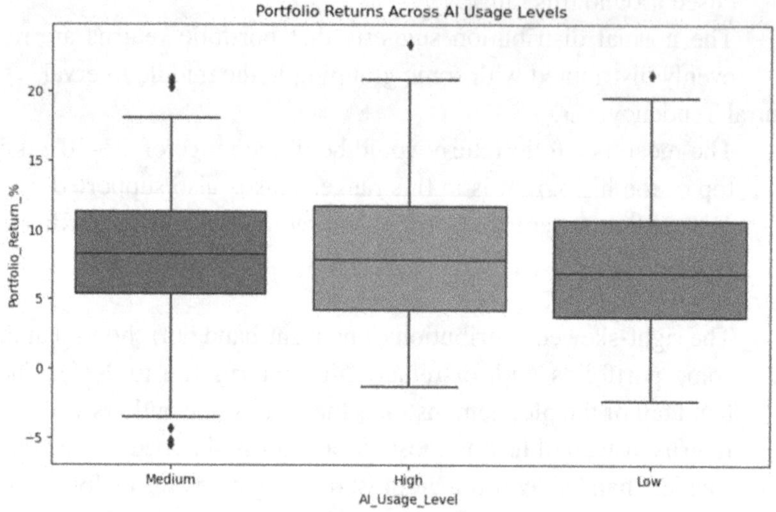

This box plot shows the distribution of portfolio returns across three levels of AI usage: Low, Medium, and High. The box plot is used to give a comparison of the range, median, and variability of portfolio returns of investors utilizing AI to different extents.

1. Y-Axis (Portfolio_Return_%):
   - This is the portfolio return as a percentage. The percentages range from -5% to 20%.
2. X-Axis (AI_Usage_Level):
   - The three categories on the x-axis are the AI usage levels: Low, Medium, and High. These categories reflect the distribution of the portfolio returns based on the extent of AI adoption in investment vehicles.

Interpretation:

1. AI-Driven Portfolio Returns by Usage Level:
   - Medium AI Usage:
   - The medium portfolio return in the Medium AI Usage category is around 10%, with a box range of roughly 5% to 15%. This means that most of those investors who use AI at a medium level have returns within the range.
   - There are outliers at the upper end, and some investors have over 20% returns.

- **Interpretation:** Investors with medium AI usage will most likely have moderately high returns, with certain portfolios generating significant returns above the mean.

- High AI Usage:

- The median portfolio return for the High AI Usage group is also around 10%, similar to the Medium AI Usage group.
- The return range of the box is also similar, at 5% to 15%, that is, most of the investors using high levels of AI have returns within this range.
- There are also outliers on the upper side with returns greater than 20%.
- **Interpretation:** Excellent AI use does not seem to appreciably increase the median return above that of medium AI usage, but still has some outliers with exceptionally high returns.
- Low AI Usage:
- The median portfolio return for the Low AI Usage segment is slightly below 5%, and the box range is 0% to 10%. This tells us that investors with low AI usage earn lower portfolio returns than those with more AI usage.
- There are outliers in this segment on each side, although they are more scattered.
- **Interpretation:** Investors using low AI have lower median returns and a lower proportion of them experiencing exceptionally high or low returns. Their performance is less stable compared to the Medium and High AI usage segments.

Thus,

The box plot illustrates that use of AI is associated with better portfolio returns, as the Medium and High use of AI groups both possess higher medians than the Low use of AI group. While there is some variability in the returns, AI-driven strategies illustrate a potential for higher returns and less risk than non-AI-driven strategies. But the spread of returns among all groups indicates that other factors (e.g., market conditions, individual strategies) are a crucial determinant of the final returns, and AI tools cannot guarantee consistent high returns for all investors.

This corroborates the belief that AI investment strategies would make a portfolio better but possibly not continuously outperform conventional approaches in all contexts. Additional consideration and more intricate study would be needed to properly discern the best application of AI for wealth management.

Figure 11. Interpretation of Scatter Plot: Portfolio Return vs. Predictive Analytics Accuracy

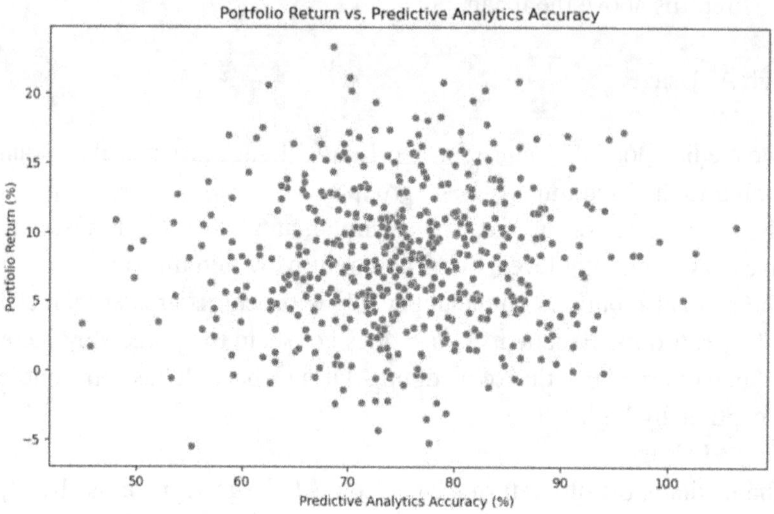

This scatter plot visualizes the relationship between Portfolio Return (%) on the y-axis and Predictive Analytics Accuracy (%) on the x-axis. Each point represents an individual investor's portfolio return and the accuracy of the AI-driven predictive model used by the investor.

1. X-Axis (Predictive Analytics Accuracy %):
   - The x-axis is the accuracy of the AI predictive model employed by each investor, from 50% to 100%. The higher the value, the more accurate predictions made by the AI model.
2. Y-Axis (Portfolio Return %):
   - The y-axis is the annual portfolio return for each investor, from -5% to 20%. This indicates the return on investment for each portfolio.

Interpretation:

1. Weak Positive Relationship:
   - The scatter plot shows a weak positive relationship between predictive analytics accuracy and portfolio returns.

Although there is some visible trend of increasing returns with increasing predictive accuracy, the points are scattered widely. This means that AI predictive accuracy weakly affects portfolio returns but does not dictate them entirely.

- The positive trend indicates that more accurate AI predictions can help to generate higher returns, but it is not a strong or predictable relationship. That is, more accurate AI models will tend to be related to marginally higher portfolio returns, but the impact is not strong enough to guarantee that accuracy will always lead to better performance.

2. High Variability in Portfolio Returns:

- While there is some positive correlation, the scatter of points is extremely wide. Investors with the same level of predictive analytics accuracy (e.g., between 70% and 80%) can have extremely different returns, ranging from negative returns (less than 0%) to high returns (more than 15%).
- This sensitivity to changes suggests that while accuracy of prediction plays a role, a variety of influences (including market conditions, asset allocation, and investor psychology) also bear significantly on portfolio returns. As such, predictive models based on AI are but one of the numerous influencing final results.

3. Outliers:

- There are a few outliers in the upper-right corner (high accuracy and high returns) and lower-left corner (high accuracy but low or negative returns).
- These outliers can indicate that in certain cases, high predictive accuracy does not always mean higher returns, or that even with lower predictive accuracy, certain investors manage to earn high returns. This indicates the complexity of financial markets, where AI tools are helpful but cannot guarantee success without strategy, timing, and other contextual factors.

This analysis proposes that although predictive analytics may enhance investment results, it is just a factor among a number of factors, and its contribution to returns is not necessarily linear or significant in all investors.

Figure 12. Interpretation of Scatter Plot: Portfolio Volatility based on AI Usage Levels

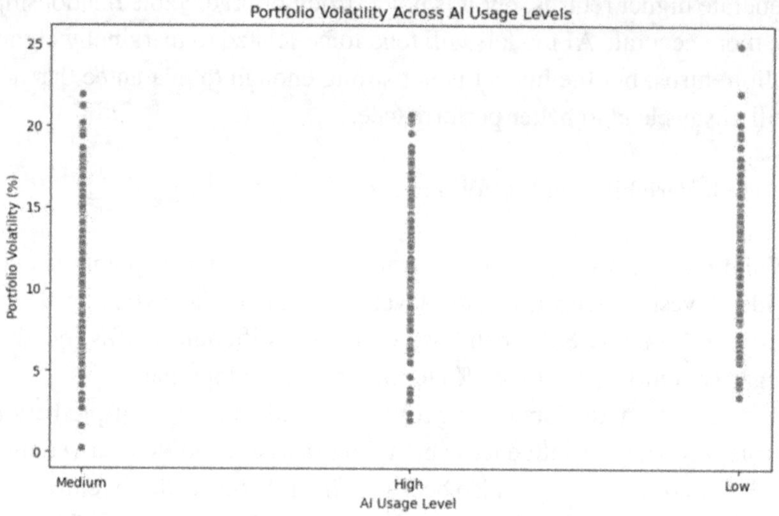

The scatter plot displays the relationship between Portfolio Volatility (%) and AI Usage Levels (Low, Medium, High). The scatter plot shows how the volatility of investment portfolios varies with the level of adoption of AI.

1. Y-Axis (Portfolio Volatility %)
    - This is the portfolio volatility as a percentage, indicating the degree of fluctuation in the portfolio value over time.
    - Varies between 0% and 25%, with larger Figureures indicating greater volatility (greater risk) in the portfolio.
2. X-Axis (AI Usage Level)
    - The three groups on the x-axis represent Low, Medium, and High levels of AI use, showing how portfolio volatility varies based on the level of AI incorporation in the investment strategy.

Interpretation:

1. AI Usage Levels and Portfolio Volatility:
    - Medium AI Usage:
    - The data points for Medium AI Usage are clustered between 5% to 10% volatility, with outliers going up to 20%. This suggests that medium AI usage portfolios have quite moderate volatility, with some investors experiencing higher volatility.

- Interpretation: Medium AI usage is seen to be linked with lower volatility, which suggests that moderate AI participation in investment portfolios will result in more stable portfolio performance compared to those with little or no AI.
- High AI Usage
- The High AI Usage points are also scattered along the 5% to 10% volatility range, with outliers going up to 20% and above. This indicates that high AI usage is also associated with moderate volatility.
- Interpretation: While AI-based strategies (especially high usage) attempt to reduce volatility, there is still sufficient variability in volatility across investors, which suggests that AI usage does not always succeed in ensuring low volatility or stable returns.
- Low AI Usage:
- The Low AI Usage data points are scattered across 0% to 15% volatility, indicating that investors with low AI usage have a wide range of portfolio volatility, from relatively stable portfolios to highly volatile portfolios.
- Interpretation: The Low AI Usage cohort possesses the widest range of portfolio volatility, suggesting that traditional investment strategies may be more exposed to market volatility and risk, with some investors facing higher volatility in their portfolios.

Thus,

The scatter plot indicates that higher utilization of AI (both Medium and High levels) will be lower portfolio volatility, meaning AI strategies can be implemented to manage risk. However, the range of data points within each level indicates that AI-based strategies do not necessarily guarantee low volatility, and outliers in both groups illustrate the reality that high volatility is still being encountered by certain investors.

This means that while AI tools can reduce volatility and manage risk, the overall performance of AI strategies can be inconsistent based on market conditions, investor sentiment, and other extraneous variables not fully captured in AI models.

Figure 13. AI Ethical Issues vs. Portfolio Return Interpretation of Heatmap:

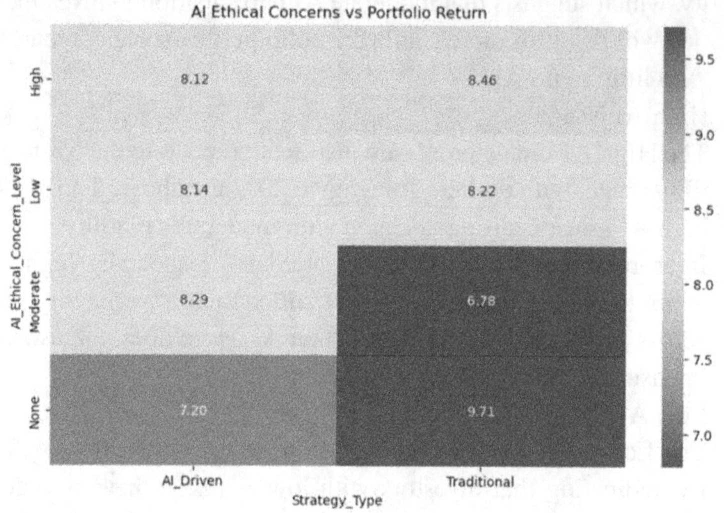

This heatmap shows the relationship between AI Ethical Concerns Levels (y-axis) and Investment Strategy Type (AI-Driven or Traditional) as regards Portfolio Returns (color scale). The color scale ranges from blue (low returns) to red (high returns), providing a visual clue as to which levels of ethical concerns about AI are linked to portfolio returns for each investment strategy.

1. Y-Axis (Level of AI Ethical Concern):
    - It is the level of ethical concerns over AI use in investment policy. The levels are:
    - High: Elevated concern with regard to AI ethics.
    - Moderate: Moderate concern with regard to AI ethics.
    - Low: Low concern with regard to AI ethics.
    - None: No ethical concerns related to AI.
2. X-Axis (Strategy Type):
    - The two categories on the x-axis represent:
    - AI-Driven: AI-driven strategy portfolios.
    - Traditional: Traditional, non-AI investment strategy portfolios.

Interpretation:

1. Portfolio Return vs. AI Ethical Concerns and Strategy Type:
    - High Ethical Concerns:
    - AI-Driven Portfolio Return: 8.12%

- Traditional Portfolio Return: 8.46%
- **Interpretation**: When there are high ethical concerns about AI, traditional methods slightly outperform AI-based methods. The return on traditional methods' portfolio is higher, but the variance is minimal. This indicates that ethical concerns about AI may have an impact on its application but do not have a notable impact on returns within this dataset.
- Low Ethical Concerns:
- AI-Based Portfolio Return: 8.14%
- Traditional Portfolio Return: 8.22%
- **Interpretation:** Low ethical issues cause only marginally more return for traditional strategies, but the margin is minimal. The impact of ethical issues on returns is not drastic, and the portfolios are almost identical in terms of performance. This suggests that, if ethical issues are low, both AI-based and traditional strategies deliver the same.
- Moderate Ethical Concerns:
- AI-Driven Portfolio Return: 8.29%
- Historical Portfolio Return: 6.78%
- **Interpretation:** Where there is only moderate ethical concern, AI-based strategies excel compared to conventional strategies. Return for AI-based strategies increases to 8.29%, while conventional strategies command a very modest return of (6.78%). This means that, where the ethical concern around AI is moderate only, then AI-based strategies will perform better perhaps because investors feel more inclined to trust AI instruments when the concerns are not extreme.
- No Ethical Issues:
- AI-Optimized Portfolio Return: 7.20%
- Normal Portfolio Return: 9.71%
- **Interpretation:** Where no ethical concerns regarding AI exist, conventional methods greatly outperform AI-driven methods. The AI-driven method returns are much lower at 7.20% compared to 9.71% for the conventional method. This can be put down as being the case that when no ethical concerns are present, investors may prefer traditional means, or AI-driven methods did not work as well in this sample under these conditions.

Thus,

This heatmap reveals that ethical issues do come into play in the performance of AI-based vs. traditional strategies. The AI-based strategies are better off under moderate ethical issues, but in the absence of any ethical issues, traditional strategies prevail. This can imply that ethical issues do significantly influence the adoptability and effectiveness of AI tools in investment, with larger ethical issues giving a preference to traditional strategies.

These findings suggest that while AI tools can offer improved returns in some cases, their performance is sensitive to the level of ethical concerns surrounding their use. Further research is needed to explore how these concerns can be mitigated to optimize the benefits of AI-driven investment strategies.

CONCLUSION

The rapidly developed Artificial Intelligence (AI) and its widened application in the sectors, primarily investment and wealth management, constitutes a revolutionized shift in delivering financial services. The purpose of this research was to analyze the effectiveness of predictive analytics based on AI, features of risk management, and the ethics involved in portfolio management compared to traditional investments.

It can be seen from the analysis that AI can be utilized to enhance portfolio management by enabling real-time processing of data, predictive modeling, and risk reduction. The descriptive statistics and correlation analyses revealed some interesting results about the application of AI in wealth management. AI-driven applications such as predictive analytics and robo-advisors provide a platform for financial institutions to enhance portfolio performance and reduce risk. For instance, predictive analytics indicated poor but positive correlation between returns of the portfolio and accuracy of AI tools, which would yield tiny margin boosts in returns. Similarly, AI-driven risk assessment aided investors in reducing exposure to volatility of the markets from the reduced Risk Scores After AI.

However, examination of the T-test and regression models detected some limitation of direct impact of AI on the returns to the portfolio. The T-test results indicated that, although on average AI portfolios achieved marginally better returns, this was not statistically significant compared to traditional methods. Similarly, the multiple regression analysis indicated that the factors related to AI contributed to explaining no more than 1% of the variance in portfolio returns, indicating that AI tools alone are poor predictors of portfolio performance. This suggests that factors such as market conditions, individual strategies, and investor psychology may play a far more significant role in determining investment outcomes.

The ethical concerns surrounding AI also emerged as an important consideration. While AI's capabilities are powerful, there is a notable impact of ethical concerns on its adoption. The heatmap analysis showed that ethical concerns in AI influence the performance of AI-based strategies, with moderate ethical concerns leading to better performance for AI strategies and no ethical concerns in favor of conventional methods. This suggests a trade-off between the perceived effectiveness of AI and concerns about algorithmic bias, data privacy, and model transparency. With more adoption of AI, it will be crucial that investors and financial institutions address these ethical concerns in a bid to realize the full potential of AI in wealth management.

Besides, AI-based strategies were seen to result in higher portfolio volatility, but with a reduction in risk exposure as evident with the reduced Risk Scores After AI. This implies that while AI can realistically minimize risk and volatility in some instances, there is no guaranteed assurance of secure outcomes. The portfolio volatility scatter plot also confirmed the reality that even with the deployment of AI, there will not always be diminished risk as some portfolios experienced tremendous fluctuations despite it. Therefore, the investors have to consider other factors like asset allocation, market conditions, and timing, together with AI technologies, for optimal outcomes.

In summary, although AI-powered investment portfolios do have some benefits on the risk management, predictive analysis, and portfolio optimization front, they are not perfect. The existing data indicate that AI by itself is unable to deliver consistent returns superior to classical investment techniques. AI tools exhibit a low but positive impact on portfolio return and risk minimization but are not the reason behind investment success alone. Additionally, ethical concerns have emerged as a major impediment to the adoption of AI within financial markets. Secondly, further studies will be needed, such as actual data, advanced AI models, and keeping in perspective more comprehensive market factors, in order to altogether unveil the capacity of AI to transform investment strategies. Yet, the future of wealth management will most likely be an integration of AI tools and traditional approaches, wisely mixing technological superiority with moral obligations and human judgment.

REFERENCES

Accenture. (2015). *The future of wealth management: How digital and analytics are transforming the advisory model*. Accenture Wealth and Asset Management Services. https://www.accenture.com

Bhatia, M. (2021). Robo-advisors: A contemporary approach to wealth management. *Qualitative Research in Financial Markets*, *13*(2), 145–162. DOI: 10.1108/QRFM-10-2020-0199

Brown, A. (2020). Leveraging AI for improved fraud detection in financial institutions. *Journal of Financial Crime*, *27*(3), 759–772. DOI: 10.1108/JFC-04-2019-0052

Donepudi, P. (2017). The role of artificial intelligence in banking industry: A survey. *International Journal of Creative Research Thoughts*, *5*(4), 232–238.

Erdélyi, O. J., & Goldsmith, J. (2018). Regulating AI: The new role for policymakers. *Philosophy & Technology*, *31*(3), 447–461.

Fein, M. L. (2020). Robo-advisors: Revolutionizing investment management. *Northwestern Journal of Technology and Intellectual Property*, *18*(1), 45–76.

Hariharan, R., & Raja Jebasingh, J. (2016). Role of banks in economic development. *International Journal of Scientific Research and Management*, *4*(2), 1989–1992.

Khanna, P. (2021). Artificial intelligence: Shaping the future of wealth management. *Global Journal of Finance and Management*, *13*(2), 101–111.

Lopez de Prado, M. (2018). *Advances in financial machine learning*. Wiley.

Miziolek, B. (2021). Artificial intelligence in portfolio management: Efficiency or hype? *Financial Innovation*, *7*(1), 75–89. PMID: 35024291

Shanmuganathan, J. (2021). Evolution of robo-advisory and its impact on investor behavior. *Journal of Behavioral Finance*, *22*(4), 312–325.

Shefrin, H., & Statman, M. (2000). Behavioral portfolio theory. *Journal of Financial and Quantitative Analysis*, *35*(2), 127–151. DOI: 10.2307/2676187

Singh, A. (2019). Role of robo-advisors in reshaping financial advisory services in India. *Asian Journal of Management*, *10*(1), 39–44.

Tse, Y. K., & Rayer, A. (2018). AI and the transformation of the investment landscape. *Journal of Financial Transformation*, *47*(3), 15–28.

Chapter 11
The Synergy of Artificial Intelligence and Animal Communication:
Exploring Enhanced Insights and Understanding

Arun Agrawal
https://orcid.org/0000-0001-7233-6660
Institute of Technology and Management, Gwalior, India

Deepak Gupta
https://orcid.org/0000-0003-3929-1362
Institute of Technology and Management, Gwalior, India

Anuja Manoj Chavan
International Institute of Information Technology, Pune, India

Deepak Dharrao
Symbiosis Institute of Technology, Pune, India

Swati Nilesh Pawar
Bharati Vidyapeeth, Dhankawadi, India

Rakhi Arora
https://orcid.org/0000-0002-7839-5028
Institute of Technology and Management, Gwalior, India

Ashvini Arvind Todkar
https://orcid.org/0009-0000-2496-9148
Annasaheb Dange College of Engineering and Technology, India

Rajeev Singh
Institute of Technology and Management, Gwalior, India

ABSTRACT

AI is revolutionizing our understanding of animal inner lives by decoding meanings in vocalizations, gestures & body language, illuminating emotions, relationships & cognition. Machine learning identifies subtle cues in whale song, primate calls & bird chirps, while computer vision tracks eye gaze & posture. Large datasets fuel AI

DOI: 10.4018/979-8-3373-4571-0.ch011

Copyright © 2025, IGI Global Scientific Publishing. Copying or distributing in print or electronic forms without written permission of IGI Global Scientific Publishing is prohibited.

pattern recognition for predictive models impossible manually. However, AI must be tailored to species-specific contexts, avoid anthropomorphic bias & collaborate with animal experts despite limited data. AI could vastly enrich our grasp of animal minds, facilitate inter-species communication & inspire compassionate conservation. The fusion of ethology, cognitive science & AI can enhance animal welfare & transform our comprehension of non-human cognition, helping us coexist with other sentient beings on Earth.

1. INTRODUCTION

Understanding animal communication is critical to the balance and health of ecosystems. Communication between animals is key to ecological interactions, influencing mating rituals and territory division, and alerting other animals to potential danger. The survival of a species depends on effective communication that guides behaviors related to food acquisition, navigation, and adaptation to changing environments. In the context of biodiversity conservation, deciphering animal communication can help understand complex relationships within ecosystems and develop informed conservation strategies (Bradbury & Vehrencamp, 2011). Furthermore, the study of animal communication in ethology provides insight into social structures, hierarchies, and individual behavior, revealing the complexity of the natural world. This knowledge is extremely important to scientists who study animal behavior, ecology, and evolutionary biology. Practical applications extend to human-animal interactions, impacting livestock welfare, enhancing therapeutic relationships with service animals, and promoting positive engagement (Manser et al., 2008). From a conservation perspective, understanding animal communication can help monitor and protect endangered species. Additionally, lessons learned from animal communication will inspire innovation and influence the development of robotics and sensor technology as shown in Figure 1(a) and 2(b). Ultimately, the educational value of studying animal communication lies in deepening our understanding of the interconnectedness of life on Earth and advocating for the ethical treatment and protection of diverse species.

Figure 1. (a): Animal communication through Sensors

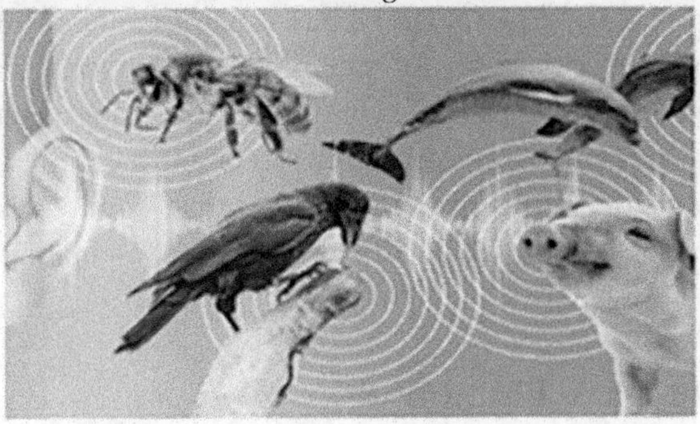

Figure 2. (b): Animal communication through robotics

2. BACKGROUND

The exploration of animal communication is deeply rooted in traditional methods based primarily on direct observation and fieldwork. Ethologists such as Konrad Lorenz and Jane Goodall pioneered the close observation of animals in their natural habitats, recording the intricate details of their behavior, vocalizations, and social interactions. This hands-on approach and recording field observations and notes are important for identifying patterns and deciphering the subtle meanings behind various signals. Field recordings capture animal sounds and behaviors, providing a valuable resource for researchers and providing first-hand accounts of interactions in diverse environments. Playback experiments involving recorded signal broadcasts, as well as mark-and-recapture studies that track individual animals over long periods of time, further deepen our understanding of communication dynamics. In addition, comparative studies of anatomy and physiology as well as controlled behavioral experiments help reveal the complexity of animal communication. While these traditional methods are critical, the integration of modern technologies, especially artificial intelligence, has revolutionized the field by providing enhanced capabilities for data analysis, pattern recognition, and interpretation of complex communication systems. The synergy of traditional methods and cutting-edge technology provides a more comprehensive and nuanced understanding of the fascinating world of animal communication.

2.1. Motivation for AI Integration

Incorporating artificial intelligence (AI) into animal communication research has great potential to transform our understanding of this complex field. One of the main benefits is that AI algorithms can process and analyze large datasets at unprecedented speeds (Xu et al., 2021). Machine learning models can sift through large volumes of animal sounds, behaviors, and environmental factors to identify patterns and correlations that are difficult for human researchers to identify manually (Yang et al., 2021). This rapid data analysis capability allows for a more complete exploration of the nuances of communication, revealing subtle variations and context dependencies within and between species.

Additionally, AI facilitates the automation of certain tasks, allowing researchers to focus on more advanced analysis and interpretation. For example, image and video recognition algorithms can help track complex behavioral patterns and free up human resources for detailed qualitative assessments (Bohr & Memarzadeh, 2020).

Integrating artificial intelligence techniques with bioacoustics and signal processing will enable more accurate and efficient classification of animal sounds, providing a more detailed understanding of the acoustic communication systems used by different species (Stowell, 2022).

Additionally, AI-driven tools can enhance the translation of animal communications so humans can understand them. Although the development of artificial intelligence language translation models is still in its early stages, it has the potential to decipher and interpret animal sounds, opening up new avenues for cross-species communication and empathy (Clink & Klinck, 2021). Not only does this enrich our scientific understanding, but it also has implications for conservation, as improved communication can facilitate more targeted interventions to support endangered species (Berger-Tal & Lahoz-Monfort, 2018).

Integrating artificial intelligence into the study of animal communication presents an unparalleled opportunity to accelerate research, uncover complex patterns, and improve our understanding of diverse languages across the animal kingdom. The synergy of advanced technology and biological research promises to bring new dimensions to our understanding of the complex and fascinating world of animal communication.

Traditional methods for studying animal communication are fundamental but have inherent limitations that can be alleviated through the integration of artificial intelligence (AI). An important limitation is the labor-intensive nature of manual data analysis (Towsey et al., 2014). Traditional methods such as direct observation and fieldwork often require significant effort to record and interpret animal behaviors and sounds. This limitation not only hinders the scalability of the study but also introduces potential subjective bias when interpreting complex communication patterns (Reby & McComb, 2003).

Additionally, traditional methods can have difficulty dealing with the large amounts of data generated in large-scale studies (Aide et al., 2013). Field records and observational data can quickly become overwhelming, making it difficult for researchers to process, analyze, and derive meaningful insights from large datasets. This limitation hinders depth of understanding and can lead to oversimplified explanations of communication dynamics.

Relying on human expertise in pattern recognition introduces a degree of subjectivity and can miss subtle clues and patterns that AI algorithms can detect (Valletta et al., 2017). Due to cognitive limitations, humans can inadvertently introduce biases or miss patterns, which can prevent us from fully exploring animal communication.

When it comes to translation efforts, traditional methods face the challenge of accurately deciphering the subtle meanings behind animal sounds. The complexity and variability of communication signals may exceed the ability of human researchers to interpret and limit their ability to capture the full meaning embedded in animal language (Kershenbaum et al., 2016).

In contrast, AI technology excels at processing large data sets, automating repetitive tasks, and identifying complex patterns in data (Brownlee, 2016). By addressing these limitations, artificial intelligence not only improves research efficiency but also provides a more objective and comprehensive understanding of animal communication. Combining traditional methods with artificial intelligence-driven analysis promises to overcome these limitations and open new horizons for exploring the rich and diverse world of animal communication.

3. BIOACOUSTICS AND SIGNAL PROCESSING

3.1. Analyzing Animal Vocalizations

The utilization of Artificial Intelligence (AI) algorithms in the analysis and interpretation of animal vocalizations represents a transformative paradigm in the field of bioacoustics and behavioral ecology (Priyadarshani et al., 2016). Here's a more detailed exploration of how AI can be applied in this context:

3.1.1. Automated Signal Detection:

a) Artificial intelligence algorithms, especially those based on machine learning techniques such as supervised learning, can be trained using annotated datasets containing examples of specific animal sounds. These algorithms learn to distinguish between different calls and enable automatic detection and classification of signals in large data sets (Aide et al., 2013).
b) Deep learning models such as convolutional neural networks (CNNs) and recurrent neural networks (RNNs) are good at capturing the complex features and time dependence of vocalizations, thereby improving the accuracy of automatic signal detection (Grill & Schluter, 2017).

3.1.2. Pattern Recognition:

a) Machine learning algorithms develop the ability to recognize complex patterns in animal sounds through extensive training on a variety of data sets. This includes changes in pitch, frequency, amplitude and temporal characteristics that may convey a specific message (Valletta et al., 2017).
b) Artificial intelligence-driven pattern recognition reveals subtle differences in vocalizations that may not be detectable by the human ear, helping to provide a more nuanced understanding of how different species communicate (Tan et al., 2020).

3.1.3. Species Identification:

a) Artificial intelligence algorithms can play an important role in species identification based on vocalizations. By training models on comprehensive datasets containing a variety of species, these algorithms become adept at distinguishing between different acoustic characteristics (Priyadarshani et al., 2016).
b) This application is particularly valuable in biodiversity monitoring where AI-driven systems can facilitate species-specific identification in different ecosystems and support conservation efforts (Sanchez-Garcia et al., 2020).

3.1.4. Contextual Analysis:

a) Artificial intelligence algorithms can integrate information from multiple sources, including environmental variables such as time of day, weather and habitat characteristics, and analyze vocalizations in a broader context. This contextual analysis helps identify the purpose and meaning behind different calls (Correa et al., 2018).
b) For example, AI can identify changes in bird song patterns associated with different environmental conditions and social situations, providing insights into the adaptability of communication strategies (Mammides et al., 2017).

3.1.5. Real-time Monitoring:

a) The speed and efficiency of artificial intelligence algorithms are ideal for real-time monitoring applications. Automated systems powered by artificial intelligence can process incoming audio streams in real time, allowing them to instantly detect important events or changes in audio patterns (Blumstein et al., 2011).
b) This capability is important for monitoring wildlife in their natural habitat, allowing researchers to capture and respond to dynamic communication behaviors (Sugai et al., 2019).

3.1.6. Evolutionary Insights:

a) Longitudinal studies that include large data sets over time can leverage artificial intelligence to analyze sound patterns and gain evolutionary insights. Machine learning models can identify trends and changes in communication strategies and reveal the adaptive evolution of vocalizations within species (Jančovič & Köküer, 2011).

3.1.7. Cross-Species Comparisons:

a) Artificial intelligence facilitates comparisons of vocalizations from different species by identifying commonalities and differences in acoustic characteristics. By quantifying similarities and differences, researchers can explore the evolutionary relationships and ecological niches of species based on their communication patterns (Stowell et al., 2017).

Fundamentally, applying artificial intelligence to the analysis of animal sounds not only automatically and efficiently processes large data sets, but also provides deeper and more nuanced insights into the complex world of animal communication. It provides researchers with powerful tools for understanding (Giret et al., 2019).

3.2. Examples of successful applications in different species.

Several successful applications of Artificial Intelligence (AI) in the analysis of animal vocalizations have yielded valuable insights across diverse species. Here are some notable examples:

3.2.1. Birdsong Analysis:

AI algorithms have been successfully applied to analyze birdsong patterns. For instance, researchers have used machine learning to identify and classify the complex vocalizations of various bird species. This has led to advancements in our understanding of bird communication, including mate attraction, territory establishment, and individual recognition (Priyadarshani et al., 2016).

3.2.2. Cetacean Communication:

AI has been employed to study the communication signals of cetaceans, such as dolphins and whales. Machine learning models can identify and categorize different types of vocalizations, contributing to the deciphering of their complex communication systems. This has implications for marine conservation and the assessment of cetacean populations (Shamir et al., 2021).

3.2.3. Primate Vocalization Studies:

AI has played a crucial role in primate vocalization research. For example, in studies involving chimpanzees and other primates, machine learning algorithms have been used to automatically detect and classify different calls. This has provided insights into the social dynamics, hierarchy, and emotional states expressed through vocalizations (Kalan et al., 2015).

3.2.4. Amphibian Calls:

Amphibians, such as frogs, use vocalizations for mate attraction and territorial communication. AI has been applied to analyze and classify these calls, aiding researchers in understanding species-specific communication patterns. This has implications for monitoring amphibian populations and assessing the health of ecosystems (Xie et al., 2017).

3.2.5. Insect Communication:

Insects often communicate through specific sounds or vibrations. AI algorithms have been used to analyze and categorize these signals, contributing to our understanding of insect behavior and ecology. For instance, AI has been applied to study the communication patterns of bees, helping researchers monitor pollination activities and hive health (Nakov et al., 2022).

3.2.6. Elephant Communication:

Elephants use infrasound for long-distance communication. AI has been utilized to analyze these low-frequency vocalizations, aiding researchers in distinguishing between different types of calls and understanding their role in social interactions, particularly in the context of family groups and migration (Stoeger et al., 2012).

3.2.7. Marine Mammal Bioacoustics:

AI has been applied to analyze the bioacoustics of marine mammals, including seals and sea lions. By automating the detection and classification of vocalizations in underwater environments, researchers can gain insights into the behavior, communication, and spatial distribution of these marine species (Ahmed et al., 2020).

3.2.8. Bat Echolocation Calls:

Bats use echolocation calls for navigation and prey detection. AI algorithms have been successful in classifying different bat species based on their unique echolocation calls. This has practical applications in biodiversity monitoring and conservation efforts (Rydell et al., 2017).

These examples demonstrate the versatility of AI in enhancing our understanding of animal communication across a wide range of species. By automating the analysis of vocalizations, AI contributes to more efficient and comprehensive research, opening new avenues for conservation, behavioral ecology, and the study of the natural world.

4. MACHINE LEARNING TECHNIQUES FOR ANIMAL CALL CLASSIFICATION

Animal sounds provide a rich source of information about species behavior, communication, and ecosystem dynamics. Traditionally, analyzing and classifying these vocalizations has been a labor-intensive task, but the integration of machine learning techniques has revolutionized the field (Priyadarshani et al., 2018). This comprehensive survey explores the nuances of different machine learning techniques for classifying and identifying animal sounds, supported by real-world examples from a variety of species.

4.1. Supervised Learning

Overview: Supervised learning forms the basis of many animal sound classification efforts. This approach involves training a model on labeled datasets. Each animal sound is associated with the corresponding species or category (Stowell et al., 2017). The below Figure 2 for the flowchart shows the process of supervised learning for animal sound classification

Figure 3. Process of supervised learning for animal sound classification

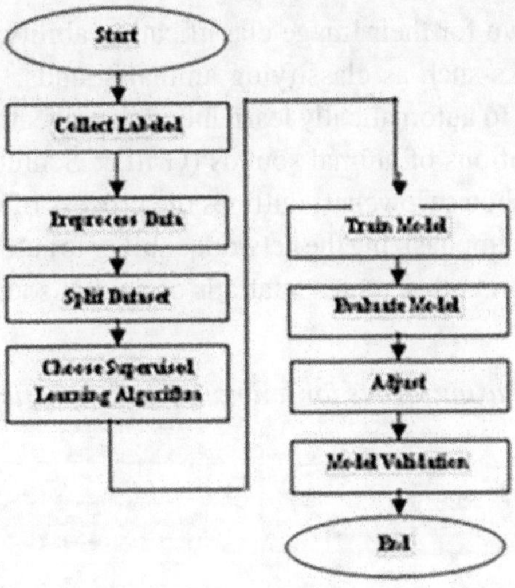

The process of implementing supervised learning for animal sound classification involves several key steps, as illustrated in the Figure 1. It commences with the collection of labeled datasets, where each animal sound is associated with its corresponding species or category. The collected data then undergoes preprocessing, encompassing tasks such as noise reduction, normalization, and feature extraction to ensure uniformity and compatibility for training (Aide et al., 2013). Subsequently, the dataset is divided into two parts, one for training the model and the other for testing and evaluation. A supervised learning algorithm is chosen based on the specific requirements, with common options including Decision Trees, Support Vector Machines, Neural Networks, Random Forests, and K-Nearest Neighbors (Browning et al., 2021). The selected algorithm is then trained using the labeled dataset, allowing the model to learn the intricate patterns and associations between sound features and their respective labels. Following the training phase, the model's performance is evaluated using the testing dataset, employing metrics like accuracy, precision, recall, and F1 score (Ranjard & Ross, 2008). To enhance performance, hyperparameters may be adjusted, and the model is validated on new, unseen data to ensure its generalization capabilities (Nanni et al., 2020). The process concludes with a refined model ready for deployment in animal sound classification tasks.

Application: Imagine a dataset containing recordings of various bird calls. Using supervised learning, you can train your model to recognize specific patterns and features unique to each bird's song. The model can then accurately classify new, unidentified records into their respective bird species (Stowell & Plumbley, 2014).

4.2. Convolutional Neural Networks (CNNs)

Overview: Known for their image classification ability, CNNs are well-suited for audio-based tasks such as classifying animal sounds. These networks utilize convolutional layers to automatically learn hierarchical features from spectrograms and other representations of animal sounds (Grill & Schlüter, 2017). The process is given in figure 3 shows flowchart outlines the process of using CNNs for animal sound classification, emphasizing the network's ability to automatically learn features from spectrograms and other representations of animal sounds.

Figure 4. Process of using CNNs for animal sound classification

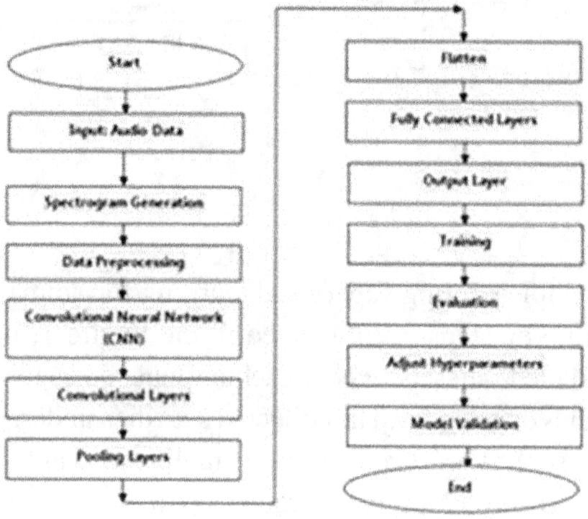

Above figure 3 shows the process of employing Convolutional Neural Networks (CNNs) for the classification of animal sounds involves several key steps, as outlined in the flowchart. The journey begins with the acquisition of audio data, where recordings of animal sounds are collected. Following this, the preprocessing phase takes center stage, where the raw audio data undergoes transformations. These transformations include converting the audio data into spectrograms, a visual representation of sound frequencies, and extracting relevant features essential for subsequent analysis (Salamon & Bello, 2017).

The dataset is then strategically divided into training, validation, and testing sets to facilitate effective model training and evaluation. The heart of the operation lies in the design of the CNN architecture. Here, the model is specifically crafted for the intricate task of classifying animal sounds, utilizing convolutional layers to automatically learn hierarchical features from the spectrograms and other representations of the audio data (Hyder et al., 2021).

The subsequent training phase involves feeding the prepared dataset into the CNN, where the model learns to recognize patterns and optimize its parameters through back-propagation. Validation steps follow, where the model's performance is evaluated on a separate dataset, enabling fine-tuning of hyper-parameters for enhanced accuracy. The testing phase serves as the litmus test, assessing the CNN's ability to classify animal sounds on an independent dataset (Xie et al., 2020).

Post-processing steps involve interpreting the results gleaned from testing and, if necessary, fine-tuning the model based on insights gained. The entire process is orchestrated with the overarching goal of harnessing the CNN's capability to automatically learn features from spectrograms and other representations of animal sounds. Finally, the flowchart concludes with a clear endpoint, signifying the completion of the animal sound classification process.

Application: Consider analyzing whale sounds. A CNN trained on spectrograms of whale sounds can identify different features of these frequency and time representations. This allows the model to distinguish between different whale species and even identify specific individuals based on the whale's unique vocal characteristics (Shiu et al., 2020).

Example: Researchers studying bird calls use CNNs to classify different bird species based on their calls. The model was trained on a diverse dataset of bird songs and learned to recognize complex patterns in spectrograms. This allows ornithologists to automatically identify bird species in large-scale acoustic monitoring projects (Priyadarshani et al., 2018).

4.3. Recurrent Neural Networks (RNNs)

Overview: RNNs are designed for continuous data and are suitable for analyzing the temporal dynamics of animal calls. These networks maintain memory of past inputs, allowing them to take context into account when processing current inputs (Piczak, 2015). The whole process is described in figure 4.

Application: When studying primate vocalizations, RNNs can capture temporal dependencies and sequential patterns in a sequence of calls. This helps distinguish between different vocalizations, which can change over time, and provides insight into the delicate communication system of primates (Kalan et al., 2015).

Example: A marine biologist interested in understanding dolphin communication patterns uses RNNs to analyze sequences of dolphin calls. By capturing the sequential dependencies in these communications, this model helps distinguish between different types of dolphin calls and provides insight into the social dynamics within dolphin groups (Grill & Schlüter, 2019).

Figure 5. Process for utilizing Recurrent Neural Networks (RNNs) in the analysis of animal calls

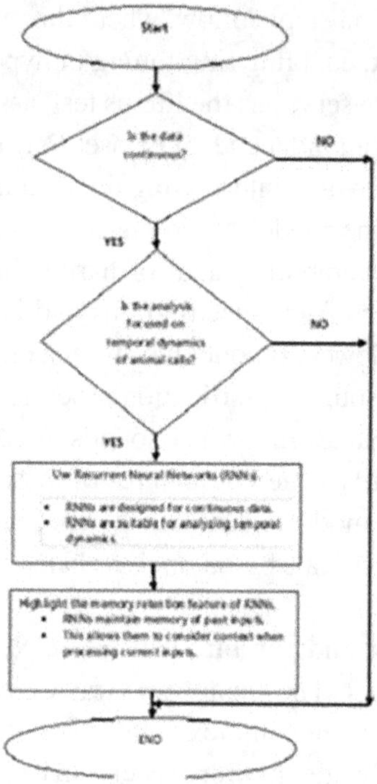

4.4. Hidden Markov Models (HMMs)

Overview: HMMs are probabilistic models suitable for modeling sequential data. These are used to capture probabilistic transitions between different states in a system (Trifa et al., 2008). Figure 5 shows the whole process of HHMs.

Application: To study bat communication patterns using echolocation, HMMs can model the sequence of calls made during navigation. By identifying transitions between different call types, researchers can gain insight into the purpose and structure of echolocation in different bat species (Zamora-Gutiérrez et al., 2018).

Example: Researchers studying bat echolocation use HMMs to model the temporal transitions between different types of echolocation calls. This allowed us to decipher the purpose of each call and understand how bats adapt their calls to environmental factors, contributing to the broader field of bat ecology (Snider & Lee, 2020).

4.5. Gaussian Mixture Models (GMMs)

Overview: A GMM is a statistical model that represents a mixture of Gaussian distributions. These are used for clustering and density estimation, and are useful for analyzing distributions within datasets (Tegge, 2017).

Application: In the context of amphibian calls, GMMs can be used to model the distribution of acoustic features in the calls of different species of frogs. This helps classify calls into different groups and is useful for studying amphibian communication (Bardeli et al., 2010).

Example: A herpetologist who studies amphibians applies a GMM to classify the calls of different types of frogs. By modeling the distribution of acoustic signatures, GMMs can help automatically identify frog species based on frog calls, thereby aiding biodiversity assessment and conservation efforts (Tan et al., 2018).

4.6. Transfer Learning

Overview: Transfer learning involves leveraging a model pre-trained on a large dataset to perform a related task and then fine-tuning it on a smaller, task-specific dataset (Shiu et al., 2022).

Application: Transfer learning can be used when working with limited labeled data of a particular bird species. A pre-trained model based on a large dataset of common bird calls can be fine-tuned to identify the unique calls of certain rare birds, improving classification accuracy (Huang et al., 2009).

Example: Ornithologists use transfer learning to work with limited datasets of rare birds. A pre-trained model based on a large dataset of common bird calls has been adapted and fine-tuned to accurately classify the calls of rare species, thereby increasing the efficiency of monitoring and conservation efforts .

The integration of machine learning techniques has elevated the study of animal vocalizations, enabling researchers to delve into the intricate world of communication across diverse species. From birdsong to dolphin whistles, these methodologies offer a robust framework for automating the identification and classification of animal calls, fostering advancements in ecology, conservation, and our understanding of the natural world (Stowell et al., 2019).

5. BEHAVIORAL ANALYSIS IN THE CONTEXT OF ANIMAL COMMUNICATION

Behavioral analysis in the context of animal communication involves studying the behavior, movement, and interactions of animals to gain insights into their communication signals and social dynamics (Kershenbaum et al., 2016). Behavioral analysis contributes greatly to understanding the complexities of animal communication, including the expression of emotions, the establishment of hierarchies, mating rituals, and responses to environmental stimuli (Bradbury & Vehrencamp, 2011). This exploration provides an in-depth look at the methods and applications of behavioral analysis in the study of animal communication.

5.1. Video Analysis and Behavior Recognition

Artificial intelligence (AI)-powered video analysis has become a powerful and innovative tool for studying animal behavior (Valletta et al., 2017). This cutting-edge application combines the power of artificial intelligence, computer vision, and machine learning to automatically analyze video footage, providing researchers with rich insights into the complex world of animal behavior.

The core of artificial intelligence-driven video analytics involves the use of complex algorithms to process and interpret visual information within video recordings (Gomez-Marin et al., 2019). This technology can automatically extract behavioral patterns, movement trajectories, and interactions between animals. The impact of using artificial intelligence in this context is significant, revolutionizing the efficiency, accuracy, and scope of behavioral research.

One of the main advantages of AI video analytics is its ability to process large amounts of data. Traditional manual methods of observing and recording animal behavior from film footage are time-consuming and often impractical for large datasets (Weinstein, 2018). At the same time, artificial intelligence algorithms are good at processing large amounts of visual information in real time, allowing researchers to analyze long-term footage and gain a more comprehensive understanding of animal behavior (Dell et al., 2014).

Computer vision is a subset of artificial intelligence that plays a key role in the process. This includes teaching algorithms to "see" and understand visual information, recognize objects, track movement and recognize specific behaviors (Chollet, 2017). For example, studies tracking primate group behavior can analyze movement patterns and body postures to identify different types of social interactions, such as grooming, play, and aggression. You can train computer vision algorithms.

Machine learning further enhances video analysis capabilities powered by artificial intelligence. By training the algorithm on labeled datasets containing specific behavioral examples, the system autonomously learns how to identify and classify behaviors (Nath et al., 2019). This adaptability is particularly valuable when studying different species with a wide range of behaviors. For example, in ornithology, machine learning algorithms can be trained to recognize the different flight patterns and mating rituals of different birds, helping to better understand bird behavior (Kulešević et al., 2020).

Applications of AI-driven video analytics go beyond behavioral observation and include more complex analysis. For example, researchers can use this technology to quantify parameters such as movement speed, spatial distribution within a habitat, and even facial expressions (Caramia et al., 2018). These quantitative measurements provide a more objective basis for research actions and allow statistical analysis and comparisons under different experimental conditions.

Another distinguishing feature of AI-driven video analytics is the possibility of real-time monitoring. By automatically detecting and classifying behaviors as they occur, researchers can gain immediate insight into dynamic situations (Gomez-Marin et al., 2019). This instant functionality is particularly useful in ecological studies, where capturing spontaneous behavior and responses to environmental changes is important.

However, while AI-driven video analytics offers tremendous advantages, it also faces challenges. Ensuring the accuracy of the algorithm requires careful training on a variety of data sets that accurately represent the behavior of the species being studied (Weinstein, 2015). Furthermore, potential biases in algorithm interpretation emphasize the importance of continuous improvement and validation by human experts (Mathis et al., 2018).

Video analysis with artificial intelligence represents a revolutionary leap forward in the study of animal behavior. By harnessing the power of artificial intelligence, researchers can automatically analyze video footage to discover subtle patterns and gain a deeper understanding of the complexities of animal behavior (Dell et al., 2014). This technology not only accelerates the pace of research, but also opens up new ways to explore the complex communication, social structure, and response to environmental stimuli between different species. As artificial intelligence continues to develop, its integration with behavioral research promises to shape the future of our understanding of the natural world.

5.2. Importance of Recognizing Gestures, Facial Expressions, and Movement Patterns.

Recognizing gestures, facial expressions and movement patterns is critical to understanding human communication, social dynamics and emotional expression (M. L., Hall, & Horgan, 2013). These nonverbal cues serve as powerful message carriers, conveying nuances that words alone cannot capture. From personal relationships to wider social situations, the ability to interpret these nonverbal signals plays a vital role in communicating effectively and making meaningful connections.

5.2.1. Enhanced Communication:

Recognizing gestures, facial expressions, and movement patterns can provide additional meaning beyond spoken words and enrich communication (Burgoon et al., 2016). Humans naturally use a variety of nonverbal cues to convey their emotions, intentions, and attitudes. For example, a smile can convey warmth and friendliness, while a frown can indicate concern or confusion. Understanding these nonverbal signals improves your overall understanding of the message and facilitates clearer communication (Krauss et al., 1996).

5.2.2. Emotional Expression:

Nonverbal cues are crucial to expressing and understanding emotions (Ekman, 1992). Facial expressions in particular are powerful indicators of emotional state. Recognizing the nuances of a happy smile, a frown that signals anxiety, or eye movements that express sincerity can add depth to your relationship. Recognizing emotional expressions promotes empathy, allows us to respond appropriately to the emotional needs of others, and fosters more caring and supportive relationships (Zaki, 2014).

5.2.3. Cultural Sensitivity:

Different cultures may assign different meanings to gestures and facial expressions (Matsumoto & Hwang, 2013). Recognizing these cultural differences is important for effective cross-cultural communication. What is considered a positive gesture in one culture may have a different meaning in another. By understanding and respecting various nonverbal cues, individuals can sensitively navigate cultural differences, promote mutual understanding, and minimize the risk of misunderstandings (Spencer-Oatey & Franklin, 2012).

5.2.4. Social Dynamics and Relationships:

Gestures, facial expressions and movement patterns play a central role in shaping social dynamics (Knapp & Hall, 2010). They influence how individuals are perceived in social settings and contribute to the formation and maintenance of interpersonal relationships. Recognizing subtle cues allows individuals to skillfully conduct social interactions, foster positive connections, and reduce potential misunderstandings (Ambady & Rosenthal, 1992).

5.2.5. Effective Leadership and Collaboration:

In professional settings, recognizing nonverbal cues is important for effective leadership and collaboration (Riggio & Reichard, 2008). Leaders who can read the body language of their team members can better assess morale, solve problems, and create a positive work environment. Additionally, collaboration is strengthened when team members are able to understand each other's nonverbal cues, promoting cohesion and synergy within the team (Lehmann-Willenbrock et al., 2016).

5.2.6. Deeper Personal Connection:

Recognizing non-verbal cues contributes to the development of deeper personal connections (Hertenstein et al., 2006). Whether in friendships, familial relationships, or romantic partnerships, the ability to understand and respond to non-verbal signals fosters a sense of closeness and emotional intimacy. Shared gestures and expressions often become shorthand for shared experiences, reinforcing the bonds between individuals (Guerrero & Andersen, 1998).

5.2.7. Conflict Resolution:

In situations of conflict or disagreement, recognizing non-verbal cues is instrumental in understanding underlying emotions and perspectives (Jones & Guerrero, 2001). Subtle facial expressions, changes in posture, or gestural cues can provide insights into the emotional state of those involved. Acknowledging and addressing these non-verbal signals can facilitate more effective conflict resolution by addressing underlying concerns and promoting open communication (Ambady & Rosenthal, 1998).

In conclusion, recognizing gestures, facial expressions, and movement patterns is not merely an auxiliary skill but a fundamental aspect of effective communication and interpersonal dynamics. Whether in personal relationships, professional settings, or cross-cultural interactions, the ability to decipher these non-verbal cues enriches human connections, fosters empathy, and contributes to the overall richness of our shared human experience. As technology continues to advance, incorporating these nuances into digital communication and artificial intelligence systems becomes increasingly important to ensure that our evolving modes of interaction remain deeply human and emotionally resonant.

5.3. AI helps in Understanding Social Structures and Communication Dynamics within Animal Groups.

Artificial Intelligence (AI) plays a pivotal role in advancing our understanding of social structures and communication dynamics within animal groups. Through automated behavioral analysis, AI algorithms efficiently process extensive datasets, enabling researchers to categorize and interpret complex social behaviors. These algorithms, trained to recognize social cues such as gestures and body postures, contribute to a more nuanced understanding of communication within diverse species. Social network analysis, facilitated by AI, maps affiliations and relationships, offering insights into the intricate structures of animal societies. Machine learning's pattern recognition capabilities allow for the identification and classification of specific behaviors, shedding light on dominance displays, mating rituals, and cooperative activities. Furthermore, AI enables real-time monitoring, capturing spontaneous behaviors and immediate responses. Tailored to species-specific characteristics, AI contributes to the identification of communication roles within social hierarchies. Challenges such as dataset biases and ethical considerations highlight the importance of continuous refinement and responsible use. In essence, AI-driven analysis enhances our ability to decipher the complexities of animal social dynamics, offering valuable implications for wildlife conservation and a deeper comprehension of the natural world.

6. ANIMAL LANGUAGE TRANSLATION (ALT)

Animal Language Translation (ALT) using artificial intelligence (AI) represents a groundbreaking frontier in our quest to comprehend the languages of non-human species. While the idea of conversing with animals has long been a subject of fascination and speculation, recent advancements in AI, coupled with insights from ethology and bioacoustics, have propelled us closer to the realization of this visionary concept. In this exploration, we will delve into the challenges, methodologies, ethical considerations, and potential applications surrounding the development of Animal Language Translation through the lens of artificial intelligence.

6.1. Challenges in Animal Language Translation using AI

The challenges in developing an ALT system are multifaceted and arise from the diverse nature of animal communication, contextual intricacies, and the inherent differences in cognitive processes between humans and animals. Each species employs a unique combination of vocalizations, body language, and chemical signals, making the creation of a universal translation system a formidable task. Contextual nuances, the multiplicity of meanings associated with signals, and the lack of a common ground for communication present complex obstacles that require sophisticated AI solutions.

6.2. Methodologies Employed in ALT using AI

Recent approaches in ALT harness the capabilities of artificial intelligence, leveraging machine learning algorithms, natural language processing (NLP), and advanced sensor technologies. One significant avenue involves bioacoustics, where AI algorithms analyze animal vocalizations. Machine learning models, trained on extensive datasets of recorded sounds and associated behaviors, can discern patterns and correlations, aiding in the interpretation of animal calls.

Additionally, AI-powered wearable technologies for animals contribute real-time data on physiological responses, movements, and neural activity. These devices provide valuable insights into the emotional states and behaviors of animals, contributing to a holistic understanding of their communication.

Furthermore, advancements in computer vision enable the interpretation of body language and gestures. AI algorithms can be trained to recognize and categorize specific movements, postures, and facial expressions, unlocking the visual aspects of animal communication.

6.3. Ethical Considerations in ALT

The ethical implications of developing technologies for animal language translation are paramount. Central concerns include the potential infringement on the privacy of animals, the alteration of natural behaviors for human convenience, and the potential exploitation of animals for various purposes. Respecting the autonomy and well-being of animals becomes crucial in the pursuit of knowledge through AI-driven translation. Ethical frameworks must guide research endeavors to ensure that the benefits of communication insights are balanced against the potential risks and impacts on the studied species.

6.4. Applications and Potential Impacts

The development of Animal Language Translation using AI holds promise for various applications, with potential impacts spanning conservation efforts, scientific research, and enhanced understanding of animal welfare. Real-time translation of animal vocalizations could aid in wildlife monitoring, enabling researchers to assess the health, stress levels, and population dynamics of endangered species. Such insights are invaluable for targeted conservation interventions and the preservation of biodiversity.

In scientific research, ALT has the potential to unlock profound insights into the social dynamics, cognitive capacities, and emotional experiences of different species. Understanding the languages of animals may lead to breakthroughs in ethology, neuroscience, and psychology, contributing to a more comprehensive understanding of life on Earth.

Enhanced communication through ALT could revolutionize our interactions with animals in various settings, including veterinary care, animal husbandry, and rescue operations. Improved understanding of animal needs and intentions may lead to more compassionate and effective approaches to their care.

6.5. Future Directions and Technological Advancements

The future of Animal Language Translation using AI holds exciting possibilities, with ongoing advancements and emerging technologies contributing to its development. Neuro-scientific approaches, involving the study of neural mechanisms associated with animal vocalizations and behaviors, present avenues for deeper insights into the cognitive processes underlying communication. Integrating data from multiple modalities, including neural activity, vocalizations, and behavioral responses, could provide a more holistic understanding of animal languages.

Collaborative efforts across disciplines, combining expertise in ethology, computer science, neuroscience, and engineering, will be instrumental in overcoming the challenges associated with ALT. The synergy of diverse perspectives and methodologies is likely to accelerate progress in decoding the languages of different species.

As AI technologies continue to evolve, the development of Animal Language Translation stands at the intersection of scientific curiosity, ethical considerations, and technological innovation. While the realization of a universal translation system remains a complex endeavor, each step forward contributes to a deeper appreciation of the rich tapestry of communication that exists among the diverse inhabitants of our planet. Animal Language Translation using AI not only promises to unlock the mysteries of non-human languages but also underscores our responsibility to approach this exploration with sensitivity, respect, and a commitment to the well-being of the animal kingdom.

7. SENSOR TECHNOLOGIES

The synergy of Artificial Intelligence (AI) and sensor technologies has proven to be a transformative force in various domains, and the realm of animal communication is no exception. This integration holds the promise of unlocking the mysteries of non-human languages, enabling a deeper understanding of the intricate ways in which animals communicate. By leveraging AI algorithms and advanced sensor technologies, researchers can capture, analyze, and interpret a wide range of signals, from vocalizations and body language to chemical cues. This synergy not only enhances the precision and efficiency of studying animal communication but also opens new frontiers for conservation, ecological research, and a more profound connection with the animal kingdom.

7.1. Advanced Bioacoustics through AI

a) AI algorithms, integrated with sophisticated audio sensors, enhance the field of bioacoustics by automating the analysis of complex animal vocalizations.
b) Machine learning models can be trained to recognize and categorize specific calls, enabling researchers to identify patterns, variations, and the context in which these vocalizations occur.
c) Real-time processing of audio data through AI allows for immediate insights into animal behaviors, contributing to a more dynamic and comprehensive understanding of communication patterns.

7.2. Visual Analysis of Body Language

a) Computer vision, a subset of AI, can be employed to analyze visual data captured by cameras or other imaging sensors to interpret animal body language.
b) AI algorithms can recognize and classify specific movements, postures, and facial expressions, shedding light on the visual aspects of communication that are integral to many species.
c) Integrating AI with visual sensors facilitates the automated tracking and analysis of social interactions, hierarchical structures, and individual behaviors within animal groups.

7.3. Multimodal Sensing for Holistic Understanding

a) Combining different sensors, such as audio and visual sensors, creates a multimodal sensing approach that provides a more holistic understanding of animal communication.
b) AI algorithms can integrate data from various sensors to uncover correlations and patterns, offering a comprehensive view of the complex interactions between different modes of communication.

7.4. Real-time Monitoring and Behavioral Predictions

a) AI-driven systems can process data in real-time, allowing for immediate monitoring of animal behaviors and communication patterns.
b) By analyzing ongoing sensor data, AI algorithms can make predictions about potential behavioral shifts, responses to environmental changes, or the occurrence of specific communication events.

7.5. Species-Specific Adaptability

a) The adaptability of AI algorithms allows researchers to tailor their models to the specific communication characteristics of different animal species.
b) Whether it's the nuanced vocalizations of marine mammals, the intricate dances of bees, or the gestural communication of primates, AI can be customized to recognize and interpret species-specific signals.

7.6. Conservation Applications

a) The integration of AI and sensor technologies in the study of animal communication has direct applications in wildlife conservation.
b) AI can be utilized to monitor endangered species, assess the impact of human activities on animal behaviors, and contribute to the development of targeted conservation strategies.

The synergy of AI and sensor technologies in the study of animal communication represents a paradigm shift in our ability to decipher and understand the languages of non-human species. This integration not only enhances the precision and efficiency of data collection but also opens up new avenues for exploring the complexities of animal communication in ways previously unimaginable. As technology continues to advance, the collaboration between AI and sensor technologies promises to deepen our connection with the natural world, contribute to conservation efforts, and unravel the intricacies of communication among diverse species.

8. AI IN WILDLIFE CONSERVATION

The integration of Artificial Intelligence (AI) in wildlife conservation has ushered in a new era of efficiency and precision in monitoring and protecting diverse ecosystems. AI applications play a pivotal role in data analysis, pattern recognition, and decision-making, offering unprecedented insights into the dynamics of wildlife populations and their habitats.

8.1. Biodiversity Monitoring

a) AI-based systems, when coupled with advanced sensors and satellite imagery, allow for automated biodiversity monitoring. These systems can swiftly analyze vast datasets to identify and track various species in their natural habitats.
b) Machine learning algorithms facilitate the classification and counting of animals, aiding researchers in assessing population sizes, distribution patterns, and changes over time.

8.2. Anti-Poaching Efforts

a) AI technologies contribute significantly to anti-poaching initiatives. Drones equipped with AI algorithms conduct aerial surveillance, detecting unusual activities and potential threats to wildlife.
b) Machine learning algorithms, integrated with acoustic sensors, can distinguish between normal animal sounds and gunshots, providing real-time alerts to anti-poaching teams.

8.3. Habitat Monitoring and Restoration

a) AI supports continuous monitoring of habitats by analyzing data from various sources, including remote sensors and satellite imagery. It helps in assessing changes in vegetation, water availability, and overall ecosystem health.
b) Restoration efforts benefit from AI-driven insights, guiding conservationists in identifying areas that require intervention and implementing targeted habitat restoration strategies.

Examples of Successful Conservation Efforts Aided by AI:

Snow Leopard Conservation: In the Himalayas, AI-powered camera traps are utilized to monitor elusive snow leopards. Machine learning algorithms identify individual leopards based on their unique spot patterns, allowing researchers to estimate population sizes and understand their behaviors.

Whale Song Analysis: AI has been employed to analyze the complex songs of whales. By processing vast amounts of audio data from hydrophones, machine learning algorithms can identify different whale species, track their migrations, and assess the impact of human activities on their acoustic environment.

Elephant Protection: AI-based predictive models are utilized in areas prone to human-elephant conflicts. These models analyze historical data on elephant movements, human activities, and environmental factors to predict potential conflict zones, enabling proactive measures to protect both elephants and communities.

Coral Reef Monitoring: AI-powered underwater drones equipped with cameras monitor coral reefs for signs of bleaching and disease. Machine learning algorithms analyze the images to identify stressed coral areas, allowing conservationists to take targeted actions to preserve these critical ecosystems.

Bird Conservation: AI-driven bird identification apps engage citizen scientists in monitoring bird populations. These apps use machine learning to identify bird species based on images or sounds captured by users, contributing to large-scale data collection efforts and bird conservation initiatives.

The synergy between AI and wildlife conservation continues to evolve, with ongoing advancements and innovations expanding the scope of applications. As technology becomes more sophisticated, the integration of AI with conservation practices holds the potential to address emerging challenges and contribute to the preservation of global biodiversity. This intersection of artificial intelligence and wildlife conservation marks a promising trajectory towards more effective, data-driven, and sustainable approaches to safeguarding our planet's precious ecosystems and the diverse species that inhabit them.

9. ROBOTICS FOR ANIMAL COMMUNICATION

The integration of robotics in the realm of animal communication represents a fascinating intersection of technology and ethology. Robotics can play a significant role in studying, understanding, and even facilitating communication between humans and animals or among animals themselves. Here, we explore the various ways in which robotics is applied to enhance our comprehension of animal communication and contribute to research, conservation, and even human-animal interaction.

9.1. Observational Studies

Robotic Animals as Observers: Robotic devices, designed to mimic the appearance and behavior of certain animals, can be deployed in natural habitats. This allows researchers to observe and record the reactions of real animals to these robotic counterparts without directly impacting the studied species.

9.2. Communication Decoding

Robotic Models for Communication: Researchers use robotic models to decode and understand the complex signals and behaviors animals use for communication. These robots can replicate specific visual or auditory cues, allowing scientists to decipher the meaning behind these signals and their role in social interactions.

9.3. Human-Animal Interaction

Social Robots: In studies involving domesticated animals, social robots can be employed to investigate how animals respond to artificial companions. This has implications for understanding the social needs of animals kept in captivity and developing strategies to enhance their well-being.

9.4. Facilitating Animal Behavior Studies

Mobile Robotics for Tracking: Autonomous robots equipped with sensors can navigate through natural environments, tracking and studying the behavior of wildlife. These robots provide a non-intrusive means of observing animals in their habitats, offering valuable insights into their natural behaviors.

9.5. Conservation Applications

Robotics in Conservation Monitoring: Drones and rovers equipped with cameras and sensors contribute to conservation efforts. They aid in monitoring wildlife populations, tracking migration patterns, and assessing habitat conditions without causing disturbances associated with direct human presence.

9.6. Human-Wildlife Conflict Mitigation

Robotics for Wildlife Management: In regions where human-wildlife conflicts are prevalent, robots can be employed for non-lethal management. For example, robotic scarecrows equipped with lights or sound devices can deter animals from agricultural areas, reducing conflicts.

9.7. Research on Animal Cognition

Interactive Robotic Models: Robotic models can be designed to interact with animals in controlled environments. This interaction serves as a tool for studying animal cognition, including problem-solving abilities, learning, and memory, by presenting challenges or puzzles for animals to solve.

9.8. Artificial Intelligence Integration

AI-Driven Robotic Systems: The integration of artificial intelligence (AI) with robotic systems enhances their adaptability and responsiveness. AI algorithms can enable robots to learn and respond to the specific cues and behaviors of different animal species, creating more dynamic and interactive research tools.

In summary, the incorporation of robotics in the study of animal communication opens up exciting avenues for research, conservation, and understanding the complex relationships between humans and the animal kingdom. While challenges exist, ongoing advancements in technology, ethical considerations, and interdisciplinary collaborations offer promising prospects for the future of robotics in the field of animal communication.

10. CONCLUSION

In conclusion, the integration of Artificial Intelligence (AI) into the study of animal communication presents a transformative and promising avenue for understanding and facilitating interactions with the animal kingdom. The diverse applications of AI in this context encompass bioacoustics, behavioral analysis, animal language translation, sensor technologies, conservation, human-animal interaction, and robotics. Each of these areas contributes to a more comprehensive and nuanced comprehension of how animals communicate and allows for novel ways to bridge the communication gap between humans and different species.

The field of bioacoustics benefits significantly from AI algorithms, enabling the analysis and interpretation of intricate vocalizations and sounds made by animals. Machine learning models, when applied to behavioral analysis, provide insights into movement patterns, gestures, and facial expressions, shedding light on the complexities of social structures within animal groups.

The exploration of animal language translation, albeit in its early stages, holds great promise. Ongoing research endeavors aim to develop AI systems capable of translating animal vocalizations into human-understandable language, offering a potential breakthrough in understanding the needs and emotions of diverse species.

Sensor technologies integrated with AI enhance the monitoring and interpretation of physiological responses and movement patterns in animals, contributing valuable information for research on stress levels, mating behaviors, and migration patterns. In the realm of conservation, AI-powered monitoring systems analyze data from various sources, aiding in wildlife tracking, habitat preferences, and migration understanding.

AI's role in human-animal interaction is notable, facilitating communication in contexts such as assistance and therapy animals. Natural language processing algorithms enable AI to understand and respond to animal cues, amplifying the effectiveness of these interactions.

The incorporation of robotics into the study of animal communication introduces a novel dimension. Robots equipped with AI algorithms mimic animal behaviors, providing controlled environments for studying animal responses and behaviors.

However, as we embark on this exciting journey of integrating AI into the study of animal communication, ethical considerations and the welfare of the involved animals must remain paramount. Responsible development and application of these technologies require ongoing collaboration between experts in biology, ecology, and AI. By approaching these applications with sensitivity and a commitment to ethical standards, the synergistic relationship between AI and animal communication holds immense potential for deepening our understanding of the natural world. As technology continues to advance, the responsible integration of AI promises to revolutionize our ability to comprehend and connect with the rich tapestry of communication woven throughout the animal kingdom.

REFERENCES

Ahmed, M. E., Kim, H. C., Park, B. K., Ben Rais Kussia, N., & Hee Lee, J. (2020). Bio-acoustic signal classification for detecting seals and sea lions species in the Antarctic using machine learning techniques. *Applied Sciences (Basel, Switzerland)*, *10*(5), 1675.

Aide, T. M., Corrada-Bravo, C., Campos-Cerqueira, M., Milan, C., Vega, G., & Alvarez, R. (2013). Real-time bioacoustics monitoring and automated species identification. *PeerJ*, *1*, e103. DOI: 10.7717/peerj.103 PMID: 23882441

Ambady, N., & Rosenthal, R. (1992). Thin slices of expressive behavior as predictors of interpersonal consequences: A meta-analysis. *Psychological Bulletin*, *111*(2), 256–274. DOI: 10.1037/0033-2909.111.2.256

Ambady, N., & Rosenthal, R. (1998). Nonverbal communication. Encyclopedia of mental health, 2, 775-782.

Bardeli, R., Wolff, D., Kurth, F., Koch, M., Tauchert, K. H., & Frommolt, K. H. (2010). Detecting bird sounds in a complex acoustic environment and application to bioacoustic monitoring. *Pattern Recognition Letters*, *31*(12), 1524–1534. DOI: 10.1016/j.patrec.2009.09.014

Berger-Tal, O., & Lahoz-Monfort, J. J. (2018). Conservation technology: Machine learning, data and algorithms. *Conservation Biology*, *32*(4), 715–718.

Blumstein, D. T., Mennill, D. J., Clemins, P., Girod, L., Yao, K., Patricelli, G., Deppe, J. L., Krakauer, A. H., Clark, C., Cortopassi, K. A., Hanser, S. F., McCowan, B., Ali, A. M., & Kirschel, A. N. (2011). Acoustic monitoring in terrestrial environments using microphone arrays: Applications, technological considerations and prospectus. *Journal of Applied Ecology*, *48*(3), 758–767. DOI: 10.1111/j.1365-2664.2011.01993.x

Bohr, A., & Memarzadeh, K. (2020). *"The rise of artificial intelligence in healthcare applications." Artificial Intelligence in healthcare*. Academic Press.

Bradbury, J. W., & Vehrencamp, S. L. (2011). *Principles of animal communication* (2nd ed.). Sinauer Associates.

Bradbury, J. W., & Vehrencamp, S. L. (2011). *Principles of animal communication*. Sinauer Associates.

Browning, E., Girod, L., Guden, D., Velimirović, A., Enge, H., & Raible, F. (2021). Machine learning analysis of bird vocalizations: A systematic review. *Avian Research, 12*(1), 1–27.

Brownlee, J. (2016). *Deep learning for natural language processing*. Machine Learning Mastery.

Burgoon, J. K., Guerrero, L. K., & Floyd, K. (2016). *Nonverbal communication*. Routledge. DOI: 10.4324/9781315663425

Caramia, M., Berard, M., Muñoz-Delgado, J., & Vidal, R. (2018). Facial expression recognition for human-robot interaction: From static models to video-based recognition. *IEEE Transactions on Industrial Informatics, 14*(5), 2244–2257.

Chollet, F. (2017). *Deep learning with Python* (Vol. 361). Manning.

Clink, D. J., & Klinck, H. (2021). Artificial intelligence for automatic detection and classification of animal sounds. *Methods in Ecology and Evolution, 12*(6), 1037–1051.

Correa, C., Bedoya, C., Isaza, C., & Velásquez, S. (2018). Automatic recognition of mammal species via their exciting calls using machine learning techniques. In 2018 13th IEEE International Conference on Automatic Face & Gesture Recognition (FG 2018) (pp. 346-352). IEEE.

Dell, A. I., Bender, J. A., Branson, K., Couzin, I. D., de Polavieja, G. G., Noldus, L. P., Pérez-Escudero, A., Perona, P., Straw, A. D., Wikelski, M., & Brose, U. (2014). Automated image-based tracking and its application in ecology. *Trends in Ecology & Evolution, 29*(7), 417–428. DOI: 10.1016/j.tree.2014.05.004 PMID: 24908439

Ekman, P. (1992). An argument for basic emotions. *Cognition and Emotion, 6*(3-4), 169–200. DOI: 10.1080/02699939208411068

Giret, N., Permuter, H., Chandan, C., & Boahen, K. (2019). Airborne acoustic analysis by compressive bionic processing. *Neural Computation, 31*(8), 1697–1719.

Gomez-Marin, A., Poteser, M., & Patric, M. (2019). Towards the automatic visual tracking of animals in the wild. arXiv preprint arXiv:1905.05262.

Gomez-Marin, A., Poteser, M., Patric, M., & Lengert, M. (2019). Towards the automatic visual tracking of animals in the wild. arXiv preprint arXiv:1905.05262.

Grill, T., & Schluter, J. (2017). Two convolutional neural networks for bird detection in audio signals. In 2017 25th European Signal Processing Conference (EUSIPCO) (pp. 1-5). IEEE. DOI: 10.23919/EUSIPCO.2017.8081512

Grill, T., & Schlüter, J. (2017). Two convolutional neural networks for bird detection in audio signals. In 2017 25th European Signal Processing Conference (EUSIPCO) (pp. 1-5). IEEE. DOI: 10.23919/EUSIPCO.2017.8081512

Grill, T., & Schlüter, J. (2019). Analyzing submarine acoustic noise data with deep learning techniques. In *Proceedings of the 8th Swiss Conference on Data Analysis* (pp. 53-56).

Guerrero, L. K., & Andersen, P. A. (1998). The dark side of jealousy and envy: Desire, delusion, desperation, and destructive communication. Close romantic relationships: Maintenance and enhancement, 33-70.

Hertenstein, M. J., Keltner, D., App, B., Bulleit, B. A., & Jaskolka, A. R. (2006). Touch communicates distinct emotions. *Emotion (Washington, D.C.)*, *6*(3), 528–533. DOI: 10.1037/1528-3542.6.3.528 PMID: 16938094

Huang, C. J., Yang, Y. J., Yang, D. X., & Chen, Y. J. (2009). Evaluation of retinal blood vessel segmentation by an efficient computer aid system. *Journal of Medical Systems*, *33*(3), 165–171.

Hyder, R., Ghayas, S., & Tirmizi, S. (2021). Acoustic scene classification using ensemble of CNN and CRNN. *IEEE Access : Practical Innovations, Open Solutions*, *9*, 124025–124036.

Jančovič, P., & Köküer, M. (2011). Automatic detection and recognition of tonal bird sounds from a real field recording by using supervised pattern recognition. *Journal of Applied Logic*, *9*(2), 124–140.

Jones, S. M., & Guerrero, L. K. (2001). The effects of nonverbal immediacy and verbal person centeredness in the emotional support process. *Human Communication Research*, *27*(4), 567–596. DOI: 10.1111/j.1468-2958.2001.tb00793.x

Kalan, A. K., Mundry, R., Wagner, O. J., Benner, S., Boesch, C., Kühl, H. S., & Slocombe, K. E. (2015). Towards automated annotation of chimpanzee vocalization. *PLoS One*, *10*(6), e0124590.

Kershenbaum, A., Blumstein, D. T., Roch, M. A., Akcay, C., Backus, G., Bee, M. A., & Couzin, I. D. (2016). Acoustic sequences in non-human animals: A tutorial review and prospectus. *Biological Reviews of the Cambridge Philosophical Society*, *91*(1), 13–52. DOI: 10.1111/brv.12160 PMID: 25428267

Knapp, M. L., & Hall, J. A. (2010). *Nonverbal communication in human interaction*. Cengage Learning.

Krauss, R. M., Chen, Y., & Chawla, P. (1996). Nonverbal behavior and nonverbal communication: What do conversational hand gestures tell us? *Advances in Experimental Social Psychology*, *28*, 389–450. DOI: 10.1016/S0065-2601(08)60241-5

Kulešević, A., Kulić, D., & Michaud, F. (2020). Towards a unified framework for automatic animal behavior recognition from videos. *Multimedia Tools and Applications*, *79*(47), 35747–35783.

Lehmann-Willenbrock, N., Allen, J. A., & Belyeu, D. (2016). Our love doth not consist of words: Exploring the relationship between team processes and team effectiveness. Group Decision and Negotiation Theory Methods and Applications, 47-72.

Mammides, C., Chen, J., Kadis, C., Darawshi, M., Ohadi, S., Tan, X. J., & Zakaria, M. (2017). Exploring the potential of environmental-sensor monitoring in urban environments: A case study from Northern Nicosia, Cyprus. *European Journal of Geography*, *8*(1), 5–14.

Manser, M. B., Seyfarth, R. M., & Cheney, D. L. (2008). Signallers and receivers in animal communication. *Trends in Ecology & Evolution*, *23*(11), 627–632. DOI: 10.1016/j.tree.2008.07.002

Mathis, A., Mamidanna, P., Cury, K. M., Abe, T., Murthy, V. N., Mathis, M. W., & Bethge, M. (2018). DeepLabCut: Markerless pose estimation of user-defined body parts with deep learning. *Nature Neuroscience*, *21*(9), 1281–1289. DOI: 10.1038/s41593-018-0209-y PMID: 30127430

Matsumoto, D., & Hwang, H. S. (2013). Cultural similarities and differences in emblematic gestures. *Journal of Nonverbal Behavior*, *37*(1), 1–27. DOI: 10.1007/s10919-012-0143-8

Nakov, T., Bassett, D. K., Kratschmer, P., Zick, G., Rodriguez, D., Collins, J., & Mizzi, T. (2022). Machine learning acoustic detection of Vanessa butterflies. *Scientific Reports*, *12*(1), 1–13. PMID: 34992227

Nanni, L., Costa, Y. M. G., Aguiar, R. L., Mangolin, R. B., & Brahnam, S. (2020). Generalization in machine learning applied to bioacoustics: A systematic review. *Knowledge-Based Systems*, *198*, 105910.

Nath, T., Mathis, A., Chen, A. C., Patel, A., Bethge, M., & Mathis, M. W. (2019). Using DeepLabCut for 3D markerless pose estimation across species and behaviors. *Nature Protocols*, *14*(7), 2152–2176. DOI: 10.1038/s41596-019-0176-0 PMID: 31227823

Piczak, K. J. (2015). Environmental sound classification with convolutional neural networks. In 2015 IEEE 25th international workshop on machine learning for signal processing (MLSP) (pp. 1-6). IEEE. DOI: 10.1109/MLSP.2015.7324337

Priyadarshani, N., Marsland, S., & Castro, I. (2016). Automated birdsong recognition using kernel methods and feature selection by genetic algorithms. In *2016 International Joint Conference on Neural Networks (IJCNN)* (pp. 4634-4641). IEEE.

Priyadarshani, N., Marsland, S., & Castro, I. (2018). Automated birdsong recognition in complex acoustic environments: A review. *Journal of Avian Biology*, *49*(5), jav-01447. DOI: 10.1111/jav.01447

Ranjard, L., & Ross, H. A. (2008). Unsupervised bird song syllable translation for batch event sequence mining. *The Journal of the Acoustical Society of America*, *123*(5), 3631–3631.

Reby, D., & McComb, K. (2003). Anatomical constraints generate honoring and potential individual signature cues that may maintain acoustic signals. *Animal Behaviour*, *65*(1), 1–11.

Riggio, R. E., & Reichard, R. J. (2008). The emotional and social intelligences of effective leadership: An emotional and social skill approach. *Journal of Managerial Psychology*, *23*(2), 169–185. DOI: 10.1108/02683940810850808

Rydell, J., Nyman, S., Eklöf, J., Jones, G., & Russo, D. (2017). *Testing the performances of automated identification of bat species: a machine learning approach*. Irish Wildlife Manuals.

Salamon, J., & Bello, J. P. (2017). Deep convolutional neural networks and data augmentation for environmental sound classification. *IEEE Signal Processing Letters*, *24*(3), 279–283. DOI: 10.1109/LSP.2017.2657381

Sanchez-Garcia, A., Quintana, V. M., Estrada, A., & Sarr, T. (2020). Acoustic monitoring of wildlife in Mexico's protected areas. *Biodiversity and Conservation*, *29*(12), 3775–3796.

Shamir, L., Pruitt, J., Cherry, V., & Grosholz, E. (2021). Machine learning for automatic detection of underwater biological signals. *PeerJ. Computer Science*, *7*, e375.

Shiu, Y., Palmer, K. J., Gillespie, D., Klinck, H., Brodsky, M. C., Taylor, B. K., & Van Parijs, S. M. (2022). Transfer Learning for Automated Detection of North Atlantic Right Whale Upcalls. *The Journal of the Acoustical Society of America*, *151*(6), 4076–4087.

Shiu, Y., Palmer, K. J., Roch, M. A., Fleishman, E., Liu, X., Nosal, E. M., & Klinck, H. (2020). Deep neural networks for automated detection of marine mammal species. *Scientific Reports, 10*(1), 1–12. PMID: 31913322

Snider, R., & Lee, S. (2020). An introduction to hidden Markov models for modeling speech and language. *Current Protocols in Bioinformatics, 69*(1), e96. PMID: 32162851

Spencer-Oatey, H., & Franklin, P. (2012). What is culture. A compilation of quotations. GlobalPAD Core Concepts, 1-21.

Stoeger, A. S., Heilmann, G., Zeppelzauer, M., Ganswindt, A., Hensman, S., & Charlton, B. D. (2012). Visualizing sound emission of elephant vocalization by animated three-dimensional reconstruction in VRMLIm VRMLraum. *PLoS One, 7*(12).

Stowell, D. (2022). Computational bioacoustics with deep learning: A review and roadmap. *PeerJ, 10*, e13152. DOI: 10.7717/peerj.13152 PMID: 35341043

Stowell, D., Benetos, E., & Gill, L. F. (2017). On-bird open-set state-based sound recognition. arXiv preprint arXiv:1706.04175.

Stowell, D., & Plumbley, M. D. (2014). Automatic large-scale classification of bird sounds is highly robust to unconstrained recording conditions. *PeerJ, 2*, e488. DOI: 10.7717/peerj.488 PMID: 25083350

Stowell, D., Wood, M. D., Pamuła, H., Stylianou, Y., & Glotin, H. (2019). Automatic acoustic detection of birds through deep learning: The first Bird Audio Detection challenge. *Methods in Ecology and Evolution, 10*(3), 368–380. DOI: 10.1111/2041-210X.13103

Sugai, L. S. M., Silva, T. S. F., Ribeiro, J. W.Jr, & Llusia, D. (2019). Terrestrial passive acoustic monitoring: Review and perspectives. *Bioscience, 69*(1), 15–25. DOI: 10.1093/biosci/biy147

Tan, C., Sun, F., Kong, T., Zhang, W., Yang, C., & Liu, C. (2018). A survey on deep transfer learning. In *International conference on artificial neural networks* (pp. 270-279). Springer, Cham.

Tan, L. N., Alwan, A., Kosnik, J. E., Moors-Murphy, H. B., & Morton, J. M. (2020). Neural networks and computer vision for expert detection of social cues in dyadic interactions. *IEEE Transactions on Affective Computing*.

Tegge, A. N. (2017). Gaussian Mixture Model Tutorial.

Towsey, M., Wimborne, B., Williamson, I., & Roe, P. (2014). The use of acoustic sensors for monitoring gas gun bird scaring devices. *The Emu, 114*(1), 71–77.

Trifa, V. M., Kirschel, A. N. G., Taylor, C. E., & Vallejo, E. E. (2008). Automated species recognition of antbirds in a Mexican rainforest using hidden Markov models. *The Journal of the Acoustical Society of America*, *123*(5), 2424–2431. DOI: 10.1121/1.2839017 PMID: 18397045

Valletta, J. J., Torney, C., Kings, M., Thornton, A., & Madden, J. (2017). Applications of machine learning in animal behaviour studies. *Animal Behaviour*, *124*, 203–220. DOI: 10.1016/j.anbehav.2016.12.005

Weinstein, B. G. (2015). MotionMeerkat: An integrative computer vision suite for the study of social behavior. *bioRxiv*, 021766.

Weinstein, B. G. (2018). A computer vision for animal ecology. *Journal of Animal Ecology*, *87*(3), 533–545. DOI: 10.1111/1365-2656.12780 PMID: 29111567

Xie, J., Towsey, M., Truskinger, A., Eichinski, P., Zhang, J., & Roe, P. (2017). Artificial Intelligence for ecosystems: Deep learning for multi-label classification of Australian frog calls. arXiv preprint arXiv:1704.04736.

Xie, J., Towsey, M., Zhu, J., Xiaodong, J., & Roe, P. (2020). Adaptive frequency shaping for recording bioacoustics in environments with multiple background noise sources. *Remote Sensing in Ecology and Conservation*, *6*(4), 482–496.

Xu, Y., Liu, X., Cao, X., Huang, C., Liu, E., Qian, S., Liu, X., Wu, Y., Dong, F., Qiu, C.-W., Qiu, J., Hua, K., Su, W., Wu, J., Xu, H., Han, Y., Fu, C., Yin, Z., Liu, M., & Zhang, J. (2021). Artificial intelligence: A powerful paradigm for scientific research. *Innovation (Cambridge (Mass.))*, *2*(4), 4. DOI: 10.1016/j.xinn.2021.100179 PMID: 34877560

Yang, X., Zhang, S., Liu, J., Gao, Q., Dong, S., & Zhou, C. (2021). Deep learning for smart fish farming: Applications, opportunities and challenges. *Reviews in Aquaculture*, *13*(1), 66–90. DOI: 10.1111/raq.12464

Zaki, J. (2014). Empathy: A motivated account. *Psychological Bulletin*, *140*(6), 1608–1647. DOI: 10.1037/a0037679 PMID: 25347133

Zamora-Gutiérrez, V., López-Lorente, C., Traba, J., Clarabuch, O., & Ecología-UAB, G. (2018). Acoustic signalling in desert bats: A trade-off between detecting resources and being too vocal? *Oecologia*, *188*(4), 1123–1134.

Compilation of References

Abdelwahab, O., & Torkamaneh, D. Refinement of genetic variants needs attention *arXiv*. (2024). https://doi.org//arXiv.2408.00659DOI: 10.48550

Abdulateef, O. G., Abdullah, A. I., Ahmed, S. R., & Mahdi, M. S. (2022). Vehicle license plate detection using deep learning. In *2022 International Symposium on Multidisciplinary Studies and Innovative Technologies (ISMSIT)* (pp. 288–292). IEEE. DOI: 10.1109/ISMSIT56059.2022.9932852

Accenture. (2015). *The future of wealth management: How digital and analytics are transforming the advisory model.* Accenture Wealth and Asset Management Services. https://www.accenture.com

Agarwal, V., & McShan, A. C. (2024). The power and pitfalls of AlphaFold2 for structure prediction beyond rigid globular proteins. *Nature Chemical Biology*, *20*(8), 950–959. DOI: 10.1038/s41589-024-01638-w PMID: 38907110

Ahmed, M. E., Kim, H. C., Park, B. K., Ben Rais Kussia, N., & Hee Lee, J. (2020). Bio-acoustic signal classification for detecting seals and sea lions species in the Antarctic using machine learning techniques. *Applied Sciences (Basel, Switzerland)*, *10*(5), 1675.

Aide, T. M., Corrada-Bravo, C., Campos-Cerqueira, M., Milan, C., Vega, G., & Alvarez, R. (2013). Real-time bioacoustics monitoring and automated species identification. *PeerJ*, *1*, e103. DOI: 10.7717/peerj.103 PMID: 23882441

Alebel, A., Wondemagegn, A. T., Tesema, C., Kibret, G. D., Wagnew, F., Petrucka, P., Arora, A., Ayele, A. D., Alemayehu, M., & Eshetie, S. (2019). Prevalence of Diabetes Mellitus Among Tuberculosis Patients in Sub-Saharan Africa: A Systematic Review and Meta-Analysis of Observational Studies. *BMC Infectious Diseases*, *19*(1), 254. DOI: 10.1186/s12879-019-3892-8 PMID: 30866836

Alizadegan, H., Malki, B., Radmehr, A., Karimi, H., & Ilani, M. (2024). Comparative Study of Long Short-Term Memory (LSTM), Bidirectional LSTM, and Traditional Machine Learning Approaches for Energy Consumption Prediction. *Energy Exploration & Exploitation*. Advance online publication. DOI: 10.1177/01445987241269496

Alzubaidi, L., Latif, G., & Alghazo, J. (2019). Affordable and portable real-time Saudi license plate recognition using SoC. In *2019 2nd International Conference on New Trends in Computing Sciences (ICTCS)* (pp. 1–5). IEEE. DOI: 10.1109/ICTCS.2019.8923064

Ambady, N., & Rosenthal, R. (1998). Nonverbal communication. Encyclopedia of mental health, 2, 775-782.

Ambady, N., & Rosenthal, R. (1992). Thin slices of expressive behavior as predictors of interpersonal consequences: A meta-analysis. *Psychological Bulletin*, *111*(2), 256–274. DOI: 10.1037/0033-2909.111.2.256

Ammar, A., Koubaa, A., Boulila, W., Benjdira, B., & Alhabashi, Y. (2023). A multi-stage deep-learning-based vehicle and license plate recognition system with real-time edge inference. *Sensors (Basel)*, *23*(4), 2120. DOI: 10.3390/s23042120 PMID: 36850714

Angelini, E. D., Yang, J., Balte, P. P., Hoffman, E. A., Manichaikul, A. W., Sun, Y., Shen, W., Austin, J. H. M., Allen, N. B., Bleecker, E. R., Bowler, R., Cho, M. H., Cooper, C. S., Couper, D., Dransfield, M. T., Garcia, C. K., Han, M. L. K., Hansel, N. N., Hughes, E., & Barr, R. G. (2023). Pulmonary emphysema subtypes defined by unsupervised machine learning on CT scans. *Thorax*, *78*(11), 1067–1079. DOI: 10.1136/thorax-2022-219158 PMID: 37268414

Angermueller, C., Pärnamaa, T., Parts, L., & Stegle, O. (2016). Deep learning for computational biology. *Molecular Systems Biology*, *12*(7), 878. DOI: 10.15252/msb.20156651 PMID: 27474269

Antar, R., Alghamdi, S., Alotaibi, J., & Alghamdi, M. (2022). Automatic license plate recognition of Saudi license car plates. *Engineering, Technology &. Applied Scientific Research*, *12*(2), 8266–8272.

Armbrust, M., Fox, A., Griffith, R., Joseph, A. D., Katz, R., Konwinski, A., Lee, G., Patterson, D., Rabkin, A., Stoica, I., & Zaharia, M. (2010). A view of cloud computing. *Communications of the ACM*, *53*(4), 50–58. DOI: 10.1145/1721654.1721672

Atzori, L., Iera, A., & Morabito, G. (2010). The Internet of Things: A survey. *Computer Networks*, *54*(15), 2787–2805. DOI: 10.1016/j.comnet.2010.05.010

Awalgaonkar, N., Bartakke, P., & Chaugule, R. (2021). Automatic license plate recognition system using SSD. In *2021 International Symposium of Asian Control Association on Intelligent Robotics and Industrial Automation (IRIA)* (pp. 394–399). IEEE. DOI: 10.1109/IRIA53009.2021.9588707

Balbin, J. R., Sejera, M. P., Valiente, F. L., Martinez, C. O. A., Cataquis, N. A., Ontog, L. M., & Toribio, J. K. (2017). Metro Manila Development Authority color coding scheme violator detection through plate recognition using image processing. In *2017 IEEE 9th International Conference on Humanoid, Nanotechnology, Information Technology, Communication and Control, Environment and Management (HNICEM)* (pp. 1–6). IEEE. DOI: 10.1109/HNICEM.2017.8269464

Bardeli, R., Wolff, D., Kurth, F., Koch, M., Tauchert, K. H., & Frommolt, K. H. (2010). Detecting bird sounds in a complex acoustic environment and application to bioacoustic monitoring. *Pattern Recognition Letters*, *31*(12), 1524–1534. DOI: 10.1016/j.patrec.2009.09.014

Barnes, H., Humphries, S. M., George, P. M., Assayag, D., Glaspole, I., Mackintosh, J. A., Corte, T. J., Glassberg, M., Johannson, K. A., Calandriello, L., Felder, F., Wells, A., & Walsh, S. (2023). Machine learning in radiology: The new frontier in interstitial lung diseases. *The Lancet. Digital Health*, *5*(1), e41–e50. DOI: 10.1016/S2589-7500(22)00230-8 PMID: 36517410

Behera, S., & Misra, R. (2021). Generative adversarial networks based remaining useful life estimation for IIoT. *Computers & Electrical Engineering*, *92*, 107195.

Bengio, Y. (2009). Learning deep architectures for AI. Foundations and Trends® in Machine Learning, 2(1), 1-127.

Benziane, S. (2024). *Innovating prosperity: Intelligent approaches*. IGI Global. DOI: 10.4018/979-8-3693-1418-0.ch009

Benziane, S., & Benyettou, A. (2013). Biometric Technology based on hand vein. *Orient J. Comput. Sci. Technol*, *6*(4), 401–412.

Berger-Tal, O., & Lahoz-Monfort, J. J. (2018). Conservation technology: Machine learning, data and algorithms. *Conservation Biology*, *32*(4), 715–718.

Bhatia, M. (2021). Robo-advisors: A contemporary approach to wealth management. *Qualitative Research in Financial Markets*, *13*(2), 145–162. DOI: 10.1108/QRFM-10-2020-0199

Bishop, C. M. (2006). *Pattern recognition and Machine Learning*. Springer.

Blumstein, D. T., Mennill, D. J., Clemins, P., Girod, L., Yao, K., Patricelli, G., Deppe, J. L., Krakauer, A. H., Clark, C., Cortopassi, K. A., Hanser, S. F., McCowan, B., Ali, A. M., & Kirschel, A. N. (2011). Acoustic monitoring in terrestrial environments using microphone arrays: Applications, technological considerations and prospectus. *Journal of Applied Ecology*, *48*(3), 758–767. DOI: 10.1111/j.1365-2664.2011.01993.x

Bohr, A., & Memarzadeh, K. (2020). *"The rise of artificial intelligence in healthcare applications." Artificial Intelligence in healthcare*. Academic Press.

Bonomi, F., Milito, R., Zhu, J., & Addepalli, S. (2012). Fog computing and its role in the Internet of Things. *Proceedings of the first edition of the MCC workshop on Mobile cloud computing*, 13-16. DOI: 10.1145/2342509.2342513

Box, G. E. P., Jenkins, G. M., Reinsel, G. C., & Ljung, G. M. (2015). *Time series analysis: Forecasting and control* (5th ed.). John Wiley & Sons.

Bradbury, J. W., & Vehrencamp, S. L. (2011). *Principles of animal communication* (2nd ed.). Sinauer Associates.

Brown, A. (2020). Leveraging AI for improved fraud detection in financial institutions. *Journal of Financial Crime*, *27*(3), 759–772. DOI: 10.1108/JFC-04-2019-0052

Browning, E., Girod, L., Guden, D., Velimirović, A., Enge, H., & Raible, F. (2021). Machine learning analysis of bird vocalizations: A systematic review. *Avian Research*, *12*(1), 1–27.

Brownlee, J. (2016). *Deep learning for natural language processing*. Machine Learning Mastery.

Bryant, P., Pozzati, G., & Elofsson, A. (2022). Improved prediction of protein-protein interactions using AlphaFold2. *Nature Communications*, *13*(1), 1265. DOI: 10.1038/s41467-022-28865-w PMID: 35273146

Burgoon, J. K., Guerrero, L. K., & Floyd, K. (2016). *Nonverbal communication*. Routledge. DOI: 10.4324/9781315663425

Buyya, R., & Dastjerdi, A. V. (Eds.). (2016). *Internet of Things: Principles and paradigms*. Elsevier.

Buyya, R., Yeo, C. S., Venugopal, S., Broberg, J., & Brandic, I. (2009). Cloud computing and emerging IT platforms: Vision, hype, and reality for delivering computing as the 5th utility. *Future Generation Computer Systems*, *25*(6), 599–616. DOI: 10.1016/j.future.2008.12.001

Caramia, M., Berard, M., Muñoz-Delgado, J., & Vidal, R. (2018). Facial expression recognition for human-robot interaction: From static models to video-based recognition. *IEEE Transactions on Industrial Informatics*, *14*(5), 2244–2257.

Carvalho, T. P., Soares, F. A. A. M., Vita, R., Francisco, R. P., Basto, J. P., & Alcalá, S. G. (2019). A systematic literature review of machine learning methods applied to predictive maintenance. *Computers & Industrial Engineering*, *137*, 106024. DOI: 10.1016/j.cie.2019.106024

Cenggoro, T. W., & Siahaan, I. (2016). Dynamic bandwidth management based on traffic prediction using deep long short-term memory. *2016 2nd International Conference on Science in Information Technology (ICSITech).*

Chai, L., Zhang, Y., & Gao, W. (2021). Comparison of ARIMA and LSTM in forecasting epidemic data: A case study on COVID-19 in China. *PLoS One*, *16*(4), e0249021. DOI: 10.1371/journal.pone.0249021 PMID: 33844695

Chaudhary, M. F., Hoffman, E. A., Guo, J., Comellas, A. P., Newell, J. D.Jr, Nagpal, P., Fortis, S., Christensen, G. E., Gerard, S. E., Pan, Y., Wang, D., Abtin, F., Barjaktarevic, I. Z., Barr, R. G., Bhatt, S. P., Bodduluri, S., Cooper, C. B., Gravens-Mueller, L., Han, M. L. K., & Reinhardt, J. M. (2023). Predicting severe chronic obstructive pulmonary disease exacerbations using quantitative CT: A retrospective model development and external validation study. *The Lancet. Digital Health*, *5*(2), e83–e92. DOI: 10.1016/S2589-7500(22)00232-1 PMID: 36707189

Chawla, N. V., Bowyer, K. W., Hall, L. O., & Kegelmeyer, W. P. (2002). SMOTE: Synthetic minority over-sampling technique. *Journal of Artificial Intelligence Research*, *16*, 321–357. DOI: 10.1613/jair.953

Chen, M., Mao, S., & Liu, Y. (2014). Big data: A survey. *Mobile Networks and Applications*, *19*(2), 171–209. DOI: 10.1007/s11036-013-0489-0

Chen, S. M. (1996). Forecasting enrollments based on fuzzy time series. *Fuzzy Sets and Systems*, *81*(3), 311–318. DOI: 10.1016/0165-0114(95)00220-0

Chen, Y.-C., Loh, C.-H., Wang, F.-C., Chen, Z.-J., Fu, S.-H., & Wang, C.-Y. (2022). Application of generative adversarial network to optimize vehicle allocation at dispatch stations of paratransit services. *Electronics (Basel)*, *11*(3), 423. DOI: 10.3390/electronics11030423

Chiroma, H., Ezugwu, A. E., Jauro, F., Al-Garadi, M. A., Abdullahi, I. N., & Shuib, L. (2020). Early survey with bibliometric analysis on machine learning approaches in controlling COVID-19 outbreaks. *PeerJ. Computer Science*, *6*, 313. DOI: 10.7717/peerj-cs.313 PMID: 33816964

Chollet, F. (2017). *Deep learning with Python* (Vol. 361). Manning.

Chui, M.. (2018). *Notes from the AI frontier: Insights for executives*. McKinsey Global Institute.

Clink, D. J., & Klinck, H. (2021). Artificial intelligence for automatic detection and classification of animal sounds. *Methods in Ecology and Evolution, 12*(6), 1037–1051.

Correa, C., Bedoya, C., Isaza, C., & Velásquez, S. (2018). Automatic recognition of mammal species via their exciting calls using machine learning techniques. In 2018 13th IEEE International Conference on Automatic Face & Gesture Recognition (FG 2018) (pp. 346-352). IEEE.

Cosentino, J., Behsaz, B., Alipanahi, B., McCaw, Z. R., Hill, D., Schwantes-An, T. H., Lai, D., Carroll, A., Hobbs, B. D., Cho, M. H., McLean, C. Y., & Hormozdiari, F. (2023). Inference of chronic obstructive pulmonary disease with deep learning on raw spirograms identifies new genetic loci and improves risk models. *Nature Genetics, 55*(5), 787–795. DOI: 10.1038/s41588-023-01372-4 PMID: 37069358

Coyle, J. R.. (2011). Social media and analytics. *Journal of Marketing, 75*(4), 20–30.

Cui, R.. (2017). Dynamic motion planning for mobile robots using reinforcement learning. *IEEE Transactions on Robotics, 33*(4), 860–873. DOI: 10.1109/TRO.2017.2701130

Cui, R., Ge, S. S., & How, B. V. E. (2010). Leader–Follower Formation Control of Underactuated Autonomous Underwater Vehicles. *Ocean Engineering, 37*(17), 1491–1502. DOI: 10.1016/j.oceaneng.2010.07.006

Dack, E., Christe, A., Fontanellaz, M., Brigato, L., Heverhagen, J. T., Peters, A. A., Huber, A. T., Hoppe, H., Mougiakakou, S., & Ebner, L. (2023). Artificial intelligence and interstitial lung disease: Diagnosis and prognosis. *Investigative Radiology, 58*(8), 602–609. DOI: 10.1097/RLI.0000000000000974 PMID: 37058321

Dastjerdi, A. V., & Buyya, R. (2016). Fog computing: Helping the Internet of Things realize its potential. *Computer, 49*(8), 112–116.

Dell, A. I., Bender, J. A., Branson, K., Couzin, I. D., de Polavieja, G. G., Noldus, L. P., Pérez-Escudero, A., Perona, P., Straw, A. D., Wikelski, M., & Brose, U. (2014). Automated image-based tracking and its application in ecology. *Trends in Ecology & Evolution, 29*(7), 417–428. DOI: 10.1016/j.tree.2014.05.004 PMID: 24908439

Ding, H., Gao, J., Yuan, Y., & Wang, Q. (2023). Boosting one-stage license plate detector via self-constrained contrastive aggregation. *IEEE Transactions on Circuits and Systems for Video Technology*, *33*(8), 4204–4216. Advance online publication. DOI: 10.1109/TCSVT.2023.3241283

Donepudi, P. (2017). The role of artificial intelligence in banking industry: A survey. *International Journal of Creative Research Thoughts*, *5*(4), 232–238.

Dooley, K. E., & Chaisson, R. E. (2009). Tuberculosis and Diabetes Mellitus: Convergence of Two Epidemics. *The Lancet. Infectious Diseases*, *9*(12), 737–746. DOI: 10.1016/S1473-3099(09)70282-8 PMID: 19926034

Duddu, V. R., Pulugurtha, S. S., Mane, A. S., & Godfrey, C. (2020). Back-propagation neural network model to predict visibility at a road link-level. *Transportation Research Interdisciplinary Perspectives*, *8*, 100250. DOI: 10.1016/j.trip.2020.100250

Duives, D. C., Wang, G., & Kim, J. (2019). Forecasting pedestrian movements using recurrent neural networks: An application of crowd monitoring data. *Sensors (Basel)*, *19*(2), 382. DOI: 10.3390/s19020382 PMID: 30669293

Eke, R. A., & Orakwue, S. I. (2023). Automatic license plate recognition system.

Ekman, P. (1992). An argument for basic emotions. *Cognition and Emotion*, *6*(3-4), 169–200. DOI: 10.1080/02699939208411068

Eraslan, G., Avsec, Ž., Gagneur, J., & Theis, F. J. (2019). Deep learning: New computational modelling techniques for genomics. *Nature Reviews. Genetics*, *20*(7), 389–403. DOI: 10.1038/s41576-019-0122-6 PMID: 30971806

Erdélyi, O. J., & Goldsmith, J. (2018). Regulating AI: The new role for policymakers. *Philosophy & Technology*, *31*(3), 447–461.

Esteva, A., Kuprel, B., Novoa, R. A., Ko, J., Swetter, S. M., Blau, H. M., & Thrun, S. (2017). Dermatologist-level classification of skin cancer with deep neural networks. *Nature*, *542*(7639), 115–118. DOI: 10.1038/nature21056 PMID: 28117445

Evans, R., O'Neill, M., Pritzel, A., & Antropova, N.. Protein complex prediction with AlphaFold-Multimer. *bioRxiv, (*2022*).* doi: https://doi.org/DOI: 10.1101/2021.10.04.463034

Fan, X., & Zhao, W. (2022). Improving robustness of license plates automatic recognition in natural scenes. *IEEE Transactions on Intelligent Transportation Systems*, *23*(10), 18845–18854. DOI: 10.1109/TITS.2022.3151475

Fein, M. L. (2020). Robo-advisors: Revolutionizing investment management. *Northwestern Journal of Technology and Intellectual Property*, *18*(1), 45–76.

Firasanti, A., Ramadhani, T. E., Bakri, M. A., & Hamidi, E. A. Z. (2021). License plate detection using OCR method with Raspberry Pi. In *2021 15th International Conference on Telecommunication Systems, Services, and Applications (TSSA)* (pp. 1–5). IEEE. DOI: 10.1109/TSSA52866.2021.9768252

Fu, Q., Hu, C., Peng, J., Rind, F. C., & Yue, S. (2019). Towards Autonomous Robotic Systems: A Robust Collision Perception Visual Neural Network with Specific Selectivity to Darker Objects. *IEEE Transactions on Cybernetics*, *50*(12), 5074–5088. DOI: 10.1109/TCYB.2019.2946090 PMID: 31804947

García Cabello, J. (2022). Mathematical neural networks. *Axioms*, *11*(2), 80. DOI: 10.3390/axioms11020080

Gavranović, B. (2024). *Fundamental components of Deep Learning: A category-theoretic approach* (PhD thesis). University of Strathclyde, Glasgow. https://arxiv.org/pdf/2403.13001

Ghosh, S. (2025). "How to Compare Machine Learning Models and Algorithms", Neptune Blog. Available: https://neptune.ai/blog/how-to-compare-machine-learning-models-and-algorithms

Giret, N., Permuter, H., Chandan, C., & Boahen, K. (2019). Airborne acoustic analysis by compressive bionic processing. *Neural Computation*, *31*(8), 1697–1719.

Gomez-Marin, A., Poteser, M., & Patric, M. (2019). Towards the automatic visual tracking of animals in the wild. arXiv preprint arXiv:1905.05262.

Gomez-Marin, A., Poteser, M., Patric, M., & Lengert, M. (2019). Towards the automatic visual tracking of animals in the wild. arXiv preprint arXiv:1905.05262.

Gonzalez, A. J., & Dankel, D. D. (2010). *The engineering of knowledge-based systems: Theory and practice*. Prentice Hall.

Goodfellow, I., Bengio, Y., & Courville, A. (2016). *Deep Learning*. MIT Press. Retrieved from http://www.deeplearningbook.org

Goodfellow, I., Bengio, Y., & Courville, A. (2016). *Deep learning*. MIT Press.

Goodfellow, I., Bengio, Y., & Courville, A. (2016). *Deep Learning*. MIT Press.

Goodfellow, I., Pouget-Abadie, J., Mirza, M., Xu, B., Warde-Farley, D., Ozair, S., Courville, A., & Bengio, Y. (2014). Generative adversarial nets. *Advances in Neural Information Processing Systems*, *27*, 2672–2680.

Graves, A., & Schmidhuber, J. (2005). Framewise phoneme classification with bidirectional LSTM networks. *Proceedings of the International Conference on Neural Networks*, 2047-2052. DOI: 10.1109/IJCNN.2005.1556215

Grill, T., & Schluter, J. (2017). Two convolutional neural networks for bird detection in audio signals. In 2017 25th European Signal Processing Conference (EUSIPCO) (pp. 1-5). IEEE. DOI: 10.23919/EUSIPCO.2017.8081512

Grill, T., & Schlüter, J. (2019). Analyzing submarine acoustic noise data with deep learning techniques. In *Proceedings of the 8th Swiss Conference on Data Analysis* (pp. 53-56).

Gubbi, J., Buyya, R., Marusic, S., & Palaniswami, M. (2013). Internet of Things (IoT): A vision, architectural elements, and future directions. *Future Generation Computer Systems*, *29*(7), 1645–1660. DOI: 10.1016/j.future.2013.01.010

Guerrero, L. K., & Andersen, P. A. (1998). The dark side of jealousy and envy: Desire, delusion, desperation, and destructive communication. Close romantic relationships: Maintenance and enhancement, 33-70.

Gupta, R., Fricker, J. D., & Moffett, D. P. (2002). Reduction of video license plate data. *Transportation Research Record: Journal of the Transportation Research Board*, *1804*(1), 31–38. DOI: 10.3141/1804-05

Gupta, R., & Gupta, P. (2019). *Industrial Internet of Things (IIoT)*. Springer.

Haas, B., Wendt, A., Jantsch, A., & Wess, M. (2021). A. Jantsch та M. Wess, "Neural Network Compression Through Shunt Connections and Knowledge Distillation for Semantic Segmentation Problems". *IFIP Advances in Information and Communication Technology*, *627*, 349–361. DOI: 10.1007/978-3-030-79150-6_28

Ha, D., & Schmidhuber, J. (2018). World models. *Proceedings of the Neural Information Processing Systems (NeurIPS)*, 1-16.

Hariharan, R., & Raja Jebasingh, J. (2016). Role of banks in economic development. *International Journal of Scientific Research and Management*, *4*(2), 1989–1992.

Hassan, A., Abuhmed, T., & El-Sappagh, S. "End-to-End Optimized Ensemble Model for Alzheimer's Disease Detection," 2025 19th International Conference on Ubiquitous Information Management and Communication (IMCOM), Bangkok, Thailand, 2025, pp. 1-8, DOI: 10.1109/IMCOM64595.2025.10857489

Haykin, S. (2009). *Neural networks and learning machines* (3rd ed.). Pearson.

He, K., Gkioxari, G., Dollár, P., & Girshick, R. *Mask R-CNN*. arXiv. (2017). https://doi.org//arXiv.1703.06870DOI: 10.1109/ICCV.2017.322

Heaton, J. B., Polson, N. G., & Witte, J. H. (2017). Deep Learning for finance: Deep portfolios. *Applied Stochastic Models in Business and Industry*, *33*(1), 3–12. DOI: 10.1002/asmb.2209

Hegazi, M. O., Almaslukh, B., & Siddig, K. (2023). A fuzzy model for reasoning and predicting student's academic performance. *Applied Sciences (Basel, Switzerland)*, *13*(9), 5140–5164. DOI: 10.3390/app13085140

He, K., Zhang, X., Ren, S., & Sun, J. (2016). Deep residual learning for image recognition. In *Proceedings of the IEEE Conference on Computer Vision and Pattern Recognition* (pp. 770–778). https://doi.org/DOI: 10.1109/CVPR.2016.90

Hertenstein, M. J., Keltner, D., App, B., Bulleit, B. A., & Jaskolka, A. R. (2006). Touch communicates distinct emotions. *Emotion (Washington, D.C.)*, *6*(3), 528–533. DOI: 10.1037/1528-3542.6.3.528 PMID: 16938094

Hochreiter, S., & Schmidhuber, J. (1997). Long short-term memory. *Neural Computation*, *9*(8), 1735–1780. DOI: 10.1162/neco.1997.9.8.1735 PMID: 9377276

Howard, A. G., Zhu, M., Chen, B., Kalenichenko, D., Wang, W., Weyand, T., Andreetto, M., & Adam, H. (2017). MobileNets: Efficient convolutional neural networks for mobile vision applications. *arXiv preprint arXiv:1704.04861*. https://arxiv.org/abs/1704.04861

Huang, C. J., Yang, Y. J., Yang, D. X., & Chen, Y. J. (2009). Evaluation of retinal blood vessel segmentation by an efficient computer aid system. *Journal of Medical Systems*, *33*(3), 165–171.

Huang, W., Xu, X., Hu, M., & Huang, W. (2022). A license plate recognition data to estimate and visualize the restriction policy for diesel vehicles on urban air quality: A case study of Shenzhen. *Journal of Cleaner Production*, *338*, 130401. DOI: 10.1016/j.jclepro.2022.130401

Huang, Y., Li, W., Ng, W. Y., Zhang, X., Xian, Y., Chiu, P. W. Y., & Li, Z. (2021). An Autonomous Robotic Flexible Endoscope System with a DNA-Inspired Continuum Mechanism. *2021 IEEE International Conference on Robotics and Automation (ICRA)*, 7657-7663. DOI: 10.1109/ICRA48506.2021.9561712

Huarng, K., & Yu, T. H. K. (2006). The Application of Neural Networks to Forecast Fuzzy Time Series. *Physica A*, *353*, 445–462. DOI: 10.1016/j.physa.2004.11.070

Hurtado, J., Salvati, D., Semola, R., Bosio, M., & Lomonaco, V. (2023). Continual learning for predictive maintenance: Overview and challenges. *Intelligent Systems with Applications*, *19*, 200251. DOI: 10.1016/j.iswa.2023.200251

Hussein, K. A., & Al-Ani, Z. T. A. (2022). Iraqi license plate recognition based on neural network technique. *Journal of Physics: Conference Series*, *2322*(1), 012025. DOI: 10.1088/1742-6596/2322/1/012025

Hyder, R., Ghayas, S., & Tirmizi, S. (2021). Acoustic scene classification using ensemble of CNN and CRNN. *IEEE Access : Practical Innovations, Open Solutions*, *9*, 124025–124036.

IEEE P7000 — Model Process for Addressing Ethical Concerns During System Design.

IEEE Std 1872-2015 — Standard Ontologies for Robotics and Automation.

ISO 13482:2014 — Robots and robotic devices — Safety requirements for personal care robots.

ISO 9283:1998 — Robots and robotic devices — Performance criteria for position, velocity, and acceleration of robotic systems.

ISO. "The basis of neural networks: Cracking the code", (2024). Available: https://www.iso.org/artificial-intelligence/neural-networks

ISO/IEC 20924:2021(en). "Information technology — Internet of Things (IoT) — Vocabulary", 2021. Available: https://www.iso.org/obp/ui/#iso:std:iso-iec:20924:ed-2:v1:en

ISO/IEC 22989:2022(en), "Information technology — Artificial intelligence — Artificial intelligence concepts and terminology", 2022. Available: https://www.iso.org/obp/ui/en/#iso:std:iso-iec:22989:ed-1:v1:en

ISO/IEC 23053:2022. "Framework for Artificial Intelligence (AI). Systems Using Machine Learning (ML)", 2022. Available: https://www.iso.org/standard/74438.html

ISO/IEC 24668:2022(en) "Information technology — Artificial intelligence — Process management framework for big data analytics", 2022. Available: https://www.iso.org/obp/ui/en/#iso:std:iso-iec:24668:ed-1:v1:en

ISO/IEC TR 24029-1:2021(en), "Artificial Intelligence (AI) — Assessment of the robustness of neural networks — Part 1: Overview", 2021. Available: https://www.iso.org/obp/ui/en/#iso:std:iso-iec:tr:24029:-1:ed-1:v1:en

ISO/IEC TR 24030:2024(en), "Information technology — Artificial intelligence (AI) — Use cases", 2024. Available: https://www.iso.org/obp/ui/en/#iso:std:84144:en

ISO/IEC. "JTC 1 Preliminary Report 2014 Internet of Things (IoT)", (2014). 17 p. Available: https://www.iso.org/files/live/sites/isoorg/files/developing_standards/docs/en/internet_of_things_report-jtc1.pdf

Jančovič, P., & Köküer, M. (2011). Automatic detection and recognition of tonal bird sounds from a real field recording by using supervised pattern recognition. *Journal of Applied Logic*, *9*(2), 124–140.

Jardine, A. K. S., Lin, D., & Banjevic, D. (2006). A review on machinery diagnostics and prognostics implementing condition-based maintenance. *Mechanical Systems and Signal Processing*, *20*(7), 1483–1510. DOI: 10.1016/j.ymssp.2005.09.012

Jasmine Pemeena Priyadarsini, M., Kotecha, K., Rajini, G. K., Hariharan, K., Utkarsh Raj, K., Bhargav Ram, K., Indragandhi, V., Subramaniyaswamy, V., & Pandya, S. (2023). Lung diseases detection using various deep learning algorithms. *Journal of Healthcare Engineering*, *2023*(1), 3563696. DOI: 10.1155/2023/3563696 PMID: 36776955

Jia, W., Zhang, H., & He, X. (2007). Region-based license plate detection. *Journal of Network and Computer Applications*, *30*(4), 1324–1333. DOI: 10.1016/j.jnca.2006.09.010

Jilani, T. A., Burney, S. M. A., & Ardil, C. (2008). Fuzzy Metric Approach for Fuzzy Time Series Forecasting Based on Frequency Density-Based Partitioning. *International Journal of Computational Intelligence*, *4*(1), 4–10.

Jones, S. M., & Guerrero, L. K. (2001). The effects of nonverbal immediacy and verbal person centeredness in the emotional support process. *Human Communication Research*, *27*(4), 567–596. DOI: 10.1111/j.1468-2958.2001.tb00793.x

Jothilakshmi, S., & Vasanthamani, G. (2015). Fuzzy neural network-based prediction model for tuberculosis. *International Journal of Soft Computing*, *10*(1), 53–58.

Jumper, J., Evans, R., Pritzel, A., Green, T., Figurnov, M., Ronneberger, O., Tunyasuvunakool, K., Bates, R., Žídek, A., Potapenko, A., Bridgland, A., Meyer, C., Kohl, S. A. A., Ballard, A. J., Cowie, A., Romera-Paredes, B., Nikolov, S., Jain, R., Adler, J., & Hassabis, D. (2021). Highly accurate protein structure prediction with AlphaFold. *Nature*, *596*(7873), 583–589. DOI: 10.1038/s41586-021-03819-2 PMID: 34265844

Kalan, A. K., Mundry, R., Wagner, O. J., Benner, S., Boesch, C., Kühl, H. S., & Slocombe, K. E. (2015). Towards automated annotation of chimpanzee vocalization. *PLoS One*, *10*(6), e0124590.

Karampitsakos, T., Sotiropoulou, V., Katsaras, M., Tsiri, P., Georgakopoulou, V. E., Papanikolaou, I. C., Bibaki, E., Tomos, I., Lambiri, I., Papaioannou, O., Zarkadi, E., Antonakis, E., Pandi, A., Malakounidou, E., Sampsonas, F., Makrodimitri, S., Chrysikos, S., Hillas, G., Dimakou, K., & Tzouvelekis, A. (2023). Post-COVID-19 interstitial lung disease: Insights from a machine learning radiographic model. *Frontiers in Medicine*, *9*, 1083264. DOI: 10.3389/fmed.2022.1083264 PMID: 36733935

Kaur, P., Kumar, Y., Ahmed, S., Alhumam, A., Singla, R., & Ijaz, M. F. (2022). Automatic license plate recognition system for vehicles using a CNN. *Computers, Materials & Continua*, *71*(1), 1303–1321.

Kershenbaum, A., Blumstein, D. T., Roch, M. A., Akcay, C., Backus, G., Bee, M. A., & Couzin, I. D. (2016). Acoustic sequences in non-human animals: A tutorial review and prospectus. *Biological Reviews of the Cambridge Philosophical Society*, *91*(1), 13–52. DOI: 10.1111/brv.12160 PMID: 25428267

Khan, M. G., Saeed, M., Zulfiqar, A., Ghadi, Y. Y., & Adnan, M. (2022). A novel deep learning based ALPR pipeline for vehicle access control. *IEEE Access : Practical Innovations, Open Solutions*, *10*, 64172–64184. DOI: 10.1109/ACCESS.2022.3183101

Khanna, C., Bish, B., Kamshetty, D., Bhardwaj, H., & Bhutani, M. (2025). Enhancing license plate recognition using YOLONAS, YOLOv8, and SORT algorithms. *Journal of Artificial Intelligence*, *2*(1), 167–174. DOI: 10.61552/JAI.2025.01.003

Khanna, P. (2021). Artificial intelligence: Shaping the future of wealth management. *Global Journal of Finance and Management*, *13*(2), 101–111.

Kim, E., Lee, Y., Choi, J., Yoo, B., Chae, K. J., & Lee, C. H. (2023). Machine Learning-based Prediction of Relative Regional Air Volume Change from Healthy Human Lung CTs. *KSII Transactions on Internet and Information Systems*, *17*(2), 576–590.

Kim, J., Park, S., Min, D., & Kim, W. (2021). Comprehensive Survey of Recent Drug Discovery Using Deep Learning. *International Journal of Molecular Sciences*, *22*(18), 9983. DOI: 10.3390/ijms22189983 PMID: 34576146

Knapp, M. L., & Hall, J. A. (2010). *Nonverbal communication in human interaction*. Cengage Learning.

Kober, J., Bagnell, J. A., & Peters, J. (2013). Reinforcement learning in robotics. *Survey (London, England)*. Advance online publication. DOI: 10.1177/0278364912439674

Kolisnyk, M., & Jantsch, A. (2024, September). ML-based fault tree analysis of Industrial Router Reliability in the System IIoT. In *2024 International Conference on Applied Mathematics & Computer Science (ICAMCS)* (pp. 173-178). IEEE.

Koul, A., Bawa, R. K., & Kumar, Y. (2023). Artificial intelligence techniques to predict the airway disorders illness: A systematic review. *Archives of Computational Methods in Engineering*, *30*(2), 831–864. DOI: 10.1007/s11831-022-09818-4 PMID: 36189431

Krauss, R. M., Chen, Y., & Chawla, P. (1996). Nonverbal behavior and nonverbal communication: What do conversational hand gestures tell us? *Advances in Experimental Social Psychology*, *28*, 389–450. DOI: 10.1016/S0065-2601(08)60241-5

Krizhevsky, A., Sutskever, I., & Hinton, G. E. (2012). ImageNet classification with deep convolutional neural networks. *Advances in Neural Information Processing Systems*, *25*, 1097–1105.

Krizhevsky, A., Sutskever, I., & Hinton, G. E. (2017). I. Sutskever та G. E. Hinton, "ImageNet classification with deep convolutional neural networks". *Communications of the ACM*, *60*(6), 84–90. DOI: 10.1145/3065386

Kucharski, A. J., Russell, T. W., Diamond, C., Liu, Y., Edmunds, J., Funk, S., Eggo, R. M., Sun, F., Jit, M., Munday, J. D., Davies, N., Gimma, A., van Zandvoort, K., Gibbs, H., Hellewell, J., Jarvis, C. I., Clifford, S., Quilty, B. J., Bosse, N. I., & Flasche, S. (2020). Early dynamics of transmission and control of COVID-19: A mathematical modelling study. *The Lancet. Infectious Diseases*, *20*(5), 553–558. DOI: 10.1016/S1473-3099(20)30144-4 PMID: 32171059

Kulešević, A., Kulić, D., & Michaud, F. (2020). Towards a unified framework for automatic animal behavior recognition from videos. *Multimedia Tools and Applications*, *79*(47), 35747–35783.

Kumar, A., Ahuja, N. J., Thapliyal, M., Dutt, S., Kumar, T., Pacheco, D. A. D. J., & Choo, K. K. R. (2023). Blockchain for unmanned underwater drones: Research issues, challenges, trends and future directions. *Journal of Network and Computer Applications*, *103649*, 103649. Advance online publication. DOI: 10.1016/j.jnca.2023.103649

Kumar, P., & Kumar, N. (2021). A predictive maintenance framework using LSTM and big data technologies for Industry 4.0. *Procedia Computer Science*, *184*, 444–451.

Kuo, R., & Zulvia, F. E. (2021). The Application of Gradient Evolution Algorithm to an Intuitionistic Fuzzy Neural Network For Forecasting Medical Cost of Acute Hepatitis Treatment in Taiwan. *Applied Soft Computing*, *111*, 107711. DOI: 10.1016/j.asoc.2021.107711

Kushwaha, M. K., & Suseela, G. (2022). Car number plate detection using Deep Learning. *2022 International Conference on Data Science, Agents & Artificial Intelligence (ICDSAAI)*, 1-4. DOI: 10.1109/ICDSAAI55433.2022.10028818

L.A. Zadeh. (1975a). The Concept of Linguistic Variable and its Application to Approximate Reasoning, Volume 8. Part 1. Pp: 199-249.

L.A. Zadeh. (1975b). The Concept of Linguistic Variable and its Application to Approximate Reasoning, Volume 8. Part 2. Pp: 301-357.

L.A. Zadeh. (1975c). The Concept of Linguistic Variable and its Application to Approximate Reasoning, Volume 8. Part 3. Pp: 43-80.

Laroca, R., Cardoso, E. V., Lucio, D. R., Estevam, V., & Menotti, D. (2022). On the cross-dataset generalization in license plate recognition. *arXiv preprint* arXiv:2201.00267. DOI: 10.5220/0010846800003124

Latrach, A. (2023). Application of deep learning for predictive maintenance of oilfield equipment. *arXiv preprint arXiv:2306.11040*.

LeCun, Y., Bengio, Y., & Haffner, P. (1998). Gradient-based learning applied to document recognition.

LeCun, Y., & Bengio, Y. (1995). Convolutional networks for images, speech, and time series. *Proceedings of the IEEE, 86*(11), 2278–2324. DOI: 10.1109/5.726791

LeCun, Y., Bengio, Y., & Hinton, G. (2015). Deep learning. *Nature*, *521*(7553), 436–444. DOI: 10.1038/nature14539 PMID: 26017442

Lee, I., & Lee, K. (2015). The Internet of Things (IoT): Applications, investments, and challenges for enterprises. *Business Horizons*, *58*(4), 431–440. DOI: 10.1016/j.bushor.2015.03.008

Lee, J., Bagheri, B., & Kao, H. A. (2015). A cyber-physical systems architecture for Industry 4.0-based manufacturing systems. *Manufacturing Letters*, *3*, 18–23. DOI: 10.1016/j.mfglet.2014.12.001

Lee, J., Wu, F., Zhao, W., Ghaffari, M., Liao, L., & Siegel, D. (2014). Prognostics and health management design for rotary machinery systems—Reviews, methodology and applications. *Mechanical Systems and Signal Processing*, *42*(1-2), 314–334. DOI: 10.1016/j.ymssp.2013.06.004

Lee, Y. Y., Halim, Z. A., & Ab Wahab, M. N. (2022). License plate detection using convolutional neural network–back to the basic with design of experiments. *IEEE Access : Practical Innovations, Open Solutions*, *10*, 22577–22585. DOI: 10.1109/ACCESS.2022.3153340

Lehmann-Willenbrock, N., Allen, J. A., & Belyeu, D. (2016). Our love doth not consist of words: Exploring the relationship between team processes and team effectiveness. Group Decision and Negotiation Theory Methods and Applications, 47-72.

Lei, Y., Li, N., Guo, L., Li, N., Yan, T., & Lin, J. (2018). Machinery health prognostics: A systematic review. *Mechanical Systems and Signal Processing*, *104*, 799–834. DOI: 10.1016/j.ymssp.2017.11.016

Lemieux, J., & Ma, Y. (2015). Vehicle speed prediction using Deep Learning. *2015 IEEE Conference.*

Leonie, F., Dominik, N., Zita, S., You-Shan, F., & Sulyok, M. (2020). Forecasting Tuberculosis using Diabetes-Related Google Trends Data. *Pathogens and Global Health*, *114*(5), 236–241. DOI: 10.1080/20477724.2020.1767854 PMID: 32453658

Liang, F. (2003). An effective Bayesian neural network classifier with a comparison study to support vector machine. *Neural Computation*, *15*(8), 1959–1989. DOI: 10.1162/08997660360675107

Liang, F. (2005). Bayesian neural networks for nonlinear time series forecasting. *Statistics and Computing*, *15*(1), 13–29. DOI: 10.1007/s11222-005-4786-8

Li, D. Z., Wang, W., & Ismail, F. (2013). Fuzzy Neural Network Technique for System State Forecasting. *IEEE Transactions on Cybernetics*, *43*(5), 1484–1494. DOI: 10.1109/TCYB.2013.2259229 PMID: 23757566

Lin, H., Zhao, J., Li, S., & Qiu, G. (2020). License plate location method based on edge detection and mathematical morphology. In *2020 IEEE 4th Information Technology, Networking,Electronic and Automation Control Conference (ITNEC)* (Vol. 1, pp. 853–857). IEEE. DOI: 10.1109/ITNEC48623.2020.9085121

Litman, T. (2021). *Autonomous vehicle implementation predictions: Implications for transport planning*. Victoria Transport Policy Institute. https://www.vtpi.org/avip.pdf

Lopez de Prado, M. (2018). *Advances in financial machine learning*. Wiley.

Lundberg, S. M., & Lee, S.-I. (2017). A unified approach to interpreting model predictions. In *Advances in Neural Information Processing Systems* (pp. 4765–4774). https://doi.org/DOI: 10.48550/arXiv.1705.07874

Lv, Y., Duan, Y., Kang, W., Li, Z., & Wang, F.-Y. (2015, April). Traffic flow prediction with big data: A Deep Learning approach. *IEEE Transactions on Intelligent Transportation Systems*, *16*(2).

Ma, S., Flanigan, K. A., & Bergés, M. (2024). State-of-the-art review: The use of digital twins to support artificial intelligence-guided predictive maintenance. *arXiv preprint arXiv:2406.13117*.

Maglogiannis, I. (2021). J. Macintyre та L. Iliadis, "*Artificial Intelligence Applications and Innovations*". Cham. *IFIP Advances in Information and Communication Technology*, *627*. Advance online publication. DOI: 10.1007/978-3-030-79150-6

Maheswari, V. U., Aluvalu, R., & Mudrakola, S. (2022). An integrated license plate recognition system through images using threshold-based methods and KNN. In *2022 International Conference on Decision Aid Sciences and Applications (DASA)* (pp. 493–497). IEEE. DOI: 10.1109/DASA54658.2022.9765218

Mahmood, Z., Khan, K., Khan, U., Adil, S. H., Ali, S. S. A., & Shahzad, M. (2022). Towards automatic license plate detection. *Sensors (Basel)*, *22*(3), 1245. DOI: 10.3390/s22031245 PMID: 35161988

Makimoto, K., Hogg, J. C., Bourbeau, J., Tan, W. C., & Kirby, M. (2023). CT imaging with machine learning for predicting progression to COPD in individuals at risk. *Chest*, *164*(5), 1139–1149. DOI: 10.1016/j.chest.2023.06.008 PMID: 37421974

Mammides, C., Chen, J., Kadis, C., Darawshi, M., Ohadi, S., Tan, X. J., & Zakaria, M. (2017). Exploring the potential of environmental-sensor monitoring in urban environments: A case study from Northern Nicosia, Cyprus. *European Journal of Geography*, *8*(1), 5–14.

Manser, M. B., Seyfarth, R. M., & Cheney, D. L. (2008). Signallers and receivers in animal communication. *Trends in Ecology & Evolution*, *23*(11), 627–632. DOI: 10.1016/j.tree.2008.07.002

Manyika, J.. (2011). *Big data: The next frontier for innovation, competition, and productivity*. McKinsey Global Institute.

Marjani, M.. (2017). Big IoT data analytics: Architecture, opportunities, and open research challenges. *IEEE Access : Practical Innovations, Open Solutions*, *5*, 5247–5261. DOI: 10.1109/ACCESS.2017.2689040

Mathew, P. A., Jagarlamudi, A., Bharathwaj, N., & Jaspin, K. (2023). Real-time license plate and helmet detection of motorcyclists using YOLOv5 and ResNet-50. In *2023 International Conference on Sustainable Computing and Data Communication Systems (ICSCDS)* (pp. 709–715). IEEE. DOI: 10.1109/ICSCDS56580.2023.10105076

Mathis, A., Mamidanna, P., Cury, K. M., Abe, T., Murthy, V. N., Mathis, M. W., & Bethge, M. (2018). DeepLabCut: Markerless pose estimation of user-defined body parts with deep learning. *Nature Neuroscience*, *21*(9), 1281–1289. DOI: 10.1038/s41593-018-0209-y PMID: 30127430

Matsumoto, D., & Hwang, H. S. (2013). Cultural similarities and differences in emblematic gestures. *Journal of Nonverbal Behavior*, *37*(1), 1–27. DOI: 10.1007/s10919-012-0143-8

Maturana, D., & Scherer, S. (2015). 3D Convolutional Neural Networks for Landing Zone Detection from LiDAR. *2015 IEEE International Conference on Robotics and Automation (ICRA)*, 3471-3478. DOI: 10.1109/ICRA.2015.7139679

Mayer, K. H., & Dukes, H. C. (2010). Synergistic Pandemics: Confronting the Global HIV and Tuberculosis Epidemics. *Clinical Infectious Diseases*, *50*(s3), S67–S70. DOI: 10.1086/651475 PMID: 20397958

Menasria, M., Baouche, A., & Ait Kaci Azzou, S. (2024). *La maintenance prédictive des machines de l'industrie 4.0*. Mémoire de Master, Université de Bejaia.

Mhatre, A., & Sharma, P. (2023). Deep learning approach for vehicle license plate recognition system with image enhancement technique. *International Journal of Intelligent Systems and Applications in Engineering*, *11*(1s), 251–262.

Milinovich, G., Magalhães, S., & Hu, W. (2015). Role of Big Data in The Early Detection of Ebola and Other Emerging Infectious Diseases. Lancet Glob Health 3:e20-e21. *The Lancet. Global Health*, *3*(1), e20–e21. DOI: 10.1016/S2214-109X(14)70356-0 PMID: 25539964

Minerva, R., Biru, A., & Rotondi, D. (2015). Towards a definition of the Internet of Things (IoT). *IEEE Internet Initiative*, *1*(1), 1–86.

Miziolek, B. (2021). Artificial intelligence in portfolio management: Efficiency or hype? *Financial Innovation*, *7*(1), 75–89. PMID: 35024291

Mnih, V.. (2013). Playing Atari with deep reinforcement learning. *NIPS Deep Learning Workshop*.

Mnih, V., Kavukcuoglu, K., Silver, D., Rusu, A. A., Veness, J., Bellemare, M. G., Graves, A., Riedmiller, M., Fidjeland, A. K., Ostrovski, G., Petersen, S., Beattie, C., Sadik, A., Antonoglou, I., King, H., Kumaran, D., Wierstra, D., Legg, S., & Hassabis, D. (2015). Human-level control through deep reinforcement learning. *Nature*, *518*(7540), 529–533. DOI: 10.1038/nature14236 PMID: 25719670

Mobley, R. K. (2002). *An introduction to predictive maintenance*. Butterworth-Heinemann.

Mohamed, N. (2020). Security and privacy in IoT systems. *IEEE Security and Privacy*, *18*(4), 58–67.

Monostori, L., Kádár, B., Bauernhansl, T., Kondoh, S., Kumara, S., Reinhart, G., Sauer, O., Schuh, G., Sihn, W., & Ueda, K. (2016). Cyber-physical systems in manufacturing. *CIRP Annals*, *65*(2), 621–641. DOI: 10.1016/j.cirp.2016.06.005

Mosalaganti, S., Obarska-Kosinska, A., Siggel, M., Taniguchi, R., Turoňová, B., Zimmerli, C. E., Buczak, K., Schmidt, F. H., Margiotta, E., Mackmull, M.-T., Hagen, W. J. H., Hummer, G., Kosinski, J., & Beck, M. (2022). AI-based structure prediction empowers integrative structural analysis of human nuclear pores. *Science*, *376*(6598), eabm9506. Advance online publication. DOI: 10.1126/science.abm9506 PMID: 35679397

Moslemi, A., Makimoto, K., Tan, W. C., Bourbeau, J., Hogg, J. C., Coxson, H. O., & Kirby, M. (2023). Quantitative CT lung imaging and machine learning improves prediction of emergency room visits and hospitalizations in COPD. *Academic Radiology*, *30*(4), 707–716. DOI: 10.1016/j.acra.2022.05.009 PMID: 35690537

Mourtzis, D., Doukas, M., & Psarommatis, F. (2019). A continuous improvement methodology for the assembly process using industrial Internet of Things (IIoT) data. *Procedia CIRP*, *81*, 797–802.

Muehlhauser, M. (2021). Data protection in IoT and AI systems. *Security Journal*, *15*(6), 400–420.

Murel, J., & Kavlakoglu, E. (2024). What is ensemble learning?.

Mushtaq, A. (2019). Tuberculosis in Diabetes: Insidious and Neglected. *The Lancet. Respiratory Medicine*, *7*(6), 483. DOI: 10.1016/S2213-2600(19)30119-5 PMID: 31003965

Naji, H. A. H., Xue, Q., Zhu, H., & Li, T. (2021). Forecasting taxi demands using generative adversarial networks with multi-source data. *Applied Sciences (Basel, Switzerland)*, *11*(20), 9675. DOI: 10.3390/app11209675

Nakov, T., Bassett, D. K., Kratschmer, P., Zick, G., Rodriguez, D., Collins, J., & Mizzi, T. (2022). Machine learning acoustic detection of Vanessa butterflies. *Scientific Reports*, *12*(1), 1–13. PMID: 34992227

Nandhakumar, R. G., Devi, K. N., Krishnamoorthy, N., Shanthi, S., Pranesh, V. R., & Nikhalyaa, S. (2023). YOLO-based license plate detection of triple riders and violators. *2023 International Conference on Computer Communication and Informatics (ICCCI)*, 1-6. https://doi.org/DOI: 10.1109/ICCCI56745.2023.10128537

Nanni, L., Costa, Y. M. G., Aguiar, R. L., Mangolin, R. B., & Brahnam, S. (2020). Generalization in machine learning applied to bioacoustics: A systematic review. *Knowledge-Based Systems*, *198*, 105910.

Nath, T., Mathis, A., Chen, A. C., Patel, A., Bethge, M., & Mathis, M. W. (2019). Using DeepLabCut for 3D markerless pose estimation across species and behaviors. *Nature Protocols*, *14*(7), 2152–2176. DOI: 10.1038/s41596-019-0176-0 PMID: 31227823

NVIDIA. developer. "Artificial Neural Network", (2024). Available: https://developer.nvidia.com/discover/artificial-neural-network

Oliveira-Neto, F. M., Han, L. D., & Jeong, M. K. (2009). Tracking large trucks in real time with license plate recognition and text-mining techniques. *Transportation Research Record: Journal of the Transportation Research Board*, *2121*(1), 121–127. DOI: 10.3141/2121-13

Oliveira-Neto, F. M., Han, L. D., & Jeong, M. K. (2013). An online self-learning algorithm for license plate matching. *IEEE Transactions on Intelligent Transportation Systems*, *14*(4), 1806–1816. DOI: 10.1109/TITS.2013.2270107

Onesimu, J. A., Sebastian, R. D., Sei, Y., & Christopher, L. (2021). An intelligent license plate detection and recognition model using deep neural networks. [AET-iC]. *Annals of Emerging Technologies in Computing*, *5*(4), 20–29. DOI: 10.33166/AETiC.2021.04.003

Otoum, Y., Liu, D., & Nayak, A. (2019). D. Liu та A. Nayak, "DL-IDS: A deep learning–based intrusion detection framework for securing IoT". *Transactions on Emerging Telecommunications Technologies*, *33*(3), e3803. Advance online publication. DOI: 10.1002/ett.3803

Pan, J., Hofmanninger, J., Nenning, K. H., Prayer, F., Röhrich, S., Sverzellati, N., Poletti, V., Tomassetti, S., Weber, M., Prosch, H., & Langs, G. (2023). Unsupervised machine learning identifies predictive progression markers of IPF. *European Radiology*, *33*(2), 925–935. DOI: 10.1007/s00330-022-09101-x PMID: 36066734

Park, H., Yun, J., Lee, S. M., Hwang, H. J., Seo, J. B., Jung, Y. J., Hwang, J., Lee, S. H., Lee, S. W., & Kim, N. (2023). Deep learning–based approach to predict pulmonary function at chest CT. *Radiology*, *307*(2), e221488. DOI: 10.1148/radiol.221488 PMID: 36786699

Pawlowski, A., Jansson, M., Sköld, M., Rottenberg, M. E., & Källenius, G. (2012). Tuberculosis and HIV Co-Infection. *PLoS Pathogens*, *8*(2), e1002464. DOI: 10.1371/journal.ppat.1002464 PMID: 22363214

Pedrycz, W. (1998). *Fuzzy modeling and control*. Springer.

Piczak, K. J. (2015). Environmental sound classification with convolutional neural networks. In 2015 IEEE 25th international workshop on machine learning for signal processing (MLSP) (pp. 1-6). IEEE. DOI: 10.1109/MLSP.2015.7324337

Poonia, P., & Jain, V. K. (2020). Short-term traffic flow prediction: Using LSTM. *2020 International Conference on Emerging Trends in Communication, Control and Computing (ICONC3)*, 1–4. https://doi.org/DOI: 10.1109/ICONC345789.2020.9117329

Poplin, R., Chang, P. C., Alexander, D., Schwartz, S., Colthurst, T., Ku, A., Newburger, D., Dijamco, J., Nguyen, N., Afshar, P. T., Gross, S. S., Dorfman, L., McLean, C. Y., & DePristo, M. A. (2018). A universal SNP and small-indel variant caller using deep neural networks. *Nature Biotechnology*, *36*(10), 983–987. DOI: 10.1038/nbt.4235 PMID: 30247488

Pranamesh, S., Rao, D., & Pati, P. (2020). Applications of Deep Learning in intelligent transportation systems. *International Journal of Big Data and Analytics*, *8*(3), 143–160. https://pranamesh.github.io/files/2020-DL-review-paper-BDAT.pdf

Priyadarshani, N., Marsland, S., & Castro, I. (2016). Automated birdsong recognition using kernel methods and feature selection by genetic algorithms. In *2016 International Joint Conference on Neural Networks (IJCNN)* (pp. 4634-4641). IEEE.

Priyadarshani, N., Marsland, S., & Castro, I. (2018). Automated birdsong recognition in complex acoustic environments: A review. *Journal of Avian Biology*, *49*(5), jav-01447. DOI: 10.1111/jav.01447

Qian, C., Yu, W., Lu, C., Griffith, D., & Golmie, N. (2022). "Toward Generative Adversarial Networks for the Industrial Internet of Things". *IEEE Internet of Things Journal*, *9*(19), 9147–19159. DOI: 10.1109/JIOT.2022.3163894

Rahman, R., Pias, T. S., & Helaly, T. (2020). GGCS: A greedy graph-based character segmentation system for Bangladeshi license plate. In *2020 4th International Symposium on Multidisciplinary Studies and Innovative Technologies (ISMSIT)* (pp. 1–7). IEEE. DOI: 10.1109/ISMSIT50672.2020.9254449

Rahman, R., Rakib, A. F., Rahman, M., Helaly, T., & Pias, T. S. (2021). A real-time end-to-end Bangladeshi license plate detection and recognition system for all situations, including challenging environmental scenarios. In *2021 5th International Conference on Electrical Engineering and Information Communication Technology (ICEEICT)* (pp. 1–6). IEEE. DOI: 10.1109/ICEEICT53905.2021.9667896

Raj, S., Gupta, Y., & Malhotra, R. (2022). License plate recognition system using YOLOv5 and CNN. In *2022 8th International Conference on Advanced Computing and Communication Systems (ICACCS)* (Vol. 1, pp. 372–377). IEEE. DOI: 10.1109/ICACCS54159.2022.9784966

Ramalingam, R., & Chinnaiyan, V. (2023). A comparative analysis of chronic obstructive pulmonary disease using machine learning, and deep learning. *International Journal of Electrical and Computer Engineering*, *13*(1), 389. DOI: 10.11591/ijece.v13i1.pp389-399

Ramya, P., Chowdary, T. H., Teja, P. K., & Hrushikesh, T. (2023). Number plate recognition using optical character recognition (OCR) and connected component analysis (CCA). In *Smart Technologies in Data Science and Communication* [Springer.]. *Proceedings of SMART-DSC, 2022*, 29–40.

Ranjard, L., & Ross, H. A. (2008). Unsupervised bird song syllable translation for batch event sequence mining. *The Journal of the Acoustical Society of America*, *123*(5), 3631–3631.

Reby, D., & McComb, K. (2003). Anatomical constraints generate honoring and potential individual signature cues that may maintain acoustic signals. *Animal Behaviour*, *65*(1), 1–11.

Ribeiro, M. T., Singh, S., & Guestrin, C. (2016). "Why should I trust you?": Explaining the predictions of any classifier. In *Proceedings of the 22nd ACM SIGKDD International Conference on Knowledge Discovery and Data Mining* (pp. 1135–1144). https://doi.org/DOI: 10.1145/2939672.2939778

Rifaioglu, A. S., Nalbat, E., Atalay, V., Martin, M. J., Cetin-Atalay, R., & Doğan, T. (2020). DEEPscreen: DEEPScreen: high performance drug–target interaction prediction with convolutional neural networks using 2-D structural compound representations. *Chemical Science (Cambridge)*, *11*(9), 2531–2557. DOI: 10.1039/C9SC03414E PMID: 33209251

Riggio, R. E., & Reichard, R. J. (2008). The emotional and social intelligences of effective leadership: An emotional and social skill approach. *Journal of Managerial Psychology*, *23*(2), 169–185. DOI: 10.1108/02683940810850808

Ronneberger, O., Fischer, P., & Brox, T. *U-Net: Convolutional Networks for Biomedical Image Segmentation*. arXiv. (2015). https://doi.org//arXiv.1505.04597DOI: 10.1007/978-3-319-24574-4_28

Ruder, S. (2016). An overview of gradient descent optimization algorithms. *arXiv preprint arXiv:1609.04747*.

Ruff, K. M., & Pappu, R. V. (2021). AlphaFold and Implications for Intrinsically Disordered Proteins. *Journal of Molecular Biology, 433*(20), 167208. DOI: 10.1016/j.jmb.2021.167208 PMID: 34418423

Russell, S., & Norvig, P. (2021). *Artificial Intelligence: A Modern Approach* (4th ed.). Pearson.

Rydell, J., Nyman, S., Eklöf, J., Jones, G., & Russo, D. (2017). *Testing the performances of automated identification of bat species: a machine learning approach.* Irish Wildlife Manuals.

Sadique, M. F., & Haque, S. R. (2019). A comparative study of license plate detection and recognition techniques. In *2019 22nd International Conference on Computer and Information Technology (ICCIT)* (pp. 1–6). IEEE. DOI: 10.1109/ICCIT48885.2019.9038583

Salamon, J., & Bello, J. P. (2017). Deep convolutional neural networks and data augmentation for environmental sound classification. *IEEE Signal Processing Letters, 24*(3), 279–283. DOI: 10.1109/LSP.2017.2657381

Samantaray, M., Biswal, A. K., Singh, D., Samanta, D., Karuppiah, M., & Joseph, N. P. (2021). Optical character recognition (OCR) based vehicle's license plate recognition system using Python and OpenCV. In *2021 5th International Conference on Electronics, Communication and Aerospace Technology (ICECA)* (pp. 849–853). IEEE.

Samek, W., Montavon, G., Lapuschkin, S., Anders, C. J., & Müller, K. R. (2021). Explaining deep neural networks and beyond: A review of explainable AI methods. *Proceedings of the IEEE, 109*(3), 247–278. DOI: 10.1109/JPROC.2021.3060483

Sanchez-Garcia, A., Quintana, V. M., Estrada, A., & Sarr, T. (2020). Acoustic monitoring of wildlife in Mexico's protected areas. *Biodiversity and Conservation, 29*(12), 3775–3796.

Sathya, D., & Uma, V. (2024). *Object detection*. Kindle Direct Publishing.

Schmidhuber, J. (2015). Deep Learning in neural networks: An overview. *Neural Networks, 61*, 85–117. DOI: 10.1016/j.neunet.2014.09.003 PMID: 25462637

Schwendemann, S., & Reinhart, G. (2020). Predictive maintenance planning: A literature review and research agenda. *Procedia CIRP*, *93*, 1137–1142.

Selvan, C., Kumar, R. S., Joseph, S. I. T., Bruntha, P. M., Amanullah, M., & Arulkumar, V. (2025). *Traffic prediction using GPS-based cloud data through RNN-LSTM-CNN models: Addressing Road congestion, safety, and sustainability in smart cities*. Springer Nature Singapore Pte Ltd.

Senior, A. W., Evans, R., Jumper, J., Kirkpatrick, J., Sifre, L., Green, T., Qin, C., Žídek, A., Nelson, A. W. R., Bridgland, A., Penedones, H., Petersen, S., Simonyan, K., Crossan, S., Kohli, P., Jones, D. T., Silver, D., Kavukcuoglu, K., & Hassabis, D. (2020). Improved protein structure prediction using potentials from deep learning. *Nature*, *577*(7792), 706–710. DOI: 10.1038/s41586-019-1923-7 PMID: 31942072

Shah, S. S., Daoliang, T., & Chandan Kumar, S. (2024). RUL forecasting for wind turbine predictive maintenance based on deep learning. *arXiv preprint arXiv:2412.17823*.

Shamir, L., Pruitt, J., Cherry, V., & Grosholz, E. (2021). Machine learning for automatic detection of underwater biological signals. *PeerJ. Computer Science*, *7*, e375.

Shanmuganathan, J. (2021). Evolution of robo-advisory and its impact on investor behavior. *Journal of Behavioral Finance*, *22*(4), 312–325.

Shashirangana, J., Padmasiri, H., Meedeniya, D., & Perera, C. (2020). Automated license plate recognition: A survey on methods and techniques. *IEEE Access : Practical Innovations, Open Solutions*, *9*, 11203–11225. DOI: 10.1109/ACCESS.2020.3047929

Shastri, S., Singh, K., & Uniyal, S. (2022). LSTM-based deep learning model for prediction of COVID-19 cases using time series data. *Materials Today: Proceedings*, *51*, 2481–2486. DOI: 10.1016/j.matpr.2021.11.265

Shefrin, H., & Statman, M. (2000). Behavioral portfolio theory. *Journal of Financial and Quantitative Analysis*, *35*(2), 127–151. DOI: 10.2307/2676187

Shiu, Y., Palmer, K. J., Gillespie, D., Klinck, H., Brodsky, M. C., Taylor, B. K., & Van Parijs, S. M. (2022). Transfer Learning for Automated Detection of North Atlantic Right Whale Upcalls. *The Journal of the Acoustical Society of America*, *151*(6), 4076–4087.

Shiu, Y., Palmer, K. J., Roch, M. A., Fleishman, E., Liu, X., Nosal, E. M., & Klinck, H. (2020). Deep neural networks for automated detection of marine mammal species. *Scientific Reports*, *10*(1), 1–12. PMID: 31913322

Shokry, A., & Moulines, É. (2021). *Le machine learning au service de la maintenance prédictive*. FX-Conseil, École Polytechnique.

Silvano, G. V. T., Silva, I., Ribeiro, V. C. T., Greati, V. R., Bezerra, A., Endo, P. T., & Lynn, T. (2020). Artificial MERCOSUR license plates dataset. *Data in Brief*, *33*, 106554. DOI: 10.1016/j.dib.2020.106554 PMID: 33344736

Silver, D., Huang, A., Maddison, C. J., Guez, A., Sifre, L., van den Driessche, G., Schrittwieser, J., Antonoglou, I., Panneershelvam, V., Lanctot, M., Dieleman, S., Grewe, D., Nham, J., Kalchbrenner, N., Sutskever, I., Lillicrap, T., Leach, M., Kavukcuoglu, K., Graepel, T., & Hassabis, D. (2016). Mastering the game of Go with deep neural networks and tree search. *Nature*, *529*(7587), 484–489. DOI: 10.1038/nature16961 PMID: 26819042

Singh, I. (2016). *Automatic vehicle detection and recognition.*

Singh, A. (2019). Role of robo-advisors in reshaping financial advisory services in India. *Asian Journal of Management*, *10*(1), 39–44.

Singh, S., Kaur, N., & Gehlot, A. (2024). Application of artificial intelligence in drug design: A review. *Computers in Biology and Medicine*, *179*, 108810. DOI: 10.1016/j.compbiomed.2024.108810 PMID: 38991316

Smith, M. (2022). Machine learning techniques for predictive maintenance in industrial IoT. *Information Sciences and Technological Innovations*, *4*(2), 33.

Snider, R., & Lee, S. (2020). An introduction to hidden Markov models for modeling speech and language. *Current Protocols in Bioinformatics*, *69*(1), e96. PMID: 32162851

Song, Q., & Chissom, B. S. (1993a). Forecasting Enrolments with Fuzzy Time Series. *Fuzzy Sets and Systems*, *54*(1), 1–9. DOI: 10.1016/0165-0114(93)90355-L

Song, Q., & Chissom, B. S. (1993b). Fuzzy Time Series and Its Model. *Fuzzy Sets and Systems*, *3*(54), 269–277. DOI: 10.1016/0165-0114(93)90372-O

Spencer-Oatey, H., & Franklin, P. (2012). What is culture. A compilation of quotations. GlobalPAD Core Concepts, 1-21.

Srivastava, S.. (2015). *Predictive analytics: Concepts and techniques*. Springer.

Stoeger, A. S., Heilmann, G., Zeppelzauer, M., Ganswindt, A., Hensman, S., & Charlton, B. D. (2012). Visualizing sound emission of elephant vocalization by animated three-dimensional reconstruction in VRMLIm VRMLraum. *PLoS One*, *7*(12).

Stowell, D., Benetos, E., & Gill, L. F. (2017). On-bird open-set state-based sound recognition. arXiv preprint arXiv:1706.04175.

Stowell, D. (2022). Computational bioacoustics with deep learning: A review and roadmap. *PeerJ*, *10*, e13152. DOI: 10.7717/peerj.13152 PMID: 35341043

Stowell, D., & Plumbley, M. D. (2014). Automatic large-scale classification of bird sounds is highly robust to unconstrained recording conditions. *PeerJ*, *2*, e488. DOI: 10.7717/peerj.488 PMID: 25083350

Stowell, D., Wood, M. D., Pamuła, H., Stylianou, Y., & Glotin, H. (2019). Automatic acoustic detection of birds through deep learning: The first Bird Audio Detection challenge. *Methods in Ecology and Evolution*, *10*(3), 368–380. DOI: 10.1111/2041-210X.13103

Stringer, C., Wang, T., Michaelos, M., & Pachitariu, M. (2021). Cellpose: A generalist algorithm for cellular segmentation. *Nature Methods*, *18*(1), 100–106. DOI: 10.1038/s41592-020-01018-x PMID: 33318659

Sugai, L. S. M., Silva, T. S. F., Ribeiro, J. W.Jr, & Llusia, D. (2019). Terrestrial passive acoustic monitoring: Review and perspectives. *Bioscience*, *69*(1), 15–25. DOI: 10.1093/biosci/biy147

Sun, T., Sun, B., Jiang, Z., Hao, R., & Xie, J. (2021). Traffic flow online prediction based on a generative adversarial network with multi-source data. *Sustainability (Basel)*, *13*(21), 12188. DOI: 10.3390/su132112188

Sun, Y.. (2018). Internet of Things and big data analytics for smart and connected communities. *IEEE Access : Practical Innovations, Open Solutions*, *6*, 72080–72089.

Susto, G. A., Schirru, A., Pampuri, S., McLoone, S., & Beghi, A. (2015). Machine learning for predictive maintenance: A multiple classifier approach. *IEEE Transactions on Industrial Informatics*, *11*(3), 812–820. DOI: 10.1109/TII.2014.2349359

Sutton, R. S., & Barto, A. G. (2018). *Reinforcement learning: An introduction* (2nd ed.). MIT Press.

Tan, C., Sun, F., Kong, T., Zhang, W., Yang, C., & Liu, C. (2018). A survey on deep transfer learning. In *International conference on artificial neural networks* (pp. 270-279). Springer, Cham.

Tang, N., Yuan, M., Chen, Z., Ma, J., Sun, R., Yang, Y., He, Q., Guo, X., Hu, S., & Zhou, J. (2023). Machine Learning Prediction Model of Tuberculosis Incidence Based on Meteorological Factors and Air Pollutants. *International Journal of Environmental Research and Public Health*, *20*(5), 3910. DOI: 10.3390/ijerph20053910 PMID: 36900920

Tan, L. N., Alwan, A., Kosnik, J. E., Moors-Murphy, H. B., & Morton, J. M. (2020). Neural networks and computer vision for expert detection of social cues in dyadic interactions. *IEEE Transactions on Affective Computing*.

Tegge, A. N. (2017). Gaussian Mixture Model Tutorial.

Thomas, A., & Nguyen, M. (2020). Ethics in AI. *AI Journal*, *12*(3), 200–220. PMID: 36456550

Towsey, M., Wimborne, B., Williamson, I., & Roe, P. (2014). The use of acoustic sensors for monitoring gas gun bird scaring devices. *The Emu*, *114*(1), 71–77.

Transportation Research Board. (2008). *Transportation applications of artificial intelligence, neural networks, and other advanced analytical techniques* (Circular E-C113). National Academies Press. https://onlinepubs.trb.org/onlinepubs/circulars/ec113.pdf

Trifa, V. M., Kirschel, A. N. G., Taylor, C. E., & Vallejo, E. E. (2008). Automated species recognition of antbirds in a Mexican rainforest using hidden Markov models. *The Journal of the Acoustical Society of America*, *123*(5), 2424–2431. DOI: 10.1121/1.2839017 PMID: 18397045

Tsai, C. W., Lai, C. F., Chao, H. C., & Vasilakos, A. V. (2015). Big data analytics: A survey. *Journal of Big Data*, *2*, 1–32.

Tse, Y. K., & Rayer, A. (2018). AI and the transformation of the investment landscape. *Journal of Financial Transformation*, *47*(3), 15–28.

Tusher, M. S. R., Rahman, N. N., Chowdhury, S., Tabassum, A., Adnan, M. A., Rahman, R., & Al Masud, S. M. R. (2023). An enhanced variational autoencoder approach for the purpose of deblurring Bangla license plate images. *International Journal of Advanced Computer Science and Applications*, *14*(6). Advance online publication. DOI: 10.14569/IJACSA.2023.01406133

Valletta, J. J., Torney, C., Kings, M., Thornton, A., & Madden, J. (2017). Applications of machine learning in animal behaviour studies. *Animal Behaviour*, *124*, 203–220. DOI: 10.1016/j.anbehav.2016.12.005

Vassilev, A., Oprea, A., Fordyce, A., & Andersen, H. (2024). Adversarial machine learning: A taxonomy and terminology of attacks and mitigations.

Vaswani, A., Shazeer, N., Parmar, N., Uszkoreit, J., Jones, L., Gomez, A. N., Kaiser, Ł., & Polosukhin, I. (2017). Attention is all you need. *Advances in Neural Information Processing Systems*, *30*, 5998–6008.

Vernova, G. E. (2025). *Brochure*. Apm Driving Reliability Forward., Available https://www.gevernova.com/software/resources/brochure/asset-performance-management-reliability

Wang, H., Kong, H., Man, Z., Tuan, D. M., Cao, Z., & Shen, W. (2014). Sliding Mode Control for Steer-by-Wire Systems with AC Motors in Road Vehicles. *IEEE Transactions on Industrial Electronics*, *61*(3), 1596–1611. DOI: 10.1109/TIE.2013.2258296

Wang, H., Man, Z., Shen, W., Cao, Z., Zheng, J., Jin, J., & Do, M. T. (2014). Robust Control for Steer-by-Wire Systems with Partially Known Dynamics. *IEEE Transactions on Industrial Informatics*, *10*(4), 2003–2015. DOI: 10.1109/TII.2014.2338273

Wang, H., Shi, L., Man, Z., Zheng, J., Li, S., Yu, M., Jiang, C., Kong, H., & Cao, Z. (2018). Continuous Fast Nonsingular Terminal Sliding Mode Control of Automotive Electronic Throttle Systems Using Finite-Time Exact Observer. *IEEE Transactions on Industrial Electronics*, *65*(9), 7160–7172. DOI: 10.1109/TIE.2018.2795591

Wang, H., Zheng, J., Man, Z., Kong, H., Zhao, Y., Yu, M., Cao, Z., & Do, M. T. (2016). Design and Implementation of Adaptive Terminal Sliding Mode Control on a Steer-by-Wire Equipped Road Vehicle. *IEEE Transactions on Industrial Electronics*, *63*(9), 5774–5785. DOI: 10.1109/TIE.2016.2573239

Wang, J. M., Labaki, W. W., Murray, S., Martinez, F. J., Curtis, J. L., Hoffman, E. A., Ram, S., Bell, A. J., Galban, C. J., Han, M. L. K., & Hatt, C. (2023). Machine learning for screening of at-risk, mild and moderate COPD patients at risk of FEV1 decline: Results from COPDGene and SPIROMICS. *Frontiers in Physiology*, *14*, 1144192. DOI: 10.3389/fphys.2023.1144192 PMID: 37153221

Wang, S., Clark, R., Wen, H., & Trigoni, N. (2017). DeepVO: Towards End-to-End Visual Odometry with Deep Recurrent Convolutional Neural Networks. *2017 IEEE International Conference on Robotics and Automation (ICRA)*, 2043-2050. DOI: 10.1109/ICRA.2017.7989236

Wang, X., Han, Y., & Zhang, H. (2018). A review of data-driven predictive maintenance: Methods, cases, and future directions. *IEEE Transactions on Industrial Informatics*, *14*(1), 24–35.

Wang, X., Ren, H., Ren, J., Song, W., Qiao, Y., Ren, Z., Zhao, Y., Linghu, L., Cui, Y., Zhao, Z., Chen, L., & Qiu, L. (2023). Machine learning-enabled risk prediction of chronic obstructive pulmonary disease with unbalanced data. *Computer Methods and Programs in Biomedicine*, *230*, 107340. DOI: 10.1016/j.cmpb.2023.107340 PMID: 36640604

Weinstein, B. G. (2015). MotionMeerkat: An integrative computer vision suite for the study of social behavior. *bioRxiv*, 021766.

Weinstein, B. G. (2018). A computer vision for animal ecology. *Journal of Animal Ecology*, *87*(3), 533–545. DOI: 10.1111/1365-2656.12780 PMID: 29111567

Weiss, J., Raghu, V. K., Bontempi, D., Christiani, D. C., Mak, R. H., Lu, M. T., & Aerts, H. J. (2023). Deep learning to estimate lung disease mortality from chest radiographs. *Nature Communications*, *14*(1), 2797. DOI: 10.1038/s41467-023-37758-5 PMID: 37193717

Weiss, S. M.. (1990). Knowledge-based systems and AI. *Communications of the ACM*, *33*(5), 576–602.

Wess, M., Ivanov, M., Unger, C., Nookala, A., Wendt, A., & Jantsch, A. (2021). A. Wendt та A. Jantsch, "ANNETTE: Accurate Neural Network Execution Time Estimation With Stacked Models". *IEEE Access : Practical Innovations, Open Solutions*, *9*, 3545–3556. DOI: 10.1109/ACCESS.2020.3047259

West, D. M. (2018). *The future of work: Robots, AI, and automation*. Brookings Institution Press.

World Health Organization. (2019). Global Tuberculosis Report 2019. Cited [2025 February 4th]. Available from: https://www.who.int/tb/global-report-2019

Wu, C., Chen, L., Wang, G., Chai, S., Jiang, H., Peng, J., & Hong, Z. (2020). Spatiotemporal scenario generation of traffic flow based on LSTM-GAN. *IEEE Access : Practical Innovations, Open Solutions*, *8*, 186191–186198. DOI: 10.1109/ACCESS.2020.3029230

Wuest, T., Weimer, D., Irgens, C., & Thoben, K.-D. (2016). Machine learning in manufacturing: Advantages, challenges, and applications. *Production & Manufacturing Research*, *4*(1), 23–45. DOI: 10.1080/21693277.2016.1192517

Xie, J., Towsey, M., Truskinger, A., Eichinski, P., Zhang, J., & Roe, P. (2017). Artificial Intelligence for ecosystems: Deep learning for multi-label classification of Australian frog calls. arXiv preprint arXiv:1704.04736.

Xie, J., Towsey, M., Zhu, J., Xiaodong, J., & Roe, P. (2020). Adaptive frequency shaping for recording bioacoustics in environments with multiple background noise sources. *Remote Sensing in Ecology and Conservation*, *6*(4), 482–496.

Xin, S., Zhaobin, P., & Jing, Q. (2022). Legal analysis of the right to privacy protection in the age of artificial intelligence. In *International Conference on Intelligent Computing* (pp. 617–626). DOI: 10.1007/978-3-031-13870-6_51

Xu, Y., Liu, X., Cao, X., Huang, C., Liu, E., Qian, S., Liu, X., Wu, Y., Dong, F., Qiu, C.-W., Qiu, J., Hua, K., Su, W., Wu, J., Xu, H., Han, Y., Fu, C., Yin, Z., Liu, M., & Zhang, J. (2021). Artificial intelligence: A powerful paradigm for scientific research. *Innovation (Cambridge (Mass.))*, *2*(4), 4. DOI: 10.1016/j.xinn.2021.100179 PMID: 34877560

Yan, H., & Li, Y. (2023). A survey of generative AI for intelligent transportation systems. *arXiv preprint arXiv:2312.08248*.https://arxiv.org/abs/2312.08248

Yang, H., Yang, J., Han, L. D., Liu, X., Pu, L., Chin, S. M., & Hwang, H. (2018). A kriging based spatiotemporal approach for traffic volume data imputation. *PLoS One*, *13*(4), e0195957. DOI: 10.1371/journal.pone.0195957 PMID: 29664928

Yang, J., & Zhang, K. (2021). Intelligent systems for big data analytics in IoT. *IEEE Transactions on Industrial Informatics*, *17*(3), 1864–1876.

Yang, L., Li, G., Yang, J., Zhang, T., Du, J., Liu, T., Zhang, X., Han, X., Li, W., Ma, L., Feng, L., & Yang, W. (2023). Deep-Learning Model for Influenza Prediction From Multisource Heterogeneous Data in a Megacity: Model Development and Evaluation. *Journal of Medical Internet Research*, *25*, e44238. DOI: 10.2196/44238 PMID: 36780207

Yang, Q., Liu, Y., Chen, T., & Tong, Y. (2019). Federated machine learning: Concept and applications. [TIST]. *ACM Transactions on Intelligent Systems and Technology*, *10*(2), 1–19. DOI: 10.1145/3298981

Yang, X., Zhang, S., Liu, J., Gao, Q., Dong, S., & Zhou, C. (2021). Deep learning for smart fish farming: Applications, opportunities and challenges. *Reviews in Aquaculture*, *13*(1), 66–90. DOI: 10.1111/raq.12464

Yang, Z., Wu, Z., Wang, Y., & Wu, H. (2024). Deep Reinforcement Learning Lane-Changing Decision Algorithm for Intelligent Vehicles Combining LSTM Trajectory Prediction. *World Electric Vehicle Journal*, *15*(4), 173. DOI: 10.3390/wevj15040173

Yin, C., Udrescu, M., Gupta, G., Cheng, M., Lihu, A., Udrescu, L., Bogdan, P., Mannino, D. M., & Mihaicuta, S. (2023). Fractional dynamics foster deep learning of COPD stage prediction. *Advancement of Science*, *10*(12), 2203485. DOI: 10.1002/advs.202203485 PMID: 36808826

Yoon, S. A., & Lee, H. (2017). Reinforcement learning for robotics. *Robotics and Autonomous Systems*, *98*, 167–178. DOI: 10.1016/j.robot.2017.06.012

Yuan, Y., Shao, C., Cao, Z., He, Z., Zhu, C., Wang, Y., & Jang, V. (2020). Bus dynamic travel time prediction: Using a deep feature extraction framework based on RNN and DNN. *Electronics (Basel)*, *9*(11), 1876. DOI: 10.3390/electronics9111876

Yue, S., Arvin, F., Xiong, C., & Hu, C. (2016). A Bio-Inspired Embedded Vision System for Autonomous Micro-Robots: The LGMD Case. *IEEE Transactions on Cognitive and Developmental Systems*, *1*(99), 1–1. DOI: 10.1109/TCDS.2016.2577021

Yu, H., Wang, X., Shao, Y., Qin, F., Chen, B., & Gong, S. (2022). Research on license plate location and recognition in a complex environment. *Journal of Real-Time Image Processing*, *19*(4), 823–837. DOI: 10.1007/s11554-022-01225-z

Yu, L., He, X., Fang, X., Liu, L., & Liu, J. (2023). Deep Learning with Geometry-Enhanced Molecular Representation for Augmentation of Large-Scale Docking-Based Virtual Screening. *Journal of Chemical Information and Modeling*, *63*(21), 6501–6514. DOI: 10.1021/acs.jcim.3c01371 PMID: 37882338

Zadeh, L. A. (1965). Fuzzy sets. *Information and Control*, *8*(3), 338–353. DOI: 10.1016/S0019-9958(65)90241-X

Zaki, J. (2014). Empathy: A motivated account. *Psychological Bulletin*, *140*(6), 1608–1647. DOI: 10.1037/a0037679 PMID: 25347133

Zamora-Gutiérrez, V., López-Lorente, C., Traba, J., Clarabuch, O., & Ecología-UAB, G. (2018). Acoustic signalling in desert bats: A trade-off between detecting resources and being too vocal? *Oecologia*, *188*(4), 1123–1134.

Zhang, G., Luo, L., Zhang, L., & Liu, Z. (2023). Research progress of respiratory disease and idiopathic pulmonary fibrosis based on artificial intelligence. *Diagnostics (Basel)*, *13*(3), 357. DOI: 10.3390/diagnostics13030357 PMID: 36766460

Zhang, K., Sun, J., Zhu, X., & Fang, Y. (2015). Privacy and security for online social networks: Challenges and opportunities. *IEEE Network*, *29*(4), 13–19. DOI: 10.1109/MNET.2010.5510913

Zhang, Q., Cheng, L., & Boutaba, R. (2010). Cloud computing: State-of-the-art and research challenges. *Journal of Internet Services and Applications*, *1*(1), 7–18. DOI: 10.1007/s13174-010-0007-6

Zhang, T., Li, H., & Zhang, Q. (2024). Deep Learning algorithms for traffic forecasting: A comprehensive review. *Journal of Transportation Engineering*, *150*(1), 1–18. https://onlinelibrary.wiley.com/doi/10.1155/2024/9981657. DOI: 10.1061/(ASCE)0733-947X(2000)126:1(1)

Zhang, W., Yang, D., & Wang, H. (2019). Data-driven methods for predictive maintenance of industrial equipment: A survey. *IEEE Systems Journal*, *13*(3), 2213–2227. DOI: 10.1109/JSYST.2019.2905565

Zhao, R., Wang, D., Yan, R., Mao, K., Shen, F., & Wang, J. (2019). Machine health monitoring using local feature-based gated recurrent unit networks. *IEEE Transactions on Industrial Electronics*, *66*(6), 4944–4953.

Zhou, X., Leung, C. K., Wang, K. I. K., & Fortino, G. (2024). Deep Learning-Optimized Editorial Analysis of Big Data in Biomedical Applications and Digital Healthcare. *IEEE/ACM Transactions on Computational Biology and Bioinformatics*, *21*(4), 516–520. DOI: 10.1109/TCBB.2024.3371808

Zhu, H., Yu, F. R., Wang, Y., Ning, B., & Tang, T. (2020). Big data analytics in intelligent transportation systems: A survey. *IEEE Transactions on Intelligent Transportation Systems*, *21*(2), 383–398.

Zonta, T., da Costa, C. A., da Rosa Righi, R., de Lima, M. J., da Trindade, E. S., & Li, G. P. (2020). Predictive maintenance in the industry 4.0: A systematic literature review. *Computers & Industrial Engineering*, *150*, 106889. DOI: 10.1016/j.cie.2020.106889

About The Contributors

Sarah Benziane is a distinguished researcher and university lecturer in computer science and distributed systems, currently based at the Computer Science Department of the University of Science and Technology in Oran, Algeria. With a strong academic foundation, she holds an engineering degree in Parallel and Distributed Systems, a Magister in Electronics specializing in Vision and Pattern Recognition, and a Ph.D. in Artificial Intelligence and Pattern Recognition. Her research has produced a wealth of publications primarily focused on biometrics, hand vein recognition, and the application of convolutional neural networks (CNNs) in image processing. In addition to her research contributions, Sarah Benziane has supervised numerous undergraduate and master's projects on topics ranging from biometric systems and irrigation optimization to intelligent asset management. She has also been actively involved in organizing national and international conferences, such as doctoral workshops and conferences on embedded and distributed systems, and has served on scientific committees for conferences focused on artificial intelligence and the Internet of Things (IoT). Sarah Benziane is the author of several academic books, including one on reactive navigation for mobile robots and another on computer networks. Her recent work includes innovative research on AI applications for weather prediction and anti-theft systems for agriculture. She is currently involved in several national and international projects related to the application of AI in smart industry automation and renewable energy systems, as well as in fundamental research in computer science.

Fatiha Guerroudji is an Associate Professor at the University of Science and Technology Mohamed Boudiaf of Oran (USTOMB), Algeria. She holds both a Magister and a Ph.D. in Computer Science from the same institution. Her research focuses on Artificial Intelligence, Data Science, Geographic Information Science, interactive cartography, and geovisualization. Dr. Guerroudji is actively involved in interdisciplinary research projects at both national and international levels. She has served as principal investigator and project leader in several initiatives dealing with the integration of AI, data science, and geospatial technologies to address complex challenges in environmental monitoring, spatial data analysis, and smart decision-making systems. Her work aims to develop intelligent, user-centered tools that enhance geospatial data interpretation and communication. She has authored and co-authored numerous scientific papers published in peer-reviewed international journals and conference proceedings. In addition to her research, Dr. Guerroudji contributes to the academic and scientific communities as a reviewer and program committee member for various national and international conferences and journals in the fields of computer science, geoinformatics, and data-driven technologies. She also supervises Master's and Ph.D. students, and is deeply committed to advancing education and innovation in intelligent systems, spatial data science, and interdisciplinary research.

***

Rakhi Arora is an Asst. Prof. at Institute of Technology and management Gwalior, specializing in Computer Science Engg. Their research focuses on Machine Learning and Data Mining.

C. Sudha working as an Assistant Professor in the Department of CSE, GITAM University, Hyderabad has about 11 years of teaching experience. She received her ME degree from Anna university regional center, Coimbatore in 2013. She received Ph.D. degree in Computer Science from Annamalai University, Tamil Nadu in 2023. She has published 18 research papers in refereed international journals and 6 research papers in the proceedings of various international and national conferences. Her areas of research include Wireless sensor network, Machine Learning, and Internet of Things.

Anuja M. Chavan is a Computer Science Engineer and currently serves as an Assistant Professor at an international Institute of Information Technology, Pune. With over eight years of dedicated teaching experience, I have consistently contributed to the academic and professional growth of my students. My core area of specialization is Cloud Computing, and I have recently developed a strong interest in Artificial Intelligence, Machine Learning, Prompt Engineering, Web Application Development. Passionate about creating engaging learning environments. This book reflects my growing curiosity in the intersection of AI and animal communication, aiming to shed light on new possibilities for understanding non-human intelligence through technology. This book reflects her commitment to academic excellence and her enthusiasm for sharing emerging trends in the field of computer science.

Sathya.D completed B.Tech in 2023 at Pondicherry Engineering College and is currently pursuing M.Tech at Pondicherry University. Their research interests include Machine Learning, Deep Learning, and Computer Vision.

Deepak Dharrao, currently working as an Assistant Professor in the Department of CSE at Symbiosis Institute of Technology, Symbiosis International (Deemed University), Pune Maharashtra, India. He is having 16 years of experience in research and academics. He has authored or co-authored over 50 technical articles in reputed journals and conference proceedings. He published 2 patents and 1 Book on current demanding research topics. Dr. Deepak is member of IEEE, ACM & Life Member of ISTE professional organizations. His research interests include the areas of image and real-time video processing, FinTech, Data Science, Artificial Intelligence and Machine Learning.

Wafaa Hanifa Guerroudji is PhD Student in Molecular and Cellular Biology at Saad Dahleb Blida 1 University

Deepak Gupta is a distinguished academician with over 20 years of teaching experience and expertise in Computer Science and Engineering. He holds a Ph.D. in Computer Engineering and has an extensive research portfolio, including 102 international journal papers, multiple conference proceedings, and several books. His research interests span machine learning, artificial intelligence, and data mining. Currently, Dr. Gupta serves as an Associate Professor and Academic Coordinator in the Department of Computer Science & Engineering at ITM Gwalior, MP, India. He has also contributed significantly to the field through patents and copyrights and actively engages as a reviewer, conference chair and editor.

Risman Mat Hasim is a senior lecturer at Department of Mathematics and Statistics, Faculty of Science, Universiti Putra Malaysia. He received his PhD from Universiti Putra Malaysia and his research interest are Differential Games, Optimization and Game Theory. Currently, he is expanding his research interest in Fuzzy Differential Game problem.

Axel Jantsch, I received a Ph.D. in Computer Sciene from TU Wien in 1992. Then I made a postdoc with Hannu Tenhunen at KTH, The Royal Institute of Technology in Stockholm, Sweden and stayed at KTH until 2014. During that time I enjoyed working with Ahmed Hemani, Zhonghai Lu, Ingo Sander, Lirong Zheng, Zhuo Zou, Dinesh Pamunuwa and many others, on topics like Networks on Chip and Models of Computation. In 2015 I moved to TU Wien and since then my main research interests are on Self-aware Cyber-physical systems, embedded machine learning, and SoCs and Embedded Systems in general. IEEE Fellow since Jan 2024.

Zeashan Khan received his PhD from University of Grenoble, France in 2010 with specilaity of Automation and Computer Integrated Manufacturing. His area of interest include computational intelligence, robotics and intelligent control. He is a member of IEEE, ASME and SIAM.

Maryna Kolisnyk, PhD (2007), Docent (2011), Associate Professor, Department of computer systems, networks and cybersecurity. Faculty of Radio Electronics, Computer Systems and Infocommunications. National aerospace university «KhAI» Laureate of Grant of the National Academy of Sciences and the President of Ukraine (2020) (the honorary title and the medal). Laureate of Grant of Austrian Academy of Sciences (2022) - JESH-fellow (Method and models of dependability assessment of Industrial Internet of Things subsystems) with TU Wien, ICT. Laureate of Grant of a Post-Doctoral Studies Scholarship in the research Group "Internet Technologien und Systeme" (01.04.2022-31.12.2022) - Hasso-Platner Institute for Digital Engineering gGmbH, Potsdam Laureate of OAEW Grant 2023, TUWien, ICT

Ata Jahangir Moshayedi, Associate Professor at Jiangxi University of Science and Technology, holds a Ph.D. in Electronics from Pune University, India. He is a senior member of IEEE, Memeber of ACM, CCF and a Life Member of the Instrument Society of India, and a Life Member of Speed society, in India. Dr. Moshayedi's contributions extend beyond academia, as he actively participates in various IEEE conferences, serving in roles such as Keynote speake and technical Chair, reviewer, and editorial team member for conferences and international journals. His scientific achievements are substantial, with over 90 articles published in prestigious national and international journals. Alongside his research publications, he has authored three books and holds two patents and 12 copyrights, showcasing his pioneering contributions. Notably, his latest book, "Unity in Embedded System Design and Robotics: A Step-by-Step Guide", published by CRC Press, is recognized as the first book to integrate VR, robotics, and embedded systems. His primary research interests include robotics and automation, sensor modeling and biomimetic robotics, mobile robot olfaction and plume tracking, embedded systems, machine vision-based systems, virtual reality, cognitive science, and bio-inspired systems.

Swati Nilesh Pawar is an Assistant Professor in the Department of Computer Science and Engineering with over 14 years of experience in teaching, research, and academic development. Passionate about advancing knowledge in the field, Prof. Swati Pawar has contributed significantly to both undergraduate and postgraduate education, mentoring numerous students and guiding them in their academic and professional pursuits. Her areas of expertise include Artificial Intelligence, Cloud Computing, Computer Networks, Data Mining and she has been actively involved in research and scholarly publications throughout her academic career. With a commitment to lifelong learning and innovation, Prof. swati pawar continues to explore emerging technologies and foster a dynamic learning environment. She has participated in various national and international conferences, workshops, and seminars, and remains dedicated to promoting excellence in education and research.

Ashvini Arvind Todkar is an Assistant Professor in the Department of Computer Science and Engineering with over 13 years of experience in teaching, research, and academic development. Passionate about advancing knowledge in the field, Prof. Todkar has contributed significantly to both undergraduate and postgraduate education, mentoring numerous students and guiding them in their academic and professional pursuits. Her areas of expertise include Artificial Intelligence, Cloud Computing, Computer Networks, and she has been actively involved in research and scholarly publications throughout her academic career. With a commitment to lifelong learning and innovation, Prof. Todkar continues to explore emerging technologies and foster a dynamic learning environment. She has participated in various national and international conferences, workshops, and seminars, and remains dedicated to promoting excellence in education and research.

Lorna Uden is Emeritus Professor of IT systems in the school of Computing, Engineering and Technology at Staffordshire University. She has published widely in conferences, journals, chapters of books and workshops. Her research interests include Learning Technology, Web Engineering and Technology, Human Computer Interaction, Activity Theory, Big Data, Innovation, E-business, Knowledge management, Health Care, Service Innovation, Social Media, Intelligent Transport Systems, Service Science, Ecosystems, Internet of Things (IOT), Artificial Intelligence Smart Cities. Neuroscience and Problem-Based Learning (PBL). She co-authored the book, 'Technology and Problem - Based Learning', published by IGI publishers. Professor Uden has been invited round the world to give workshops in Problem Based Learning and Research seminars as visiting professor as well as keynote speaker at many international conferences. She also co-authored a book, the Future of Intelligent Transport System published by Elsevier. Professor Uden is program committee member for many international conferences and workshops. She is on the editorial board of several international journals. She is founder and editor in chief of the International Journal of Web Engineering and Technology (IJWET) and the International Journal of Learning Technology (IJLT), published by Inderscience, UK. She is Listed in the ScholarGPS 2024 of the Top 0.5% Scientists in the world.

V. Uma is an Associate Professor in the Department of Computer Science, Pondicherry University. She received her M.Tech and Ph.D. in Computer Science from Pondicherry University in 2007 and 2014, respectively, and was awarded the university gold medal for her M.Tech. She has over 15 years of teaching experience at the postgraduate level. Her research interests include Machine Learning, Deep Learning, Knowledge Representation, Reasoning, and Sentiment Analysis.

Suzelawati Zenian is a Senior Lecturer in the Mathematics Computer Graphics Programme at the Faculty of Science and Natural Resources, Universiti Malaysia Sabah. She earned her B.Sc. and M.Sc. degrees in Mathematics from Universiti Kebangsaan Malaysia, followed by a Ph.D. in Mathematics from Universiti Teknologi Malaysia. She has teaching experience in various mathematics courses such as Fuzzy Mathematics, Control Mathematics, Discrete Mathematics, Mathematical Programming, Differential Equations, Advanced Calculus, and Real Analysis. Her research interests span a broad range of disciplines, with a primary focus on fuzzy theory and image processing. She brings a multidisciplinary approach to her work, contributing to the advancement of knowledge at the intersection of mathematics and computer graphics. In recognition of her dedication to the field, she holds lifetime memberships with the Persatuan Sains Matematik Malaysia (PERSAMA) and the Persatuan Matematik dan Grafik Berkomputer Sabah (MAGRAPH).

Index

A

B

C

D

E

F

G

I